Apartheid in Indian Country?

SEEING RED OVER BLACK DISENFRANCHISEMENT

HANNIBAL B. JOHNSON

EAKIN PRESS ❦ Fort Worth, Texas

FIRST EDITION
Copyright © 2012 by Hannibal B. Johnson
Published in the United States of America
By Eakin Press
An Imprint of Wild Horse Media Group
P.O. Box 331779
Fort Worth, Texas 76163
1-888-982-8270
www.EakinPress.com
ALL RIGHTS RESERVED
1 2 3 4 5 6 7 8 9
ISBN 13: 978-1-935632-34-4
ISBN 10: 1-935632-34-5
Library of Congress Control Number 2012949237

Contents

Acknowledgments v
Introduction 1

CHAPTER
   I. Pre-Removal, Removal, War and Treaties:
      To the Victor Go the Spoils 13
        A. The "Trail of Tears" / 13
        B. The American Civil War / 31
        C. The Treaty of 1866 / 38

   II. Relations Between Africans and Native Americans
       in the Five Civilized Tribes: Deep and
       Intertwined Roots 53

   III. A Legacy of Mixing and Matching:
        Debunking the Purity Premise. 101

   IV. Post-Civil War Adaptation, Indian Enrollments
       and the Allotment Process: The Erosion of
       Indian Territory 118

   V. The Impact of Racism and Jim Crow:
      "Blacklash" in Indian Country 127

   VI. Money Talks: The Changing Economics
       of Tribal Membership 149

CHAPTER
  VII. Fighting for the Franchise: The African-
American Struggle for Tribal Rights 165
      A. In the Cherokee Nation / 165
      B. In the Muscogee (Creek) Nation / 204
      C. In the Seminole Nation / 234
      D. In the Choctaw Nation / 241
      E. In the Chickasaw Nation / 248

Conclusion 263

Appendices
    A. Having Their Say: The Freedmen
        Respond to Detractors 275
    B. The Voice of a Freedmen Advocate:
        Marilyn Vann, in Her Own Words 280
    C. The Cherokee Nation Perspective
        on the Freedmen 284
    D. A Conversation with David Cornsilk 287
    E. Epochs and Signposts in Native American History . . . 292
    F. Federally Recognized Indian Tribes in Oklahoma 305
    G. African-American Civil Rights in the
        United States: A Timeline 307
    H. State of the Union Address: President Andrew
        Jackson (December 6, 1830) 326

Endnotes 331
Index 393

Acknowledgments

I offer special thanks to several individuals: Martin H. Belsky, Dean, the University of Akron School of Law, for his thoughtful and detailed editorial comments; David Cornsilk, former Managing Editor, *Cherokee Observer*, and founding member, Cherokee National Party, for offering his keen insights on Cherokee history; Ron Graham, Founder/President, Muscogee (Creek) Indian Freedmen Band, for providing historical and personal materials relating to the status of the Muscogee (Creek) Freedmen; Eli Grayson, President of the California Muscogee (Creek) Association, for enlightening me on his considerable efforts in behalf of the Muscogee (Creek) Nation Freedmen; Davis D. Joyce, Ph.D., historian, for his engagement around issues of purpose and perspective, as well as his critical commentary; Robert Littlejohn, African-American Historical Society, Tulsa, for sharing his extensive collection of references and detailed knowledge of the African-American experience in Indian Country; and Marilyn Vann, President of Descendants of the Freedmen of the Five Civilized Tribes, for allowing me access to her impressive cache of documents and records and, more generally, for her passion for the Freedmen.

Thanks also to: Reuben Gant, Chief Executive Officer, Greenwood Chamber of Commerce; George Getchow, The Mayborn Literary Nonfiction Writers Conference of the Southwest at North Texas State University; Vanessa Adams-Harris, Muscogee (Creek) Nation citizen, advocate, and actress; Terry J. Ligon, Director of the Choctaw-Chickasaw Freedmen Project; Jeremy Lynch, Park Ranger, Fort Smith National Historic Site, National Park Service, U.S. Department of the Interior; Calvin C. Moore, J.D., Ph.D., Cleveland State University; Larry O'Dell, Historical

Collections Specialist, Research Division, Oklahoma Historical Society; Loretta F. Radford, Esq.; Osman Sheikh, University of Oklahoma graduate student; Monetta Trepp, Muscogee (Creek) Nation citizen; Robert Trepp, Muscogee (Creek) Nation citizen and historian; Verdie Triplett, Founder and Contact Person, Choctaw-Chickasaw Freedmen Association; Angela Y. Walton-Raji, Webmaster and Editor, The African-Native American History and Genealogy Web Page; and Corporal Steve Wood, Tulsa Police Department.

Introduction

*"We learn from history that
we learn nothing from history."*
—George Bernard Shaw

Apartheid in Indian Country?: Seeing Red Over Black Disenfranchisement focuses on the long and storied relationship between persons of African ancestry and Native Americans,[1] particularly in the United States. This longstanding bond has been recognized in segments of the African-American community for generations. Only of late have scholars taken a keen interest in uncovering evidence of these interrelationships and analyzing how African- and Native-American intersections shaped our history.[2] As scholar William Loren Katz pointed out:

> Those who have put history into books have emphasized differences between Africans and Native Americans. For example, they have stressed that Europeans encountered Indians as distinct individuals and members of proud nations, and Africans as nameless slaves. Little mention is made of the enslavement of Native Americans and nothing is said about the cultural similarities between the two dark peoples.[3]

Katz asserts that this hypersensitivity to differences, real or imagined, between red and black people worked to the advantage of the dominant culture. Whites, he argues, exploited both populations.[4]

Dr. Carter G. Woodson,[5] noted African-American historian, journalist, and author, also reflected upon the paucity of historical information focused on red/black interaction. He observed: "[O]ne of the longest unwritten chapters of the history of the United States is that treating of the relations of the [N]egroes and the Indians."[6]

2 Apartheid in Indian Country?

Others echo these same sentiments. For too long, critics urge, historians cast African Americans as bit players on the stage of the American drama, no less so in the acts recounting the Native-American experience.

> [I]n the telling of Native-American history . . . historians have rendered African-American members of the Five Nations of the Southeastern United States [Cherokee, Choctaw, Muscogee (Creek), Seminole, and Chickasaw] as passive "objects" swept along in the tides of the great drama which is Native-American history. Existing solely as the reason for the struggle that led up to the Civil War in Indian Territory, they are seldom given their proper place as moral guides and political instigators in the struggle which came to define a people. This [is an] a historical and immoral treatment of history.[7]

Recent developments further cloud our understanding of the enduring, nuanced relationship between persons of African ancestry and Native Americans. Controversy swirls around the tribal exile of African Americans with blood, cultural, and/or treaty ties to various Native-American tribes. Ties once thought to bind have loosened and frayed along color lines. Some cite ignorance of history, political demagoguery, and racism as among the chief facilitators of this unraveling of relations.[8] How the United States dealt with these dynamic populations lies at the heart of the story.

The centuries-old interactions between the United States and various Native-American tribes have been fundamentally political—government to government—in nature. The European colonists who settled here regarded the original indigenous tribes they encountered as sovereign nations. That early solicitude for indigenous sovereignty[9] continues. Indeed, in 2010, President Barack Obama announced the United States' support for the United Nations Declaration on the Rights of Indigenous Peoples,[10] an affirmation of indigenous sovereignty.[11] Native Americans enjoy peculiar legal and political relationships with the federal government.

However, Native-American sovereignty, the subject of considerable scholarship and popular discourse, is both malleable and ephemeral. In the final analysis, this "special kind of non-sovereign sovereignty"[12] goes only as far as Congress allows. In *United States v. Blackfeet Tribe*,[13] a 1973 case, a federal court described the special status of Native-American tribes:

> No doubt the Indian tribes were at one time sovereign[,] and even now the tribes are sometimes described as being sovereign. The blunt fact, however, is that an Indian tribe is sovereign to the extent that the United States permits it to be sovereign—neither more nor less.
>
> . . . .
>
> While for many years the United States recognized some elements of sovereignty in the Indian tribes and dealt with them by treaty, Congress[,] by Act of March 3, 1871, prohibited the further recognition of Indian tribes as independent nations. Thereafter the Indians and the Indian tribes were regulated by acts of Congress. The power of Congress to govern by statute rather than treaty has been sustained. *United States v. Kagama* (1886). That power is a plenary power (*Matter of Heff* (1905)) and[,] in its exercise[,] Congress is supreme. *United States v. Nice* (1916).[14] [citations omitted]

In relating to tribal governments, the federal government acts under authority of provisions of the Constitution. In Article I, Section 8, the Constitution states: "The Congress shall have power . . . to regulate commerce with foreign nations, among the several states, and with Indian tribes." Moreover, treaties, agreements made with the Indian tribes, are part of our nation's supreme law in furtherance of the federal government's powers with respect to dealing with Indian commerce. Article VI of the Constitution notes: "This Constitution, and the laws of the United States which shall be made in pursuance thereof; and all treaties made, or which shall be made . . . shall be the supreme law of the land. . . ."[15]

Indians are the only group specifically identified in the Constitution. Indian tribes are distinct political entities—governments with executive, legislative, and judicial powers. Tribal members may hold dual citizenship (i.e., tribal and United States).

On account of their unique status, members of federally recognized Native-American tribes, by virtue of group affiliation, receive certain services and preferences from the government that members of other racial and ethnic "minorities" do not (e.g., health care through Indian Health Services). Indeed, owing to the special posture of Native Americans, legislation passed for the benefit of Indian tribes does not constitute racial discrimination in violation of the Due Process Clause of the Fifth Amendment to the United States Constitution.

In *Morton v. Mancari*,[16] the United States Supreme Court considered whether an employment preference for members of federally recognized tribes constituted racial discrimination in violation of the Fifth Amendment. The Court began its analysis by noting "[t]he plenary power of Congress to deal with the special problems of Indians is drawn both explicitly and implicitly from the Constitution itself."[17] Deferring to Congress's broad power under the Indian Commerce Clause, the Court explained:

> Literally every piece of legislation dealing with Indian tribes and reservations, and certainly all legislation dealing with the BIA [Bureau of Indian Affairs],[18] singles out for special treatment a constituency of tribal Indians living on or near reservations. If these laws, derived from historical relationships and explicitly designed to help only Indians, were deemed invidious racial discrimination, an entire Title of the United States Code (25 U.S.C.) would be effectively erased and the solemn commitment of the Government toward the Indians would be jeopardized.[19]

The Court concluded that the legislation under consideration was not directed toward a racial group of "Indians," but rather was limited to recognized tribal governments, and therefore constituted a political classification.[20]

In addition to the special, official *political* relationship between Native Americans and the United States, a tacit *racial* relationship has also evolved. Slavery, American racism, and "Jim Crowism" (i.e., rigid, forced racial segregation at all levels of society—in effect, a racial caste system)[21] infected Native-American interactions, not only with the federal government, but with other demographic groups as well.

Evidence suggests initial encounters between Africans and Native Americans date back to the pre-Columbus era, well before the beginning of the sixteenth century.[22] Later, European influence and American-style slavery molded black-red[23] interactions. Color-based fault lines embedded in the American foundation both firmed and fractured African-American/Native-American relations.

Enslaved Africans began to supplant Native-American bondservants[24] in the mid-seventeenth century. This shared experience of enslavement resulted in powerful connections: common work experiences, communal living, shared folklore, and intermarriage.[25]

In time, however, these potent cultural intersections began yielding to the irresistible ideology of racial hierarchy.[26] Pushed toward assimilation by dominant whites, some Native American tribes embraced the "peculiar institution" that once ensnared them. Captive became captor. Red enslaved black.

Only a minority of Native Americans, mostly "mixed-bloods," held slaves. This mighty minority, however, accumulated disproportionate political and economic power, particularly among the Cherokees, Chickasaws, and Choctaws.[27]

Post-Civil War treaties between the federal government and Indian slaveholders freed enslaved Africans, granted them tribal citizenship, and offered them the illusory promise of parity. In some ways, Native American tribes both ratified and expedited the social, political, and economic aspirations of the Africans with whom they lived and toiled for decades (e.g., the provision by some tribes of schools for persons of African ancestry). In others ways, tribal actions impeded black progress (e.g., the enactment of anti-black laws by some tribes).

Near the turn of the twentieth century, the federal government implemented an Indian census process that fomented discord between African Americans and Native Americans. That process produced the "Dawes Rolls." The Dawes Rolls were intended not determine tribal citizenship status, but to facilitate tribal land allotment.

Agents working for the Dawes Commission, a federal body named for a United States Senator, undertook a survey that resulted in the disintegration of tribal lands facilitated through an Indian allotment system. Under the allotment system, the federal government granted individual acres of land to those Native Americans and "Freedmen"—those freed Africans who had been held in bondage by particular Indian tribes and other persons of African descent who had tribal affiliations*—listed on census rosters.

The federal government kept segregated lists, placing most persons with even a hint of African ancestry on a "Freedmen Roll" and those considered "real" Indians on a "Blood Roll." Government agents routinely consigned individuals with discernible "African blood" (i.e., as detectable through visible Negroid features) to the Freedmen Roll even in the face of evidence indicating Indian ancestry. The Freedmen Roll omitted reference to any "Indian blood" a

---

*The term "Freedmen," as used here, refers both to the persons of African ancestry with blood, cultural and/or treaty-based ties to the Five Civilized Tribes at the conclusion of the Civil War and to their descendants. As used in this book, "Freedmen" embraces both the singular and the plural and the term is gender-neutral.

6   Apartheid in Indian Country?

registrant may have had, focusing exclusively on his/her African ancestry, however small.

In practical effect, the rigid bifurcation of the Dawes Rolls, these allotment lists, denied the reality of widespread "race mixing" among African Americans and Native Americans. This cavalier inattention to the richness of Freedmen ancestry by federal allotment agents more than one hundred years ago is now being used by some tribes as a basis for the denial of tribal citizenship to the Freedmen.

Despite misgivings about the Dawes Commission enrollment process, the allotted land afforded the Freedmen economic and political opportunity. Some tribes made bold and salutary strides toward incorporation of persons of African descent, and even adopted them as full tribal citizens. This progressive attitude soon gave way to American racism, which grew especially blatant and virulent in the nineteenth and early twentieth centuries, a critical period in African-American and Native-American interface.[28] In myriad ways, Indians yielded to the prevailing race theory predicated on white hegemony and black inferiority.

In turn, this "modern" racial response ushered in renewed tensions associated with the tribal citizenship status of the Freedmen within the "Five Civilized Tribes" or "Five Tribes" (i.e., the Cherokee, Choctaw, Chickasaw, Muscogee [Creek], and Seminole). Today, an epic clash looms between Indian tribes' sovereign prerogative to determine tribal membership and the century-and-a-half-old, treaty-based, tribal citizenship guarantee to descendants of the Freedmen.

Complicating matters further is the rationality, relevance, and role of blood quantum—percentage of tribal blood by lineage—in determining tribal membership status.[29] Blood quantum is not a Native-American concept, but rather one foisted upon, and subsequently adopted by, some tribes.[30] Persons of mixed ancestry, and even those with no Indian ancestry, have long been considered tribal members.[31] The case of the Cherokee Freedmen puts the matter in stark relief.

On the one hand, some Indian leaders and scholars argue that sovereignty encompasses the right to make unfettered tribal citizenship decisions. To them, decisional authority includes: (1) the right to exclude persons who lack a direct link to an Indian ancestor on the Dawes "Blood Rolls"; and (2) the right to exclude persons who, by virtue of treaty rights, would otherwise be entitled to such citizenship.

On the other hand, the Cherokee Freedmen and their allies

wonder aloud whether Freedmen exclusion amounts to a "redwashing" of history. They ponder whether Indian Nations actually dishonor their ancestors by refusing to recognize select descendants and reneging on treaty obligations.[32] A particular case in point, the subject of recent focus, is the treatment of the Cherokee Freedmen.

The posture of the Freedmen among the Cherokees is, at best, incongruous. Present-day disenfranchisement efforts belie the Cherokees' long history of Freedmen inclusion. The active engagement of the Freedmen in Cherokee affairs for more than 150 years offers a compelling counter-narrative to the move toward expulsion.

The Cherokees signed a treaty with the United States government in 1866 that incorporated the Freedmen into the tribe. That same year, the tribe amended its 1839 Constitution to guarantee the Freedmen full rights as citizens. Cherokee courts subsequently ratified the status of the Freedmen among the Cherokee Nation and, in fact, enlarged the class of Freedmen citizens.

Cherokee censuses in the late nineteenth century listed two classes of citizens: (1) citizens by birth (i.e., by blood); and (2) citizens by adoption. The latter category encompassed the two groups of Indians, the Shawnee and the Delaware tribes, as well as the Freedmen and intermarried whites. All these were Cherokee citizens. At the other end of the spectrum, the Cherokees maintained lists of persons who were considered intruders or imposters. The Cherokee Freedmen have never been considered mere poseurs.

Cherokee Freedmen have consistently participated in all aspects of Cherokee life, from the social/cultural to the political to the economic.[33] As historian Dr. Daniel Littlefield pointed out, "The Cherokee Nation was, in fact, a multi-racial, multi-cultural constitutional nation, whose citizenship was based not on blood or culture but on either birth or adoption."[34]

Despite this history, present Cherokee leadership persisted in contesting the citizenship claims of the Freedmen. On February 3, 2009, the Tahlequah, Oklahoma-based Cherokee Nation filed suit in the United States District Court for the Northern District of Oklahoma against the United States Department of Interior, the federal agency in charge of Indian affairs, and five Cherokee Freedmen. The suit seeks a declaration that "non-Indian" Cherokee Freedmen have no federal claim to citizenship in the Cherokee Nation. On July 2, 2010, Judge Terrance Kern transferred the case, known as *The Cherokee Nation v. Nash et al.*, to Washington, D.C.[35] The case was to be tried together with an earlier-filed case raising many of the same issues (i.e., matters regarding the rights of Cherokee Freedmen under an 1866 treaty between the United States of America and the Cherokee Nation). The first-filed Washington, D.C., case was *Vann et al. v. Salazar*,[36] pending before Judge Henry H. Kennedy, Jr., in the United States District Court for the District of Columbia.

Vann was a suit initially filed on August 11, 2003, by six individual plaintiffs against the United States Department of the Interior and its head, the Secretary of the Interior. Plaintiffs in *Vann* were descendants of persons listed on the 1907 "Freedmen Rolls" of the Cherokee Nation, one of two lists (i.e., the "Blood Roll" and the "Freedmen Roll") compiled by the Dawes Commission.

The *Vann* plaintiffs claimed their exclusion from participation in two 2003 Cherokee Nation tribal elections on account of the lack of an ancestral link to the "Blood Roll" violated their rights under the Thirteenth and Fifteenth Amendments to the United States Constitution, an 1866 treaty between the Cherokee Nation and the federal government, and other federal laws. Moreover, the *Vann* plaintiffs argued that the recognition of the elections by the Secretary of the Interior further trampled on their protected rights.

The *Vann* plaintiffs sought a declaration overturning federal recognition of the 2003 Cherokee Nation elections. They also urged the reviewing court to enjoin recognition of any future elections from which they were excluded.[37]

Jonathan Velie, lead counsel for the Freedmen in both cases, summed up the posture of the controversy:

> The Northern District [of Oklahoma] decision to transfer the case brought by the Cherokee Nation of Oklahoma against five individual Freedmen turned on the fact that the case had essentially the same issues as the case brought by the Cherokee Freedmen Band and several individual Freedmen in Washington, D.C., which was the first case filed. Another matter of interest was that the court's finding that the [Cherokee Nation of Oklahoma] had waived sovereign immunity by filing the case, especially while the D.C. court action was still pending. The D.C. Court of Appeals has previously held, in 2008, that the Thirteenth Amendment and the Treaty of 1866 have whittled away the tribe's right to discriminate against the Freedmen.[38]

During the pendency of the *Vann* case, a class action lawsuit in the District Court of the Cherokee Nation, *Raymond Nash v. Cherokee Nation Registrar*,[39] held that the Freedmen are, based on the Treaty of 1866, entitled to Cherokee Nation citizenship. Almost immediately, the Cherokee Nation appealed the decision to the Cherokee Nation Supreme Court. That Court reversed and vacated the lower court's decision, thereby terminating the tribal citizenship of the Cherokee Freedmen.[40]

Legal maneuvering in the *Vann* case resulted in a temporary reinstatement of Freedmen citizenship rights.[41] Thereafter, Judge Henry H. Kennedy dismissed *Vann* on technical grounds and the case with which it had been consolidated, *Nash*, was transferred back to federal district court in Tulsa.[42] The *Nash* court will determine the citizenship status of the Cherokee Freedmen.

The Cherokee Nation, numbering about 280,000 members, claims there are some 2,800 known Cherokee Freedmen, while most experts believe there are thousands more.[43] A significant number of these Freedmen are "Indian"—that is, they have a demonstrable blood nexus to an Indian ancestor. Others base their claims to tribal citizenship on the post-Civil War treaty executed in 1866.

Why now the press to remove the Freedmen, not just within the Cherokee Nation, but generally among the Five Civilized Tribes? Questions of race and racism lurk behind the curtain of rationales and ratiocinations. In some quarters, race and racism have been catapulted prominently into the foreground:

> Over forty years after the landmark Civil Rights and Voting Rights Acts, there is a place in the United States that African Americans cannot vote or receive federal benefits as a matter of law. The victims of this racial oppression are known as freedmen, who are descendants of African slaves owned by Indians. They are called freedmen, but they are anything but free.[44]

Robert Littlejohn, a retired petroleum geologist living in Tulsa, was but one of many "bi-cultural" Oklahomans longing for full recognition. He recalled the exhortation of his family elders during his boyhood: "One of these days you're going to have to prove who you are." At the time, he dismissed it.[45]

Back then, family storytellers imparted a smidgen about his Creek and Cherokee ancestors: Creek on his mother's side; Cherokee on his grandfather's side. His Aunt Atlanta, the family

10 Apartheid in Indian Country?

Tulsa World, *March 8, 2007, at A12*

griot, regaled the children with tales of generations past. Stories typically began with Aunt Atlanta's signature prelude, "They say, they say, they say."

Littlejohn, an African American to the casual observer, had always considered himself a Native American of African ancestry.[46] He spent decades confirming his past. What he confirmed has yet to be fully affirmed by his Native-American kin. He stood ready, willing, and able to prove who he was.[47]

Like Robert Littlejohn, the Freedmen in some ways seek birthright and belonging.[48] As historian Celia E. Naylor pointed out: "Just as descendants of African-American freedpeople continue to fight for their rightful place within American society, the descendants of African-Indian freedpeople of the Five Civilized Tribes of Oklahoma struggle for recognition as citizens of their respective tribal nations."[49]

Like Robert Littlejohn, other African Indians still face persistent questions about authenticity by virtue of their blackness and the American racial narrative. Neither factor—blackness nor the American racial narrative—should be underestimated:

> Indians who appear to have black ancestry bear a unique burden in being discriminated against even within their own tribes and families. Doubts about tribal authenticity that are linked to accusations of blackness are placed on their shoulders, or more accurately, on their faces. Such is the power of race that it leads us to disown our own kin, undermining the most basic human bond and principles of tribal people.[50]

This book explores the quarrel over Freedmen citizenship through the primary prism of race. It is virtually impossible to understand fully the dimensions of the present controversy without some appreciation of the role race has played in calibrating relationships between and among Native Americans, persons of African descent, and those of European heritage. Context is key.

Grappling with the nettlesome issues surrounding Freedmen identity and rights will help advance the American dialogue about race and culture—past, present, and future. That dialogue, which seems to occur only in fits and starts, is in need of a catalyst.

 CHAPTER I

Pre-Removal, Removal, War and Treaties: To the Victor Go the Spoils

> *"History teaches us that men and nations behave wisely once they have exhausted all other alternatives."*
> —ABBA EBAN

A. Trail of Tears

The whites are already nearly a match for us all united, and too strong for any one tribe alone to resist; so that unless we support one another with our collective and united forces[,] unless every tribe unanimously combines to give check to the ambition and avarice of the whites, they will soon conquer us apart and disunited, and we will be driven away from our native country and scattered as autumnal leaves before the wind. But have we not courage enough remaining to defend our country and maintain our ancient independence? Will we calmly suffer the white intruders and tyrants to enslave us? Shall it be said of our race that we knew not how to extricate ourselves from the three most dreadful calamities—folly, inactivity and cowardice? But what need is there to speak of the past? It speaks for itself and asks where today is the Pequo[t]? Where the Narragansetts, the Mohawks, Pocanokets, and many other once powerful tribes of our race? They have vanished before the avarice and oppression of the white men, as snow before a summer sun.[1]

—TECUMSEH, *Sleep Not Longer, O Choctaws and Chickasaws*
(Excerpt from speech before a joint council of the Choctaw and Chickasaw nations [1811])

Native-American upheavals at the hands of interlopers are nothing new. Native Americans suffered immeasurably at the hands of early European explorers in the "New World." One truth emerged: white dominance and hegemony—viewed through a Eurocentric lens as "progress"—meant land loss and cultural degradation.

As naturalist and writer William Bartram observed in the late eighteenth century, Native Americans did not cede these things lightly:

> Surely it is very absurd to suppose they would give all their Country away, abandon their aged Parents, & consign themselves & Posterity to slavery, for the purpose of gratifying the evil & caprice of avaricious Strangers. We might almost as easily imagine that these innocent People, would tamely suffer those Strangers to cut off their Arms & Legs, or deprive them of their Members, which are necessary for procreation. We find, as they ever have been, that they now are most tenacious of their freedom, independence & other unalienable rights of Men.[2]

Once begun, the European onslaught forever changed "Native America." The process began in 1526 with the Spanish exploration and attempted colonization of what is now the southeastern United States. Europeans then first encountered the aborigines of that area, Native Americans or "Indians."[3]

The early Spanish explorers found advanced natives who, for example, kept and grazed deer, which they milked like cattle. They even made cheese from the deer milk. Maize and potatoes were also prevalent.

Some of these sixteenth-century natives shared folkways with persons of African descent. The Spanish took note:

> The color of the inhabitants is dark brown. None of them have any system of writing, but they preserve traditions of great antiquity in rhymes and chants. Dancing and physical exercises are held in honor, and they are passionately fond of ball games, in which they exhibit the greatest skill. The women know how to spin and sew. Although they are partially clothed with skins of wild beasts, they use cotton . . . and they make nets of the fiber of certain tough grasses. . . .[4]

The Spanish tasked Hernando de Soto with conquering *La Florida*. In this vast territory that covered the area from the

Chesapeake Bay to northeastern Mexico, Hernando de Soto was to establish settlements and return to Spain with hoped-for riches. His ship, which carried 600 people, livestock, and supplies to establish settlements, landed in Tampa Bay on May 30, 1539.

By October 1539, the de Soto party reached the Tallahassee area. At the time, some 30,000 Native Americans lived in the Apalachee Province, the capital of which was the village of Anhaica.

Aware of de Soto's impending arrival, the Apalachee abandoned Anhaica, its 250 buildings, and its storehouse of foodstuffs. Upon arrival, de Soto seized control. His men occupied the Apalachee village for the winter, despite persistent resistance from the indigenous population.

The Spaniards left Anhaica in March 1540. They continued on their expedition throughout the southeastern United States, as far west as Texas and Oklahoma. Over a four-year period, the expedition traveled 4,000 miles.

De Soto often captured Native-American leaders, holding them until his conquistadors gained safe passage through the territory. At times, pitched battles ensued. The Spanish massacred Native Americans and burned their villages. Spaniards, too, died in these clashes. European-borne diseases, far more insidious than combat-related wounds, also infected and decimated local populations.

Hernando de Soto died on May 21, 1542. He was buried in the Mississippi River to prevent his body from being desecrated by Indians. Survivors of the de Soto party left *La Florida* in July 1543. From the vantage of the Spanish Crown, de Soto's expedition proved to be a failure. No new settlements resulted. No booty accompanied the returnees.[5]

White settlers intensified their onslaught over the next two centuries. By the mid-eighteenth century, white supremacist ideology increasingly gained a foothold. Over time, the ascendancy of whiteness (or at least non-blackness) drove a wedge between black and red.[6]

Early colonists realized that sheer numbers signaled a black-red alliance could spell trouble for whites. In some quarters, concerns arose that persons of African ancestry might join forces with the Indians against whites. In parts of the South, the combined population of African Americans and Native Americans, if unified, threatened to form a critical, oppositional mass.

The colonists took action. Slave codes began to distinguish between African Americans and Native Americans. Miscegenation laws prevented black-red intermarriage. Colonists played these two "races" against each other. They used African Americans to quell "Indian uprisings" and engaged Native Americans to cap slave revolts, offering bounties for runaway slaves. These strategic deployments helped foment mistrust—even hatred—between African Americans and Native Americans in some parts of the South.[7]

The ideology of white supremacy[8] lies at the core of much of the historic tension and social distance that existed, and to some extent, still exists, between African Americans and Native Americans.[9]

Rooted in the Euro-American desire for social, political, and economic domination,[10] race became a convenient mechanism to relegate non-whites to inferior, sometimes subhuman, status. In time, Samuel Morton's racial pseudo-science (1831-1851) created a hierarchy of the so-called races based on the physiognomy of human skulls. Not surprisingly, the architects of this hierarchical racial ladder occupied the top rung, with Indians and other non-black people inhabiting the intermediate stratum, and blacks at the bottom as the lowest form of human existence.[11] Morton's work conveniently dovetailed with the racist view of Southern planters, who needed a scientific foundation upon which to morally justify involuntary servitude, and thereby fulfill their economic manifest destinies.[12]

Later, Lewis Henry Morgan proposed racial Darwinism. The races, he argued, compete for survival. Innate qualities allow the fittest among us to thrive and, ultimately, prevail. The inherently weaker races falter.[13] Morgan's theory worked to justify the status quo, ignoring the historical and environmental factors that brought it into being. Morgan evaded counter-narrative facts, such as the magnificent pre-Conquest civilizations developed by Native Americans and the post-Conquest depredations visited upon them by the conquerors. He discounted the impact of American slavery, racism, and "Jim Crowism" on African Americans.

Morgan, too, found many a listening ear. His views seemed to mirror the reality of the American experience. Whites prospered. Non-whites lagged behind. Blacks pulled up the rear.

Others allowed assumptions about race to shape their interactions. Native Americans, realizing the profound nature of "white privilege" and the risks attendant to mixing with blacks, often chose "whitening" over "blackening." They imposed restrictions upon social intercourse with blacks, while simultaneously encouraging, if sometimes tacitly, all manner of engagement with whites.

> Black and Indian communities have undermined each other's best interests many times over. Why? Typically because we have failed to recognize the unique but common impact white supremacy has had on each of our communities. Thinking about why Indians in the South have consistently sought to separate themselves politically from African Americans obliges us to grapple with issues that touch on our most sensitive nerves, our most basic sense of who we are.
>
> . . . .
>
> The origin of anti-black racism among southern Indians clearly rests in Anglo-American racism and colonialism, two phenomena that are based on an ideology of white supremacy—one in which white people are understood to be morally, intellectually, politically, and spiritually superior to non-whites and therefore entitled to various forms of privilege, power, and property. [footnote omitted][14]

Historian Howard Zinn offers an example of how whites encouraged friction between African Americans and Native Americans. He points to mid-eighteenth century developments in South Carolina:

> In the Carolinas . . . whites were outnumbered by black slaves and nearby Indian tribes; in the 1750s, 25,000 whites faced 40,000 black slaves, with 60,000 Creek, Cherokee, Choctaw, and Chickasaw Indians in the area. . . . The white rulers of the Carolinas seemed to be conscious of the need for a policy, as one of them put it, "to make Indians & Negroes a checque upon each other[,] lest by their Vastly Superior Numbers we should be crushed by one or the other." And so laws were passed prohibiting free blacks from traveling in Indian country. Treaties with Indian tribes contained clauses requiring the return of fugitive slaves. Governor Lyttletown of South Carolina wrote in 1738: "It has allways [sic] been the policy of this government to create an aversion in them [Indians] to Negroes."
> Part of this policy involved using black slaves in the South Carolina militia to fight Indians. . . . Blacks ran away to Indian villages, and the Creeks and Cherokees harbored runaway slaves by the hundreds. Many of these were amalgamated into the Indian tribes, married, produced children. But the combination of harsh

slave codes and bribes to the Indians to help put down black rebels kept things under control.

It was the potential combination of poor whites and blacks that caused the most fear among the wealthy white planters.[15]

Following the Revolutionary War, Native Americans succumbed to the intense pressure to assimilate, in part to salvage what remained of indigenous cultures.[16] Cherished traditions declined precipitously.

Indian tribes often became enmeshed in deadly European colonial wars. Losing those conflicts generally entailed surrendering parts of their homelands.

Some Indians, loath to concede the superiority of white ways, held fast to centuries-old traditions as long as they could. As a result, whites questioned their ability to assimilate into "civilized" society:

> The term "civilized" was originally applied to them in contradistinction to the life of the wild Indian tribes, but as a whole their condition is not the civilization of the Anglo-Saxon. The Indians of The Five Civilized Tribes, or a large number of them, are quarter or half-breeds; in fact, are white men in features. They are generally progressive; but the most obstinate opponents of change are found among them.
> . . . .
> The civilization of The Five Civilized Tribes has not been accomplished without a vast expenditure of time and money by white people. No Indians in the United States have received such care from the whites or have been aided so much by the United States.[17]

"Civilization" implied Christianization, the adoption of an agrarian lifestyle, the embrace of Eurocentric education, and the codification of American-style laws.

> The Five Tribes "performed whiteness" by modifying their form of government, as well as their language, attire, religion, education, laws, and even [whom] they married. This emulation of whiteness earned the Five Tribes the title of being "civilized," setting them apart from other Indians and making them even more acceptable as marriage partners for whites. Additionally, the adoption of white sexual mores was another way that the tribes performed whiteness. . . . Through the adoption of [tribal anti-black miscegenation] laws, the tribes gave yet another signal to whites that

they were advancing toward civilization, and hence deserving of equality with whites.[18] [footnotes omitted]

Civilization policy, implemented in part by Christian missionaries, resulted in encroachments on Indian sovereignty and decreased Indian land holdings. For Indians, the perceived benefits of the civilization bargain included semi-autonomy and enhanced opportunities for upward social and economic mobility within the "white world."[19]

The lure of Indian "civilization" proved to be a classic "racial bribe"[20]—a systematic way of offering advancement along the black/white racial continuum toward the presumed ideal: whiteness. The racial bribe arrogates whiteness to supremacy, elevates "otherness" to normalcy, and relegates blackness to inferiority.[21]

Scholars have pointed to the perversity of Indians' simultaneous and paradoxical desires to retain vestiges of sovereignty for themselves and to deny basic freedom to persons of African ancestry:

> Cherokees adopted black slavery in part to demonstrate their level of "civilization" in the hopes of forestalling further encroachment by white America. Thereafter the Cherokee Nation legalized slavery and black exclusion to maintain economic growth and independence and to demonstrate a social distance from the subjugated African race. In its qualified support of the Confederacy during the American Civil War[,] the Cherokee Nation again opposed black liberation and Cherokee independence, since many Cherokee leaders had come to view slavery as a core feature of their national character and a key sign of their sovereign rights.[22]

White purveyors of the racial bribe sought to: (1) blunt the push for cultural preservation and continued communal land ownership; (2) dissuade associations, particularly sexual liaisons, with blacks, deemed members of a veritable "under-caste"; (3) secure for Indians social and economic advancement and an intermediate, quasi-white status through, in part, intermarriage with whites; and (4) broaden "whiteness" to include non-black people beyond Caucasians, and thereby deflect charges of racism.[23] Acceptance of this racial bribe only further ensconced the black/white racial duality, creating, in effect, two nations: one black, one white; separate, hostile, and unequal.[24]

Indians' acquiescence in the racial bribe, with its false promise of honorary "whiteness," resulted in the dilution of native culture.

Indians often lost their traditional identity in ways enslaved Africans, some of whom toiled for Indians, did not.

> [C]ontrary to the Indians, black slaves had never had the means, nor the opportunity, "of assuming the prestigious attributes of an alien culture," and had therefore managed "to preserve their own cultural identity." Compared to them, the slaveholding Indians of North America were clearly losers on two essential scores: they had, at least in part, lost their original identity, and they had not become "white," i.e.[,] socially, culturally, and politically equal to their white models. They were at best a surrealistic caricature of the dominant group. . . .[25]

As Negrophobia—contempt for blackness—spread, the enduring racial epithet "Nigger" emerged in the early-to-mid 1800s as a common slur against persons of African ancestry. This "ethnophaulism"—this verbal picture of negative stereotypes—became the linguistic embodiment of racism and racial hatred.[26] In time, the analogous term "Prairie Nigger," a similar invective aimed at Native Americans,[27] evolved as a reminder of the rigidity of the prevailing social order and the elusive character of "whiteness."

Economics impelled the racial bribe. Early on, whites coveted Indian lands in the Southeast. As historian Angie Debo pointed out, conquest sometimes comes in other than militaristic ways:

> Indian warfare was a perpetual accompaniment of American pioneering, but the second stage in dispossessing the Indians is not so generally and romantically known. The age of military conquest was succeeded by the age of economic absorption, when the long rifle of the frontiersman was displaced by the legislative enactment and court decree of the legal exploiter, and the lease, mortgage, and deed of the land shark. As a preliminary to this process[,] the Indians were persuaded or forced to surrender their tribal organization and accept United States citizenship and to divide their communal holdings into individual allotments. Because of the magnitude of the plunder and the rapidity of the spoliation[,] the most spectacular development of this policy occurred with the Five Civilized Tribes of the Indian Territory.[28]

Whites felt a sense of entitlement—of manifest destiny—to long held Indian plots. Moreover, some whites perceived Indians's humane treatment of African Americans[29] and the presence of abolitionist missionaries among some of the tribes as threats to chattel slavery, a foundational element in Southern society.

The "manifest destiny" concept became established public policy. In 1803, the United States purchased the French territory of *Louisiane* for just over $23 million. *Louisiane* encompassed portions of fifteen current states and two Canadian provinces. Following the "Louisiana Purchase," white immigration to the area pushed the United States government to develop a federal policy on native presence in the region. Not surprisingly, a pro-white immigration policy emerged, with scant regard for Native American rights. Indeed, Indian removal had been discussed at high levels of the United States government since its inception.[30]

In 1825, the United States government formally decided to free up lands in the Southeast for white settlement by removing the native population. Presidents Andrew Jackson[31] and Martin Van Buren executed this removal policy[32] in the 1830s and 1840s.

The federal government uprooted Indians who occupied the Southeastern United States—primarily the Cherokees, Chickasaws, Choctaws, Muscogee (Creek), and Seminoles—and then transplanted them to Oklahoma, an unfamiliar, faraway land. White settlers, desiring Indian land holdings, spurred on the removal effort. Their covetousness, rather than any kind of social or economic necessity, held sway.[33] Incredible suffering ensued, both to Native Americans and the persons of African ancestry who lived among them.

Many scholars cite political, economic, nationalistic, and/or imperialistic motives as key catalytic factors that pushed the federal government toward a policy of Indian removal. An alternative narrative focuses on Native, mostly oral, sources that have not been roundly mined. Using such sources, Donna L. Akers shed light on what forced removal meant to Native people, particularly the Choctaws. She found that Choctaw religious beliefs about appropriate care for the bones of ancestors helped explain that tribe's refusal to sell tribal lands, sometimes even upon pain of death. She argued that this alternative narrative, this shift in perspective, enhances our understanding of Indian removal.[34]

> The story of the American policy of Indian Removal must be reexamined and retold. It was not merely an official, dry, legal instrument[,] as it often is portrayed. Removal, as experienced by Native people, was an official U.S. policy of death and destruction

that created untold human pain and misery. It was unjust, inhumane, and a product of the worst impulses of Western society. Indian Removal cannot be separated from the human suffering it evoked[—]from the toll on the human spirit of the Native people. It cannot be remembered by Americans as merely an official U.S. policy, but must be understood in terms of the human suffering it caused, and the thousands of deaths and lives it destroyed.[35]

The Cherokees suffered a particularly tragic fate upon removal. As former Cherokee Nation Principal Chief Wilma Mankiller observed: "[W]e [must] never forget what happened to our people on the Trail of Tears. It was indeed our holocaust."[36]

The federal government extricated the Cherokees from their homes, herded them into internment camps, and forcibly evicted them to a foreign land along *Nunna daul Tsunyi*, "the trail where we cried."[37] Removal proved all the more bitter and ironic for the Cherokees, who had largely succeeded at Eurocentric assimilation.

The word "Cherokee" is the anglicized version of *Tsalagi*, meaning "cave people," a word that has been spelled a variety of ways throughout history.[38] Traditionally, the Cherokees, woodlands people, lived in villages in the southern Appalachians, in present day Virginia, West Virginia, Kentucky, Tennessee, western North Carolina, South Carolina, northern Georgia, and northeastern Alabama. The Cherokees availed themselves of the diverse topography in the region to create a culture rife with farming, hunting, and fishing.

The Cherokees constructed European-style homes and farmsteads. They laid out European-style fields and farms. They developed a written language based on the syllabary created by Sequoyah. They established a newspaper, the *Cherokee Phoenix*. They wrote a constitution. Some of them, a relative few, undertook human bondage; they embraced slavery.

Cherokee assimilation, however successful, failed to stave off white land-lust. Neither did it guarantee the Cherokees equal protection under the law.

Beginning in 1791, a series of treaties between the United States and the Cherokees explicitly recognized the Cherokee Nation as a separate sovereign. Despite this official recognition, however, subsequent treaties and agreements gradually whittled away at the Cherokee land base.

In the late 1700s, some Cherokees sought refuge from white interference in Northwest Arkansas, between the White and Arkansas rivers. As the United States government increasingly foisted land cessions upon the Cherokees during the first two decades of the 1800s, more Cherokees moved west of the Mississippi River. Federal government agents had begun encouraging individual Cherokees to migrate west during this period. Some Cherokees relocated to the west as early as 1808.

In 1819, the Cherokee National Council notified the federal government that the Cherokee Nation would no longer cede land. Thus began the ossification of the Cherokee resolve to maintain cultural homelands.

States' rights and a prolonged dispute between Georgia and the federal government further complicated the Cherokee situation. In 1802, Georgia became the last of the original colonies to give its western lands over to the federal government. Georgia expected all titles to land held by Indians to be extinguished, but the Cherokees continued to occupy their ancestral, treaty-protected homelands.

White Georgians resented Cherokee land ownership and self-governance. They continued to encroach on Cherokee and neighboring Muscogee (Creek) lands.

Finally, in 1828, Georgia passed a law pronouncing all laws of the Cherokee Nation to be null and void as of June 1, 1830. Prospectors' discovery of gold on Cherokee land in northern Georgia in 1829 intensified the efforts to dislodge the Cherokees.

Meanwhile, President Andrew Jackson, a noted Indian fighter and slaveholder, moved aggressively to implement a sweeping policy of extinguishing Indian land titles in affected states and relocating the Indian population. On May 26, 1830, Congress passed the Indian Removal Act[39] to open up for settlement Indian lands, primarily in Georgia, Tennessee, Alabama, Mississippi and North Carolina. President Andrew Jackson applauded passage of the Act as a means to enhance wealth, grow population, and consolidate power.[40]

Passage of the Indian Removal Act, the discovery of gold, and continued hostility from the State of Georgia prompted the Cherokee Nation to bring suit in the United States Supreme Court in 1831. Fundamental notions of sovereignty rested at the core of the Cherokee claims.

Frustrated by persistent incursions by whites upon their lands, the Cherokees sued the State of Georgia to restrain the execution of laws allowing whites to inhabit and explore Native American territory. The United Stated Supreme Court indicated its sympathy for the Cherokee Nation on sovereignty grounds in *Cherokee Nation v. Georgia*.[41] The High Court subsequently affirmed Cherokee Nation sovereignty vis-à-vis Georgia law in *Worcester v. Georgia*.[42]

In *Cherokee Nation v. Georgia*,[43] Chief Justice John Marshall, writing for the majority of the United States Supreme Court, addressed the issue of whether the Court had original jurisdiction to hear a case filed by a tribe against a state. Under Article III of the United States Constitution, such jurisdiction existed only in cases between a state and another state or a foreign nation and its citizens. The Court held that the Cherokee Nation was a "domestic dependent nation." It would not be treated as a sovereign state or foreign nation. The Court, though sympathetic to the Cherokee Nation's concerns, decided it simply did not have original jurisdiction to resolve the dispute. As such, Georgia state law applied to the Cherokee Nation.

The United States Supreme Court followed up its *Cherokee Nation v. Georgia* decision the following year, in *Worcester v. Georgia*.[44] Under an 1830 law, Georgia required all white residents in Cherokee country to secure a license from the governor and to take an oath of allegiance to the state. Missionaries Samuel Austin Worcester and Dr. Elizur Butler, highly visible opponents of Indian removal, refused. State authorities arrested, convicted, and imprisoned them. The State of Georgia sentenced both men to years of hard labor.

Worcester appealed to the United States Supreme Court, claiming the laws leading to his conviction were unconstitutional. States, he argued, had no authority over sovereign Indian nations. This time, the Court, with appellate jurisdiction, held that: (i) Indian nations are capable of making treaties; (ii) under the Constitution, treaties are the supreme law of the land; (iii) the federal government had exclusive jurisdiction within the confines of the Cherokee Nation; and (iv) state law had no force within the Cherokee boundaries. The decision resulted in the release of the two men.

President Andrew Jackson, an architect of Indian removal, ignored the Supreme Court's edict and pressed forward with abandon. Indians tribes "traded" land desired by the United States for largely unknown lands west of the Mississippi River. Those Indians who did not take the "deal" became ordinary citizens of the states in which they remained.

Some tribes, including the Cherokee Nation, resisted. The Cherokees based their anti-removal stance on pre-existing treaty guarantees, their ancestral connection to the southern lands, the unfamiliarity of the new world promised in the West, and the prospect of facing hostile Indians from other tribes already inhabiting their proposed new home. Cherokee resistance met with some initial success.

Like the American president, the State of Georgia all but ignored the decision of America's highest court. In due course, the federal government approached the Five Civilized Tribes with new treaty offers. Tribal reactions varied: the Chickasaws acquiesced; the Seminoles fought removal for almost three decades; and a group of Cherokees, thought by some to be renegades, ultimately signed a removal treaty, the Treaty of New Echota, disclaimed by most of their brethren.

Seeing removal as imminent, a Cherokee faction known as the "Treaty Party" began negotiating with the federal government. The group, led by Major Ridge, and including his son, John, Elias Boudinot, editor of the *Cherokee Phoenix*, and Boudinot's brother, Stand Watie, signed a treaty at New Echota, the Cherokee Nation capital, in 1835. The Treaty Party sold the eastern lands of the Cherokees for $5 million in exchange for seven million acres of land in present-day Oklahoma. The "National Party," led by Cherokee Principal Chief John Ross, and supported by the majority of the Cherokee Nation, considered the Treaty Party traitorous.

The United States Senate ratified the Treaty of New Echota despite knowledge that only a minority of Cherokees had accepted it. Within two years, the federal government slated the Cherokees for removal. By the 1830s, removal pressure had reached a crescendo.[45]

President Martin Van Buren ordered the implementation of the Treaty of New Echota in 1838. United States Army troops, under the command of General Winfield Scott, rounded up the Cherokees and moved them into fort stockades in North Carolina, Georgia, Alabama, and Tennessee. Builders positioned all of the posts, intended only as temporary housing, proximate to Cherokee towns.

Authorities soon transferred the Indians from the removal forts to several internment camps more centrally located. In North Carolina, for example, Cherokees at the removal forts were sent initially to Fort Butler and, by the second week in July, on to the principal agency at Fort Cass. By late July 1838, most Cherokees remaining in the east inhabited these internment camps.

One group of Cherokees did not leave the mountains of North Carolina. This group, the Eastern Band of Cherokee Indians, or the "Oconaluftee," traces its origins to an 1819 treaty that provided for the occupation of lands separate and apart from the parcel occupied by the Cherokee Nation. That treaty also provided for American citizenship.

At the initiation of forced removal in 1838, the Eastern Band of Cherokee Indians held fast. The Treaty of New Echota, they asserted, did not apply to them since they no longer lived on Cherokee lands. The argument succeeded. North Carolina ultimately recognized the rights of the Eastern Band of Cherokee Indians. Fugitive Cherokees from the Cherokee Nation joined them. Today, the Eastern Band of Cherokee Indians resides on the Qualla Reservation in North Carolina.[46]

During the roundup, intimidation and acts of cruelty at the hands of the troops, along with theft and destruction of property by local residents, further alienated the Cherokees. A frustrated Principal Chief John Ross appealed to President Van Buren to permit the Cherokee to oversee their own removal. Van Buren acquiesced, and Ross and his brother, Lewis, administered the effort.

Cherokee leaders divided the tribe into sixteen detachments, each composed of approximately 1,000 persons. Three detachments of Cherokees—some 2,800 persons in all—traveled by river to Indian Territory. The first of these groups left on June 6, 1838, by steamboat and barge from Ross's Landing on the Tennessee River, present-day Chattanooga. They followed the Tennessee as it wound across northern Alabama, including a short railroad detour around the shoals between Decatur and Tuscumbia Landing. They headed north through central Tennessee and Kentucky to the Ohio River, the Mississippi River, and on to the mouth of the Arkansas River, which led northwest into Indian Territory. They arrived aboard a steamboat at the mouth of Sallisaw Creek near Fort Coffee, Oklahoma, on June 19, 1838.

The remainder of the Cherokees traveled to Indian Territory overland on existing roads, organized into detachments ranging in size from 700 to 1,600. A conductor and an assistant conductor appointed by Principal Chief John Ross headed each grouping. People routinely walked. A separate unit led by John Bell and administered by United States Army Lieutenant Edward Deas included the Treaty of New Echota signatories.

A physician, and oftentimes a clergyman, accompanied these detachments. The travelers generally carried supplies and low-grade foodstuffs, including flour and corn, and occasionally salt pork, coffee, and sugar. Drought and the sheer number of migrants substantially reduced forage for the beasts of burden that hauled possessions.

Enslaved Africans stocked the wagons and cleared the trails for the brutal trek. They suffered the highest mortality of all of the Trail of Tears migrants.[47] For those who survived, freedom would be the ultimate reward, but it would be a generation in coming.

An African living among the Cherokee at the time of the removal recalled its horrors:

> The weeks that followed General Scott's order to remove the Cherokees were filled with horror and suffering for the unfortunate Cherokees and their slaves. The women and children were driven from their homes, sometimes with blows and close on the heels of the retreating Indians came greedy whites to pillage the Indian[s'] homes, drive off their cattle, horses, and pigs; and they even rif[f]led the graves for any jewelry, or other ornaments that might have been buried with the dead.
>
> The Cherokees, after having been driven from their homes, were divided into detachments of nearly equal size[,] and late in October, 1838, the first detachment started, the others following one by one. The aged, sick and young children rode in the wagons, which carried provisions and bedding, while others went on foot. The trip was made in the dead of winter and many died from exposure to sleet and snow, and all who lived to make this trip, or had parents who made it, will long remember it as a bitter memory.[48]

Such were the horrors endured by the Cherokees and the persons of African ancestry living among them. As former Cherokee Nation Principal Chief Joe Byrd pointed out:

> The Freedmen came with us on the Trail of Tears. They delivered babies with us. They died with us. They lived and ate with us. They buried our dead and they persevered with our people [i.e., with Native Americans] just to stay alive during a time that we today can hardly imagine. They were one with us.[49]

Similarly, former Principal Chief of the Cherokee Nation, Wilma Mankiller,[50] reflected: "Although we know about the terrible human suffering of our native people and the members of other tribes during the removal, we rarely hear of those black people who also suffered."[51]

African Americans constituted a significant minority of those forcibly marched to Oklahoma.[52] Indeed, some claim African Americans made up some fifteen percent of those who died on the Cherokee Trail of Tears:[53]

> [W]e can rest assured that whenever faces gathered around the campfire, there were Africans there to serve as spiritual guides into a different kind of wilderness. When there were dances to celebrate, deaths to mourn, or festivals to mark the passing of the seasons, there were Africans present. In addition, we must never forget that on the "trail where we cried," there were also African tears. This we can never forget.[54]

The arduous journey that became the Trail of Tears traversed a number of paths. The most commonly used overland route followed a northern alignment. This northern route started at Calhoun, Tennessee, and crossed central Tennessee, southwestern Kentucky, and southern Illinois. After crossing the Mississippi River north of Cape Girardeau, Missouri, these detachments trekked across southern Missouri and the northwest corner of Arkansas. Other routes, notably those led by John Benge and John Bell, followed more southern routes. Still others followed slight variations on these principal courses.

Unforgiving terrain and the harshness of winter complicated the migration. Cherokees in southern Illinois, for example, waited in freezing temperatures for thawing conditions that would enable them to traverse the then-frozen Mississippi River. Illness was rampant. Death became a daily occurrence.

Removal mortality rates mounted to a staggering 4,000 persons by one account.[55] Cold numbers, however, scarcely paint the total picture. Among the personal chronicles that shed additional light on the twists and turns of removal is that of Lucy Butler.

Lucy Ames Butler wrote a letter to Drusilla Burnap of Lowell, Massachusetts, on January 2, 1839, and posted it a week later from Cleveland, Tennessee. The letter explained the forbidding conditions faced by the removed Cherokees. Ms. Butler, a Presbyterian missionary, was the second wife of Dr. Elizur Butler.

As previously noted, Dr. Butler and Samuel Worcester had been incarcerated by the State of Georgia for entering Indian Territory without proper authorization. After Chief Justice John Marshall ordered their release in *Worcester v. Georgia*,[56] Lucy's husband accompanied the Cherokees to present-day Oklahoma. At the time she wrote the letter, Dr. Butler had almost completed his journey with the Cherokees.

Lucy Ames Butler's 1839 letter reads:

> My husband has been engaged in camp, preaching and attending on the sick Cherokees, since they were first taken. He was appointed to serve as Physician in one of the first companies. He also preaches in camp on the Sabbath as they have made arrangements not to travel on that day. We have heard from several companies, and understand they have considerable sickness. Twenty-five in a company of seven hundred had died, when they had proceeded three hundred miles. In another, which numbered about the same, in two hundred miles, eighteen had been laid in their graves. I have not heard particularly from others. When these companies arrive in their new country, the greatest part will be without shelters as they were in this [place], after they were prisoners; and it is to be feared many will be cut down by death, as has been the case with new emigrants in the country. It is estimated about two thousand died while in camp in this country. Will not the people in whose power it is to redress Indian wrongs awake to their duty? Will they not think of the multitudes among the various tribes that have within a few years been swept into Eternity by the cupidity of the "white man" who is in the enjoyment of wealth and freedom on the original soil of these oppressed Indians? I know many friends of the Indians have set down in despair, thinking oppression has been carried so far, nothing now can be done. I will mention one person who thinks otherwise; and it may surprise you when I tell [you] it is John Ross, the principal Chief of these oppressed Cherokees. In speaking of the distresses of his people, I have heard him with subdued agitation of feeling, with calmness and confidence say, "Though for years, the Press has been closed against us, and the few friends we have left[] have[,] at times, been ready to think we must sink to ruin unheard; yet I cannot think the United States' Government is so lost to all justice that our wrongs will not be redressed, if the truth is fairly set before those[] who have the power to do it." With these feelings, this man has presented himself at our seat of Government year after year; and though false reports, in almost every form, have been circulated against him, and indignities heaped on him and his associates, and withal being

told by the highest Authorities of our Government, that he must accept [the] terms already offered, that nothing more favourable would ever be granted, yet the returning Congress has again found him at Washington pleading for his people. It may now be thought as his people have actually been driven from their native country, and one eighth of them already cut off by death, that he will think nothing can be gained by further intercession; but probably, if his life is spared, he will again be seen pleading with Government, for those that remain.[57]

Lucy's husband, Dr. Elizur Butler, went on to become the first religion instructor at the Cherokee Female Seminary in Tahlequah, Oklahoma, one of the first boarding schools for Native Americans. Founded in 1851, the seminary produced a cadre of women integral to the acculturation of the Cherokees.[58]

Most of the land route detachments entered present-day Oklahoma near Westville. Often a detachment of United States troops from Fort Gibson on the Arkansas River received the Cherokees. The new arrivals generally went to live with those who had already arrived, or awaited land assignments while camped along the Illinois River and its tributaries east of present-day Tahlequah.

Upon arrival in Indian Territory, a palpable schism soon arose between new arrivals and existing settlers. On June 22, 1839, angry Cherokees exacted retribution upon the Treaty of New Echota signing party, killing[59] Major Ridge, John Ridge, and Elias Boudinot for what they viewed as a treasonous transfer of Cherokee land to the federal government. Stand Watie escaped death, and became a lifelong adversary of Cherokee Chief John Ross. Tensions mounted.

As the transition to Oklahoma smoothed, the Cherokees continued to adapt to their new homeland. They re-established their own governance structure, patterned after that of the United States and based in Tahlequah.

The 1827 Cherokee Constitution divided responsibilities among an elected principal chief, an elected legislature known as the National Council, and a supreme court with lesser courts. Local districts with elected officials, similar to counties, rounded out the Cherokee Nation governance structure.[60]

Article III, Section 7 of the 1827 Constitution denied persons of African ancestry the franchise.[61] This denial of the franchise to persons of African ancestry may have been attributable to the American institution of slavery generally, and its characterization of the enslaved as chattel. Later, after the end of slavery, the Cherokee Nation enfranchised the Africans living within its borders.

Beyond government, the Cherokees concentrated on building an educational infrastructure. They operated a bilingual school system.

The Cherokees and, arguably to a lesser extent, other Indians, came to embrace the divisive concept of race promoted by whites. First in subtle ways, and then roundly, Cherokees came to view whiteness as the coin of the realm in the dominant "white world." Some Cherokees even assumed a mysterious "Black Dutch" heritage—pseudo-Eurocentric ancestry—in order to purchase land. They feared their actual Indian identity would make them vulnerable to land seizure.[62]

With self-preservation among its principal aims, the Cherokee Nation pushed forward with assimilation. The Cherokees' dutiful adoption of white culture and their reliance on the American judicial system to vindicate their rights fell short of the mark. Nothing could forestall the erosion of Indian sovereignty attendant to the removal process.[63]

The federal government uprooted some 46,000 Indians from the east side of the Mississippi River and transplanted them to the west side. By removing these Indians, the government freed up about twenty-five million acres of land for white settlement and, in some cases, for settlement by the Africans they enslaved.[64]

Though the dust of the forced migrations of Indian Nations had barely settled, the American Civil War would break out in a matter of decades. With that, tribal life would be disrupted once again, alliances frayed, and loyalties questioned. Friction between Native Americans and persons of African descent flared.

B. The American Civil War

Generally speaking, Native Americans were reluctant warriors. Some aligned themselves with the Union in the hope of federal protection from further land loss. Others saw the Civil War as an economic opportunity. Compensated military service was a way out of dire poverty. For all, the Civil War provided further proof of the law of unintended consequences.

Though titular allies of the Confederacy in the Civil War, the Confederate-aligned Five Civilized Tribes did relatively little actual fighting. Such alliances developed, in part, around a shared interest in the maintenance of the institution of slavery to further economic interests.[65]

The Choctaw Nation, for example, replicated slavery as it had existed in the South. The Choctaws enacted a plethora of legislation to cement the inferior status of Africans among them, including laws prohibiting co-habitation of tribesmen with enslaved Africans; banning intermarriage; denying, generally, the ability of enslaved Africans to own property; and barring the teaching of reading and writing to enslaved Africans.[66]

According to some estimates, the Cherokees ranked as the largest holders of enslaved Africans—some 4,600 by 1860.[67] These Cherokee slaveholders relied upon chattel slavery to bridge them over to white society. Some enslaved Africans provided interpretation and translation services, but most worked at menial tasks—as farm laborers, housemaids, or servants.

Indian Territory, situated between slaveholding Texas and the battleground state of Kansas, became a hotbed of activity for enslaved Africans. Its general reputation for lawlessness and its lack of a coherent, cohesive stance on the issue of slavery made it a natural haven for surreptitious activity. While some Africans fled bondage in Indian Territory by making their way to Kansas, others found their way to Indian Territory as fugitives from other areas. Though not celebrated as such, Indian Territory evolved into a veritable whistle-stop along the Underground Railroad.[68]

Potential revolts by these enslaved Africans cast a pall over the Cherokee Nation. On the morning of November 15, 1842, the worst fears of these Cherokee overlords materialized in Webbers Falls, Oklahoma.

Some twenty-five African rebels, primarily from the Joseph Vann[69] plantation, locked their Cherokee owners in their homes and cabins while they slept. The escapees purloined guns, horses, mules, ammunition, food, and supplies.

At daybreak, this rag-tag contingent of men, women, and children headed to Mexico, a recognized safe haven for such escapes. The party added to its numbers as it descended south of the border. Similarly situated Africans in the Creek Nation joined the fleeing group. Some thirty-five strong, the fugitives repelled a number of pursuers. They killed two bounty hunters (a.k.a., "patrollers" or "patty rollers") in the Choctaw Nation.

The Cherokee Nation, under the auspices of the Cherokee National Council in Tahlequah, dispatched eighty-seven men from the Cherokee Militia in an effort to capture the runaways. This official posse located its targets, by then worn and weak, seven miles north of the Red River on November 28, 1842. Overmatched, the escapees offered scant resistance.

On December 8, 1842, the entire party returned to Tahlequah. The Cherokees executed five slaves. Joseph Vann, the overseer from whom a number of the Africans had escaped, assigned most of his rebellious charges to work on a fleet of steamboats in his public ferry operating along the Arkansas, Mississippi, and Ohio Rivers.

The Cherokees blamed what is now known as the Slave Revolt of 1842 on free, armed African Seminoles living in close proximity to the African Cherokees at Fort Gibson, and sought to eliminate such corrupting influences from the Cherokee Nation. On December 2, 1842, the Cherokee Nation passed "An Act in Regard to Free Negroes," a law banishing all free Africans except those formerly enslaved within the Cherokee Nation.[70]

For the Choctaws, the Cherokees, and other tribes, chattel slavery provided the common bond that tipped the scales in favor of Civil War pacts with the South—the Confederacy.[71] There would be a price to pay.

Regular United States Army troops amassed in the East, the locus of the skirmishes and pitched battles that defined the Civil War. Their departure left some western posts manned by motley local militia. One such militia unit, under the command of John Chivington, attacked a peaceful band of Cheyenne Indians at Sand Creek in Colorado in November 1864. Chivington's forces slaughtered hundreds of people, largely women and children, and mutilated their bodies.[72]

Indians in the South, recalling the federal government's treaty relationship with them, initially wished to maintain neutrality in this internecine family feud. Again, the actions of the Cherokee Nation are illustrative.

At first, the Cherokees maintained neutrality. On the recommendation of Principal Chief John Ross, the tribe adopted a neutrality resolution at Tahlequah, Oklahoma, on August 21, 1861. Ross had impressed upon the Cherokees "the importance of non-interference in the affairs of the people of the States and the observance of unswerving neutrality between them."[73] Principal Chief Ross saw the impending Civil War as potentially catastrophic, and hoped to spare his vulnerable Nation its ravages.

> Weak, defenseless, and scattered over a large section of country, in the peaceful [pursuit] of agricultural life, without hostility to any State and with friendly feelings toward all, [the Cherokee people] hope to be allowed to remain so, under the solemn conviction that they should not be called upon to participate in the threatened fratricidal war between the "United" and the "Confederate" States, and that persons gallantly tenacious of their own rights will respect those of others.[74]

This neutrality would be short lived. Both South and North exerted immense pressure on the tribes to join their respective causes.

Confederate leaders aggressively courted Indian alliances. Attractive propaganda swayed Native Americans to align with one side or the other during the course of the Civil War.

Instructions dated May 14, 1861, from the Confederate Secretary of War, L. P. Walker, to the Superintendent of Indian Affairs, David Hubbard, made clear the Confederacy's intention to tap into manpower from the Five Civilized Tribes in connection with its war effort:

> Let them know that our agents are now actively employed in procuring rifles and providing ammunition to be immediately forwarded to Fort Smith [Arkansas], for the purpose of supplying [Indian] regiments as soon as they shall have been organized, one of which will be raised among the Choctaws and Chickasaws, another among the Cherokees, and the third from among the Creeks, Seminoles, and other friendly tribes entertaining the proposition.
> In addition to these things, regarded of primary importance, you will, without committing the Government to any especial conduct, express our serious anxiety to establish and enforce the debts and annuities due to them from the Government at Washington, which otherwise they will never obtain, as that Government would, undoubtedly, sooner rob them of their lands, emancipate their slaves, and utterly exterminate them, than render to them justice.[75]

Eventually, some tribes in Indian Territory, buoyed by

Confederate propaganda, took up arms for the South. In addition, they were motivated by anger, based on the resurfaced memories of the brutal removal process. Many felt a victory for the North in the American Civil War would lead to further land cessation and displacement.

Beyond concerns over the North's motives, some southern tribal leaders had cultural affiliations with the South. There were, after all, enslaved Africans living among the tribes.

On October 28, 1861, the Cherokee Nation ratified a treaty with the Confederacy, breaching its neutrality pledge. In so doing, the Cherokees felt compelled to justify reneging on that earlier promise:

> Whatever the cause the Cherokee people may have had in the past to complain of some of the Southern States, they cannot but feel that their interest and their destiny are inseparably connected with those of the South. The war now raging is a war of Northern cupidity and fanaticism against the institution of African servitude; against the commercial freedom of the South, and against the political freedom of the States, and its objects are to annihilate the sovereignty of those States and utterly change the nature of the Gen. Government.
>
> The Cherokee people and their neighbors were warned before the war commenced that the first object of the party which now holds the powers of government of the United States would be to annul the institution of slavery in the whole Indian country, and make it what they term free territory and after a time free State; and they have been also warned by the fate which has befallen those of their race in Kansas, Nebraska, and Oregon that at no distant day they too would be compelled to surrender their country at the demand of Northern rapacity, and be content with an extinct nationality, and with reserves of limited extent for individuals, of which their people would soon be despoiled by speculators, if not plundered unscrupulously by the State.
>
> Urged by these considerations, the Cherokees, long divided in opinion, became unanimous, and like their brethren, the Creeks, Seminoles, Choctaws, and Chickasaws, determined, by the undivided voice of a Gen. Convention of all the people . . . to make common cause with the South and share its fortunes.[76]

Historian Theda Perdue cites the introduction of European value systems that justified African slave labor as a defining moment in the Cherokee Nation. The institution of slavery divided the Nation:

> The issue of slavery had not been hotly contested in the [Cherokee] Nation before the outbreak of war, but the institution immediately came to represent all that the traditionalists despised in the white man's "civilization." Despite a forced treaty with the Confederacy and active participation on that side by many Cherokee leaders, the conservative majority repudiated the alliance and the way of life that it symbolized and joined the Union cause.[77]

As Perdue pointed out with respect to the Cherokees, many Indians refused to embrace the official tribal alliances with the Confederacy. In the end, Indian units fought on both sides of the conflict, often with distinction.

During the Civil War, persons of African ancestry and Native Americans shared the battlefield, both as comrades and as combatants. In Oklahoma, one deadly skirmish loomed large. Rentiesville, Oklahoma, one of the dozens of all-black towns that have historically dotted the Oklahoma landscape, was the site of the Battle of Honey Springs, the so-called "Gettysburg of the West," on July 17, 1863.

Outnumbered Union troops routed Confederate troops from Texas. At stake was control of Fort Gibson, a strategically important site along the Arkansas River. Indian fighters engaged in the conflict on both sides. Black troops, the First Kansas Colored Volunteer Infantry Regiment, sealed the Union victory.

The First Kansas Colored was the second "Negro" unit organized after President Abraham Lincoln breeched the color barrier. President Lincoln authorized Union commanders to recruit and arm black soldiers to face a pesky and determined Confederate adversary.[78]

The racial/ethnic composition of the Confederate and Union forces at the Battle of Honey Springs bears examination. On the Confederate side, troops from the Creek, Cherokee, Choctaw, and Chickasaw tribes constituted the majority of the soldiers. The smaller contingent of Union troops, 3,000 strong, consisted of whites, Native Americans, and formerly enslaved Africans.[79]

Curiously, the last Confederate general to surrender was a Native American: Stand Watie, the Cherokee leader of the Indian brigades of the Army of the Trans-Mississippi. Watie gave up the fight on June 23, 1865, two months after General Robert E. Lee's surrender on April 9, 1865.[80]

The Civil War exacted a terrible toll on the nation. Native Americans could not escape the suffering. Virtually all the tribal communities that fought in the Civil War suffered death and destruction as a direct consequence. In fact, greater losses occurred in Indian Territory than in any state.[81] Of the 3,530 men from Indian Territory who served in the Union Army, a staggering 1,018—nearly one-third—died during enlistment.[82]

Such massive deaths left large numbers of widows and orphans in many Indian communities. Rebuilding seemed virtually impossible. Many Native Americans succumbed to poverty and despair.

Post-Civil War, the federal government made manifest the initial fears of retaliation against Native Americans. The western tribes faced intense pressure to give up lives of relative freedom on the plains and move to reservations. Despite loyal service during the Civil War, the Oneida, Seneca, and Ojibwe Indian communities, with little federal protection, continued to face hostile neighbors.

The Five Civilized Tribes executed new treaties with the federal government at the conclusion of the Civil War. As a prelude to the execution of these treaties, the federal government convened The Peace Council at Fort Smith, Arkansas, in 1865. This collective, made up of representatives of the Five Civilized Tribes and federal Indian agents, discussed post-Civil War peace treaty terms.

On September 9, 1865, United States agents announced the official policy of the government as to these treaties. Post-War treaties had to include: (1) a commitment to permanent peace, internally, in relation to other tribes, and as respects the United States; (2) assistance with keeping the peace among the Plains Indians; (3) the abolition of slavery, the emancipation of all enslaved Africans, and the incorporation of the emancipated into the various tribes on par with original members; (4) a permanent ban on slavery; (5) the ceding of lands for occupation by other tribes; (6) the organization of the tribes occupying Indian Territory into a consolidated government, unless otherwise stipulated in the future; and (7) the expulsion of all white persons, except certain authorized personnel, unless such white persons be incorporated into some tribe.[83]

Based on this federal policy, the 1866 treaties further diminished Indian land bases and chipped away at Indian sovereignty. That said, the treaties also had significant salutary effects: emancipating enslaved Africans and, with the notable exception of the Africans living among the Chickasaw Nation, according them citizenship rights.[84]

C. The Treaty of 1866

After the American Civil War, the Five Civilized Tribes signed treaties of reunification with the United States. The post-Civil War Treaty of 1866 guaranteed most of the 7,000 emancipated persons of African descent tribal citizenship rights within the Five Civilized Tribes. As earlier noted, the Chickasaws were the only tribe to refuse citizenship rights to their formerly enslaved Africans, though the Choctaws also resisted temporarily.[85]

Under a deal with the Chickasaws, the federal government pledged to relocate freed Africans whom the tribes refused to adopt, using monies the tribes would otherwise have been paid for the ceded lands. In the end, the Chickasaws held firm. They refused to adopt the Chickasaw Freedmen. They called the government's bluff. The federal government balked, never following through on its pledge to remove the unwanted Freedmen from the bosom of the Five Civilized Tribes.[86]

Within the Five Civilized Tribes, African Americans faced varying degrees of acceptance:

> Among the Seminoles, blacks were immediately liberated and six were elected to the forty-two-seat Seminole Council. Blacks were also elected as representatives to the Creek Council in Okmulgee. By the end of freedom's first year, African-Seminoles were building homes, churches, schools, and businesses, as well as planting and harvesting crops.
>
> Black members of other Indian Nations worked vigorously for equality, land ownership, and education. Very few left their host nation. Whatever unfairness they felt among their Indian friends could not match what they would experience among whites. They knew this and stayed. Here were a people who would never lynch or brutalize their sons and daughters.
>
> Among Creeks, Seminoles, and Cherokees, black people made economic strides they could rarely duplicate in U.S. society. African-Cherokees owned barbershops, blacksmith shops, general stores, and restaurants. Some had become printers, ferry-boat operators, cotton-gin managers, teachers, and postmasters.[87]

In the Cherokee Nation, as in other tribes, the internal damage occasioned by the embrace of chattel slavery would not soon be undone.

> The treaty made with the United States after the war superficially reunited the Nation but social and economic class distinctions and conflicting values continued to divide the Cherokees. This division, which exists today long after the dissolution of tribal government, has its roots in the institution of slavery and the economic inequality and cultural dichotomy that slavery produced.[88]

The Treaty of 1866 with the Cherokee Nation, reproduced below in pertinent part, is typical of the various post-Civil War treaties between the federal government and the constituent members of the Five Civilized Tribes (referred to both individually and collectively as the "Treaty of 1866"). The federal government negotiated similar treaties with the Muscogee (Creek), Choctaw, Chickasaw, and Seminole Nations after the Civil War.

> 1866 Treaty with Cherokee Nation: Articles Pertaining to African Cherokee Citizens and Ending Slavery in the Nation (July 19, 1866. Ratified July 27, 1866. Proclaimed Aug. 11, 1866)
>
> ARTICLE 4.
> All the Cherokees and freed persons who were formerly slaves to any Cherokee, and all free negroes not having been such slaves, who resided in the Cherokee Nation prior to June first, eighteen hundred and sixty-one . . . shall have the right to settle in and occupy . . . a quantity of land equal to one hundred and sixty acres for each person who may so elect to reside in the territory above-described in this article. . . .
>
> . . . .
>
> ARTICLE 9.
> The Cherokee Nation having, voluntarily, in February, eighteen hundred and sixty-three, by an act of the national council, forever abolished slavery, hereby covenant and agree that never hereafter shall either slavery or involuntary servitude exist in their nation otherwise than in the punishment of crime, whereof the party shall have been duly convicted, in accordance with laws applicable to all the members of said tribe alike. They further agree that all freedmen who have been liberated by voluntary act of their former owners or by law, as well as all free colored persons who were in the country at the commencement of the rebellion, and are now resi-

dents therein, or who may return within six months, and their descendants, shall have all the rights of native Cherokees: Provided, That owners of slaves so emancipated in the Cherokee Nation shall never receive any compensation or pay for the slaves so emancipated.

ARTICLE 10.
 Every Cherokee and freed person resident in the Cherokee Nation shall have the right to sell any products of his farm, including his or her live stock, or any merchandise or manufactured products, and to ship and drive the same to market without restraint, paying any tax thereon which is now or may be levied by the United States on the quantity sold outside of the Indian Territory.[89]

In addition to the foregoing, the Treaty of 1866 gave Freedmen the right to elect officials, and to representation "according to numbers" on the national council.[90] It provided the right to sue in federal court in the event of an actionable dispute between Freedmen and other members of the Cherokee Nation.[91] It guaranteed that laws in the Cherokee Nation "shall be uniform throughout said nation," warning that if "any law, either in its provisions or in the manner of its enforcement, in the opinion of the President of the United States, operate unjustly in [the Freedmen] district, he is hereby authorized and empowered to correct such evil."[92] Finally, the Treaty of 1866 unambiguously declared: "No law shall be enacted inconsistent with the Constitution of the United States, or laws of Congress, or existing treaty stipulations with the United States."[93]

After more than a century, the Treaty of 1866 still matters, especially to the Freedmen. That pact is central to the present-day struggle for Freedmen citizenship rights. Anthropologist Circe Sturm interviewed an African-American Indian in Tahlequah, Oklahoma, the headquarters of the Cherokee Nation, and asked her subject a simple question: "What do you think I should write about?"[94]

The question elicited an impassioned response about race and racism within native tribes and beyond:

> I think you should write about the racism that permeates these Indian programs [re: tribal benefits and who qualifies for them], and point out that many of the so-called Indians running the Oklahoma tribes are exclusive if the hyphenated Indian is Black, and inclusive if the hyphenated Indian is White. I think you should

go back to the Dawes process and point out how degree of Indian blood was ignored among black people just as degree of European blood did not and does not today affect one's status if one is Black. I think you need to argue that these programs need to be made realistic.... It is ridiculous to allow White people to take advantage of Indian programs because they have blood on a tribal roll a hundred years ago, when a Black person who suffers infinitely more discrimination and needs the aid more is denied it because his Indian ancestry is overshadowed by his African ancestry. Few Blacks are 100 percent African, and to be frank about it, few Europeans whose ancestors come from the South are 100 percent European.... Either the descendants of freedmen should be allowed to take advantage of benefits, or the federal government, not these cliquish tribes, should set new standards for who is an Indian—and save [themselves] some money. [footnote omitted][95]

Beyond questions about the Treaty of 1866, some observers see larger social and political forces at play in the Freedmen citizenship debate. David Cornsilk, a Cherokee nationalist and activist, framed the disenfranchisement question as one of race-tinged power and politics:

One of the main proponents of the drive to eliminate the Freedmen is a Cherokee Nation councilwoman with a blood degree of 1/256. The president of the Freedmen Association is 1/8, but cannot get a CDIB ["Certificate of Degree of Indian Blood," a document issued by the Bureau of Indian Affairs indicating entitlement to certain governmental services] card because the Dawes Commission, while aware of the blood, did not permit it to be recorded. If we are to throw out the less connected individual, it should be the former....

[T]his controversy... begs the question of when can a people, once made citizens of a nation, finally rest. The Freedmen were made citizens of the Cherokee Nation 140 years ago by a treaty with the United States and amendment to our Constitution. What right does any Cherokee have to look at their fellow man and say "I have the right to destroy your heritage and steal away your rights[?]"[96]

Cornsilk's observations about the perversity of blood works within the Cherokee Nation are neither new nor novel. At the turn of the twentieth century, ethnographer James Moody noted:

> [W]e find the destinies of the nation guided henceforth by shrewd mixed-blood politicians, bearing white men's names and speaking the white man's language, and frequently with hardly enough Indian blood to show itself in the features. The change was not instantaneous, nor is it even yet complete, for although the tendency is constantly away from the old things, and although frequent intermarriages are rapidly bleaching out the brown of the Indian skin, there are still several thousand full-blood Cherokee....[97]

David Cornsilk, whose father is 7/8 Cherokee and whose mother is white, views membership in the Cherokee Nation as a matter of nationality—a political determination, not a racial one. After all, he says, Cherokees adopted outsiders into the fold as early as the 1700s, thus negating any claim of ethnic purity. "Indianness," on the other hand, is, in Cornsilk's worldview, a racial construct.

Cornsilk thus de-couples the issue of whether the Freedmen are members of the Cherokee Nation—a question of nationality—from whether the Freedmen are Indians—a question of "race." The Freedmen are, in his mind, members of the Cherokee Nation based on history and extant law. Many are not, however, "Indian" based on their lack of acculturation in Cherokee tradition, custom, and heritage.[98]

Some scholars share Cornsilk's concerns over equating Indian authenticity with blood quantum—with defining Indianness in racial terms instead of political ones. The issue, however, is not without complexity:

> Scott B. Vickers argues, "the criterion of blood quantum must be reconsidered and eventually disavowed as a meaningful marker of Indian identity." Yet, he contends, "the fact remains that without a certain quantity of Indian blood, such human beings will in scientific fact cease to belong to the racial group presently called "Indian." Thus the blood quantum argument is a major conundrum that vexes Indian identity at its very core."[99]

Similarly, Cornsilk is not alone in his musings about the racial makeup of the Cherokee tribe.

> Today, one of the most striking things about Indian country is the faces. Some prominent Cherokees of the past were products of intermarriage, and now a fair number of those who count themselves

as Cherokee have fair skin or blue eyes or blonde hair—and limited Indian blood. Just 6,000 of the Cherokee Nation's 260,000 citizens speak Cherokee.[100]

Any quest for purity of racial identity, at least in some imagined biological sense, seems to have been long ago abandoned.

As an enrolled member of the Cherokee Nation, Teresa Rendon, an attorney and professor, has given thought to the whole notion of Indian identity. Citing DNA mapping from the Human Genome Project, she echoed that group's conclusions that: (1) there are no "pure, distinct races";[101] and (2) there is as much genetic diversity within so-called racial groups as between and among them. However, she, too, acknowledges race as a powerful and persistent social construct.[102]

Tribal membership is generally defined, she noted, with reference to three salient factors: (1) descendancy (i.e., the ability to trace lineage back to an ancestor listed on the official rolls of the tribe—the Dawes Roll, tribal census rolls, tribal town rolls, or any other official roll); (2) dual enrollment (i.e., the refusal of some tribes to enroll persons who are already enrolled in another tribe): and (3) blood quantum. The latter definitional element has allowed some to sneak race back into the identification equation.[103]

Rendon questioned the peculiar posture of Indians, who are often asked to delineate their blood quantum, if not for tribal membership, then for federal services. "Imagine asking a white person, 'How much white blood do you have in you?' It sounds ludicrous, doesn't it? How odd would it be to ask an African-American person, 'How black are you?' In her tribe, the Cherokee Nation, blood quantum runs the gamut from 'full blood' to $1/2,048$th, a level on the magnitude of the contents of an eyedropper."[104]

The United States Supreme Court has likewise viewed race as a contextually bound legal construct. The Court has held that discrimination against Arabs and Jews qualifies as *racial* discrimination even though neither Arab nor Jew constitutes a typically conceived racial group.[105] Race, then, has both cultural and legal determinants in addition to its celebrated, if flawed, biological ones.

The Treaty of 1866 forever altered the relationships between the Cherokees (and the other members of the Five Civilized Tribes) and the Freedmen who so long lived among them. The pact forever ended slavery and began to chip away at its racist and dehumanizing features. Given the historic significance of the Treaty of 1866, particularly in the realm of human rights, unilateral abrogation, a policy presently being pursued by the Cherokee Nation, must be carefully considered. Indeed, such action warrants both legal and moral scrutiny.

Some contemporary opponents of Freedmen citizenship suggest that the federal government coerced the Five Tribes into executing the Treaty of 1866. Others contend that, in contract law parlance, the constituent members of the Five Tribes executed the 1866 treaties under duress. Once again, the case of the Cherokees is instructive.

Fort Smith, Arkansas, hosted the negotiations between the Cherokee Nation and federal authorities leading up to the Treaty of 1866. These talks, begun in 1865, concluded in Washington, D.C., in 1866. The incorporation of Freedmen into the tribe, consolidation of all tribes in Indian Territory, and territorial government were among the negotiated provisions. In the end, tribal negotiators did not object to the provision providing for Freedmen rights in the Treaty of 1866. The Cherokee negotiators acceded to the agreement voluntarily.[106]

Cherokee Nation v. United States, a 1963 case before the Indian Claims Commission, explicitly examined and rejected Cherokee claims that the negotiation process that culminated in the Treaty of 1866 was flawed:

> [The Cherokee Nation] has not proved that the 1866 treaty or its antecedent 1865 and 1866 negotiations were attended by duress, fraud, intimidation, falsehood, or mistake.
>
> . . . .
>
> [The Cherokee Nation] has not proved that the 1866 treaty or its antecedent 1865 and 1866 negotiations were tainted by unfair or dishonorable dealings on the part of [The United States].[107]

In the end, peace treaties are not standard contracts. Rather, they are agreements made under special and extenuating circumstances. Indeed, some have argued that duress attends to all such contracts.

> [H]olding contracts made under duress unenforceable…[is not advisable] under all circumstances. A peace treaty is a contract made

under duress; yet most of us think that a world where nations can sign peace treaties and be bound by them is better than a world where the victor must annihilate the vanquished before he can be sure the war is over.[108]

This much is axiomatic: The vanquished are never on equal footing with the victors. Some pressure is necessarily brought to bear on "the loser" to accede to the demands of the winner. As between sovereigns, this seems neither novel nor persuasive as a ground upon which to vitiate a treaty.

The level of accession to a victor's demands need not be complete and total. The Chickasaw Nation, for example, never accepted Chickasaw Freedmen as citizens pursuant to its version of the Treaty of 1866. Federal government wishes notwithstanding, the Chickasaws never acquiesced. Inclusion of the Freedmen as citizens, then, was not "a given." Rather, Freedmen acceptance was a condition pressed hard upon the tribes by the federal government and acquiesced in by all but one of said tribes.

William Potter Ross, a Princeton-educated lawyer and the nephew of famed Cherokee leader John Ross, led the Treaty of 1866 Cherokee negotiating team. The Cherokee delegation accepted, without reservation, citizenship for the Freedmen as proposed by the Federal government.[109]

Other opponents of Cherokee Freedmen citizenship brand the Treaty of 1866, as respects "forcing" the adoption of Freedmen by the tribes, "unconscionable." Freedmen advocates argue that the contract law doctrine of unconscionability, holding only contracts that "shock the conscience" unenforceable, is inapposite. Typical cases require that the agreement be grossly imbalanced both in its bargaining and in its substance.[110]

Most war-ending bargains—peace treaties—reflect a power imbalance between the parties to the pact. However, as previously indicated, such agreements serve the paramount interest of the parties in ceasing hostilities on terms to which the parties themselves assent.

The Treaty of 1866 served just such a greater interest: cessation of Civil War hostilities on terms acceptable to the parties. That, to Freedmen advocates, trumps any contention that it is somehow invalid as a matter of contract law.

Moreover, Freedmen allies insist, the "shocks the conscience" test used in unconscionability analysis might well be turned on its head in the case of Freedmen disenfranchisement. The equities favor a positive resolution of the *substantive* rights of the Freedmen over the *procedural* rights of those who would disavow them.

For these Freedmen supporters, what would really shock the conscience is: (i) A Native American tribe's reneging, with impunity, on a longstanding, equality-based treaty obligation; and (ii) The federal government's acceding to the demands of a Native American tribe to cast aside persons of longstanding affiliation with blood, treaty, and affinity ties to such tribe.

In *Seminole v. Norton*,[111] a 2002 case involving the Seminole version of the Treaty of 1866, the court recognized that it had a duty to uphold the Seminole Nation's right to self-determination and integrity. However, the court agreed with the findings of the Department of Interior and Judge Kollar-Kotelly in an earlier iteration of *Seminole v. Norton*[112] ("Seminole I") that the Seminole Treaty of 1866 "secures the rights of the [Seminole] Freedmen to be a part of the nation."[113] The posture of the Department of the Interior and the federal courts in continuing to recognize the Seminole Freedmen's right to citizenship within the Seminole Nation was dictated by a single, indisputable fact: The Seminole Treaty of 1866 has not been expressly abrogated by Congress, as would be required to sustain a different result.[114]

In the end, American enterprise and industrial development posed a greater threat to Native American sovereignty than "forced" adoption of the Freedmen did. In addition to Freedmen citizenship rights, the Treaty of 1866 contained one ostensibly benign provision that opened the floodgates of change. The Treaty of 1866 granted railroad rights-of-way through Indian Territory.[115] This caused great consternation within Indian Territory.

> In the decades following the Civil War, a new foe—the railroad corporation—joined the grasping frontier whites and border-state congressmen on the Cherokees' list of enemies . . . The railroad appeared in Cherokee writings as the center of a conspiracy to defraud the Indians and dismantle their governments.[116]
>
> . . . .
>
> [I]t became clear that the railroad companies [in fact] favored the dismantling of the tribal governments and the opening of the country to non-Indian settlement. The revival of the railroad issue

coincided with the intensification of efforts to territorialize the Five Tribes, to subject them to a United States territorial government and allow unrestricted non-Indian settlement on at least some of their lands.[117]

The coming of the railroads would, in some ways, be the beginning of the end of any true "Indian Territory":

> The treaties of 1866, with the Cherokee, Creek, Seminole, Choctaw, and Chickasaw Nations giving their consent, provided for rights of way for railroads through these nations.... With these railroads ... and with towns springing up, noncitizens pouring into the Territory from every direction, and land increasing in value by the hour, every chance for the lands of these Nations to remain in the hands of the Indians "as long as grass grows and water runs"[118] disappeared forever.[119]

Years later, the 1899 Omnibus Railroad Act addressed the acquisition by the railroads of rights of way "through Indian reservations, Indian lands, and Indian allotments...."[120]

Enterprising railroad companies cut swaths through once sacred lands. With railroads came the crush of white settlement, increasing crime and, gradually, the erosion of Indian sovereignty.[121] The railroads, then, expedited the ascension of white culture.[122]

As noted in an early chronicle of the new State of Oklahoma:

> [I]t is clear that railroads, as an institution, and especially the first railroads, were among the important forces of disintegration. From the point of view of modern civilization, the railroad has done more to develop and build up Oklahoma than any other material factor, but in considering this country with reference to its origin and the purposes for which it was founded, it is evident that the existence of rail thoroughfares through Indian Territory was an inconsistency, unless accompanied by a productive and superior civilization.[123]

Paradoxically, some of the Freedmen affiliated with the tribes who were reluctant to honor the Treaty of 1866 (e.g., the Choctaw Freedmen) welcomed the movement toward modernization represented by railroad expansion. They viewed the eventual takeover of Indian Territory by the United States government as a way to ensure

48   Apartheid in Indian Country?

the protection of their own rights. Federal control, they thought, would offer them protections under the Fourteenth (e.g., due process and equal protection) and Fifteenth (voting rights) Amendments to the United States Constitution.[124] Time would surely tell.

Sketch of Fort Smith, Arkansas, circa 1848.
—Courtesy Fort Smith National Historic Site

Fort Smith, Indian Territory, site of the Great Indian Council gathering.
—Courtesy Fort Smith National Historic Site

Pre-Removal, Removal, War and Treaties 49

Old Fort Smith, built in 1830; destroyed in the Civil War.
—Courtesy Fort Smith National Historic Site

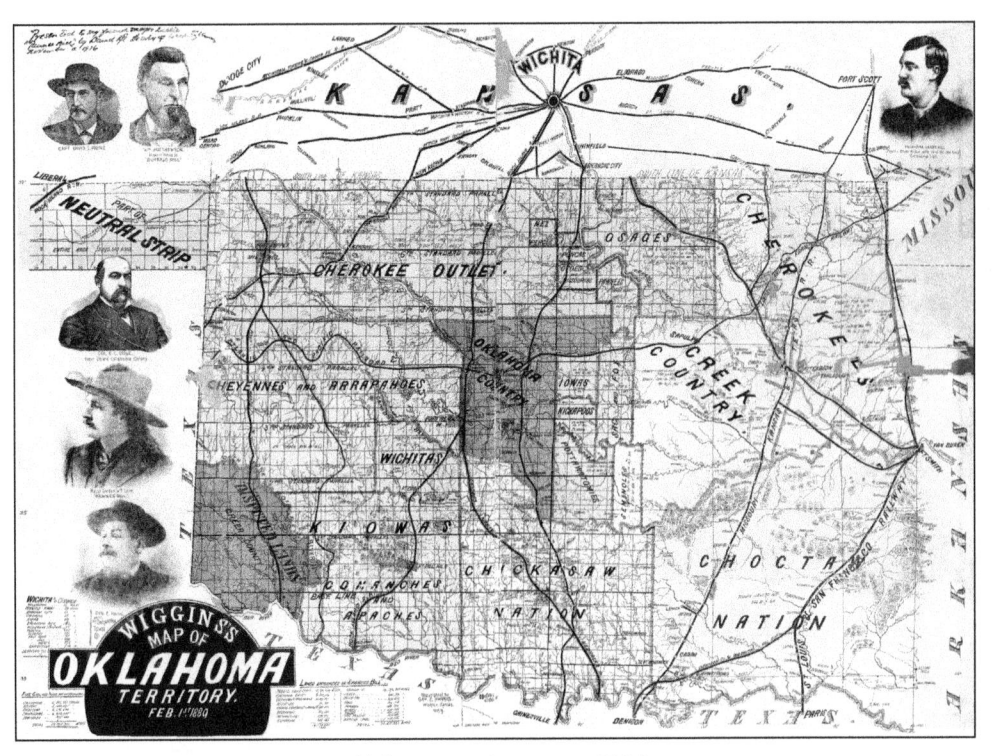

Oklahoma Territory map, 1880
—Courtesy Fort Smith National Historic Site

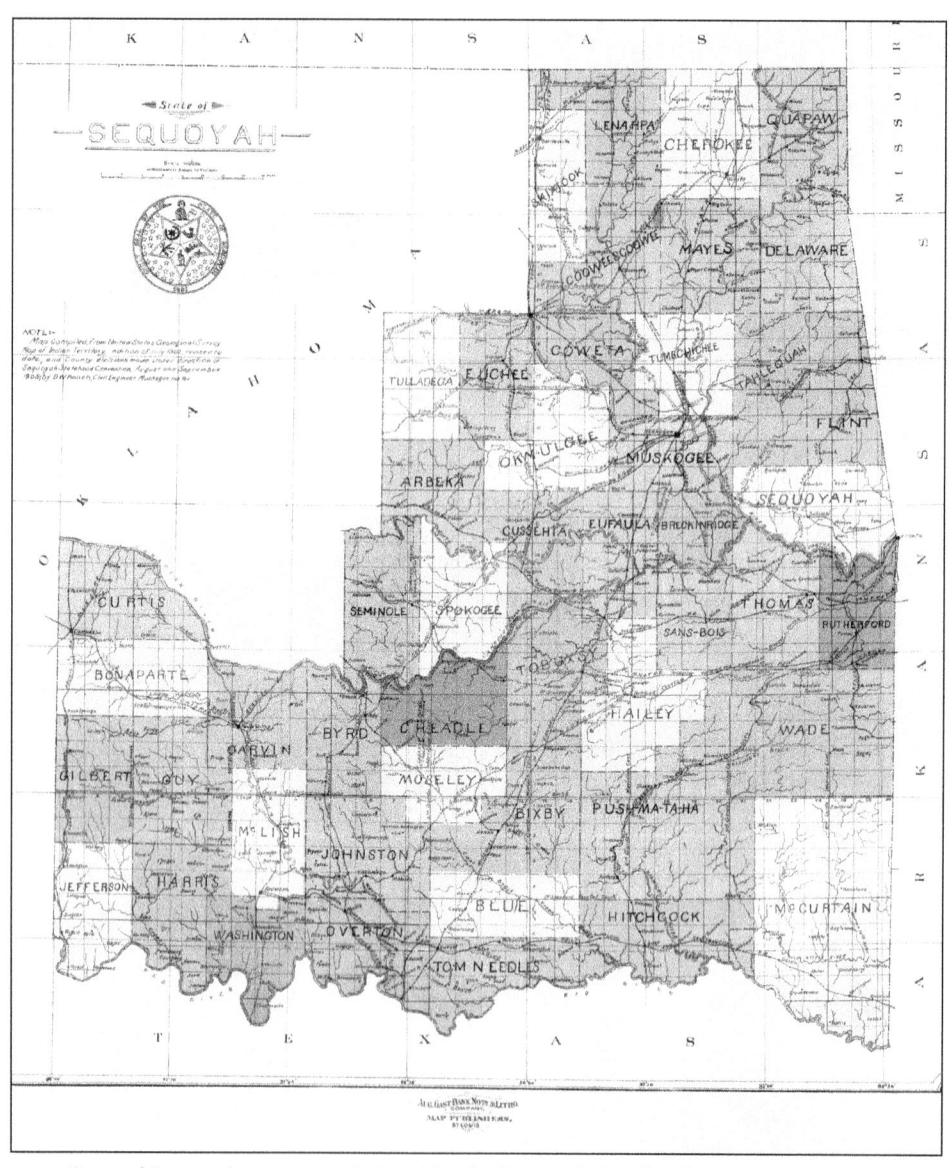

50   Apartheid in Indian Country?

State of Sequoyah map commissioned by the Sequoyah Statehood Commission, 1905
—Courtesy Fort Smith National Historic Site

Pre-Removal, Removal, War and Treaties 51

Indian Territory scene along the M.K.&T. Railway, circa 1890.
—Courtesy Fort Smith National Historic Site

Creek Council House, 1832.
—Courtesy Fort Smith National Historic Site

52   Apartheid in Indian Country?

Delaware-Cherokee Delegation to Washington, D.C., 1867. Left to right, seated: James Ketchum, James Connor, John Connor (Principal Chief), Charles Journeycake, Isaac Journeycake, John Sarcoxie, Sr.; standing: James McDaniel, Black Beaver, Henry Tiblow (Interpreter), John G. Pratt (U.S. Indian Agent), Charles Armstrong, and John Young.
—Courtesy Fort Smith National Historic Site

Cherokee Delegation to Washington, D.C., 1866. Left to right: John Rollin Ridge, Saladin Watie, Richard Field, E. C. Boudinot, and W. P. Adair.
—Courtesy Fort Smith National Historic Site

CHAPTER II

Relations Between Africans and Native Americans in the Five Civilized Tribes: Deep and Intertwined Roots

> *"I do not want my house to be walled in on all sides and my windows to be stuffed. I want the cultures of all the lands to be blown about my house as freely as possible. But I refuse to be blown off my feet by any."*
> —MAHATMA GANDHI

The shared roots of Africans and Native Americans run deep. Miles beneath the surface, they intertwine in ways often unrecognized and unappreciated. These embedded and sometimes gnarled intersections have yielded fruit both bitter and sweet:

> Generalizations about the relationships between American Indian and African Americans are difficult to make. Time, place, and circumstance shaped specific interactions, but European imperialism and colonization set the overall parameters. The nature of relations was neither inevitable nor uniform, and interactions ran the gamut from amity to enmity. European power in the South rested initially on African labor and Indian land, so from the very beginning colonizers had a vested interest in regulating the races. By the time the United States emancipated its slaves, a pattern of interaction had developed that pitted the two people[s] against each other.[1]

Consider the adventures of Lucas Vasquez de Ayllon, a wealthy Spanish official in the city of Santo Domingo on the island of Hispaniola. During the summer of 1526, Ayllon set sail for what is now the southeastern United States, landing in present-day South Carolina. Decades before Jamestown, he founded the first European colony in the United States. Ayllon seeded the short-lived settlement in an area south of his party's initial point of entry. The town, *San Miguel de Guadalpe*, sat at or near modern-day Georgia's Sapelo Sound.

The Ayllon expedition included six vessels and several hundred colonists, some five hundred Spanish men and women, and about a hundred enslaved Africans. Mishap and disaster plagued the mission. Ayllon died in 1526. Factionalism set in. In the end, the surviving Spanish explorers abandoned the enterprise.[2]

According to William Loren Katz, the enslaved Africans remained to live among the Native Americans:

> In distant South Carolina forests, two and a half centuries before the Declaration of Independence, two dark peoples first lit the fires of freedom and exalted its principles. Though neither white, Christian, nor European, they became the first settlement of any permanence on these shores to include people from overseas. As such, they qualify as our earliest inheritance.[3]

Theda Perdue generally confirms Katz' account, and sheds additional light on when and how Indians, particularly Cherokees, came into contact with Africans. The Cherokees' initial reaction to their new-found neighbors seems to have been benign.

> The Cherokees encountered Africans at least as early as they did Europeans and may have seen blacks even before the conquistadors visited their towns. When the black slaves in Lucas Vasquez de Ayllon's ill-fated colony on the Pedee River [a.k.a. the "Pee Dee River," a body of water originating in North Carolina and flowing into South Carolina named for the Pedee Indians] revolted in 1526, some of the rebels fled to the Indians, and it is at least possible that the Cherokees saw these Africans or their offspring. Black slaves later accompanied Spanish expeditions to the Cherokees including those of Hernando de Soto in 1540 and Juan Pardo in 1567. When de Soto's prize prisoner, the Lady of Cofitachequi, escaped from the Spaniards, a black slave belonging to one of his officers accompanied her to Xuala [The "Xuala" were

a tribe of Siouan-speaking Amerindians first encountered by Hernando de Soto in 1540.], where they "lived together as man and wife." Although the initial reaction of Cherokees to Africans with their black skin[] is unknown, the cohabitation of the Lady of Cofitachequi and the Spaniard's black slave indicates that the Indians probably regarded Africans simply as other human beings who were either traversing or invading their territory. Since the concept of race did not exist among Indians and since the Cherokees nearly always encountered Africans in the company of Europeans, one supposed that at first Cherokees equated the two and failed to distinguish sharply between the races. Soon after their first contact with Africans, however, the Cherokees no doubt realized that Europeans regarded blacks as inferiors and that they were in danger of receiving the same treatment.[4] (footnotes omitted)

Those fears of enslavement at the hands of Europeans proved prophetic. In time, Cherokee slaves worked alongside African bondsmen. The Europeans came to favor the enslavement of Africans over that of Indians for a number of pragmatic reasons, including: (1) Indians' proximity to their kinsmen/tribesmen; (2) the likelihood of successful revolts by the Indians given the positioning of probable allies to the Indians' cause; and (3) the cognitive dissonance between Indian slavery and the pursuit of an overarching Indian pacification policy by the United States government. As Indian slavery waned, African slavery intensified.[5]

Such is the depth and complexity of the African/Native American connection in the United States. One thing is certain: black chattel slavery deeply influenced the relationship. In Oklahoma—"Indian Country"—connections between persons of African ancestry and Native Americans became particularly pronounced.[6] Prominent African-American families spoke openly of their ties to Native-American ancestors.

> My people came from Mississippi. My grandfather belonged to the Burneys back there and when they came to this country in the [18]40's they brought my grandfather with them, as a slave. My father, David, belonged to Wesley C. Burney, brother of Ben Burney, who later became governor of the Chickasaws. My mother was Minnie; she was a most unusual colored woman. She was owned by the Colberts and Pitchlynns of Mississippi. They were Choctaws. They raised my mother and allowed her every privilege of their own people. She was a Bible student. My parents were married

after the war. I received my first schooling at the Dawes academy [the first Negro school in the Chickasaw Nation], twelve miles north of Ardmore. This [N]egro school was founded by white missionaries of the Baptist church. We had some white missionary teachers. After that I attended Roger Williams University at Nashville, Tennessee. It burned down and the site was bought by whites and the Peabody Institute is there today. My wife was a teacher. We are both college graduates. I completed my law course long ago. We have three children of which I am very proud. Mozella Franklin Jones, A.B. West Virginia State College, a teacher at Dunbar School, Tulsa, Oklahoma, for four years; Buck Colbert Franklin, Jr., an A.B. from Fiske University and a principal of a six-room school at Bixby; John Hope Franklin, twenty-three and got his A.B. from Fiske in 1935, master's degree from Harvard in 1936, has completed his residence work at Harvard and is now ready to get his Ph.D. That is not a bad record for grandchildren of slaves.[7]

—BUCK COLBERT FRANKLIN,
Oklahoma Slave Narratives

Buck Colbert Franklin, son of enslaved parents, was born on May 6, 1879, near Homer, a small country village in Pickens County, Chickasaw Nation, Indian Territory (the eastern portion of present-day Oklahoma). Franklin became a prominent Tulsa lawyer, even representing African-American survivors of the cataclysmic 1921 Tulsa Race Riot.[8] He died on September 24, 1960.[9]

The son of Buck Colbert Franklin, John Hope Franklin, Ph.D., rose to prominence as one of America's foremost historians and scholars of the African-American experience. Dr. Franklin taught at Fisk University, Howard University, Brooklyn College (where he became the first African-American department chair at a white college), the University of Chicago, Duke University, and other prominent academic institutions. He served as the first African-American president of the American Historical Association. His seminal book on the African-American experience, *From Slavery to Freedom: A History of African Americans*,[10] remains a critical favorite and a best-seller long after its initial publication in 1947.[11] Dr. Franklin served as chairman of President Bill Clinton's Initiative on Race, known as "One America in the 21st Century." He died on March 25, 2009, at age 94.

Dr. John Hope Franklin's family tree offers a striking example of generational affinity between Native-American and African-

American families. The brother of a Chickasaw governor enslaved his paternal grandfather. Choctaws enslaved his paternal grandmother. This celebrated African American traced his roots back to Native-American slaveholders.

The Choctaws treated Dr. Franklin's paternal grandmother like a member of the family:

> My [grand]mother was one-fourth Choctaw Indian blood, the other three-quarters Negro; but she never knew the meaning of slavery in her early childhood days; for she was born in the home of her Indian kin; she ate, slept, played and attended their tribal school and church and spoke their language.[12]

Like Dr. Franklin's lineal ancestors, some enslaved Africans fared better with Native Americans than they did under the yoke of Southern-style chattel slavery. Slavery was, in the final analysis, a relative concept.

The recollections of an African woman enslaved within the Muscogee (Creek) Nation address both the suffusion in Indian culture many enslaved Africans experienced and the relative degrees of harshness exercised by some Native American slave-masters.

Lucinda Davis, interviewed at age eighty-nine by the Work Projects Administration in Tulsa, recounted her experiences growing up within the Muscogee (Creek) Nation. Davis initially spoke only the tribal tongue. While she heard English from time to time, she found the language puzzling and unintelligible.

Davis recalled the home in which she spent her formative years, as well as the foods on which she was weaned. Those fond memories mounted in spite of her status as the property of a "full-blood" and his "mixed-blood" wife. "Master had a good log house and a bresh shelter out front like all de houses had."[13] She recalled meals of roasted and fried green corn, mixed greens, pork, deer, turkey, fish, and turtle. Sofkey, a traditional Indian corn dish, served as a family staple.[14]

Davis described her parents' ties to prominent Muscogee (Creek) families and recounted how the brand of enslavement they knew differed from the chattel slavery practiced by whites and by some other Native Americans:

> My own pappy was name Stephany. I think he take dat name 'cause when he little his mammy call him "Istifani." Dat mean a skeleton,

and he was a skinny man. He belong to de Grayson family and I think his master name George, but I don't know. Dey big people in de Creek, and with de white folks too. My mammy was Serena and she belong to some of de Gouge family. Dey was big people in de Upper Creek, and one de biggest men of the Gouge was name Hopoethleyoholo [the famous Opothleyoholo or "Old Gouge"] for his Creek name. He was a big man . . . in de War and died up in Kansas, I think. Dey say when he was a little boy he was called Hopoethli, which mean "good little boy," and when he git grown he make big speeches and dey stick on de "yoholo." Dat mean "loud whooper."

. . . . . .

My mammy and pappy belong to two masters, but dey live together on a place. Dat de way de Creek slaves do lots of times. Dey work patches and give de masters most all dey make, but dey have some for demselves. Dey didn't have to stay on de master's place and work like I hear de slaves of white people and de Cherokee and Choctaw people say dey had to do.[15] (footnotes omitted)

Davis' account suggests that the nature of slavery among the Five Civilized Tribes varied. Relatively speaking, slavery rested lightly upon some; brutally upon others.

As indicated by the recollections of both B. C. Franklin and Lucinda Davis, the often complicated interrelationships between and among African Americans, European Americans, and Native Americans make Oklahoma history fascinating. Native Americans came first on the Oklahoma scene. Archaeological evidence indicates that Native Americans inhabited what is now Oklahoma thousands of years ago. That habitation was not sustained, although now, eons later, Native Americans have re-inhabited that same ground

European explorers, first the Spanish in the 1500s, and then the French in the 1700s, visited Oklahoma and interacted with these early tribal denizens. Persons of African ancestry first arrived on Oklahoma soil in the 1500s, as fellow travelers with Spanish explorers. They, too, would revisit the area in subsequent waves.

As earlier noted, the United States government's forced removal policy of the 1830s and 1840s wreaked havoc on Indian nations. Suffering and death characterized the migrations. The disease and exposure attendant to the journey and resettlement killed roughly one-third of each of the migrating tribes.[16]

Native Americans within the uprooted "Five Civilized Tribes" found a new home in "Indian Territory"—Oklahoma. Decades later, these Indians would seek, unsuccessfully, to create an Indian state—"Sequoyah"—in order to hold on to sovereignty and self-governance. Instead, the federal government combined Indian Territory, which by that time included only the eastern half of what is now Oklahoma, with the land to its west, "Oklahoma Territory," to create the State of Oklahoma in 1907.

Persons of African ancestry, some enslaved, some free, lived among the Native-American tribes who were forced to emigrate. The lives of these Africans and their Native-American hosts became enmeshed.[17]

> Slaves owned by the tribes often felt multifaceted connections to their homes in Indian Territory, as evidenced by [those] who were fluent in tribal languages. They shared cultural and often family connections with their Indian owners, bonds that seem[ed] stronger than those of white-owned slaves and their masters. After the Civil War ended, former slaves of the Cherokees particularly expressed a connection to the Cherokee Nation in the Indian Territory. That was the only home many of these people had ever known, and they identified closely with the tribe.[18]

Post-manumission, and after the collapse of Reconstruction in the late 1870s, still more persons of African ancestry migrated to Oklahoma. They sought escape from the stifling social, economic, and political conditions in the Deep South.

Eventually, white political leaders began a push to control the new Indian homeland. In 1878, leaders of the Five Civilized Tribes—P. P. Pitchlynn of the Choctaws; W. P. Adair and Daniel H. Ross of the Cherokees; John R. Moore, P. Porter, D. M. Hodge, and Yarteker Harjo of the Muscogee (Creek); John F. Brown and Thomas Cloud of the Seminoles; and B. F. Overton, Governor of the Chickasaws—became concerned. They beseeched Congress to oppose measures that would: (1) open the land to white settlement; (2) extend United States legal jurisdiction to matters between and among Indians; (3) abolish tribal relations and grant United States citizenship to Indians; and (4) move Indians from a communal property system to a private property system.[19] With arguable prescience, the tribal leaders asserted that the proposed actions would violate extant treaties and, if implemented, would ultimately devastate the Five Civilized Tribes. Their plea went unheeded.

By the late 1880s, whites, also seeking to escape harsh economic conditions in the East, moved west. These white settlers successfully pressured the federal government to open up for white settlement land that had been reserved for Native populations in Oklahoma. Before long, whites dominated Oklahoma in all spheres—social, economic, and political.

African Americans, Native Americans, and whites, seekers all, found their way to Oklahoma. Oklahoma promised opportunity—a fresh start; a new way of life. All three groups accepted her offer. For Native Americans, African Americans, and some European Americans, the story unraveled in the breach—the legacy of promises broken. Present reality cannot be separated from those initial bargains.

Native Americans yearned for sovereignty and a fresh start in a new land on the heels of forcible removal from their homelands in the southeastern United States. African Americans hoped to snare the full citizenship and economic parity denied them in the post-Reconstruction South. Whites, meanwhile, longed for a chance to fulfill their manifest destiny—to push forward with westward expansion and exploit newfound economic opportunities. As David A. Chang noted in his book on land ownership in early, pre-statehood Oklahoma:

> "Oklahoma" means "red man" in the Choctaw language, is run through by a "Black Belt," and has been claimed by some as "white man's country." It has been termed an Indian homeland, a black promised land, and a white heartland. All these competing racial claims to one place . . . reveal[ ] much about how the struggle over land has given shape to the way Americans—indigenous, black, and white—created and gave meaning to races and nations.[20]

After the Civil War, the United States government secured promises from the Five Civilized Tribes to incorporate within their midst the emancipated persons of African descent whom they had enslaved prior to and during the Civil War (i.e., the Freedmen). As noted previously, only the Chickasaws rejected Freedmen citizenship outright.

Officially, the Five Civilized Tribes fought on the side of the vanquished Confederacy. Some Indians felt that the federal government foisted non-Indian people (i.e., Freedmen) upon them as punishment for their tribal alliances with the defeated South. For that reason, they resented the grant of Freedmen citizenship. Others frowned upon the influx of African Americans from the South, who they believed sought to "colonize" Indian Territory after Reconstruction.[21]

Whites quickly dominated Oklahoma, both numerically and politically. Generally speaking, whites attempted to remake Native Americans in their own image—to assimilate them. Conversely, whites went to great lengths to set African Americans apart—to segregate them.[22]

Whites routinely intermarried with Native Americans, sometimes as a ruse to obtain land. By contrast, whites strictly forbade miscegenation—intermarriage with persons of African ancestry. Laws enforcing this taboo, as well as other forms of white/black social intercourse, soon proliferated.

A pattern thus emerged. Whites sat at the peak of a seemingly intractable tri-level racial pyramid. Native Americans occupied the middle tier. African Americans formed the base. These three groups struggled to define the relationships between and among one another.

In the modern era, a trilateral jockeying for power and privilege continues. It is more than just the relationships between African Americans and whites on the one hand, and Native Americans and whites on the other. Such a Eurocentric bent gives short shrift to the complex interactions between the two minority (i.e., non-dominant culture) groups, African Americans and Native Americans. Moreover, a black/white, red/white emphasis—an undue focus on dyads—tends to minimize the extent to which institutional racism—white supremacist ideology—molded race relations in Oklahoma from the beginning, with consequences not yet undone.

The onslaught of white migration into Oklahoma in the late 1800s hastened the reshaping of relations between African Americans and Native Americans. As whites ascended, key Native-American leaders aligned themselves with the expanding institutional power base these Sooners represented.[23]

Prior to the rush of whites into Oklahoma Territory, persons of African ancestry and Native Americans had, to some extent, peaceably coexisted, and sometimes even collaborated and commingled.[24] Indeed, before the Civil War, some Muscogee (Creek) and Seminoles secreted African fugitives from surrounding slave states.[25] Some Cherokees participated in the Keetoowah Society, a furtive abolitionist organization.[26] The Keetoowah Society organized, at least in part, to preserve Native culture in the face of assimilationist forces:[27]

> The Keetoowah [S]ociety in the Cherokee Nation west was organized shortly before the civil war by John B. Jones, son of the missionary Evan Jones, and an adopted citizen of the Nation, as a secret society for the ostensible purpose of cultivating a national feeling among the full-bloods, in opposition to the innovating tendencies of the mixed-blood element. The real purpose was to counteract the influence of the "Blue Lodge" and other secret secessionist organizations among the wealthier slave-holding classes, made up chiefly of mixed-bloods and whites.[28]

White hegemony, both within Oklahoma and in the United States more broadly, cast Native Americans alternatively as incorrigible savages or cultural and social infants in need of paternalistic care. In either case, under the prevailing racial pecking order, "Indianness" implied inferiority vis-à-vis whiteness. White blood acted, however, as an antidote—a decontaminant. Thus, individuals of mixed Indian/white ancestry generally occupied a higher status in the larger society than did full-bloods.

At the time of Oklahoma statehood, whites conferred upon Native Americans honorary whiteness. They regarded Native Americans as "white" for purposes of Oklahoma's black/white segregation laws. In exchange for this concession, however, Native Americans ceded a measure of sovereignty and self-governance. White powerbrokers, including some in Congress, denied them "Sequoyah"[29]—the Indian state within Oklahoma for which they had lobbied. Voters in Indian Territory had approved the Constitution of the proposed State of Sequoyah by a large margin, but political considerations doomed the initiative.[30]

Whites, and some Indians, relegated African Americans to the lowest rung on the racial ladder. African Americans were widely considered ignorant, debauched, and incapable of reaching the Eurocentric ideal of a "civilized" being. Such characterizations dogged "Negroes" for decades. Perverted images of blacks pervaded both press and politics as Oklahoma lunged toward statehood.[31]

Both whites and Indians feared an influx of black immigrants from the oppressive Southern states. Overwhelming numbers of

African Americans, they argued, would lead to a state overrun with self-interested blacks. That is, both whites and Indians worried that a too-attractive Oklahoma might become irresistible to downtrodden blacks from the Deep South. A significant black onslaught, they conjectured, might lead to a numerical and, possibly, political, black majority in the area. In their view, that majority would work against both Indian and white social and economic interests.[32]

African Americans in the Oklahoma Territories experienced virtually every imaginable abuse. Whites orchestrated the vast majority of this campaign of terror,[33] but they did not act alone. Acts of violence and intimidation upon African Americans were also committed by Native Americans, though this happened less often.[34]

This was "the nadir of American race relations."[35] Racism—not just individual, but systemic and institutional—ran rampant during the period from the late eighteenth through the early twentieth century. This racism manifested itself in the wholesale denial of black rights, sometimes including the right to life itself. Segregation, discrimination, lynchings, and "race riots" became the norm as white supremacist ideology gained a foothold among laypersons and leaders alike.

The odious racial attitudes that prevailed in the Oklahoma Territories hardened by the time Oklahoma statehood arrived on November 16, 1907. Such attitudes would be decades in the undoing.

On November 16, 2006, Oklahoma, "land of the red people"[36] in the Choctaw language, began a yearlong celebration of her centennial. She had joined the United States of America as its forty-sixth state. With parades and proclamations, speeches and sermons, meals and merriment, Oklahomans heralded their first hundred years of statehood.

The moniker "Oklahoma" remains apt. The state boasts more individual Native Americans and more Native-American tribes than any other state in the Union. More than thirty-nine distinct tribal cultures and sixty-seven tribes claim some historical relationship to what is today the state of Oklahoma.[37]

That said, many Oklahomans—Native Americans, African Americans, and even some whites—still debate the extent to which Oklahoma is, in any meaningful sense, "Native America," as its tourism motto boasts. The fitful relationship between the "Natives" and the state named for them has often been less than salutary. Asked about the Oklahoma centennial celebration, former Principal Chief of the Cherokee Nation, Wilma Mankiller, lamented:

> [N]ot everyone was caught up in the revelry. I feel sure that Cherokee families gathered in countless rural homes to talk about the illegitimate birth of Oklahoma. Perhaps they discussed the federal government's long-forgotten promise that in exchange for the loss of our ancestral homeland, we would be left alone in Indian Territory. Statehood day was a sad day for the Cherokee Nation. Some people even erroneously assumed that the Cherokee Nation has ceased to exist.[38]

By contrast, historian Angie Debo recounted the giddiness and frenzy that white settlers experienced at the time of statehood.

> Although statehood has represented the most ardent aspirations of every new American community, it is doubtful if any other people ever longed for that magic goal with the intensity of the white inhabitants of the Indian Territory. A white population very much larger than that of any state at the time of its admission to the Union had been living under conditions of political dependence never experienced before by a frontier settlement.[39]

Debo also took note of the price of statehood—a price to be paid, in her estimation, largely by the new state's Indians.

> The plunder of Indians was so closely joined with pride in the creation of a great new commonwealth that it received little condemnation. The term "grafter" was applied as a matter of course to dealers in Indian land, and was frankly accepted by them. The speculative fever also affected Government employees so that it was almost impossible to prevent them from making personal investments.[40]

Oscar Ameringer (1870-1943) arrived in Oklahoma in 1907. Ameringer, born in Achstetten, Germany, on August 4, 1870, helped organize one of the United States' largest socialist movements. A staunch supporter of the rights of the disadvantaged, he helped found the Oklahoma Renters Union in 1909 to promote the rights of sharecroppers. In 1910, he led the fight against the "grandfather clause" that disenfranchised African-American voters. He vehemently opposed World War I, even establishing, in 1917, the *Oklahoma Daily Leader* to promote a peaceful anti-war movement.[41]

In Oklahoma, Ameringer found and described an overpopulated and underdeveloped landmass, replete with impoverished and forlorn souls. From his vantage in 1907, the new State of Oklahoma seemed far from paradise.

> I found toothless old women with sucking infants on their withered breasts. I found a hospitable old hostess, around thirty or less, her hands covered with rags and eczema, offering me a biscuit with those hands, apologizing that her biscuits were not as good as she used to make because with her sore hand she no longer could knead the dough as it ought to be. I saw youngsters emaciated by hookworms, malnutrition, and pellagra, who had lost their second teeth before they were twenty years old. I saw tottering old male wrecks with the infants of their fourteen-year-old wives on their laps. I saw a white man begging a Choctaw squaw man who owned the only remaining spring in that neighborhood to let him have credit for a few buckets of water for his thirsty family. I saw humanity at its lowest possible level of degradation and decay. I saw smug, well dressed, overly well fed hypocrites march to church on Sabbath day, Bibles under their arms, praying for God's kingdom on earth while fattening like latter-day cannibals on the share croppers. I saw wind-jamming, hot-air-spouting politicians geysering Jeffersonian platitudes about equal rights to life, liberty and the pursuit of happiness without even knowing, much less caring, that they were addressing as wretched a set of abject slaves as ever walked the face of the earth, anywhere or any time. The things I saw on that trip are the things you never forget.[42]

Ameringer was not alone in his bleak portrait of the new state. Beneath the effusive "Statehood Day" centennial celebration lurked an undercurrent of ambivalence and detachment among Oklahoma's reds and blacks. For many of Oklahoma's Native Americans and African Americans, Statehood Day represented something sinister, rather than celebratory.[43]

Oklahoma's children of color dusted off an alternative script from a different historical narrative.[44] November 16, 1907, the date on which Oklahoma became a state, spelled the sunset of a way of life for Native Americans and the reawakening of Southern-style racial politics for African Americans:

> By 1907, the date of unification of Indian and Oklahoma Territories and their admission to the Union as Oklahoma, the five tribes had lost political and economic control of the region prom-

ised exclusively to them by the federal government in 1830. They had witnessed the land's inundation by white and black settlers and heard the newcomers' demands that the region by given to them with little regard for the fate of the Indian residents. Native Americans reacted with hostility and bewilderment as their lands, tribal authority, and ultimately, tribal existence, were systematically dismantled by the federal government. Much of this hostility was directed at blacks, both freedmen and "state Negroes" [i.e., Southern blacks without Native American ties].[45]

As previously referenced, the United States government involuntary uprooted five Indian tribes from their homelands in the Southeast in the 1830s and 1840s and assigned them to Indian Territory. The government encouraged these Indians to become Anglicized. In fact, the "Five Civilized Tribes" were deemed "civilized" precisely because of their adroitness at white acculturation. They felt betrayed by removal. In essence, they were punished with loss of power in a now white-dominated state because of their success at "whitening" themselves.[46]

These formidable challenges notwithstanding, Native Americans regained a modicum of independence in Oklahoma. The federal government encouraged agrarian pursuits and sought to inculcate European values further. Some members of the Five Civilized Tribes flourished. Unlike the Plains tribesmen brought into Oklahoma Territory, they readily accommodated to the Eurocentric acculturation demanded by federal policymakers.

Just as white politicians decided the fate of Oklahoma Indians, Oklahoma Indians controlled the fate of a number of African Americans. Like the Southern whites among whom they had lived, the Five Civilized Tribes enslaved African Americans. While some contrast black enslavement to Indians with black enslavement to whites, a leading scholar reminds us of a simple yet profound point: slavery is slavery.

> Although some scholars have contended that Cherokee slave owners practiced a "benign" form of slavery, such a proposition would have failed to reflect or alter the reality of enslaved African Cherokees in the Cherokee Nation who fully recognized that they were enslaved human beings. Enslaved African Indians in the Cherokee Nation, and in Indian Territory in general, were always acutely aware that neither they nor their offspring were free.[47]

These African captives, as well as some free persons of African descent, crossed geographic boundaries in their travels with the Five Civilized Tribes to Oklahoma. Decades passed, however, before those in bondage crossed over into freedom.

"Mixed-blood" Indians, products generally of unions between white men and Indian women, were the primary slaveholders among Oklahoma tribes. Mixed-bloods mastered the economics of slavery, and helped mediate between white settlers and Indian communities. In some tribes, enslaved Africans—English speakers—assisted with interpretation and translation.

The 10,000 or so enslaved African Americans in Oklahoma in 1860 experienced treatment running the gamut from harsh to hospitable. The Chickasaws, for example, were known as avid slave-catchers, hunting down black fugitives with special vigor. The Seminoles, by way of contrast, never practiced chattel slavery. In the Seminole Nation, enslaved African Americans participated in the military and intermarried with tribespersons. Moreover, unlike other tribes, the Seminoles never enacted slave codes (i.e., sets of restrictions on the liberties of enslaved Africans, such as bars to owning weapons or property).[48]

To some extent, these tribes mimicked the attitudes of the dominant white culture when it came to racial hierarchy. Some Indians saw persons of African descent as inferior, even subhuman, but by no means all Indians did.

Clan and national identities, rather than race, defined individuals in early native cultures.[49] Whites infected Native Americans with the plague of racism. Once exposed, too few Native Americans sought to check the spread of this scourge.

By virtually all measures, the swift march to Oklahoma statehood dimmed African-American prospects. At Oklahoma statehood, Oklahoma Territory and Indian Territory, until then under federal control, merged into the State of Oklahoma. Statehood celebration planners staged a mock wedding between a white man (representing Oklahoma Territory) and a Native-American woman (representing Indian Territory) in Guthrie, the Territorial Capital and site of the Constitutional Convention.[50] The new Governor, a lawyer named Charles Nathaniel Haskell, regaled the inaugural crowd with a vision of Oklahoma as a land of collaboration between red and white denizens. Indeed, Governor Haskell saw in the American flag a metaphor for the newfound unity of the red man and the white man under the canopy of an azure blue sky.[51]

This symbolic union between the white and Native-American cultures and the Pollyannaish remarks by Governor Haskell foreshadowed harsh days to come for Oklahoma's African Americans. Excluded from this unification ritual, African Americans would likewise be excluded from full and equal participation in many facets of Oklahoma life.

In the end, the fast train to statehood constrained Native-American sovereignty and diminished Native-American influence. The Curtis Act of 1898—officially, the "Act for the Protection of the People of Indian Territory"[52]—ended tribal rule in substantial respects. That federal law prescribed the division of the Five Civilized Tribes' communal land holdings into individual allotments and placement of those tribes under the jurisdiction of the federal (United States) courts, effectively abolishing tribal courts and governments in Indian Territory.

The Five Civilized Tribes, like many indigenous cultures, viewed land under a system of usufructuary, as opposed to proprietary, rights. "Usufruct," a legal term, refers to a property system wherein individuals possess rights to use and enjoy property of another, so long as the property is not impaired or altered. The individual in a tribal usufructuary system is essentially a steward of property. The tribe as a whole "owns" the property (i.e., communally), but individuals may use parcels. If the individual dies, abandons the property, or otherwise surrenders use/possession, the property reverts to the tribe for possible reallocation.[53] This differs from the more familiar proprietary, or "fee simple," concept of property, under which land is owed privately without any necessary requirement of use and with the right to convey or alienate.[54]

Many Native Americans resigned themselves to what they viewed as inevitable. Indeed, for a host of complex reasons, the official newspaper of the Cherokee Nation Tribal Council, the *Cherokee Advocate*, became a pro-allotment propaganda vehicle.

> In the early twentieth century[,] the *Cherokee Advocate* consistently urged its readers to come to terms with allotment. Most of its arguments focused upon the necessity rather than the benefits of such a policy. The paper described the certainty of unilateral governmental action, the futility of resistance, and the need to pre-

serve at least some Cherokee lands. These arguments frequently exposed contradictions because the publication's editorials required a belief that the federal government would protect individual allotments more successfully than it preserved tribal holdings. The newspaper praised the efforts of the Dawes Commission, for this group's efforts would help eliminate non-Cherokees from the tribal rolls. As its positions reflected the views of the Tribal Council, the *Cherokee Advocate*...highlight[s] the efforts of Cherokee leaders to win the support of their people.[55]

At least as regards the inevitability of it all, the *Cherokee Advocate* got it right. The allotment era proved unstoppable. Together with Oklahoma statehood, it changed Indian Country forever.

Statehood also meant changes for persons of African ancestry in Oklahoma. In many respects, statehood squelched African-American aspirations. The new Oklahoma constitution and key laws relegated African Americans to second-class citizenship. Black citizens, segregated from whites and Native Americans in ways great and small, got short shrift. For example, renowned African-American Deputy United States Marshal[56] Bass Reeves, a stalwart protector of the region from marauding criminals, lost his job at statehood.[57] He was not alone. Jim Crow saw to that.

African-American/Native-American relations also took a particularly hard turn south at the time of statehood. Native Americans, beguiled by racist propaganda and political shenanigans, increasingly embraced white supremacist strains transplanted from the Deep South.

As increasing numbers of African Americans discovered Oklahoma, tensions mounted. In addition to the Freedmen, other persons of African descent made their way to Oklahoma. Seduced by the twin attractions of freedom and opportunity, they poured out of the South and into Kansas and Oklahoma in an 1879 post-Reconstruction diaspora.

They sought to escape the post-Reconstruction tide of political powerlessness and social repression of the American South. They ached for relief from numbing poverty produced by closed economic markets and unwavering institutional inequities. They longed for a chance to prove their mettle, unimpeded by the shackles of Southern-style racism.

By demonstrating worthiness, African Americans felt they would speed their full integration into mainstream American society. They believed that the myth of inherent black inferiority, a primary rationale for the ill treatment to which African Americans had become all too accustomed, could be debunked by a solid showing of industriousness.

Personal anecdotes and polished propaganda proved irresistible to those in the market for change. An illustrative circular proclaimed: "What will you be if you stay in the South? [You will be] [s]laves liable to be killed any time and never treated right. But if you come to Oklahoma you will have equal chances with the white man, free and independent."[58] The Oklahoma odyssey had begun.

These weary Southern migrants, voluntarily uprooted from home and hearth, formed their own largely self-sustaining communities. Prominently in Kansas, then principally in Oklahoma, all-black towns proliferated in the post-Reconstruction era.[59]

The all-black towns symbolized the African-American Beulah Land, Shagri-la, and Elysian Fields of the day. Black colonies rested on the premise of hope—hope of full citizenship; hope of self-governance; and hope of full participation, through land ownership, in the American dream. Oklahoma—then the "Twin Territories" of Oklahoma Territory and Indian Territory—became a destination of choice.

To the skeptics, it all seemed too good to be true. But the pulsating "go west" cadence composed by Oklahoma boosters tapped into the souls of black folk. For many, it removed all doubts about the daunting trek to this far-away heaven.

African Americans could be counted "in that number" when the homesteaders came marching into Oklahoma Territory during the land runs of the late 1800s. Black "Sooners" joined the hordes of whites who arrived prior to the inaugural land run on April 22, 1889, at high noon. Some 50,000 people took a chance on securing plots of up to 160 of the two million acres of "Unassigned Lands" up for grabs. Hannibal C. Carter, a Mississippi Republican legislator during the Reconstruction era,[60] helped create The Freedmen's Oklahoma Immigration Association to encourage black migration into the area:

> The Freedmen's Oklahoma Immigration Association has been formed in St. Louis. The association promises every freedman who will go to Oklahoma 160 acres of land free, and it is said too that agents have been sent into the Southern states to start an emigra-

tion movement to the Indian Territory among the colored people. The Freedmen's association bases its claim to entry on the lands of the Indian Territory on the treaties of 1866, made by the government with the [Muscogee (Creek)] and Seminoles.[61]

The premise for this migration proved false. The Freedmen's Oklahoma Immigration Association assumed, erroneously, that the Treaty of 1866, granting certain rights and reparations to the Africans enslaved by tribal members, applied to all newly freed Africans, not just those freed from Indian bondage. Curtis W. Holcomb, commissioner of the general land office, informed Secretary of the Interior Samuel J. Kirkwood of that false impression and its implications:

> The treaty stipulations, as uniformly understood and construed, have no application to any other freemen than those persons freed from Indian bondage. They relate exclusively to friendly Indians and to Indian freedmen of other tribes in the Indian Territory whom it was the desire of the United States to provide with permanent homes on the lands ceded for that purpose. The "freedmen of the United States" are not comprehended within the policy of intention of the treaty provisions, and said lands have accordingly not "been purchased for the use and occupation" of the colored people of the United States. The present attempt to make use of the colored people of the country in the same direction, by dividing them with fictitious assurances that new and congenial homes can be provided for them within the Territory, deserves special reprobation, since its only effect must be to involve innocent people in a criminal conspiracy, and to subject them to disappointment, hardship, and suffering.[62]

In addition to the black homesteaders, some African Americans prospered in Oklahoma through affiliation with Native Americans. Principally in Indian Territory, the eastern portion of modern-day Oklahoma, African Americans developed black colonies.

One man, more than any other, crafted a luminous portrait of Oklahoma. That man, Edward P. McCabe, emerged as the father of the all-black town movement in Oklahoma. McCabe first gained notoriety as a respected African-American member of the Republican Party, both in Kansas and in Oklahoma. He lived for a time in all-black Nicodemus, Kansas, one of the early stops on the Black Diaspora express.[63]

McCabe came to Oklahoma in 1889 for the opening land run. He founded Langston, Oklahoma, the home of Langston University, and a townsite company to spur real estate development. He started the town's newspaper, the *Langston City Herald*, as a propaganda vehicle with Langston boosterism as its chief focus. McCabe himself became the paper's principal beneficiary.

McCabe spun a utopian web of tales about the beauty and bounty of this western frontier. Ensnared by his sales pitch, and under siege during freedom's tenuous post-Civil War reign, starry-eyed African Americans came en masse.

In 1890, McCabe visited with President Benjamin Harrison, intent on convincing him of the wisdom of creating a black state in Oklahoma—a haven for African Americans. A black state, he argued, would allow African Americans to demonstrate their industriousness to whites without unwarranted white interference. McCabe reportedly saw himself as a modern-day Messiah—governor of the proposed new state and leader of a downtrodden but hopeful people.

Many whites welcomed the proposal of a black state. They saw it as a timely and appropriate solution to America's perceived "Negro problem."

This separation/isolation logic appealed to some whites. Indeed, it mirrored the logic underlying the catastrophic "Trail of Tears" separation and isolation. Though death and disease plagued the Trail of Tears journey, the ultimate end was served. The migration both freed up valuable land in the Southeast for white settlement and concentrated a significant number of Native Americans in a discrete, largely unsettled, manageable area.

In like manner, separating the Negroes from the white population on parcels in the unsettled Oklahoma Territory, so this thinking went, would rid whites of what they regarded as a social menace. They would be free of Negroes once and for all.

On the other hand, opponents opined that an all-black state within Oklahoma would extend the welcome mat to disaffected African Americans in the Deep South. African Americans would descend upon Oklahoma in droves, dominating the social, economic, and political spheres. This, in turn, would threaten neighboring white and Native American communities.

A wholly black state within Oklahoma, from an opportunist's point of view, would frighten away white investors and drag down nearby property values. Moreover, an all-black enclave, if successful, would also challenge the white supremacist ideology undergirding the American caste system.

McCabe could not surmount the growing chorus of naysayers. Black state momentum slowed, and eventually his black state proposal failed. Undeterred, McCabe succeeded in drawing enormous attention to this new, unspoiled land called Oklahoma, even in the absence of its designation as an all-black state.

African Americans took notice. Like moths to a fire-red flame, they swarmed into Oklahoma on the wings of hope. They sought new lives. They sought to replace suffering with sustenance. They created bustling all-black towns.

The very existence of these black-dominated enclaves said something about race. The felt need for these towns—from the black perspective, as a proving ground; from the white perspective, as another wall of social separation—suggests the prominence of race as an overarching social, political, and economic dynamic.

Despite the hyperbolic promotions, the Oklahoma frontier proved forbidding for black migrants. More than a few African Americans arrived in Oklahoma without the necessary provisions to sustain them during a rugged beginning. Frustrated, some returned home. Others abandoned America altogether, retreating south to Mexico or north to Canada. Among those who stayed planted in Oklahoma, however, a series of success stories took root.

African-American land ownership burgeoned. Blacks with Indian ties received parcels of land for occupation and use under the Treaty of 1866 and allotments pursuant to the 1898 Curtis Act that subdivided the communal lands of the Five Civilized Tribes. Other African Americans purchased land secured in the Oklahoma land runs.[64] In fact, in 1900, proportionately more African Americans (75.2%) owned farms in the Twin Territories—in pre-statehood Oklahoma—than did whites (46.1%).[65]

In addition to land, most Freedmen in pre-statehood Oklahoma enjoyed more citizenship rights within the Indian nations than did African Americans in the Southern states. By 1889, Freedmen held the franchise, gained access to tribal education, and, arguably, received substantial equality under tribal justice systems. Oklahoma Freedmen, then, reached a level of social, economic, educational, and political participation unmatched elsewhere in the land for African Americans.

The relatively improved social and economic conditions persons of African ancestry enjoyed in Oklahoma heightened calls for self-help and self-reliance. Opinion leaders preached black economic solidarity in the face of white resistance. *The Langston City Herald*, McCabe's newspaper, editorialized in 1893:

> Our people are always growling, bringing suits and fighting about their being refused at the first class hotels, barbershops, restaurants, theaters, saloons, and riding in first class cars. Now if they want a free access to all these things, knowing that the white man will never make concessions, why in the mischief don't they put their minds and their money together and build them.[66]

Many African Americans did just that. They met the McCabe challenge head-on, founding more than fifty all-black towns and settlements in Oklahoma between 1865 and 1920. Many sprang up near Freedmen-occupied lands. These towns created a mystique that would later be recounted in song by artists like Bessie Smith.[67]

In addition to creating insular, all-black towns, African Americans, together with European and Native Americans, pioneered other noteworthy Oklahoma towns. Consider the case of Broken Arrow, a suburb just south and east of Tulsa, founded in 1902 and incorporated in 1903:

> A city built on the open prairie by pioneers who were Native American, Scottish, German and African-American, and who knew how to work the land and make it prosper. Stalwart pioneers built log cabin homesteads, planted trees, grew the "three sisters" of corn, beans, and squash, and hunted the banks of the Arkansas and Verdigris. [They] built cattle ranches so large that they covered a hundred square miles. [Broken Arrow was] once promoted as a county seat in the Native[-]American "State of Sequoyah."[68]

African-American success in this racially repressive era could scarcely go unnoticed, and unchecked, by whites. As historian Danney Goble noted: "It was, in fact, because some Oklahoma Negroes were so 'progressive,' so forward-looking, prosperous, urban, and vigorous that they represented such a great threat."[69]

As previously indicated, African Americans with Native-American ties often had advantages over African Americans lacking such connections. Frequently, red blood ran through black veins. Among persons of African ancestry, distinctions developed.

Mixed-blood African-American/Native-American individuals and Freedmen generally were commonly known as "Natives." These Natives competed with African-American immigrants from other areas who lacked Native-American ties, known as *Watchina* (meaning, roughly, "white man's Negro") or "State Negroes." Natives deemed *Watchina* too servile, and considered them interlopers.[70]

To persons without African ancestry, "Native" or "Watchina" status mattered little. As Oklahoma strode toward statehood, any Negro ancestry became an albatross.

Representative of a widespread racist sentiment in Oklahoma are the words of Roy E. Stafford, writing in the September 13, 1907, issue of *The Daily Oklahoman*:

> It was never intended by the Almighty that the races should be placed upon social equality and the foolish ideas that are being placed in the black man's head to the contrary, by designing politicians, bode no good to either race. For the negro is an infant, figuratively, in intellect. His understanding of things is easily influenced. He is but so much putty in the hands of those of greater intelligence and he believes what he is told to believe. His mind is as much a slave to masters who owned it before the war.[71]

Perhaps as much as anything else, this stifling air of white superiority led to unspeakable carnage and depravity: the 1921 Tulsa Race Riot, the worst incident of its kind in the early twentieth century. Commonly called a "race riot," observers, historians, and commentators have alternatively dubbed the event a "disaster," "tragedy," "burning," "holocaust," "massacre," "pogrom," and "race war." Even former Oklahoma Governor Frank Keating eschewed the term "race riot." He proclaimed: "It was not a race riot. It was an assault on the black community."[72]

At the time, however, some local leaders blamed the horrors in Tulsa on the devastated black community. They christened it a "Negro uprising."[73]

Sociologist James W. Loewen asserts the 1921 Tulsa Race Riot was a not-so-subtle attempt to create a "sundown town." A sundown town is a jurisdiction that intentionally, through exclusionary policies and practices, is essentially "all-white." Sundown jurisdictions, as the name implies, barred non-whites (typically, African Americans) after sundown—non-whites simply could not live in such towns. Historically, larger cities like Tulsa, according to Loewen, found the task of wholly eliminating African Americans virtually impossible, but some residents were nonetheless willing to give it a shot.[74]

That a teeming white mob destroyed Tulsa's prosperous but segregated Greenwood District, the African-American community, suggests the intentionality of which Loewen speaks. Post-Riot souvenir postcards further suggest intentionality in terms of the displacement of the African-American population. One such postcard reads: "Runing [sic] the Negro out of Tulsa." Others bear captions such as "Charred Negro" and "Little Africa on Fire: Tulsa Race Riot."[75]

The white supremacist, avowedly Christian clique known broadly as the "KKK" (short for the "Ku Klux Klan") gained prominence during the 1920s. The popularity of the KKK in Tulsa also lends credence to claims that at least some townsfolk sought to intimidate, if not expel, African Americans. Historian Scott Ellsworth noted that the "Tulsa Klan grew so solvent that it built its own brick auditorium, Beno Hall—short, it was said, for 'Be No Nigger, Be No Jew, Be No Catholic'—on Main Street just north of downtown."[76]

The 1921 Tulsa Race Riot capped a spate of race-based civil unrest in the United States that included major eruptions during the summer and fall of 1919. James Weldon Johnson, Executive Secretary of the National Association for the Advancement of Colored People (NAACP), coined the term "Red Summer" to describe the particularly brutal and bloody period in 1919 during which the nation witnessed more than twenty-six documented "race riots."[77] It was Johnson who notified President Warren G. Harding (March 4, 1921, to August 2, 1923), Woodrow Wilson's successor, of the 1921 Tulsa Race Riot. In response to Johnson's June 2, 1921, telegram seeking his intercession, President Harding, on June 7, 1921, publicly expressed his "regret and horror at the recent Tulsa tragedy."[78]

In the midst of the mayhem, Jamaican-born author and poet Claude McKay penned a sonnet that helped ignite the Harlem Renaissance:

IF WE MUST DIE

If we must die—let it not be like hogs
Hunted and penned in an inglorious spot,
While round us bark the mad and hungry dogs,
Making their mock at our accursed lot.

> If we must die—oh, let us nobly die,
> So that our precious blood may not be shed
> In vain; then even the monsters we defy
> Shall be constrained to honor us though dead!
> Oh, Kinsmen! We must meet the common foe;
> Though far outnumbered, let us show us brave,
> And for their thousand blows deal one death-blow!
> What though before us lies the open grave?
> Like men we'll face the murderous, cowardly pack,
> Pressed to the wall, dying, but fighting back![79]

In addition to the "race riots," lynching became an ever-present threat to African-American safety and security during this era. In 1921, the year of the Tulsa Race Riot, scores of African Americans died at the hands of lynch mobs around the country.

Lynching became the hallmark of the KKK. Marauding members of the group regularly terrorized black citizens. Infamous KKK "night riders" fomented fear among African Americans, especially in the South.

The release of D. W. Griffith's celebrated 1915 silent film, *The Birth of a Nation*, helped swell the rosters of the KKK nationwide, and particularly in Oklahoma. The film lionized the KKK as protectors of white values and white female virtue from black savages. Even America's twenty-eighth President, Woodrow Wilson (March 4, 1913, to March 3, 1921), a former Princeton history professor, joined the film's hallelujah chorus. During a private screening at the White House on the evening of March 21, 1915, President Wilson reportedly heaped praise on the work: "It's like writing history with lightning. And my only regret is that it is all terribly true."[80] *Birth of a Nation* was based on a novel, *The Clansman*,[81] by President Wilson's friend, Thomas Dixon.[82] In Tulsa, KKK members included doctors, lawyers, teachers, and preachers—members of all professions and occupations, from all social strata.[83]

African Americans understandably took umbrage at their portrayal in *Birth of a Nation* and the literary works that inspired it. Oklahoma's own Drusilla Dunjee Houston (1876-1941) led a chorus of condemnation. She was the sister of famed Oklahoma journalist and civil rights activist Roscoe Dunjee (1883-1965), who founded the *Black Dispatch* in Oklahoma City in 1915. The paper rose to national prominence. An activist in her own right, Drusilla engaged in an eclectic array of intellectual pursuits. She crafted an unpublished screenplay, *Spirit of the South—The Maddened Mob*, in response to D. W. Griffith's *Birth of a Nation* and the racist writings of Thomas Dixon, primary source material for the celebrated movie.[84]

Birth of a Nation offered a rationale for the subjugation of African Americans. Not surprisingly, KKK members, supporters, and sympathizers employed a variety social control mechanisms, both overt and covert, to keep African Americans in their proper place. The most brutal of these was lynching.

Lynching, a form of domestic terrorism primarily aimed at African Americans, emerged as a perverse American ritual beginning in the late nineteenth century. This form of vigilantism involved abduction, torture, and brutal death, by all manner of mayhem—hanging, shooting, stabbing, mutilation, burning, or some combination of these. Gleeful crowds, sometimes including children, bore witness in a macabre, carnival-like atmosphere as happy henchmen brutalized black bodies. Like vultures on carrion, spectators fought over souvenirs such as scraps of a victim's clothing. Photographers made postcards of these spectacles.

These cruel murders served as retribution for real or imagined social or legal infractions, and also sent the message that the victims and their like were inferior and should be subjugated. Lynchings helped preserve the existing social order and white supremacy by directing social friction and frustration toward convenient, often helpless scapegoats.

Some 4,700 lynchings occurred in America between 1882 and 1968, with African Americans constituting almost three-quarters of the victims. African-American activists such as Ida B. Wells Barnett, a journalist, and Walter White, Executive Secretary of the NAACP, railed against this practice early in the twentieth century, but their voices fell on deaf ears. Congress did nothing, and the lynchings continued.[85]

Harlem Renaissance poet Claude McKay dissected the festive intergenerational practice of lynching with piercing precision:

THE LYNCHING

> His spirit in smoke ascended to high heaven.
> His father, by the cruelest way of pain,
> Had bidden him to his bosom once again;

The awful sin remained still unforgiven.
All night a bright and solitary star
(Perchance the one that ever guided him,
Yet gave him up at last to Fate's wild whim)
Hung pitifully o'er the swinging char.
Day dawned, and soon the mixed crowds came to view
The ghastly body swaying in the sun:
The women thronged to look, but never a one
Showed sorrow in her eyes of steely blue;
And little lads, lynchers that were to be,
Danced round the dreadful thing in fiendish glee.[86]

Lynching as a means of white dominance and social control gained traction as Oklahoma achieved statehood. Prior to that time, a number of lynching victims were white, some were Native American, and a few were of other or unknown racial identity. The overwhelming majority of post-statehood lynching victims, however, were black.

Thus lynching reinforced white supremacy and helped suppress African-American rights—political, social, and economic—as Oklahoma embraced the "Jim Crowism" of her southern sisters. The federal government did little to protect against lynching, at least as regards African-American targets. By contrast, a notable 1897 lynching of two Seminole boys near Wewoka in Oklahoma Territory seems to demonstrate at least a slight increase in federal government willingness to intervene on behalf of Native-American lynching victims.

On December 30, 1897, a mob burned two Seminole boys at the stake for allegedly raping a white woman. A federal investigation, indictments, convictions, and compensation to the boys' families followed. Such justice could scarcely have been imagined had those boys been black.

> This case is instructive in that it shows that white settlers were just as ready to lynch Native Americans as African Americans suspected of raping white women. At the same time, however, it demonstrates that the federal government did not condone the use of vigilante law upon Native Americans as it did with respect to African Americans. If the defendants had been African American in this case rather than Native Americans, the lynching probably would have occurred without repercussions.[87]

Between 1907 and 1915, Oklahoma produced its share of "strange fruit."[88] During that period, more than a dozen African-American Oklahomans succumbed to lynchings. A cruel, ad hoc pogrom often followed a lynching. White mobs drove African-American families from the towns where lynchings occurred.[89]

Among Oklahoma lynching victims were a mother, Laura Nelson, and her son, L.W., of Okemah. In an incident as brazen as it was ghastly, a white mob hanged the two from a bridge over the Canadian River on May 25, 1911.[90]

Despite the racial crucible that enveloped African-American life in early Oklahoma, notable success stories did take place. In politics, two extraordinary black men made their marks.

Green I. Currin, an emancipated slave, became the first African American to serve in the Oklahoma territorial legislature in 1890. He came to Oklahoma during the 1889 land run and staked a claim to land in Kingfisher County.

The day after Currin's election, white men bludgeoned a black man in Kingfisher, an incident illustrative of swelling racial violence. In response, Currin introduced Oklahoma's first civil rights bill. The Currin measure proposed penalties for race-based violence. It failed by one vote.

In 1908, Oklahomans elected the state's first African-American legislator, A. C. Hamlin, a Republican from Logan County. Hamlin's legislative efforts helped establish a school for disabled and orphaned children in Taft, one of Oklahoma's all-black towns. Hamlin lost his bid for re-election in 1910, and another black Oklahoma legislator would not be seated for more than a half-century—until 1964.[91]

Beyond matters of race and politics, Oklahoma became synonymous with one of the most remarkable economic booms of the twentieth century. It all began with the discovery of black gold. Oil fueled a boomtown. Tulsa, incorporated in 1898, morphed into "The Magic City." Soon, opportunity abounded for people of all persuasions. A number of the early black Tulsa pioneers boasted Freedmen connections.[92]

> In the beginning, there was no segregation or apparently any thought of segregation of the races [in Tulsa]. They lived together and were buried together. This was due, mostly, to the fact that the Indians and [F]reedmen owned most, if not all, of the land. The

federal government was in sole control of the titles to these lands, either directly or indirectly, and did not concern itself with the separation of the races.[93]

Among the Muscogee (Creek) Nation, it is widely believed that many of the Greenwood pioneers built their economic success on foundations laid in the Muscogee (Creek) Nation. As Freedmen, they received the same 160-acre parcels that all Muscogee (Creek) citizens got, and they were educated by the tribe at places such as the Tullahassee Mission. Many spoke the tribal language.[94]

Thelma DeEtta Perryman Gray, a 1921 Tulsa Race Riot survivor, described her family's Native-American/African-American connections:

> In the early 1900s, Daddy moved his family to Tulsa where he owned a large spread of farm land at Mingo Creek. How we fourteen children loved that place...! Daddy tried to pass on his "Indian ways" to us children, especially to my brothers.
>
> . . . .
>
> The saddest event in my life was when my Daddy got killed. My Dad was the lighter-skinned son in his family; he took mostly after the Indian side of the family. Unlike his darker-skinned brothers, he could pass for Indian and he was allowed into the white hotels. One day some white oil men, who knew about Daddy's large landholdings, took him into the Mayo Hotel in downtown Tulsa and got him drunk. Then they talked him into signing his land over to them. When my Dad sobered up, he regretted what he had done and he sought a lawyer to help him get his land back. [H]e found a Jewish lawyer [in Oklahoma City] who sympathized with him and took the case. That lawyer said Daddy had a strong case and he worked very hard preparing for court. The day before Daddy was to testify, he was found dead. The official ruling was "accidental death due to hit-and-run vehicle." But everyone knew that he had been murdered for his land.[95]

Against seemingly insurmountable odds, African-American Tulsans, beginning in 1905, created a burgeoning entrepreneurial community, purchased homes, and built schools and churches across the Frisco tracks in the segregated Greenwood District. Their bustling "Black Wall Street" clashed with the prevailing social headwinds.[96]

The Greenwood pathfinders parlayed Jim Crow into an economic advantage. They seized the opportunity to create a closed market system that defied Jim Crow's fundamental premise of African-American incompetence and inferiority.

Fear and jealously swelled over time. African-American success, including home, business, and land ownership, caused increasing consternation and friction. The ascendancy of the Greenwood District could scarcely be tolerated, let alone embraced, by the larger community. Race theory—white supremacy—dictated white hegemony in every sphere.

Black World War I veterans, having tasted true freedom only on foreign soil, came back to America with heightened expectations. Valor and sacrifice in battle earned them the basic respect and human dignity so long denied them in America—or so they thought. But America had not yet changed. Oklahoma proved no exception.

The breadth of racial oppression, often translating into violence, facing African Americans in the United States prior to and during 1921 is almost unfathomable today. Yet in America in the early twentieth century, it was open season on African Americans.

Despite rampant racial violence directed toward African Americans, the United States government did little to protect her dark-skinned denizens. Indeed, the Senate three times failed to pass measures making lynching a federal offense.[97]

In Tulsa, a seemingly random encounter between two teenagers lit the fuse that set Greenwood alight. The alleged assault on a young white woman, seventeen-year-old divorcee Sarah Page, by a nineteen-year-old African-American bootblack, Dick Rowland, triggered unprecedented civil unrest. That event became the catalyst for the 1921 Tulsa Race Riot (the Riot). Fueled by sensational reporting in *The Tulsa Tribune*, jealousy over black economic success, desire for valuable real estate, and a racially hostile climate in general, mob rule held sway.

Authorities arrested Dick Rowland. A white mob threatened to lynch him. African-American men, determined to protect the teen from the rumored lynching, marched to the courthouse that held young Rowland. Law enforcement authorities asked them to retreat, assuring Dick's safety. They left, but the lynch talk persisted.

A second group of African-American men from the Greenwood District proceeded to the courthouse. The black men exchanged words with the swelling group of white men gathered on the courthouse lawn. A gun discharged. Soon, thousands of weapon-wielding white men, some of them deputized by local law enforcement, invaded Greenwood, looting pawnshops for weapons en route.

In less than twenty-four hours, people, property, hopes, and dreams vanished. The Greenwood District burned to the ground. Hordes of agitated white rioters prevented Tulsa firefighters from dousing fast-spreading flames.

Property damage ran into the millions of dollars. By most accounts, hundreds of people died. Scores lay injured. Many fled, never to return to Tulsa. In an instant, Tulsa was defiled.

Courageous Greenwood District pioneers tried to rebuild the community from the ashes, but Tulsa leaders hindered their efforts, blaming black citizens for their own plight. They rebuffed offers of charitable financial contributions toward the rebuilding. They erected roadblocks to reconstruction (e.g., a strengthened fire code that made rebuilding cost-prohibitive for many African Americans). All the while, Tulsa's city fathers sounded a reconciliatory, if not entirely sincere, tone.

A few white families hid distraught African Americans in their homes or spirited them out of town during the Riot. Once the violence subsided, some white families helped Riot victims cope with the devastation. Some downtown churches morphed into safe havens, providing both an escape from the Riot fallout and attending, too, to immediate survival needs. The American Red Cross, called "Angels of Mercy" by many, took care of victims' immediate needs, providing medical care, food, shelter, and clothing.

The law firm of Spears, Franklin & Chappelle provided legal assistance with Riot-based claims. These African-American barristers filed lawsuits against the City of Tulsa and insurance companies for damage occasioned by the Riot. Beyond legal representation, the firm counseled and consoled Riot survivors, and made urgent appeals to African Americans nationwide for aid. One of these men, attorney B. C. Franklin, father of famed scholar and historian John Hope Franklin, led the charge.

Remarkably, and in stunningly short order, the Greenwood District came alive again, bigger and better than ever, after the 1921 calamity. In 1925, the area hosted the annual conference of the National Negro Business League, the chamber of commerce-like organization founded by Booker T. Washington with the support of Andrew Carnegie. Greenwood was back.

By 1942, scores of businesses called the Greenwood District home. The new Greenwood exceeded all expectations. The Greenwood renaissance speaks to the triumph of the human spirit. It reinforces the timeless, universal virtues of determination, integrity, humility, and compassion.

Integration, urban renewal, a new business climate, and the aging of the early Greenwood pioneers caused the community to decline. That descent began as early as the 1960s, and continued throughout the 1970s and early 1980s.[98]

The State of Oklahoma formed "The Commission to Study the Tulsa Race Riot of 1921" in 1997. The eleven-member commission, made up of six African Americans and five European Americans, conducted a probing review of the facts underlying the decades-old tragedy. Its deliberations drew international attention, and its 2001 final report chronicled the critical facts surrounding the 1921 Tulsa Race Riot.[99] The commission's work provided still more evidence that racial violence in Oklahoma, sometimes organized and, arguably, institutionalized, has been a formidable obstacle to African-American progress.

Today, the Greenwood District is in the midst of a reincarnation, not as an African-American business haven, but rather as a cultural, arts, educational, and entertainment complex. The Greenwood Cultural Center, the Greenwood Chamber of Commerce, Oklahoma State University–Tulsa, Langston University–Tulsa, ONEOK Field (the venue for the Tulsa Drillers, a minor league baseball team), John Hope Franklin Reconciliation Park, and a handful of small businesses are among the major attractions.[100]

The John Hope Franklin Reconciliation Park (JHF Park) is part of the John Hope Franklin Center for Reconciliation (the JHF Center). The JHF Center, with reconciliation at the heart of its mission, may provide an institutional vehicle through which to facilitate dialogue between Native Americans and African Americans. Decades—centuries—of history insufficiently understood and, at times, intentionally miscast, have pushed these groups apart. The JHF Center affords an opportunity for some much-needed constructive engagement.

By way of background, the JHF Center was established to recast the tragedy of the 1921 Tulsa Race Riot into a triumph of reconciliation for the Tulsa community. Honoring eminent historian and near-native son, the late Dr. John Hope Franklin, the JHF Center seeks "to transform society's divisions into social harmony through the serious study and work of reconciliation."

Dr. Franklin dedicated a lifetime to the work of societal transformation and racial reconciliation. His landmark book, 1947's *From Slavery to Freedom: A History of Negro Americans*,[101] has sold more than 3.5 million copies in eight editions. Ranking among the seminal works on African-American history, *From Slavery to Freedom* helped revolutionize teaching about the black experience in the United States, and it continues to transform how we view our racialized past.

Dr. Franklin accumulated a wealth of awards and accolades. Two presidential honors stand out. He received the *Presidential Medal of Freedom*, the nation's highest civilian honor, in 1995. Then, in 1997, President Bill Clinton selected him to head the Advisory Board to the President's Initiative on Race, which was formed to stimulate dialogue on America's race matters.

As part of the JHF Center, the JHF Park incorporates a memorial to African Americans' struggle for survival, including the destruction and rebuilding from the 1921 Tulsa Race Riot. The JHF Center programs affirm Dr. Franklin's lifelong devotion to study, reasoned analysis, and social progress. A public-private partnership, the City of Tulsa owns the overall project, which is managed by a 501(c)(3) foundation, the John Hope Franklin Center for Reconciliation, Inc.

Many Tulsans realize the City of Tulsa cannot achieve social harmony without an appropriate setting where the full community—including white, black, Native American, Hispanic, Asian-American, and other racial/ethnic groups and minorities—can reflect, study, and understand social issues. The JHF Center, designed to promote dialogue and foster reconciliation, is intended to be that place.

The JHF Center's principal projects include: (i) gathering documentary evidence to be used by scholars and students in establishing the historical record; (ii) documenting the energy and resilience of the people of Tulsa's Greenwood District, both before and after the 1921 Tulsa Race Riot; (iii) creating opportunities for high school and university students to participate in historical research; and (iv) sponsoring community programs that create knowledge and understanding of the full richness of Tulsa's history.[102]

The Tulsa story—that of the Greenwood District and the 1921 Tulsa Race Riot—is, in part, a testament to the power of race and racism to warp and corrupt. A mob virtually extinguished a black community that was nationally renowned. That kind of hostility is not congenital; rather, it evolves through indoctrination. In Oklahoma, as earlier noted, the indoctrination began before statehood.

From the outset, just a trace of African ancestry made one a "Negro" in Oklahoma. Indeed, the State of Oklahoma, in its original constitution, divided its citizens into two classes: those with African ancestry and those without it. Classification as the former subjected one to all manner of official maltreatment and discrimination. Classification as the latter entitled one to "white privilege."

Drafters crafted Article 23, Section 11, of the Oklahoma Constitution, "Definition of Races," to secure Native-American support for the Democrats. Oklahoma's first constitution proclaimed: "Wherever in this Constitution and laws of this state, the word or words, 'colored' or 'colored race,' 'negro' or 'negro race,' are used, the same shall be construed to mean or apply to all persons of African descent. The term 'white race' shall include all other persons."[103] The phrase "All other persons" included Native Americans.

Democrats dominated the 1906 Constitutional Convention in Guthrie, the territorial capital. The "Definition of Races" provision also worked to ensure that mixed white/Indian children, like those of the Convention's elected leader, a teacher, lawyer, and politician named William H. "Alfalfa Bill" Murray of Tishomingo, would escape the cruelties of anti-black Jim Crow legislation.[104]

For purposes of race-based matters, the Constitution identified Native Americans with the dominant class of whites. African Americans and African Indians became the disfavored minority—in effect, second-class citizens. Alfalfa Bill, an avowed racist with close business and familial ties to the Chickasaw Nation, later became Speaker of the Oklahoma House of Representatives, United States Representative, and the ninth Governor of Oklahoma.[105]

In the first campaign in the new State of Oklahoma, Democrats worked assiduously to stoke Indian/black tensions, and thereby sway Indian voters. A 1906 article in the *Daily Oklahoman*, entitled "The Negro and Indian to Figure as Political Issues," noted:

> "Jim [C]row cars" and slavery will be the issues of the first campaign in the new state of Oklahoma in that portion known now as the five civilized nations. Separate cars for the negroes is the scare-

crow held up to the colored population of the new state, and a reminder of the slave days, and what was done to the Indians when the slaves were freed are the levers that the two parties expect to handle to the very uncertain elements in the new state.

At the close of the war of 1861, the Indians held many slaves — more [N]egroes than there were Indian owners. This was true of all of the civilized tribes, and when the Indians were given the land now known as Indian Territory, they were forced to divide the lands and property with the former slaves, creating a class known as [F]reedmen. This is the foundation of the [D]emocratic campaign committee in the first battle. It has been determined to make a house-to-house canvass of every district and make a direct appeal for votes for the [D]emocratic party and ticket on the grounds that it was the [R]epublican party that compelled the Indians to give up their property to the former slaves. This is being talked [about] already, and is having its effect.

The [N]egroes are being thoroughly aroused and alarmed over the prospects of a strictly southern state of Oklahoma. They are being warned not only by the white men that "[J]im [C]row cars" and disfranchisement are possibilities, but the [N]egro leaders are appealing to their brothers to stick to the [R]epublicans, as therein lies their safety.

. . . .

It is shown by the census of 1900 that Indian Territory had 36,853 [N]egroes, with 9,846 of voting age. The census gave 52,500 Indians, with about 15,000 of voting age, making about 25,000 votes out of a total vote of 97,361, or about one-fourth of the whole, which is a demonstration of the importance of securing this uncertain vote. On the Oklahoma side, the [N]egroes and Indians do not play such an important part.[106]

For her black pilgrims, Oklahoma statehood spelled the beginning of a jagged journey back to bedrock reality. Mimicking their Southern kin, the inaugural Oklahoma Legislature made rigid "Jim Crow" mandates into law.

The inaugural act of the Oklahoma Legislature, Senate Bill One, mandated segregated railcars and rail facilities. Earmarked funds collected pursuant to Senate Bill One went into the common school fund. Oklahoma segregated her "common schools."[107]

One drop of Negro blood doomed a person to a life of state-sanctioned oppression, hostility, and second-class citizenship. Fear, intimidation, and discrimination followed those African Americans who left the Deep South for Oklahoma in search of something better.

Moreover, the other significant minority in Oklahoma, Native Americans, beneficiaries of some "white privileges," too often embraced the notion of African inferiority written into Oklahoma law and practiced by whites in Oklahoma. Some Native Americans became "civilized" in the art of American racism.

Traditional indicia of tribal affiliation had been more cultural and psychological than biological—acceptance of tribal culture, knowledge of tribal language, recognition of tribal customs, and submission to tribal authority. "Blood quantum"—the minimum measure of blood lineage to a particular tribe sometimes considered for tribal membership and benefits—rarely mattered. Indeed, free persons of African descent, enslaved Africans, whites and other Indians from other tribes routinely joined various tribes with little fanfare and with full acceptance.

Blood degree requirements emerged only after the United States government formulated policy guidelines for gaining highly prized federal recognition of tribal governments that included blood quantum standards. Race played a role in how federal agents recorded such blood quantum.

The federal government charged the Dawes Commission with taking a census of Native Americans in connection with the land allotment process in the early 1900s. It injected the element of race into its work. Under the allotment model, the federal government parceled out tribal lands, theretofore held communally,[108] to individuals—which marked a transition to a capitalistic, private ownership model. The shift had racial overtones from the start.

Some allotment proponents justified the process, in part, on a benevolent, redistributive basis. Some mixed-bloods of Indian and white ancestry, they argued, had amassed vast property holdings despite communal land tenure systems. "Real Indians," the full-bloods, were being squeezed out by this growing aristocracy. Allotment and private ownership of land would help level the playing field among Native Americans.[109] In the end, however, it became clear that a racial stratification system persisted.

> "Intruder[s]" [unauthorized immigrants into Indian Territory] and Boomer[s] [homesteaders and land speculators in Indian Territory] aimed to achieve their right, as white American men, to

own lands and to govern them. For their part, the reformers wished to transform "the Indian" into a proper American and a proper man and to reduce his racial liability of difference, tasks they believed entailed "giving" him private property in land while taking away his self-government.[110]

During the enrollment process, Dawes Commission workers used the term "Freedmen" to describe *any* person of African descent living among the Indians. Native-American lineage was not included. The bureaucrats did not list Native-American blood degree for *any* of the Freedmen. David A. Chang explained the profound impact this had on Freedmen within the Muscogee (Creek) Nation:

> U.S. policy...used allotment to impose its racial categorizations far more systematically and rigidly than the Creeks had ever done.... [T]he Dawes Commission considered that any individual with any African ancestry would be enrolled as a "Freedman," no matter what the other elements of his or her ancestry. Thus in cases in which the commission placed a woman on the "Creek by blood" rolls and her husband on the "Creek Freedman" rolls, the couple's children would be recorded as Creek Freedmen—racial status thereby overriding the generally matrilineal rule of Creek enrollment. Whether or not one had white or indigenous ancestry, the Dawes Commission made a policy of registering any person with known African ancestry as a Freedman.... [A]s a general rule, enrollment established a more rigid racial order that differentiated people of African descent sharply from other Creek citizens on the basis of "blood" and differentiated among non-black Creeks on the basis of "blood quantum."

The rigid profiling of the Freedmen by Dawes Commission agents had far-reaching consequences on Africans with Native American ties. The rolls created by the Dawes Commission would later be used as a basis for entitlement to governmental goods and services, and even tribal citizenship. The absence of a recorded blood degree would be used by some within the Five Civilized Tribes to justify the denial and exclusion of Freedmen.[111]

Freedmen in Oklahoma varied in terms of circumstance. Some were enslaved Africans held by one Native-American tribe or another and emancipated pursuant to the Treaty of 1866.[112] Some were free Africans who enjoyed familial and affinity relationships with the tribes. Still others were products of intermixing and intermarriage with members of the tribes, and thus possessed "Indian blood."

Present-day efforts to remove Freedmen from the various tribes often turn on sanguinity—on blood ties. Because of the Dawes Commission's century-old racial classification scheme, Freedmen still encounter great difficulty proving such ties. That, however, in no way diminishes the existence of those blood ties.

By way of example, the cultural interchange between Native American and African Americans has been reflected in the literature of both groups:

> Through the lines of black novels, short stories, poetry and theatre, [N]ative Americans emerge only occasionally as savage jokes; most frequently they are honored as ancestors, mourned as victims and delighted in as co-conspirators in the daily struggle against domination by whites. In a similar way Indian authors regard blacks as kindred spirits with an abiding affinity in the face of exploitation by whites.[113]

Bound by the shackles of slavery and linked by the bonds of kinship, African Americans and Native Americans have shared more than territory. Together and apart, they have shared life and living from a minority, "outsider" perspective.[114]

Wilma Mankiller, former Principal Chief of the Cherokee Nation, spoke of the depth, breadth, and the vicissitudes of this black-red relationship. Addressing a session at the National Congress of American Indians, she acknowledged the impact of racism: "Society tends to accept tribal people when mixed with white people…[b]ut, if you find someone who says I am half black and half [Indian], people have more difficulty with that."[115]

Dr. David Wilkins, a professor of Indian Studies at the University of Minnesota and a member of the Lumbee Tribe, echoed that view at the same conference. Professor Wilkens cited a compelling personal example.

The Lumbee Tribe has sought full federal recognition for more than a hundred years. Attaining federal recognition is a long and cumbersome process.

Federal recognition refers to the official acknowledgement by the United States of the political status of a Native-American tribe as a government.[116] Indians who are members of federally recognized tribes are eligible for programs such as health-related services designed to fulfill the federal government's trust responsibility to the tribes.[117]

Generally speaking, federal "trust responsibility" emanates from the fiduciary or "trust" relationship between the United States and the Native-American tribes. That relationship has been likened to that of a trustee and a beneficiary. This special status for federally recognized tribes affords them federal protection of their sovereign status, lands and tribal property, and rights as members of domestic dependent nations.

The federal government holds in trust status the vast majority of Indian lands, money, and resources. The United States' trust responsibility obligates it to manage those assets in ways that are most beneficial to the Indian tribes and the individual Indian people for whom they are held.[118]

Under the 1956 Lumbee Act,[119] Congress simultaneously recognized and terminated the Lumbee Tribe. That duality persists. The federal government recognizes the Lumbee Tribe, but neither extends trust responsibility nor provides federal services to the group.[120]

Federal recognition is important to Indian tribes. Such recognition allows a tribe to establish its own government and secure for that tribal government a modicum of sovereignty. Tribes not recognized by the federal government may form tribal organizations, but they lack sovereign powers. They may own land corporately, but the federal government will not put these lands into trust for the tribe.

Professor Wilkins believes his tribe hangs in the curious legal limbo of being both recognized and terminated in part because of its strong African-American ties.

> [O]ne of the primary reasons the Lumbees have been denied federal recognition is that we are said, very quietly these days, to exhibit too much of an ad-mixture of non-Indian racial characteristics, with an emphasis being placed almost exclusively on our perceived, and real, mixtures with African-Americans. This is interesting, since the documentary and oral evidence of my people points to the Lumbees having intermarried actually more with whites than with African-Americans. . . . [I]ndian[-]white intermarriage . . . has been acceptable historically while Indian[-]black involvement . . . was deemed to dilute or to corrupt the tribe's cultural or genetic identity.[121]

The concerns about race expressed by Professor Wilkins emanate from the historical record. An early twentieth century anthropologist employed by the Bureau of Indian Affairs studied the Lumbee people to determine whether they were black or Indian. Phenotype—observable physical characteristics—ruled his assessment, with particular weight given to hair texture.

The evaluator placed a pencil in a subject's hair. If the pencil slipped readily through the hair, he recorded the subject as Indian. If, however, the pencil got caught in the subject's hair, the anthropologist listed the individual as "Negroid."[122]

Native-American connections with African Americans, then, are both deep and consequential. Those connections continue into the present. Again, former Principal Chief of the Cherokee Nation, Wilma Mankiller:

> I [have seen] people who appeared to be African-American, who[m] I could absolutely look at and say "that person is Creek, or that person is Cherokee." And, I [have seen] three or four people like that, and I thought that the whole area of family connections between African Americans and Native Americans was very interesting.
>
> [T]here were many connections in this country between African Americans and Native Americans, some positive and some not so positive. In some of the large southeastern tribes, the mixed-blood population were slaveholders, and there was and continues to be what I would describe as almost a class system in the southeastern tribes. And by and large the full blood people were absolutely opposed to holding of human beings in bondage. And so we have that history. On the other hand, we have a history of a great deal of intermarriage; we have a history of our people joining abolitionists in their struggle. It is a complicated history.[123]

The complexity of that history is illustrated by recent moves to disenfranchise black tribal members, most evident in the Cherokee Nation. Some see the divestiture of the Freedmen as a mere unfortunate consequence of tribal sovereignty. That sovereignty, they argue, trumps all else, as "no right is more integral to a tribe's self governance than its ability to establish membership, [which] has long been recognized as central to its existence as an independent political community."[124]

Heather Williams, an African-American Cherokee who traces

her lineage back to non-Freedmen ancestors, embraces that view, at least implicitly. "If I said life is fair, I'd be lying. It is an unfortunate situation [the position of the Freedmen]. Maybe I would have thought differently if on my mother's side they were on the Freedmen roll, but they were not."[125]

Recall that the "Freedmen Roll" was one of the early twentieth century federal Indian census listings—"rolls"—reserved for persons of African ancestry. That and other "rolls" were used to allot Indian lands and are presently used by some tribes, including the Cherokee Nation, to determine citizenship status.

Ms. Williams works for the Cherokee Nation. Some see her role as that of a token, mere diversity window dressing designed to deflect charges of racism levied on account of the Freedmen issue.[126]

The sovereign power to determine tribal citizenship status, while roundly acknowledged, is not unfettered. An opinion rendered by Nathan R. Margold, Solicitor, United States Department of the Interior, Office of the Solicitor, on October 25, 1934, articulated the limitations pertinent to this sovereign prerogative. In essence, the opinion is a recitation of post-reorganization tribal power/authority under the Wheeler-Howard Act (a.k.a., the Indian Reorganization Act of 1934).[127] Solicitor Margold noted that tribal authority (sovereignty) over membership is broad, but limited:

> The question of what powers are vested in an Indian tribe or tribal council by existing law cannot be answered in detail for each Indian tribe **without reference to hundreds of special treaties and special acts of Congress**. It is possible, however, on the basis of reported cases, the written opinions of the various Executive departments, and those statutes of Congress which are of general import, to define the powers which have heretofore been recognized as lawfully within the jurisdiction of an Indian tribe. My answer to the propounded question, then, will be general, and subject to correction for particular tribes **in the light of the treaties and statutes affecting such tribe wherever such treaties or statutes contain peculiar provisions *restricting* or *enlarging*** the general authority of an Indian tribe.[128] (emphasis added)

The Treaty of 1866, arguably, qualifies as a "special treaty" limiting the otherwise broad authority of the tribal signatories over internal membership. The ability of the Cherokee Nation and other tribes to exclude the Freedmen would thus be circumscribed by that pact. Indeed, the United States Court of Appeals for the D.C. Circuit noted in a recent case involving the Cherokee Freedmen:

> The Cherokee Nation [claims] special interests in controlling internal governance and defining tribal membership.... The Cherokee Nation has no interest in protecting a sovereignty concern that has been taken away by the United States.... [T]he Thirteenth Amendment and the 1866 Treaty whittled away the tribe's sovereignty with regard to slavery and left it powerless to discriminate against the Freedmen on the basis of their status as former slaves. The tribe does not just lack a "special sovereignty interest" in discriminatory elections—it lacks any sovereign interest in such behavior.[129]

Freedmen advocates and allies argue that Congress, federal agencies, and the federal courts should countermand tribal sovereignty when a federally recognized tribe exercises its unquestioned citizenship power[130] in a racially discriminatory fashion. Under this view, Freedmen citizenship should be required where "self-determination becomes an oppressive tool used to exclude some Indians on the basis of race.... [W]hen the restriction or limitation on tribal membership is rooted in notions of racial superiority, it does not serve any legitimate purpose."[131]

The word "sovereignty" has a number of meanings. Basic tenets of tribal sovereignty include the power to regulate tribal lands, levy taxes, oversee zoning, manage resources, and regulate the conduct of tribal members. At its core, some argue, Indian tribal sovereignty means the right to decide who is a member of a tribe. However, there is an unspoken racial element inherent in Freedmen membership decisions. Should the burden of this sovereignty dilemma rest on the backs of black Indians, given their historical relationships with the various tribes and the nature and extent of the likely collateral damage? To what extent should the civil rights—indeed, the human rights—of the Freedmen factor into the recognition equation?

Efforts by some tribal leaders to exclude their brothers and sisters of African descent merit, at a minimum, scrutiny. Are the Five Civilized Tribes enmeshed in an apartheid-like push to purge African-American Indians from tribal citizenship rolls?

"Apartheid" is admittedly a strong, emotion-laden word, particularly as applied in twenty-first century America. Yet it can be argued that there are notable parallels between apartheid and use of the cloak of "sovereignty"[132] to purge African Americans from tribes.

Notably, the Cherokee Nation has found itself in recent tussles over sovereignty that have implications for the Freedmen. Among other examples, the Cherokee Nation amended its 1975 Constitution on June 23, 2007, so as to eliminate Section 10 of Article XV, which required review and approval of all Constitutional amendments by the Secretary of the Interior. The Chief of the Bureau of Indian Affairs (BIA), Carl J. Artman,[133] emphasized, however, that the amendment did not authorize the Cherokee Nation to act in ways inconsistent with federal law. Some saw this latter statement as an allusion to the Freedmen controversy and the amendment itself as designed to facilitate Freedmen disenfranchisement.

Increasingly, the conflict over Cherokee Nation tribal citizenship has been framed in sweeping terms. Marilyn Vann, a self-described Cherokee Native American with African blood, serves as president of the Descendants of Freedmen of the Five Civilized Tribes.

A petroleum engineer from Oklahoma City, Vann is possessed of a prodigious knowledge of Cherokee and Freedmen history. She laments her tribe's machinations aimed at removing her from its citizenship roster: "[I want to] have a voice in the affairs of the tribe. I did not come to my tribe to get something. This is a fight for justice to stop these crimes against humanity.[134] Modern nations don't de-nationalize their long-term citizens." Ms. Vann peppers her stance with footnotes about the international furor over historical attempts to strip the oppressed of citizenship: black South Africans via the Bantu Homelands Citizens Act of 1970; Gypsies in Romania; Jews in Nazi-era Germany. Something has to give, she demands, when sovereignty and human rights collide. That "something" should be the over-extension of concepts of independence and sovereignty.[135]

Native-American sovereignty has been and remains constrained by federal tribal policy. In the nineteenth century, such policy "reflected a mix of benevolent, pragmatic and manipulative impulses, whose contradictions were painstakingly glossed over in laws, treaties and policy discussions."[136] The federal government, intent on preserving the Union, at first acceded to state demands for land and for regulation of the tribes. Federal tribal policy shifted in 1934 to restore tribal autonomy.[137]

Freedmen advocates note that implicit in the notion of sovereignty is the standing to make and honor solemn commitments. The Treaty of 1866 was the post-Civil War manumission treaty that granted Freedmen citizenship rights. To them, it is one such sacrosanct commitment.

In this view, any attempt to exclude Freedmen or restrict their rights amounts to reneging on sacred promises at the expense of a whole class of citizens. Attempts to erase significant numbers of African-American Indians from tribal rosters—to deny their heritage, to withhold from them the franchise, and to sever their access to tribal services—tarnishes tribal integrity, and thus tribal independence and sovereignty.[138]

Some within the Cherokee Nation, including The United Keetoowah Band (UKB), representative of the majority of the higher degree of Cherokees, see Freedmen disenfranchisement as divisive and destructive. The UKB received federal recognition after the Indian Reorganization Act of 1934. Its members descend from the "Old Settlers," Cherokees who moved west before forced removal. The UKB requires a quarter blood quantum for enrollment. Members must have at least one ancestor listed on the final Cherokee Dawes Roll.

Beyond tribal sovereignty, more tangible costs are potentially in the offing if the Cherokee Nation expels its Freedmen from the tribe. For example, the federal government could step in and deny the Cherokee Nation federal recognition on account of black disenfranchisement.[139] This could mean loss of federal subsidies, grant monies, health care, housing, tribal citizenship, and gaming opportunities.[140] Moreover, economic boycotts of lucrative Indian casinos, smoke shops, and other business enterprises by angry African Americans and their ideological supporters could wreak financial havoc.

Leaving aside psychic and financial costs, however, there is an even more costly potential outcome of the conflict over Freedmen citizenship. The fight over black disenfranchisement threatens to unravel cultural ties that were centuries in the making at a time when coalitions and collaborations have taken on renewed urgency and importance.

Litigation and the threat of Congressional action continue to force the matter of black disenfranchisement to a head. The former eats up tribal funds and spawns adverse publicity; the latter may lead down an endless path of governmental scrutiny, oversight, and entanglement.

Freedmen supporters crafted a petition urging Congress to affirm the rights of the Freedmen, enforce the Treaty of 1866, and eschew the race-based disenfranchisement.

To the Lawmakers of the United States of America:
We, the descendents of Freedmen of the Five Civilized Tribes (Cherokee, Chickasaw, Muscogee [Creek], Seminole, and Choctaw), as well as their supporters, call for legislation to enforce the rights of descendents of Freedmen which were agreed on between the United States and the Five Civilized Tribes in the treaties of 1866. (Prior to 1866, the five tribes did not allow persons of African descent to become tribal citizens, regardless of their "blood" Indian descent). These 1866 treaties required that the five tribes give the Freedmen and their Descendents rights of native tribal citizens.

The Freedmen and Freedmen Descendents were adopted by the tribes to comply with the treaties. Freedmen and Descendents of the Freedmen of the five tribes were separately listed on the Dawes Rolls from other tribal citizens (who were "full bloods") or were mixed bloods (Indian and Caucasian mixture), whom [sic] were listed on "Indian by blood" rolls, in which an Indian blood degree was listed. Again, we emphasize that many of these Freedmen descendents did have Indian blood, although blood degrees were not listed on the Dawes Freedmen Rolls.

At the present time, the Bureau of Indian Affairs (BIA) refuses to issue certificate of Indian blood (CDIB) cards to Freedmen Descendents, which are required to participate in BIA administered programs. Furthermore, the five tribes, in violation of the 1866 treaties, have passed tribal constitutions and tribal acts which specifically require potential enrollees to provide CDIB cards prior to enrollment and/or specifically allow the enrollment of only those descended from the Dawes "Blood Rolls."

We call on lawmakers to pass legislation which will establish a blood quantum of "full blood" equivalent to those Freedmen Descendents whom [sic] are listed on the Dawes Rolls of the five tribes for purposes of the U.S. Government. Furthermore, we call on the U.S. Government to not recognize those tribal governments which currently refuse to allow the enrollment and which do not allow participation in tribal elections for the descendents of those tribal citizens who were listed on the Freedmen rolls by the Dawes

98   Apartheid in Indian Country?

Commission, and for the BIA to directly administer tribal programs for these illegal tribal governments.[141]

In August of 2007, both United States Senator Tom Coburn (R-Oklahoma), a member of the Senate Indian Affairs Committee, and BIA head Carl J. Artman announced their support of continued Freedmen citizenship in an ongoing controversy in the Cherokee Nation. Both men cited the Treaty of 1866 as controlling. Both men alluded to enforcement of the Treaty of 1866 should voluntary compliance not be forthcoming. Senator Coburn raised the specter of withholding federal funds from the Cherokee Nation. BIA Chief Artman hinted at possible court action.[142]

In 2009, a number of African-American members of Congress implored United States Attorney General Eric Holder to look into the issue of Freedmen disenfranchisement.

We the undersigned members of Congress request that the

Enlisted men from Troop C, 5th U.S. Cavalry, with squatters they arrested in Indian Territory prior to the opening of Oklahoma. On the left are two Native American scouts. (Photo appears in The United States Cavalry: An Illustrated History, 1776-1944 *by Gregory J. W. Urwin, printed by the University of Oklahoma Press in Norman, Oklahoma, in 2002, page 152.)*
—Courtesy Fort Smith National Historic Site

Department of Justice Civil Rights Division commence a full-scale investigation into what we believe are the Five Civilized Tribes' systematic expulsion of its [sic] freedmen citizens in violation of their treaty, voting, and civil rights. The illegal actions of the leadership of the Five Tribes, some of which are the wealthiest tribes in Indian Country, have resulted in the freedmen's inability to access federal benefits and programs, totaling in the hundred[s] of millions of dollars annually, in the areas of housing, education, health, and public works. In many instances, the illegal expulsions of the freedmen occurred decades ago.

. . . .

[I]t is our firm belief that [the] Department of Justice Civil Rights Division must be charged by you to investigate all efforts past and present to disenfranchise the freedmen and that any investigation it undertakes must not be short-circuited by forces that seek to use tribal sovereignty as a justification for inaction. We believe that tribal efforts to disenfranchise the freedmen transcend the scope of tribal courts and law and that incidents of tribal packing of courts to disenfranchise the freedmen and violations of the Principal Chiefs Act [1970 law requiring the approval of the Secretary of Interior for voting procedures in the Five Civilized Tribes] warrant federal investigation and possible intervention.[143]

How did we descend to these depths of rancor and mistrust? How do we repair the fissures separating Native America tribes and the offspring of the Africans who once lived among them? What is the price of allowing such disputes to fester and spread?

These questions are perhaps best answered by looking in the rearview mirror; by taking a searching and honest walk through a shared history. The past illuminates the present and informs the future.

CHAPTER III

A Legacy of Mixing and Matching: Debunking the Purity Premise

"In every conceivable manner, the family is link to our past, bridge to our future."
—ALEX HALEY

I was born in the Creek Nation, March 1, 1856. My mother was named Thamore Franklin, she was one-fourth Creek Indian and was married to a negro slave, Fred Franklin, who was a slave of James Yargee of the Creek Nation. I am one-eighth Creek Indian and seven-eighths negro. My father was born in the Creek Nation and he, with nine other slaves, worked on the farm of Jim Yargee in the Creek Nation until 1867 when the Civil War was over. My mother was allotted one hundred and sixty acres of land near Canadian [sic] and moved on it with me when I was eleven years old. My mother drew Indian money under the Creek Treaty of 1866, when the Government agreed to pay the Creeks for all damage done in the war and also allot them land. I worked with my father until I was twenty years old and applied to the government for an allotment and they gave me one hundred and sixty acres of land in the Creek Nation.[1] I was married to Fannie Franklin in 1876 and moved on my farm and we had seven children.[2]
—RICHARD FRANKLIN,
Oklahoma Slave Narratives

The concept of race helps facilitate the categorization and identification of groups. This convenient, if pernicious, shorthand amplified in importance as groups began to cross the artificial lines of difference. Rather than an overarching, impenetrable barrier, race became a fluid social construct used to impose command and control. The taboo against race mixing, or "miscegenation," has been embedded in the American psyche for centuries. Actual practice, however, never fully squared with the anti-miscegenation pronouncements and prohibitions. What has changed over the last few decades is the extent to which we acknowledge and legitimize these trans-racial involvements. Understanding the web of complex social relationships between and among European Americans, African Americans, and Native Americans is essential to grasping Oklahoma history in general and the Freedmen narrative in particular.

Prior to European incursions, the Five Civilized Tribes enjoyed virtually unthreatened habitation of the southeastern United States. As matrilineal societies, the tribes passed citizenship through an Indian mother, through marriage to a tribal member, and through the adoption of captives into a particular tribe. Tribal members fished, operated small farms, and hunted small game.

European-Americans employed a variety of approaches to deal with the Native Americans they encountered: collaboration, conquest, "civilization," and co-optation through land policy. In 1892, Captain Richard Henry Pratt, founder of the Carlisle Industrial Indian School, captured the sentiments of many of his American contemporaries: "[A]ll the Indian there is in the race should be dead. Kill the Indian in him and save the man."[3] This deep-seated, palpable disdain for native traditions and culture sullied United States policy with respect to Native Americans for decades.

The mere whitening of the Native-American population would not be sufficient. As previously noted, the forced removal of Native Americans to modern day Oklahoma constituted another subjugation stratagem.

Beyond removal, whites consolidated power in another strategic way. Europeans intermarried into the Five Civilized Tribes. These mixed marriages, primarily between white men and Indian women, brought significant changes to the old tribal ways, as native customs and traditions faded into history in emerging blended families.

Even as formal red/white bonds grew, less formal red/black ties remained strong. Early on, African-American and Native-American relations in Indian Country continued to be close. Religious practice offers a window into the interdependence of the two groups:

> [T]he first Baptist Churches—Amohee Baptist Church within the

Cherokee Nation and Ebenezer Baptist Church within the Creek Nation—were mixed congregations often led by Black Baptist preachers. Without the Black Baptist preachers who were fluent in both English and Native tongues, the gospel of the Christian faith within the Indian Territory would have fallen on deaf ears; without Indian communicants, the traditionally defined historic "Black" congregations would have had much more serious birth pangs. The "beloved community" was much more culturally complex than we have been led to believe.[4]

Eventually, white supremacist philosophy gained a foothold among Indians.

Indians occupied an ambiguous position in a legal system structured around a binary conception of racial identity, and thus not equipped to cope with racial ambiguity. The southern tribes, therefore, were forced to choose a side. It is not surprising that they would align themselves with whites; the experience of power and privilege is always more attractive than the experience of subjugation and oppression. Whites perceived tribal imitation of whiteness as evidence of the tribes' civilized status. (footnote omitted)[5]

Most of the Five Civilized Tribes enacted tribal constitutions and other measures that restricted the rights of people among them who were of African descent (e.g., barriers to citizenship). These impediments applied even to individuals of African descent whose fathers were tribal citizens.

The Five Civilized Tribes generally prohibited outright intermarriage between African Americans and tribesmen. The proscription or regulation of black-Indian sexual relations and marriage, it was believed, would obviate the inconvenience of mixed-race offspring who would corrupt Indian identity. Moreover, pre-emancipation, anti-black miscegenation laws sought to strengthen and protect the distinction between free persons and chattel slaves. Absent miscegenation, slaves could readily be identifiable with reference to physiognomy and other physical characteristics.[6] Examples of anti-black miscegenation laws include:

(1) An 1825 Muscogee (Creek) law provided for disinheritance or divestment of family property for any Indian who married an African American, noting, "[I]t is a disgrace to our Nation for our people to marry a Negro."[7]

(2) An 1839 Cherokee law—the first post-removal law passed by the Cherokee Nation[8]—proscribed marriages between African Americans and Cherokees on pain of corporal punishment not to exceed fifty lashes. An African-American male violator of this law, however, would be subject to one hundred lashes.[9]
(3) An 1859 Chickasaw law banned interracial marriage, even providing that a white man living among the tribe who took a black wife would be subject to payment of a fine and banishment.[10]
(4) An 1885 Choctaw law condemned Choctaw/African-American marriages, imposing upon violators a punishment of fifty lashes on the bare back.[11]

Official tribal efforts to prevent intimate relationships between African Americans and Native Americans reinforced the racial hierarchy already extant outside Indian Country:

> First, the tribes' internalization of the racialization of Indian identity is evident from [Indian miscegenation laws], in that the tribes did not seek to regulate inter-ethnic relations. Each tribe's laws allowed Indian members of the tribe to marry an Indian from another tribe. This suggests that the tribes were more concerned with preserving Indianness in racial terms than they were with preserving their members' individual ethnic identity as "Cherokee" or "Choctaw." Second, the tribes did not seek to ban Indian marriage to whites. The tribes were only concerned with race mixing when it came to Indians mixing with blacks. This suggests that the tribes' leadership did not identify the bleaching of the tribe as a threat to tribal existence, whereas the blackening of the tribe was perceived as such.[12]

Following the Civil War, the Choctaw Nation reluctantly adopted the Choctaw Freedmen into the tribe. As earlier noted, the Chickasaw Nation never adopted the Chickasaw Freedmen after the Civil War.[13] Moreover, while the Choctaw Nation did provide segregated schooling for its Freedmen, the Chickasaw Nation took no such initiative. Other nations within the Five Civilized Tribes proved more accommodating on matters of race.[14]

African Americans fared substantially better within the Seminole and Muscogee (Creek) Nations. Intermarriage flourished. Indeed, white settlers considered these tribes less civilized, on account of perceived black contamination, than the other three nations of the Five Civilized Tribes.[15]

Prior to the Civil War, the Seminoles treated African Americans with a level of dignity and equality unparalleled within the Five Civilized Tribes.[16] Whites adopted into the tribe, or their progeny, owned the vast majority of enslaved Africans living among the Seminoles.

As previously suggested, the concept of "slave" in the context of Native American "masters" sometimes took on a markedly different meaning than it did in connection with chattel slavery, Deep South style. Southern white slave-masters treated enslaved Africans as "things." Some Native Americans who enslaved Africans objectified them; others took pains to preserve the humanity, personhood, and dignity of their charges.[17] Some persons of African ancestry became engines of economic exploitation; others grew as branches on Native American family trees.[18] Their owners' proclivities notwithstanding, these persons of African ancestry shared a singular horror—the absence of freedom—and its accompanying indignities.

In the mid-1800s, only a miniscule number of tribal citizens owned slaves, members of the Chickasaw Nation being a notable exception. Yet at the dawn of the Civil War in 1861, each of the Five Civilized Tribes signed treaties with the Confederacy. These treaties notwithstanding, loyalties within the tribes remained divided.[19]

In light of the recent controversy over Cherokee Freedmen citizenship, it is interesting to note during the Civil War, the Cherokee Nation stood alone in explicitly repudiating its Confederate alliance. The Cherokees freed the enslaved Africans among them in 1863, and ceased enforcing discriminatory laws against people of African descent as the post-Civil War era dawned. These early Cherokee concessions on the issue of slavery, however, would not be enough. There would be a price to pay for the unholy and unsuccessful alliance with the Confederacy.

After the Civil War, the United States government seized vast swaths of land as the spoils of victory over the Confederate-allied Five Civilized Tribes. This post-War land acquisition allowed the federal government to open land on which to move Plains Indians. It also allowed settlement by land-hungry whites eager to move into Indian Territory.

The Civil War itself exacted a terrible toll, wiping out more than one-third of the Cherokees, Muscogee (Creek), and Seminoles.[20] But it also brought emancipation—albeit at the hands of a foreign, colonial, and conquering power—to those African Americans still in bondage among the tribes.

As previously noted, in 1866, each of the Five Civilized Tribes entered into an agreement with the United States. The tribes agreed to end slavery forever and to treat the formerly enslaved Africans among them (and free African Americans) equally. The Cherokee, Muscogee (Creek), and Seminole Nations immediately accepted the Freedmen, granting them tribal citizenship. The Choctaw Nation failed to accept the Freedmen as citizens until the 1880s. The Chickasaw Nation at one point adopted the Freedmen as citizens, but later rescinded that acceptance.

After the Civil War, and up until Oklahoma achieved statehood in 1907, Freedmen generally flourished among the Indians. They received, and took advantage of, equal educational opportunities. They held positions in tribal government, and they shared in the tribal resources in the Cherokee, Choctaw, Muscogee (Creek), and Seminole Nations. Despite a modicum of internal calm, however, threats from outsiders loomed.

In the post-Civil War period, white marauders regularly invaded the lands of the Five Civilized Tribes. White Southerners placed extreme pressure on the United States government to disband tribal governments and confiscate tribal lands and minerals. These assets, they argued, should be placed in white hands.

Eventually, the federal government forced the Five Civilized Tribes to sell vast amounts of land for minimal payment. Prior to the land sale, the government empowered the Dawes Commission to set up rolls of tribal citizens so each tribal citizen would receive a share of the tribal resources in accordance with agreements between the tribe and the government. This alien system of individual land ownership, the hallmark of "civilization" and a cornerstone of assimilation policy, struck at the heart of Indian history and culture.

Traditionally, tribes owned land communally. The transition to an individual-based land ownership system facilitated the erosion of a "we-based" social philosophy to a "me-based" one.

President Theodore Roosevelt, in 1901, hailed the Dawes Act as "a mighty pulverizing engine to break up the tribal mass."[21] Truth be told, the Dawes Act broke up much more.

The Dawes Commission used the earlier citizenship rolls of the tribes in determining who would be placed on the government roll for each tribe; this was known officially as the "Final Rolls of the

Citizens and Freedmen of the Five Civilized Tribes in Indian Territory." General categories of tribal citizens included citizens by blood, citizens by marriage, minor citizens, Freedmen citizens, and adopted citizens. The federal government used the resulting "Dawes Rolls" to allot individual parcels of land in return for a tribe's abolition of its tribal government and recognition of the laws of the United States of America.

Traditional tribal rolls did not record the degree of Indian blood for tribal citizens (i.e. percentage of genetic connection, measured in blood relationships, to a particular tribal heritage); rather, tribal rolls delineated two simple categories, "citizen" and "non-citizen." The notion of "blood quantum" in the Five Civilized Tribes surfaced in earnest only at the dawn of the twentieth century.

Dawes Commission workers characterized virtually all individuals believed to be of African descent as "Freedmen." They listed no degree of Indian blood on such individuals' Dawes applications. That said, many Freedmen identified an Indian father on their Dawes enrollment applications. Others orally attested to having an Indian father or grandfather. Still, Dawes Commission agents relegated the Freedmen to separate rolls. They refused to list degrees of Indian blood, even if the Freedmen registered that way.

The Dawes Commission treated individuals with mixed Indian and white ancestry more favorably. The Commission listed such individuals as "Indians," with varying degrees of Indian blood. This double standard echoed the racial politics of the day. It fueled the myth that Indian ancestry is, in effect, "Africanless." African ancestry—any African ancestry—trumped all other heritage.

> The Dawes Commission . . . used a eugenics-based methodology to determine the racial identity of mixed-race individuals: anyone of exclusively Indian ancestry—or both European and Indian ancestry—was considered "Indian" and consequently placed on the "blood roll." The blood roll listed the individual's name, tribe, and their percentage of Indian blood based on ancestry. Those individuals who were not "full blood" Indians, but who also had European ancestry, could be listed on the blood roll as "Indian." This is because the eugenics theory of race dictated that mixed race offspring took the racial identity of the "racially inferior" parent. Accordingly, the Commission categorized individuals of mixed Indian and African ancestry as "Negro" and placed them on the "freedmen roll," which included freed slaves and their descendants.

The freedmen roll listed the names of the tribes' freed slaves regardless of whether they were of Indian ancestry. It also did not record which freedmen had Native American blood. Rather, it merely listed their names and the tribal affiliations of their former slavemaster[s]. Thus, the tribes and the federal government recognized people with Indian and European ancestry as Indian and those of Indian and African ancestry as Negro.[22] (footnotes omitted)

This bifurcated registration system prevailed in Indian Country. The completed and approved Dawes Rolls for Oklahoma's largest tribe, the Cherokees, were filed in 1907, listing 41,798 total citizens: 8,698 full-bloods; 31,400 Cherokees by blood; 197 registered Delaware-Cherokees; 286 intermarried Whites; 4,991 Cherokee minors; 4,305 Cherokee Freedmen; and 619 Cherokee Freedmen minors.[23]

Reliance on the Dawes Rolls as surrogate determinant of an individual's "Indian blood" is fraught with peril, as illustrated in the case of the Cherokees. First, many of the individuals whose names appear on the Freedmen Roll descended from people with "Indian blood." They simply were not given the opportunity to present evidence of that fact. Second, the Dawes Rolls are race-matrilineal with respect to the Cherokees—that is, they only recorded proof of "Cherokee blood" via the applicant's mother. Thus a descendant of an African mother and a Cherokee father, though possessed of "Cherokee blood," found himself/herself on the Freedmen Roll. Finally, some of those eligible for the Dawes Rolls refused to participate in what they considered an ill-conceived land severance policy that violated the fundamental tenets of Cherokee society. These "irreconcilables," often full-bloods, steadfastly resisted enrollment. The Dawes Rolls are thus an incomplete and inaccurate recording of "Cherokees by blood."[24]

Black Indians protested their segregation on the tribal enrollment rosters. Their objections notwithstanding, these Freedmen failed to persuade the Dawes Commission or, later, the federal courts to reclassify them as tribal citizens by blood.

Examples of Freedmen challenges to the Dawes classification scheme may be found in allotment litigation in the first half of the twentieth century. The Oklahoma Supreme Court established early on that the Dawes Rolls were not legally determinative of Indian ancestry. Rather, the rolls had a singular purpose: to facilitate Indian land allotment.

As noted in the 1924 and 1926 cases, *Rowe v. Sartain*[25] and *Sango v. Willig*,[26] respectively, placement on the Freedmen Roll fixed one's status as lacking Indian blood *only for purposes of allotted lands*. In both cases, Muscogee (Creek) Freedmen plaintiffs sought, unsuccessfully, to invalidate sales of their lands. They argued that restraints on alienation provided by law to Indians on the Dawes "blood rolls" vitiated the sales. Federal law made land held by "blood Indians" less marketable because of restrictions on its sale.

In both cases, the Freedmen in question demonstrated Indian "by blood" ancestry, but to no avail. Their listing on the Freedmen Roll meant, for land allotment purposes, they had no Indian blood as a matter of law. The *Rowe* and *Sango* decisions made clear, for purposes beyond Indian land allotment, that these Freedmen could be classified as Indians "by blood."

Examples of the Dawes agents' rush to judgment in terms of racial classification also abound. One such illustration is the case of Mary Walker, an African-Cherokee who attempted to enroll with the Dawes Commission on the "by blood" roll. She duly recited her Cherokee ancestry to the Commission agents. One of the agents bristled: "She ain't no Cherokee. She's a nigger. That woman is a nigger and you are going to put her down as a nigger [on the Freedmen Roll]."[27]

A listing on the Freedmen Roll did confer some benefit. Each of the Freedmen received between 40 and 160 acres, depending on the tribe, as his/her share of the tribal assets. Choctaw and Chickasaw Freedmen received 40 acres, although Choctaw and Chickasaw tribe members "by blood" received 320 acres. In the other three of the Five Civilized Tribes, all tribal citizens received the same amount of tribal land.[28]

Alienability—the right to transfer allotted land—became a driver for placing a Dawes applicant on the Freedmen Roll. By recording the blood quantum, Congress sought to enforce its paternalistic land alienation/land trust system, which had been designed especially for Native Americans. Blood quantum determined which tribal citizens were restricted with respect to land alienation. The federal government allowed full-bloods and Indians with substantial blood quantum to alienate (i.e., to sell) their allotments and mineral rights only with permission from the Indian Bureau (now in the Department of the Interior). "Restricted Indians" included those having a blood quantum of greater than one-half Indian blood.

Unlike the case of Restricted Indians, Freedmen land was more readily alienable, thus more accessible to land-hungry white prospectors and settlers. This duality gave an incentive to the enrollment agents to ghettoize anyone who appeared to be of African ancestry onto the Freedmen Roll. Freedmen land came onto the open market more quickly: "The most unfriended were the Freedmen, coddled by speculators eager to protect their 'rights' in the division of tribal property, and regarded by the general population with hate and envy while they owned their allotments, and with hate and contempt after they lost them."[29]

Oklahoma statehood also raised questions about the meaning of American citizenship for the Freedmen. In fact, Oklahoma statehood became a watershed both for the so-called "Freedmen" and for the tribes with whom they were affiliated.

The new state of Oklahoma subjected Freedmen—indeed, all persons of African descent—to rigid segregation laws and racially discriminatory practices. Like other people of African descent, the Freedmen felt compelled to fight fundamentally un-American measures and the onslaught of race-based violence and terror that accompanied them. Court challenges and grassroots political activity were among the methods chosen by African Americans to combat Jim Crow laws, lynchings, and electoral disenfranchisement.

Contemporaneously with this assault on African Americans, Native-American tribal leaders sought to reestablish tribal governments. At first, the Freedmen tribal citizens received the same tribal payments for minerals and the same educational benefits as other tribal members from the Indian Bureau. Beginning in the 1960s, however, the United States government, through the Department of Interior, began issuing a document called a Certificate of Degree of Indian Blood (CDIB) as a prerequisite for participation in federal government programs established for Indians.[30]

The CDIB is an official federal government document (a card) certifying that an individual possesses a specific degree of Indian blood of a federally recognized Indian tribe, band, nation, pueblo, village or community. The BIA issues these cards to applicants who supply completed genealogies with supporting legal documents, sometimes including birth certificates.

The documents submitted in connection with the CDIB application must show descent, through one or both parents, from an enrolled Indian or an Indian listed in a base roll such as the Dawes

Rolls. Blood degree cannot be obtained through adoptive parents. The BIA may use the blood degree on a previously issued CDIB or on a base roll in the applicant's ancestry to determine the blood degree of the applicant.

The CDIB may show only the blood degree of one tribe or the total blood degree from all tribes in the applicant's ancestry. Some tribes require a specific minimum degree of tribal ancestry before an applicant can attain membership. Such a requirement may necessitate the first type of certificate. On the other hand, some federal government programs require only the second type of certificate for qualification.

CDIB cards do not establish tribal membership. Tribal membership is determined by tribal laws and may not require a CDIB. Moreover, tribal membership may require a separate tribal determination of ancestry or blood degree.

The issuance of CDIB cards by the federal government is not without controversy, in part because of the racial eligibility component inherent in the existence of the cards. Freedmen, even those otherwise eligible for tribal membership, may not be eligible for CDIB cards. Many are simply not Indians by blood, but rather by treaty and affinity relationships. Among those who are blood Indians, most do not have a recorded blood degree on a base roll. Recall that the Dawes process created a separate "Freedmen Roll" that does not delineate the existence or extent of blood degree among its registrants.

The CDIB program, to the extent it relies on the blood quantum listed on the Dawes Rolls as a mechanism to determine Indian ancestry and eligibility for tribal benefits, promotes friction. Intentionally or not, the regime results in the exclusion of most African Indians from participation in such programs as Indian Health Service (IHS) and, in some cases, even from tribal membership.

In the Cherokee Nation, for example, Freedmen have the right to apply for membership in the tribe. That right of application, however, is not unfettered. A Cherokee Tribal Council measure requires the applicant for enrollment to receive a CDIB card as part of the enrollment process. Because the Dawes Rolls do not list the blood quantum of the Freedmen, such CDIB cards are, for most of the descendants of the Freedmen, almost impossible to attain.

The CDIB card requirement has sparked controversy in other

arenas, too. Some organizations use the CDIB as a proxy for evidence of "Indianness."

Evan White, a Shawnee Indian, takes great pride in his cultural heritage. He participates in a variety of Native-American rituals and traditions. Now a collegian, White played an active role in his high school Native-American Student Association at Edison High School in Tulsa, Oklahoma. However, he abruptly resigned from that organization over the implementation of a new policy requiring CDIB cards for membership. For White, the requirement erected an unnecessary and unwise barrier.

White, who has a CDIB card, explained that he felt anyone with an interest in Native-American history and culture should be welcomed by the club. Such an inclusive spirit would help demystify Native Americans and thereby diminish stereotypes and prejudices. Moreover, he emphasized that the absence of a CDIB card does not necessarily mean the absence of Indian blood or "Indianness."[31] Controversy over the use of CDIB cards persists.

In addition to the CDIB program, the reestablished governments of some of the Five Civilized Tribes have enacted constitutions with restrictive citizenship provisions. Some such constitutions include a limitation on tribal membership to individuals with an ancestor on the so-called "blood rolls." Again Freedmen, because of the absence of the most widely accepted legal evidence of blood quantum—occasioned by the absence of a listing of Freedmen blood quantum on the Dawes Rolls—are thus excluded.

By way of example, in 2000 the Seminole Nation enacted a constitutional change that would have removed Seminole Freedmen from the tribe by virtue of a blood quantum requirement. The BIA—the Bureau of Indian Affairs—refused to recognize the new constitution. The Seminole Nation Tribal Council relented, enrolling Freedmen in late 2002 so as to regain federal recognition.

Still, blood quantum looms large as a threat to relations between African Americans and Native Americans. A decades-long Civil Rights Movement in the twentieth century muted, but did not eliminate, the pernicious role of race in American society. African-American relations with Native Americans proved no exception. While the Five Civilized Tribes have abandoned their antimiscegenation laws, work remains to be done.

The Civil Rights Movement and modern efforts to combat racism have secured Indian identity in law as a sovereign, political (and not necessarily racial) identity while simultaneously securing basic state and federal civil rights for blacks. Nevertheless, the struggle for black civil rights in Indian Country has only just begun. It remains to be seen whether the tribes will . . . exercise their sovereignty to challenge racial hierarchy and forge new meanings of Indian identity. . . .[32]

Indeed, even while patently anti-black miscegenation laws no longer exist in Indian Country, the ill effects of those laws echo throughout. The notion of racial phenotype resounds, and that notion informs some decisions about intimate associations.[33] "The number of Indian-black marriages remains low and is only slightly higher than black-white marriage levels. This indicates a potential racial boundary between blacks and Indians as deep as that between whites and blacks."[34] Perhaps the time has come to renegotiate any such boundaries with a view toward their elimination.

As President Barack Obama noted in a 2008 pre-election campaign speech on race:

> [T]he complexities of race in this country [have] never really [been] worked through— [they are] a part of our union that we have yet to perfect. And if we walk away now, if we simply retreat into our respective corners, we will never be able to come together and solve [our] challenges. . . .
>
> Understanding this reality requires a reminder of how we arrived at this point. As William Faulkner once wrote, "The past isn't dead and buried. In fact, it isn't even past." We . . . need to remind ourselves that so many of the disparities that exist in the African-American community today can be directly traced to inequalities passed on from an earlier generation that suffered under the brutal legacy of slavery and Jim Crow.[35]

On the narrow issue of Freedmen citizenship, perhaps President Obama's senior policy adviser on American-Indian issues, Kimberly Teehee, will blaze a unifying trail. Teehee, a citizen of the Cherokee Nation of Oklahoma, speaks fluent Cherokee and boasts extensive experience both in Indian Country and on Indian issues.[36]

On the broader issue of race-based division and discord, perhaps we should ask: How do we move forward in light of this tragic and traumatic past? Where do we go from here?

The possible answers to those questions are several and soul-searching: We look at the notion of race with a discerning and critical eye. We own our history. We acknowledge our mistakes. We make reparations. We envision and embrace our shared future.

Some believe the race paradigm under which we have heretofore operated has outlived its usefulness. Is it finally time to acknowledge that America is, by definition, an admixture of different peoples and cultures united around shared ideals and aspirations?[37]

We know, for example, that as far back as the 1700s, the Cherokees intermixed with explorers, hunters, and trappers in this new land. We know, too, that Cherokees shared DNA with persons of African ancestry, both enslaved and free, centuries ago. How much blood is enough to qualify a person as a member of this race or that, particularly given the folly of notions of racial purity in the first instance?

> [It is] more likely that Cherokee or other Indian DNA is within many of today's American families.
>
> Many don't know about a Cherokee or Indian ancestor because that side of the family sometimes may not have detailed written records. Maybe the family didn't talk about it or the connection was forgotten or overlooked.
>
> In addition, some families may prefer to self-identify as "white," "black," or "brown" as a primary ethnic and racial background.
>
> . . . .
>
> Some tribes use what is called "blood quantum" to identify who has enough Indian "blood" in them to be tribal members. Often, one-sixteenth blood quantum will qualify a person for membership in the official tribal rolls.
>
> . . . .
>
> To say that someone who is one-eighth is more Cherokee or Native American than a person who is one-sixteenth makes us wonder about the validity of looking at this in terms of percentages.[38]

The issue of race purity is even more perverse when applied to citizenship. It confuses the biological or, more correctly, the "pseudo-biological" with the political.

Even those sympathetic to concerns about tribal sovereignty implore the Cherokee Nation and, by way of extension, other tribes grappling with Freedmen citizenship, to see beyond the blood.

As one commentator noted:

> [B]y introducing this new concept of race—a system based solely on ancestry—the U.S. government had devised a way to whittle down the tribes and their subsequent obligations to them over time. Faced with what happened to be an arbitrary requirement[,] the tribes adopted blood quantum requirements.
>
> . . . .
>
> The fallacy of blood quantum has had tremendous repercussion over the last century. In many ways[,] it has divided tribes and created a class system where a person's degree of "Indian blood" is what determines [his/her] status in a community. Before [blood] quantum, tribal members were accepted based on their willingness to sacrifice for and support the tribe[,] and leaders were chosen because of their values and character rather than racial purity.
>
> . . . .
>
> As our world becomes smaller, tribal nations will find that we have tribal members with African, European American and even Asian descent. Tribal sovereignty must be respected and[,] as [President] Obama has said[,] the tribes must not be interfered with in their process of determining membership. But the termination policies of the past, including blood quantum[,] must be abolished or they will continue to divide and conquer our communities, family by family. It is time for us to make a change. It is time . . . for our tribal nations to evolve back.[39]

A closer look at the work of the Dawes Commission offers a window into the relations between and among the African-American, Native-American, and European-American populations in what is now the State of Oklahoma. As will be shown, the allotment process added additional instability to an already combustible mix.

116 Apartheid in Indian Country?

Four members of the Choctaw Lighthorsemen, law enforcement agents. Left to right, seated: Ellis Austin and Stanley Benton; standing: unknown and Peter Conser, circa 1928.
—Courtesy Oklahoma Historical Society

A Legacy of Mixing and Matching 117

Black school in 1890 taught by Mrs. D. C. Constant (Antoinette Snow), a missionary to the Seminole Indians.
—Courtesy Oklahoma Historical Society

Oklahoma Territory land opening: Scouts capturing the Boomers west of Oklahoma Station, March or early April, 1889.
—Photo by Ernest C. Hamill
Courtesy Oklahoma Historical Society

CHAPTER IV

Post-Civil War Adaptation, Indian Enrollments and The Allotment Process: The Erosion of Indian Territory

> *"It is from numberless diverse acts of courage and belief that human history is shaped. Each time a man stands up for an ideal, or acts to improve the lot of others, or strikes out against injustice, he sends forth a tiny ripple of hope."*
> —ROBERT FRANCIS KENNEDY

The demographics in Indian Territory between 1870 and 1910 illustrate a surge in the white population. In 1870, there were 2,407 whites in Indian Territory. In 1910, there were 1,444,531. The white population in Indian Territory mushroomed by 87% between 1900 and 1910. During the same period, the Indian population grew by a scant 5% and the black population by slightly greater percentage (8%).[1] Freedmen ties to land in Indian Country and an unprecedented southern diaspora spurred the increase in the black population.

Indian Territory, which formally disappeared with the advent of Oklahoma statehood in 1907, had, in terms of political, social, and economic dominance, effectively ended years earlier. With increased white migration into Indian Territory came numerical and, more importantly, political, dominance. As Jim Crow took hold, non-whites, particularly persons of African ancestry, became increasingly marginalized.

Table 1:
Indian Territory Population Growth, 1870-1890

	1870	Percentage	1890	Percentage
Indians	59,367	87%	50,055	28%
Blacks	6,378	10%	18,636	11%
Whites	2,407	3%	109,393	61%
Total	68,152	100%	178,097	100%

Source: U.S. Bureau of the Census, 20-21 *Compendium of the Ninth Census of the United States, 1870* (Washington, D.C.: Government Printing Office 1872); Bureau of the Census, 4 *Extra Census Bulletin: The Five Civilized Tribes* (Washington, D.C.: Government Printing Office 1894).

Table 2:
Oklahoma Population, 1900-1910

	1900*	Percentage	1910	Percentage
Indians	64,445	8%	74,825	5%
Blacks	55,684	7%	137,612	8%
Whites	670,204	85%	1,444,531	87%
Asians	27	.01%	187	.01%
Total	790,360	100%	1,647,155	100%

*Includes Indian Territory and Oklahoma Territory. Source: Bureau of the Census, 464, 466 Thirteenth Census of the United States: 1910, Population (Washington, D.C.: Government Printing Office 1913).

Table 3
Final Rolls of the Five Civilized Tribes, March 4, 1907
(Individuals Entitled to Allotments)

	Indians	Percent	Freedmen	Percent	Whites	Percent	Total
Cherokees	36,619	87.5%	4,919	11.8%	286	0.7%	41,824
Choctaws	17,488	69.5%	6,029	23.9%	1,651	6.6%	25,168
Miss. Choctaws	1,660	100.0%	—	—	—	—	1,660
Chickasaws	5,659	51.6%	4,662	42.5%	645	5.9%	10,966
Muscogee (Creek)s	11,952	63.7%	6,809	36.3%	—	—	18,761
Seminoles	2,141	68.2%	996	31.8%	—	—	3,137
Total	75,519	74.4%	23,415	23.1%	2,582	2.5%	101,516

Source: Angie Debo, *And Still the Waters Run* (Princeton, NJ: Princeton University Press 1940), at 47.

Indian tribes in "pre-allotment" Indian Territory held land title for the common use of their respective citizens. By way of example, the Muscogee (Creek) Nation held legal title to all Muscogee (Creek) lands. The Nation permitted an individual Muscogee (Creek) citizen to occupy such lands as he could fence and cultivate, with or without tenants. The land so marked could be used for life, passed down to heirs, and even sold or given to another Muscogee (Creek) citizen. Abandonment, however, resulted in a reversion to the Muscogee (Creek) Nation. This is an example of the usufructuary land use system mentioned previously.

Federal law prohibited an individual Muscogee (Creek) citizen from selling his/her land (i.e., the land he/she occupied or worked) to a United States citizen. However, a land tenure system soon developed whereby individual Indian citizens employed white laborers pursuant to a permit and fee system arranged by the Muscogee (Creek) Nation. This de facto sharecropper system allowed a white man to live with his family in Indian Territory, work the land, and share his crop with his Indian host. The system eventually resulted in the occupation and use of prime real estate by a relative few Indians and their white proxies. The traditional practice of holding lands in common—for the common good—began to fade.[2]

The federal government's allotment mandate struck the final blow to the concept of common lands. The allotment process—dividing Indian lands held in common into individual parcels—triggered "an orgy of plunder and exploitation."[3] Black, white, and even red—all manner of people devised ways to gain access to the newly divided lands.[4]

Some Indians specifically resented the tribal land allotments to the Freedmen. The sheer number of Freedmen entitled to the parcels only exacerbated the hostility. Others fretted over the proliferation of new arrivals of African descent (often, black Southerners) who sometimes intermarried with Freedmen to gain access to land. Only the Freedmen listed on the Dawes Rolls received tribal allotments. Non-tribal land offerings under the Homestead Act of 1862[5] or other federal legislation may have been available for some non-Freedmen African Americans seeking solace and economic opportunity in Oklahoma.

Chitto Harjo, a Muscogee (Creek) statesman, helped organize and lead opposition to the allotment system, under which tribal governments were to be dismantled and collectively held lands parceled out to individuals. This effort, known as the Snake Rebellion, consisted of reported "uprisings" in 1901, 1902, and, finally, in 1909.[6]

Notably, Harjo expressed his consternation at the federal government's perceived cultivation of black landholders.

> I hear that the Government is cutting up my land and is giving it away to black people. I want to know if this is so . . . These black people, who are they? They are negroes that came in here as slaves. They have no right to this land. It never was given to them. It was given to me and my people and we paid for it with our land back in Alabama. . . . Then can it be that the Government is giving it—my land—to the negro? I hear it is, and they are selling it. . . . I am informed and believe it to be true that some citizens of the United States have titles to the land that was given to my fathers and my people by the Government.[7]

Noticeably missing from Harjo's indictment are the rapacious white settlers and corporate railroad interests who ultimately ruled his land. Whites' vice-like grip on the soon-to-be State of Oklahoma included control over the lion's share of its realty.

The post-Civil War General Allotment Act of 1887[8] authorized the President of the United States to survey Native American tribal lands and to divide the area into allotments for individual Native Americans. Enacted on February 8, 1887, and named for its sponsor, Republican United States Senator Henry Laurens Dawes of Massachusetts (1816-1903), this "Dawes Act" was amended in 1891 and again in 1906 by the Burke Act.[9] The Dawes Act, as amended, remained in effect until 1934. Though the Dawes Act did not affect the Five Civilized Tribes, subsequent legislation would achieve the same objectives.

On November 1, 1893, retired United States Senator Henry L. Dawes of Massachusetts, the author of the legislation, became chairman of the three-member Commission to the Five Civilized Tribes (the Dawes Commission) and served in this capacity for ten years. The Dawes Commission negotiated with the Five Civilized Tribes for the extinction of the communal title to tribal land. Under the agreed-upon plan, each tribal member would have ownership and possession of an individual tract. The Dawes Commission also worked to dissolve tribal governments. These twin policies of land and tribal government dissolution served the ultimate goal of swallowing up the tribes within the context of the greater United States of America.

The Commission to the Five Civilized Tribes, created by Congress in 1893 to negotiate with Indian tribes over allotment issues, found unexpected bounty and order in Indian Territory.

> Instead of an arid western plain, occupied by the savage of tradition, as many suppose, the Commission found a territory not greatly smaller than the State of Maine, rich in mineral and agricultural resources and in valuable timber; a country which has been occupied and cultivated for over a half century, whose fertile valleys yielded bountiful harvests of southern products, and on whose prairies grazed a quarter of a million cattle yearly; where cities had sprung up; through which railroads had been constructed and where five distinct modern governments existed, independent of the sovereignty of the United States.[10]

The Dawes Commission chose Muskogee, Indian Territory, as its headquarters. It added two members in 1895, for a total of five. Tams Bixby replaced Henry Dawes as chairman upon Dawes' death in 1903.

From 1894 to 1896, Commissioner Dawes and his colleagues, Meredith Helm Kidd of Indiana and Archibald S. McKennon of Arkansas, achieved little. They failed to convince tribal leaders to accede to the federal government's allotment policy.

In 1896, frustrated by the lack of progress, Congress passed the initial salvo in a fusillade of legislation that expanded the powers of the Dawes Commission and altered its essential role. No longer focused on diplomacy, the Dawes Commission emerged as a judicial tribunal empowered to decide eligibility for tribal membership and the nature of the benefits of that membership in terms of land.

The Curtis Act of 1898[11] granted the Dawes Commission the authority to process the enrollment applications of more than 250,000 people. The enrollment process was closed as of March 4, 1907, by act of Congress approved on April 26, 1906. An additional 312 persons were enrolled under an act approved on August 1, 1914.

To prove tribal membership under the Dawes Commission enrollment process, an applicant had to declare affiliation with a single tribe. In turn, that declaration would, be listed on the Dawes Rolls, a national registry.

The Dawes Commission enrolled individuals as tribal citizens based on the following categories: (i) Citizen by Blood; (ii) Citizen by Marriage; (iii) New Born Citizen by Blood; (iv) Minor Citizens by Blood; (v) Freedmen (persons of African descent formerly enslaved by a tribal member); (vi) New Born Freedmen; and (vii) Minor Freedmen.

Delaware Indians adopted by the Cherokee tribe were enrolled as a separate group within the Cherokee population. Shawnee Indians adopted by the Cherokees were enrolled as "Citizens by Blood."

The Dawes Commission typically maintained three types of cards within each of the above-enumerated categories: (i) "Straight cards" for persons whose applications were approved; (ii) "D cards" for persons whose applications were considered doubtful; and (iii) "R cards" for persons whose applications were rejected.

The Dawes Commission deliberated the claims of persons with provisional or "D cards." Those persons were subsequently given either a "Straight card" or an "R card," depending on the outcome of those deliberations. Ultimate authority for decisions rested with the Secretary of Interior.[12]

A Dawes Commission enrollment card, also called a "census card," recorded the information elicited from individual applications submitted by members of the same family group or household. The information given for each applicant included: name; roll number (individual's number, if enrolled); age; sex; degree of Indian blood; relationship to the head of family group; parents' names; and references to enrollment on earlier rolls used by the Dawes Commission for verification of eligibility. Each enrollment or census card also denoted the final action taken by the Dawes Commission.

A number of individuals shunned the registration process out of a fear of government persecution based on ethnicity. Moreover, like black and white persons, many Indians were of "mixed blood," a common colloquialism for a person with diverse ancestry. This posed identity challenges, as the Dawes system required the choice of a single ethnic identity. For example, the Dawes Commission would force a man with 1/4 Cherokee and 1/4 Muscogee (Creek) ancestry to choose between the two, thus officially denying part of his heritage. Even more disturbing, as noted earlier, the system dictated that African blood countermanded—trumped—any other ancestry. Dawes Commission agents relegated those registrants with African blood to a separate "Freedmen Roll."

This Hobson's Choice of ethnic identity ran counter to Indian culture. Indeed, many Indian tribes considered blood relationships simply one of many criteria for tribal membership.

In the end, the Dawes Commission approved more than 101,000 names for the so-called "Final Rolls of the Five Civilized Tribes." Notwithstanding their intended role as merely a census for the federal allotment process, the Dawes Rolls became a definitive source on eligibility for membership in each of the Five Civilized Tribes.

In order to allot the Indian Territory land, the Dawes Commission surveyed and appraised the 19,525,966 acres of tribal land and allotted 15,794,000 acres to enrollees. The individual allotments encompassed a range of sizes, depending on the appraised value of the land. Some allotment-eligible individuals received cash in lieu of land.

Enrollment and allotment rules varied by tribe and depended on specific tribal agreements negotiated between 1897 and 1902 and subsequently ratified by the tribes and by Congress. Claimants sometimes contested allotments. The Dawes Commission ruled on some 10,952 disputed plots.

The following table[13] indicates the final disposition of the lands in Indian Territory held by the Five Civilized Tribes.

Tribe	Total Acreage	Allotted Acreage	Segregated and Unallocated Acreage
Choctaw-Chickasaw	11,660,951	8,091,517.48	3,569,432.52
Cherokee	4,420,068	4,346,145	73,923
Muscogee (Creek)	3,079,095	2,997,114	81,981
Seminole	365,852	359,575	6,277
Total	19,525,966	15,794,351.48	3,731,613.52

The Dawes Commission reserved tens of thousands of acres for mixed uses (e.g., railroad rights-of-way, townsites, churches, schools, and cemeteries). The Commission set aside huge tracts in the Choctaw and Chickasaw Nations for the potential exploitation of coal and asphalt deposits, and it segregated vast swaths of timber-rich land in these same Nations.[14] The United States first leased, and then auctioned off, these holdings. The government sold the lands remaining post-allotment.

The Dawes Commission tracked and accounted for revenues attendant to its various transactions (e.g., land sales and leases). It certified and recorded a patent—documentary evidence of right, title and/or ownership to a tract of land—for each parcel of land with which it dealt.

Congress abolished the Dawes Commission on August 1, 1914. The federal government charged the Five Civilized Tribes Agency in Muskogee, Oklahoma, with winding up its remaining work.[15]

In the final analysis, the Dawes Commission oversaw the loss of vast amounts of Indian lands held by the Five Civilized Tribes, to white settlers who had come to Oklahoma in search of fertile fields and black gold. Through settlement, purchase, intermarriage—by any means necessary—white settlers acquired land, established communities, and seized political power. Oklahoma—"Native America"—would never be the same.

126   Apartheid in Indian Country?

Bass Reeves (front row with cane), Muskogee, Indian Territory. White and black policemen, circa 1900.
—Courtesy Western History Collections, University of Oklahoma Library

Below: *Bass Reeves, U.S. Deputy Marshal, circa 1890 (born July 1840, died January 12, 1910)*
—Courtesy Fort Smith National Historic Site

Bass Reeves (second row, left), pictured with federal official family, including U.S. Marshals, U.S. Commission, and U.S. District Attorney, on November 16, 1907, in Muskogee, Oklahoma.
—Courtesy Fort Smith National Historic Site

CHAPTER V

The Impact of Racism and Jim Crow: "Blacklash" in Indian Country

> *"History, despite its wrenching pain, cannot be unlived[;] but[,] if faced with courage, [it] need not be lived again."*
> —MAYA ANGELOU

The State of Oklahoma, sometimes dubbed "Indian Country" for its historic role as the relocation destination for the Five Civilized Tribes (including the persons of African ancestry among them), once held high promise for African Americans, too. They flocked to Oklahoma in droves, seeking an escape from Southern racism and oppression. They sought to prove their mettle, both to themselves and to whites, as successful farmers, entrepreneurs, and everyday Americans in this new land. Over time, however, the promise of Oklahoma dimmed for these migrants. Indeed, a racial "blacklash" ensued.

Early in the twentieth century, Oklahoma came to mirror the racial crucible that many African Americans had so desperately sought to escape. Virtually all aspects of life in Oklahoma soon became rigidly segregated: where people lived, attended school, shopped, recreated, worshipped, spent the night, boarded a train, and more.

Whites and some white-aligned Indians urged the notion that a too-black Oklahoma would undercut the prevailing, white-dominated political power structure. As a result, these individuals propagated a rigorous system of institutional racism, invidious discrimination, and uncompromising segregation that would be decades in the undoing. As one scholar noted, "[T]he fear that if Oklahoma failed to adopt the segregationist stance of its southern neighbors it would become a promised land attracting thousands of African Americans from the Deep South states led to de facto segregation."[1]

In the end, the white supremacists won out, even taking control of writing the new state's constitution. Not surprisingly, these anti-black Democrats pushed the segregation and disenfranchisement of African Americans as far as they could.[2] They convinced more than a few influential Indian leaders to align with them. At the time, some Native Americans worried that a fast-growing Freedmen population and a decreasing full-blood Indian population would eventually result in the usurpation of political power in the tribes. As a matter of perceived self-interest, they made race-based appeals to constituents.[3] In exchange for their political support, Oklahoma's founding fathers accorded Indians "constitutional whiteness"—a pass from the imposition of state sanctioned, race-based disabilities like those imposed on African Americans.[4]

At the national level, too, the legacy of slavery bedeviled persons of African descent. That legacy is arguably still being addressed.

In a remarkable gesture, the United States Senate recently offered up an official apology for African chattel slavery and the oppressive Jim Crow regime that supplanted it. The 2009 Senate Resolution disclaimed any governmental responsibility for reparations. Even so, the apology itself, coupled with the recitation of the ugly acts that precipitated it, explained a great deal about race and racism in America. It harked back to the root cause of so much race-based strife and disparity: slavery. It acknowledged that slavery and its legacy have shaped, and to some extent still shape, interrelations and dynamics between and among all demographic groups in America, not just between blacks and whites. For that reason, the full text of the June 11, 2009, Senate Congressional Resolution 26, "Apologizing for the enslavement and racial segregation," follows:

CONCURRENT RESOLUTION

Apologizing for the enslavement and racial segregation of African-Americans.

WHEREAS, during the history of the Nation, the United States has grown into a symbol of democracy and freedom around the world;

The Impact of Racism and Jim Crow

WHEREAS the legacy of African-Americans is interwoven with the very fabric of the democracy and freedom of the United States;

WHEREAS millions of Africans and their descendants were enslaved in the United States and the 13 American colonies from 1619 through 1865;

WHEREAS Africans forced into slavery were brutalized, humiliated, dehumanized, and subjected to the indignity of being stripped of their names and heritage;

WHEREAS many enslaved families were torn apart after family members were sold separately;

WHEREAS the system of slavery and the visceral racism against people of African descent upon which it depended became enmeshed in the social fabric of the United States;

WHEREAS slavery was not officially abolished until the ratification of the 13th [A]mendment to the Constitution of the United States in 1865, after the end of the Civil War;

WHEREAS after emancipation from 246 years of slavery, African-Americans soon saw the fleeting political, social, and economic gains they made during Reconstruction eviscerated by virulent racism, lynchings, disenfranchisement, Black Codes, and racial segregation laws that imposed a rigid system of officially sanctioned racial segregation in virtually all areas of life;

WHEREAS the system of de jure racial segregation known as "Jim Crow," which arose in certain parts of the United States after the Civil War to create separate and unequal societies for Whites and African-Americans, was a direct result of the racism against people of African descent that was engendered by slavery;

WHEREAS the system of Jim Crow laws officially existed until the 1960s—a century after the official end of slavery in the United States—until Congress took action to end it, but the vestiges of Jim Crow continue to this day;

WHEREAS African-Americans continue to suffer from the consequences of slavery and Jim Crow laws—long after both systems were formally abolished—through enormous damage and loss, both tangible and intangible, including the loss of human dignity and liberty;

WHEREAS the story of the enslavement and de jure segregation of African-Americans and the dehumanizing atrocities committed against them should not be purged from or minimized in the telling of the history of the United States;

WHEREAS those African-Americans who suffered under slavery and Jim Crow laws, and their descendants, exemplify the strength of the human character and provide a model of courage, commitment, and perseverance;

WHEREAS, on July 8, 2003, during a trip to Goree Island, Senegal, a former slave port, President George W. Bush acknowledged the continuing legacy of slavery in life in the United States and the need to confront that legacy, when he stated that slavery "was . . . one of the greatest crimes of history . . . The racial bigotry fed by slavery did not end with slavery or with segregation. And many of the issues that still trouble America have roots in the bitter experience of other times. But however long the journey, our destiny is set: liberty and justice for all.";

WHEREAS President Bill Clinton also acknowledged the deep-seated problems caused by the continuing legacy of racism against African-Americans that began with slavery, when he initiated a national dialogue about race;

WHEREAS an apology for centuries of brutal dehumanization and injustices cannot erase the past, but confession of the wrongs committed and a formal apology to African-Americans will help bind the wounds of the Nation that are rooted in slavery and can speed racial healing and reconciliation and help the people of the United States understand the past and honor the history of all people of the United States;

WHEREAS the legislatures of the Commonwealth of Virginia and the States of Alabama, Florida, Maryland, and North Carolina have taken the lead in adopting resolutions officially expressing appropriate remorse for slavery, and other State legislatures are considering similar resolutions; and

WHEREAS it is important for the people of the United States, who legally recognized slavery through the Constitution and the laws of the United States, to make a formal apology for slavery and for its successor, Jim Crow, so they can move forward and seek reconciliation, justice, and harmony for all people of the United States: Now, therefore, be it

RESOLVED *by the Senate (the House of Representatives concurring)*, That the sense of the Congress is the following:

(1) APOLOGY FOR THE ENSLAVEMENT AND SEGREGATION OF AFRICAN-AMERICANS—The Congress—

    (A) acknowledges the fundamental injustice, cruelty, brutality, and inhumanity of slavery and Jim Crow laws;

(B) apologizes to African-Americans on behalf of the people of the United States, for the wrongs committed against them and their ancestors who suffered under slavery and Jim Crow laws; and

(C) expresses its recommitment to the principle that all people are created equal and endowed with inalienable rights to life, liberty, and the pursuit of happiness, and calls on all people of the United States to work toward eliminating racial prejudices, injustices, and discrimination from our society.

(2) DISCLAIMER: Nothing in this resolution—

(A) authorizes or supports any claim against the United States; or

(B) serves as a settlement of any claim against the United States.[5]

Even as our nation's founders espoused noble and inclusive ideals, they, too, embraced white supremacy. "We hold these truths to be self-evident, that all men are created equal, that they are endowed by their Creator with certain unalienable Rights, that among these are Life, Liberty and the pursuit of Happiness."[6] The "all men" in the Declaration of Independence meant neither "all people" (i.e., both genders) nor "all men" (i.e., it excluded male people who were other than white).

The principal architect of the Declaration of Independence understood the tacit omissions embedded within seemingly inclusive language:

> Jeffersonians saw "the people" as a culturally homogeneous mass of equals, a national community sharing uniform political institutions and internalizing uniform moral values so thoroughly that no coercion would ever be required, all bound together by a republican social contract that required its participants to have achieved the state of civilization. Those residents who could not participate fully in the civilized republic, either because of gender (women were barred from voting or holding office), racial inferiority (in the case of black Africans and their slave descendants), or cultural incompatibility (as in the case of Native Americans who remained in "the hunter state"), were excluded or marginalized.[7]

African Americans, from the country's beginnings, struggled to span the gulf between the new nation's shiny ideals and their own dingy day-to-day lives. The American South earned a reputation for expanding that chasm into an abyss.

African Americans once perceived Oklahoma as a veritable paradise in comparison to the rigidly race-conscious South they knew all too well. As earlier noted, pre-statehood Oklahoma consisted of "Oklahoma Territory," the western portion opened for general settlement by federal authorities in 1889, and "Indian Territory," the eastern portion that became the resettlement home of the Five Civilized Tribes during the 1830s and 1840s.

The 1890 Organic Act that established the Oklahoma Territory imposed no disabilities on African Americans based on race. Indeed, an early statute provided: "There shall be no denial of the elective franchise or of holding office, to a citizen, on account of race, color, or previous condition of servitude."[8] Despite Oklahoma's relatively progressive beginnings, she would soon become engulfed in the tidal wave of racial animus washing over the country. The chilly waters of racism would drench all aspects of life in Oklahoma, and forever alter relations among her African-American, Native-American, and European-American denizens.

The last quarter of the nineteenth century and the first quarter of the twentieth revealed an America in the depths of racial depravity. Lynchings, normalized terrorism, primarily against African Americans, went unchecked. Vigilantes hanged or shot or burned or castrated or dismembered or disfigured or otherwise tormented their victims. These summary capital punishments for putative crimes or breaches of the race-based mores served their intended purpose: They intimated African Americans and emboldened white racists.

Social stratification and racial strife knew few bounds. Atrocities against African Americans, viscerally associated with the "Deep South," occurred all over the nation, and in Oklahoma, too. So-called "race riots" during this era, including the 1921 Tulsa Race Riot, the most devastating of them all, operated as pushback on black progress, mechanisms by which to keep the Negroes "in their place." These incidents, these assaults on African-American communities nationwide, became emblematic of the systematic oppression African Americans faced.

Most of the major race riots of the era shared several common threads: (i) In the vast majority of cases, whites started these eruptions; (ii) Extraordinary social conditions relating to war or economic distress constituted contributing factors; (iii) The disturbances occurred during the hot summer months; (iv) Rumors turned white mobs on the black community; (v) Law enforcement, by commission or omission, contributed to the unrest or failed to mitigate its effects; and (vi) The destruction occurred almost entirely within the black community.[9]

Despite lynchings, race riots, and the generally stifling racial climate that suffocated the America of that era (or perhaps because of these conditions), African Americans managed to cope. In some places, mere coping morphed into capitalistic success. One strategy involved relative social isolation in all-black enclaves.

As noted earlier, all-black towns founded by black seekers mushroomed in the post-Reconstruction era. Oklahoma laid claim to the lion's share of these towns. Weary southern migrants formed their own frontier communities, most of which were largely self-sustaining. Black towns offered hope—hope of full citizenship; hope of self-governance; and hope of full participation, through land ownership, in the American dream.[10] But Oklahoma increasingly toed the color line.

Indeed, as reported in the *New York Times* on February 2, 1907, delegates to the Oklahoma Constitutional Convention provoked a confrontation with President Theodore Roosevelt over Jim Crow laws—the rigid separation of Negroes and whites in social, economic, and political spheres. President Roosevelt threatened to veto Oklahoma statehood if comprehensive racial segregation measures were included in the proposed state's constitution.

> The convention was in a difficult position. The Democrats carried Oklahoma on the race questions, and were expected by the people to lose no time in making good the issue on which they were elected. They hit upon this happy method of getting themselves out of the dilemma and at the same time drawing the President's fire.
> . . . .
> The anti-negro provisions which are proposed are simply the "Jim Crow" provisions which are in force in the Southern States, and as these have stood the test in the courts it is argued that the President could not possibly decide them to be unrepublican or unconstitutional if adopted by the new State.[11]

In the end, Constitution Convention delegates included a separate schools provision in the Oklahoma Constitution. They were not, however, successful in their efforts to incorporate the across-the-board social segregation measures desired by many whites.

Race matters escalated during the Oklahoma territorial era (1890-1907) despite a proportionately small African-American presence. African Americans constituted 3.8% of the population of Oklahoma Territory in 1890 and 4.3% by the time of statehood, 1907. By contrast, African Americans constituted 10.3% of the population of Indian Territory in 1890 and 11.8% by the time of statehood, 1907.[12]

Politics became increasingly entrenched and skewed toward the Democrats. Republican power diminished and, with it, the push for African-American civil rights.

> [The] transformation [from the Oklahoma territorial era to Oklahoma statehood] was political, a product of Oklahoma's Constitutional Convention and the ensuing race politics of statehood that effectively removed Republicans from government until 1921. Republicans had a negligible presence at the Constitutional Convention. In the first seven state legislatures they averaged fewer than one-fourth of the members and never came close to a majority in either house. During this time terrible things happened, among them the Tulsa Race Riot, and the legislature regularly added to the state's segregation laws. Nevertheless, Oklahomans, white and African American, fought back. Racial demagogues did not speak for all, or even for the majority of Oklahomans.[13]

As noted, Oklahoma, emulating her southern sister states, took her seat in Jim Crow's corner, passing nearly a score of edicts between 1890 and 1957. Hypersensitivity to the mixing of races escalated to ludicrous extremes. A 1925 local ordinance in Oklahoma City even forbade black bands and white bands to march together.

A survey of Oklahoma's Jim Crow laws[14] reveals a breathtakingly broad sweep of legislation that reinforced black inferiority and bolstered white dominance. From education to transportation, voting rights to public accommodations, adoption to marriage, Oklahoma erected a wall of separation between black and white.[15] It is not possible to understand the Freedmen controversy without a basic understanding of the evolution of race relations in America in general, and in Oklahoma in particular.

As noted, the original 1907 Oklahoma Constitution authorized the Oklahoma Legislature to provide separate schools for white and "colored" children.[16] Such schools were to be offered on a "separate-but-equal" basis. The phrase "separate schools" referred to the schools maintained for the minority race in particular districts. Different funding streams financed regular schools and separate schools.[17]

"Separate but equal," with emphasis on the "separate" and little attention to the "equal," became the state of the state in America's number forty-six. As a consequence of Constitutional and statutory Jim Crowism, blacks languished educationally in Oklahoma for decades.

> Many of the separate school buildings are unsuitable. [S]ome of them are more shacks that are not fit for housing human beings and should be condemned and replaced. [M]uch of the approximately $2,000,000.00 being spent for education of the Negro children in Oklahoma is being wasted under the present plan of poor housing, inadequate supervision, and failure to provide school facilities for all districts having Negro pupils enumerated.[18]

In the early 1900s, these glaring disparities in educational funding between the white schools, on the one hand, and the "separate" (i.e., generally, black) schools on the other, captured the attention of a leading American capitalist. Julius Rosenwald (1862-1932),[19] a Jewish-American philanthropist and a former president of Sears, Roebuck & Company, took a special interest in the education of African-American children.

Rosenwald is as important as he was unusual—a prominent white patrician who recognized and acted upon gross racial disparities in education. He staked his good reputation and his considerable financial means on marginalized African Americans. In Rosenwald, we see that kind of spirit of shared humanity that is at the crux of Freedmen claims over dispossession (at least in the minds of Freedmen supporters and advocates).

Rosenwald made Sears, Roebuck & Company a retail legend. Along the way, he amassed an enormous personal fortune. He kept company with America's business elite.[20] Beyond the business sphere, two men helped shape and mold Rosenwald's social consciousness with regard to African Americans. The first, William Baldwin, Jr., was a Boston railway executive and a founder of the National Urban League. Booker T. Washington, a former slave, became Rosenwald's second and more lasting influence.

Washington, then America's leading proponent of education as the solution to the country's "Negro problem," led Tuskegee Institute, a school for African Americans established in 1880 with skeletal facilities and a meager budget. Rosenwald and Washington became close friends. Rosenwald acted as a Tuskegee Institute trustee from 1912 until his death in 1932.

Rosenwald, in a bid to diminish "race prejudice"[21] and ameliorate the educational shortcomings African-American students faced,[22] established a fund dedicated primarily to providing facilities grants for African-American schools in the American South. By 1930, twenty years after he started, Rosenwald financed 5,295 school buildings. He contributed, primarily by way of the construction of schools for African Americans, close to $700 million in present-day purchasing power.[23]

Julius Rosenwald left his mark on Oklahoma, too. Recall that race prejudice led Oklahoma to create a rigid separate school system. The Rosenwald Fund, established in 1917, assisted in the building of 198 educational facilities in forty-four Oklahoma counties between 1920 and 1932. Among those structures were 176 schoolhouses of varying sizes, sixteen teacher-training facilities, and six vocational shops. All told, contributions from the Rosenwald Fund benefited nearly 200 African-American schools in Oklahoma during the first half of the twentieth century.[24]

African Americans not only appreciated the beneficence of Julius Rosenwald, they also respected him—the man—as a compassionate human being. In many African-American institutions, his portrait hung alongside those of Abraham Lincoln and Booker T. Washington. Grief-stricken African Americans joined the sad chorus of mourners all across America when Julius Rosenwald died in 1932.

Rosenwald credited his synagogue and his rabbi, Emil G. Hirsch, for molding his thoughtful philanthropic philosophy. His sense of *noblesse oblige* likely emanated from his Jewish roots and its emphasis on *chesed*, or lovingkindness.[25]

Jewish morning prayers emphasize creating opportunities for the needy rather than simply providing handouts. Moreover, the Jewish concept of *Tzedakah*—literally, "righteousness"—stresses doing the right thing, and is distinguishable from charity.[26] Rosenwald made this commitment to the others with whom he shared the world.

United States Representative and Civil Rights veteran John

Lewis said, "Two unlikely partners, a Jewish businessman and philanthropist, Julius Rosenwald, and a man born in slavery, Booker T. Washington, formed a unique partnership more than seventy years ago to help African Americans achieve educational equality. It is a story that needs telling."[27]

The often overlooked and underappreciated contributions of Julius Rosenwald to primary and secondary educational opportunities for African Americans in Oklahoma cannot be denied. Rosenwald's munificence, however, neither wholly remedied educational inequity nor stanched the racism underlying it.

Beyond the primary and secondary levels, higher education in Oklahoma offered a different set of challenges for African Americans. The prospects for higher education proved elusive. Dr. John Hope Franklin, an Oklahoma native son, carried the emotional scars of his Jim Crow-era upbringing for a lifetime.

> When I graduated from college in 1935 and was headed for graduate school, the only gesture that my state of Oklahoma extended to me was to bar me from studying for my doctorate at the state university, and provide a portion of my out-of-state tuition expenses if I was successful in my course work. Thus I was not only deprived of the equal opportunity to succeed or fail at the university which was financed by taxpayers such as my parents, but was sent into exile at Harvard University, so alienated by my state's action that I never returned there to live.[28]

Unequal access to education, while disappointing, comported with the prevailing winds of discrimination and denial. Against such gusts, African Americans showed remarkable resilience—bending, but not breaking. For some, efforts at Freedmen exclusion looked like one more instance of denial; one more opportunity to stand firmly planted on hallowed ground.

Unlike the Jim Crow-from-the-start approach in education, the original Oklahoma Constitution extended the franchise to African Americans. Oklahoma saw fit to enfranchise her citizens over the age of twenty-one, with exceptions for felons, paupers, and lunatics.[29]

Soon thereafter, the Oklahoma Legislature passed literacy requirements that curtailed black voting. Oklahoma demanded its potential voters be able to read and write any section of the state Constitution. Those whose ancestors had either been enfranchised on January 1, 1866, or had been residents of "some foreign nation" on that date, were exempted—"grandfathered."[30] The statute effectively enfranchised illiterate white voters while disenfranchising illiterate black voters. The Supreme Court, in the unanimous 1915 decision *Guinn v. United States*, declared this law—known commonly as the "grandfather clause"—unconstitutional. It violated the right to vote provisions of the Fifteenth Amendment to the United States Constitution.[31]

Undeterred, Oklahoma legislators responded to the High Court's decision with new voter literacy legislation that mirrored the old in its blatant racial discrimination. The new registration law explicitly exempted all persons who had voted in 1914 (i.e., whites). Other persons who were qualified to vote in 1916, but who failed to register between April 30, 1916, and May 11, 1916 (i.e., blacks), would be perpetually disenfranchised (with a few exceptions for the sick and those absent from the state, who received a short additional time period in which to register).

In effect, the statute gave African Americans twelve days within which to register, while allowing the white beneficiaries of the unconstitutional *Guinn* grandfather clause to vote unimpeded by any such registration requirement.[32] It took some twenty-three years to overturn this obstacle to black political participation.

Iverson "I. W." Lane challenged the restrictive registration requirement. Lane, the mayor of Red Bird, one of the dozens of Oklahoma all-black towns, became legend. The United State Supreme Court found that the law, like the one in *Guinn*, effectively disenfranchised black voters, and thus violated the Fifteenth Amendment.[33]

In addition to the black codes—the rigid segregation laws on the books—an accompanying social etiquette emerged under the Jim Crow regime. By way of example, blacks in conversation with whites were to adhere to the following rules:

> Never impute dishonorable intentions to a white person.
> Never assert or even intimate that a white person is lying.
> Never suggest that a white person is from an inferior class.
> Never lay claim to, or overtly demonstrate, superior knowledge or intelligence.
> Never curse a white person.
> Never laugh derisively at a white person.
> Never comment upon the appearance of a white female.[34]

These examples, laughably absurd, are all too real manifestations of an unsustainable and indefensible system. Jim Crow exacted a powerful and painful toll, directly and indirectly, on all Americans. African Americans were only its most obvious victims.

A 1964 survey of black civil rights in Oklahoma City, the state's largest city, is revealing for its candor with respect to historical and then-present challenges to racial equality.

> In the past, members of racial minority groups in Oklahoma City have endured many and varied forms of discrimination. State restrictions on voting disenfranchised many Negro voters until the court decision in the I.W. Lone [sic] Case in the 1930s. About the same time, the Jess Hollis case set a precedent for the right of Negroes to sit on juries. Racial bombings still occurred [sic] in the late '30[]s and one in 1940. Less than a generation ago, Negroes could not eat in the downtown areas, or use rest room facilities (with the exception of one segregated rest room).
>
> Lincoln Park Zoo was not open to them. Negro schools often had few books and few teaching aids. Negro physicians could not practice in the hospitals. Northwest 4th Street served as a boundary, north of which no Negro could live, or work, or operate a business. Job opportunities were very limited, mostly in the service category. These facts can be humanized by the statement of one educated Negro woman [who exclaimed] "I felt like I was in a pen."
>
> Various factors, such as court decisions, the population increase, and negotiation have combined to change this picture. The "sit-ins" originated in Oklahoma City and Wichita, Kansas, in the summer of 1958, along with boycotts and picketing, focused the attention of the city on the discrimination in public accommodations. By June[] 1964, when the City Council passed a public accommodations ordinance, most eating establishments had done away with racial barriers. At the time of this writing, there have been no formal protests of discrimination in public accommodations.[35]

For decades in Oklahoma, Jim Crow laws and companion social etiquette regulated black/"other" social relations in general, and black/white social relations in particular. In terms of determining race, the rule of hypodescent reigned in Oklahoma. The rule of hypodescent, also referred to as the one-drop rule, deemed any amount of black ancestry sufficient to warrant black racial identity.

"Mixed-race" children inherited the status of the parent deemed to be racially inferior. Societal norms deemed African stock to be subordinate.[36] As statesman and educator Booker T. Washington adroitly observed, "As you know we are a mixed race in this country. Whenever the black man intermingles his blood with that of any other race the result is always a Negro, never a whiteman [sic], Indian or any other sort of man."[37]

One drop of black blood marginalized and minimized a person's worth and value in society. These restrictions also relegated African Americans to the social, political, and economic nadir of American society. Hypodescent thus became a mechanism by which whites exerted near-absolute social control over persons of *any* African ancestry whatsoever.

> Though skin color came to assume importance through generations of association with slavery, white colonists developed few qualms about intimate contact with black women. But raising the social status of those who labored at the bottom of society and who were defined as abysmally inferior was a matter of serious concern. It was resolved by insuring [sic] that the mulatto [i.e., person of mixed African and European ancestry] would not occupy a position midway between white and black. Any black blood classified a person as black; and to be black was to be a slave. . . . By prohibiting racial intermarriage, winking at interracial sex, and defining all mixed offspring as black, white society found the ideal answer to its labor need, its extracurricular and inadmissible sexual desires, its compulsion to maintain its culture purebred, and the problem of maintaining, at least in theory, absolute social control.[38]

As previously mentioned, Native Americans in Oklahoma held honorary "white" status for Jim Crow purposes.[39] This was due, at least in part, to a political calculus on the part of the Democrats who led Oklahoma in the run-up to statehood. Democratic officials persuaded Indian leaders to support the Democratic Party rather than the rival Republican Party, at the time aligned with African-American interests (and, presumably, the interests of the Freedmen living among Native-American tribes).[40] African-American and Native-American marriages were typically frowned upon and, at one point, proscribed outright.

An early twentieth century Tulsa case illustrates the import of that proscription on black/red marriages. Sam Ispocogee, a full-blood Creek Indian, sought marital dissolution when he began to suspect that his wife, Sammie, had black blood. Sammie denied the then scandalous accusation, but stipulated that the marriage would be void were the charge to be true.

In her defense, Sammie pointed to her full-blood Creek father, Samuel C. Beaver, and her "full-blood white person" mother, Ollie V. Beaver. She cited her enrollment as a member of the Creek Nation, appearing on the Minor Creek Indian Roll, No. 364, with a one-half blood degree.

In an application to the Tulsa County District Court, Sammie sought funds to cover her legal defense and living expenses. She had two young children to support. She urged the court to consider the dire consequences of her husband's charge. Were the court to determine that she, in fact, possessed African ancestry, her world would never be the same. Sammie, speaking through her attorney, pressed her case:

> [T]he charge now made by this defendant [Sam Ispocogee] affects both her social and political status in the state and in society; that she denies the allegations made in said answer and will to the utmost of her ability defend against said charge for the sake of herself and of her children; that to permit such charge to be sustained in the courts will change her social and political status and the social and political status of said children.[41]

Judge Thomas D. Lyons awarded Sammie Ispocogee a divorce on the grounds of "adultery, cruelty, and habitual drunkenness." He granted Sammie custody of the two children, together with a generous property settlement.[42]

In the divorce decree, Judge Lyons addresses the then-scurrilous allegation that Sammie had African ancestry.

> [T]he court announced his findings of fact and conclusions of law, as follows, to-wit:
>
> > The Constitution of Oklahoma provides: "Wherever in this constitution and laws of this state the word or words 'colored or colored race, negro or negro race' are used[,] the same shall be construed to mean or apply to all persons of African descent. The term 'white race' shall include all other persons.["] Section 7499, Compiled Statutes, 1921, provides that "the marriage of a person of African descent with a person not of African descent shall be unlawful and is prohibited within this state."
> >
> > 1. I find that the plaintiff [Sammie Ispocogee] in this case,

within the meaning of the constitution, is a member of the white race. She has the appearance of a refined, educated, cultured young American matron of [C]aucasian blood. The testimony of J. M. Hall and Robert Fry disposes me completely in this matter and leaves it free from doubt. The testimony to the contrary is unsatisfactory, and I may say frankly that it weighs as dust in the balance with me.[43]

Both Sammie Ispocogee and Judge Lyons understood the racial climate of their time and place. They embraced and internalized the rigid social hierarchy all too prevalent then.

Only decades later would racial restrictions be removed from marriage and divorce as a matter of law. In *Loving v. Virginia*,[44] a unanimous United States Supreme Court declared Virginia's anti-miscegenation law, called the "Racial Integrity Act of 1924," unconstitutional. This landmark civil rights case overturned *Pace v. Alabama*,[45] an 1883 case in which the United States Supreme Court upheld the constitutionality of Alabama's anti-miscegenation statute. *Loving* ended all race-based legal restrictions on marriage in the United States of America.

Social barriers notwithstanding, relations between African Americans and Native Americans had not always been so artificially constrained. Professor Tiya Miles of the University of Michigan notes that well before the Civil War, Cherokee masters and the Africans they enslaved sometimes enjoyed relationships that confounded then-prevailing stereotypes. They prayed together. They danced together. They raced one another. Africans taught Cherokee children.

White missionaries, bent on rigid caste relations and Southern-style chattel slavery, grew weary and frustrated. Jim Crow all but alleviated their concerns,[46] fashioning a hidebound system of white supremacy and social separation that tainted those it touched.

Trying to "fit in," Native Americans adopted some of the prevalent stereotypes about African Americans. These toxic misconceptions and myths have been allowed to poison the debate over tribal citizenship requirements even today.

The story of the Cherokee Freedmen, for example, is bound up in this often conflicted and contradictory racial history:

> The Cherokee freedmen continue to be one of the most marginalized groups in Native North America, and their story has never re-

ceived the attention it deserves, in part because many people would prefer that it remain buried.

....

At the center of this story is an absence, an exclusion, a silence where the Cherokee freedmen might have been. The reason for this absence is clear: Where Cherokee citizens conflate blood, color, race, and culture to demarcate their sociopolitical community, they often exclude multiracial individuals of Cherokee and African ancestry, who are treated in both discourse and practice in qualitatively different ways from multiracial individuals with Cherokee and White ancestry.[47]

What is behind this seemingly illogical and uncharitable treatment of Cherokee Freedmen? Is it simply a matter of race, or is there something more to the story? One possible driving force, some argue, is money.

Choctaw execution at Wilburton, Indian Territory, November 5, 1894.
—Courtesy Oklahoma Historical Society

Edward P. McCabe, father of Oklahoma's all-black town movement, circa 1890.
—Courtesy Oklahoma Historical Society

Members of the Town Council of Boley, Oklahoma, one of America's premier all-black towns, circa 1906.
—Courtesy Oklahoma Historical Society

The Impact of Racism and Jim Crow   145

SAMPLE DAWES ENROLLMENT CARD
Dawes enrollment card for Ambrose Crain, Seminole Nation
—Source: Archival Research Catalog,
http://www.archives.gov/research/arc/,
last viewed March 4, 2010.

Chickasaw Freedmen filing on allotments, Tishomingo, Oklahoma, Indian Territory, 1899-1928.
—Courtesy Oklahoma Historical Society

146   Apartheid in Indian Country?

Above and below: *Oklahoma land run, circa 1889.*
—Courtesy Oklahoma Historical Society

The Impact of Racism and Jim Crow   147

Hon. Joe McNeal's Talk to His Colored Brother's Son

"NEVER MIND, SONNY, AFTER NOVEMBER 8TH, I'LL PUT YOU IN WITH THAT POOR WHITE TRASH"

Cartoon at time of Oklahoma statehood (1907)
—Courtesy Oklahoma Historical Society

148 Apartheid in Indian Country?

Cartoon, Mangum Greer County, Oklahoma Territory, August 30, 1906, with caption reading: "The democracy favors laws providing for separate schools, separate coaches and separate waiting rooms for the negro race. The democratic party will lift the Indian and white race to a plane above that to which it has fallen under republican rule."
—Courtesy Oklahoma Historical Society

Cartoon, date unknown.
—Courtesy Oklahoma Historical Society

CHAPTER VI

Money Talks: The Changing Economics of Tribal Membership

> *"Collective fear stimulates herd instinct, and tends to produce ferocity toward those who are not regarded as members of the herd."*
> —BERTRAND RUSSELL

That old saw, "money talks," rings as true in the context of tribal governments as it does anywhere else. Some people argue that money drives the debate over the citizenship of the Freedmen. Kenneth Payton, a Cherokee Freedmen, believes that the fight over Freedmen citizenship has always been about money: "It's not red or brown. It's green."[1] Likewise, Eli Grayson, a Muscogee (Creek) citizen who champions Freedmen rights, protests:

> That's what this is about. There had never been a problem with their citizenship until the casinos came about[,] and now they are being booted out because the tribes don't want to share the money with them. Today[,] because of the casinos and the amount of money that these tribes make[,] they think they have to kick out the minority for the pie to be larger for the Indian. So the first people to get kicked out happen to be the descendants of slaves.[2]

Grayson shares these sentiments with Jim Pathfinder Ewing (*Nvnehi Awatisgi*), who views casinos as having a corrosive effect on venerable cultural traditions:

> Casinos have accelerated the dis-enrollments, with tribes tightening blood-quantum requirements so that fewer people share

more of the profits, even if hundreds of members, even elderly and long-standing families, are summarily wiped off the rolls. Not only are these people no longer eligible for federal protections, but [also] they are no longer legally "Native American." With casinos, in addition, the imposition of non-traditional ways of thinking and alien social structure are as damaging as the federally imposed tribal government system itself.

Traditional ways are inclusive, the tribe and family first, care of the elderly, women and children. With casinos, greed comes foremost: inequality of the distribution of resources, every one for him[self] or herself first, profits rule, and with it comes graft with government (such as the Abramoff scandal), influence-peddling, cronyism. Whereas the traditional tribal structure (throughout time, among all groups, bands, tribes) has been communal with "giveaway" and shared decision-making, the casino culture promotes separation, fracturing of families, promotion of self-interest[,] and favoritism on reservations that already are fragmented and rife with social ills. Whereas traditional tribal communities were spirit-based, with leaders chosen for the wisdom and the retention of practices favorable to keeping communities together, inclusive and healthy for generations to come, with spiritual values at their core, the modern reservation/casino culture promotes only material values that are, at heart, the worst of short-sighted Western culture.[3]

Once again, controversy surrounding Cherokee Freedmen citizenship provides illumination. Cherokee Freedmen attorney Jonathan Velie likens the actions of the Cherokee Nation toward his clients to "an ethnic cleansing."[4]

Velie, a Freedmen advocate, grew up in the Absentee Shawnee tribal community. That group's origins merit mention. A band of Shawnee Indians accepted a reservation in Kansas in 1825. Some members, however, found their way to Indian Territory. These Shawnees, absent from the Kansas reservation, became known as Absentee Shawnees.[5]

Velie eschews claims that tribal sovereignty is somehow under attack. He asserts that by interposing the bar of sovereignty in support of Freedmen exclusion, tribes may unwittingly be chipping away at the very precept they seek to protect.

> My position is that I am a supporter of tribal sovereignty. I believe in [tribal] self-government. I am opposed to government corrup-

tion. If a tribal official wants to hide behind the concept of [sovereignty] to oppress other people[,] then I'd like to stop that. Indians and tribes aren't corrupt[,] but corrupt people have discovered the pocket where jurisdiction doesn't exist. They aren't more a part of the tribe than the people they have kicked out. As wrong as it would be for the chief to take money and leave, it is just as wrong to violate their treaties. When they do it, it is a slippery slope. This can really hurt [the tribes] by violating the treaty. If a tribal official feels that I am the person hurting sovereignty, the real person hurting it is someone hiding behind sovereignty to break laws. I feel no loyalty to them.[6]

Jonathan Velie and others see Freedmen disenfranchisement efforts as watershed moments in Native-American history. Velie has expressed as much with characteristic candor:

This is one of the blackest hours in Indian Law. This is not the United States['] termination of a tribe. Individual Indians are terminating the identity of other Indians. If certain tribal officials are angry at me for calling that up[,] then I'll take that. Whether it is Indians oppressing other Indians or black Indians or white Indians oppressing black Indians, their rights are worth fighting for. It's like the United States government saying you are no longer an American and taking away your status.[7]

Historically, economic factors have been linked to the Cherokee Nation's attempts at Freedmen exclusion. Dating back to the last quarter of the nineteenth century, the Cherokee Nation took actions to deny the Freedmen citizenship, and thus a portion of the proceeds from land sales. Though Cherokee Chief Dennis Wolf Bushyhead, who led the Cherokee Nation from 1879-1887, resisted these efforts, the legislative bodies of the Cherokee Nation prevailed. Ultimately, Congress and the federal judiciary stepped in to insist upon Freedmen rights.[8]

According to some, that seemingly ancient tribal history of parsimony, at least as regards the Freedmen, continues. Economic considerations remain a potent driving force behind tribal decision-making, when it comes to persons of African descent among them. In the modern Cherokee Nation, the economic spoils are considerable.

The Cherokee Nation, the second largest Indian tribe in the nation, with some 300,000 members, is at the center of about $1 billion worth of annual economic activity. The Nation: (1) employs some 8,500 people, having created more than 5,000 jobs since 2000; (2) maintained a 2009 payroll of more than $241 million; (3) paved more miles of road than the fourteen Oklahoma counties in its jurisdiction, spending $26.2 million on roads in 2009; (4) provides health care coverage for thousands, operating the largest tribal health care system in the nation; (5) funded 2,512 scholarships in 2009, and contributed more than $19 million to more than 100 local school districts; (6) serves as a source of capital in the region; (7) provides millions in revenue to the State of Oklahoma through, for example, gaming compacts; and (8) owns significant riparian rights.[9] According to Ross Swimmer, former Cherokee Nation Principal Chief: "All in all, [the Cherokee Nation is] a big enterprise, employs a lot of people, provides a lot of revenue in the community and [is] very, very important to the future of eastern Oklahoma."[10]

Traditionally, the federal government has provided the lion's share of tribal funding, but tribal economies are rapidly changing. Even with a recent infusion of federal economic stimulus funds into Native-American tribal coffers, tribal economic self-sufficiency continues to expand.

In 2009, Oklahoma's American Indian tribes received more than $135 million in federal stimulus money. The Cherokee Nation, Oklahoma's largest tribe, received the largest share, some $37.7 million. The tribe earmarked the money for housing, water, road, childcare, and energy conservation projects. Other tribes receiving more than $10 million include: the Muscogee (Creek) Nation ($15.3 million); the Choctaw Nation ($15.2 million); and Chickasaw Nation ($13.4 million).[11]

The one-time federal stimulus dollars doled out in 2009 aimed to shore up tribal infrastructure. Those dollars did not supplant the more long-term, non-federal funding strategies toward which tribes continue to move.

Increasingly, Indian tribes preach and practice economic diversification. Tribal enterprises now include golf resorts, energy companies, banks, and community development financial institutions.[12] Tribes have begun to leverage their lucrative gaming operations to create new jobs, fund essential government services, and promote the welfare of local communities.[13]

In Oklahoma alone, Native-American casinos employ thousands. To be sure, these enterprises primarily benefit their tribal sponsors. But casinos also pump much needed revenues into local economic coffers. They employ workers, let construction contracts, purchase equipment and supplies, and support, indirectly, other businesses that benefit from casino traffic. Consider, once again, the case of the Cherokees.

According to a 2007 annual report called *Where the Casino Money Goes: Planting Seed Corn for our Children's Future*, Cherokee Nation Enterprises, a wholly owned business arm of the Cherokee Nation, raked in a whopping $418.6 million in gaming revenues that year and employed more than 3,000 people. The Nation accounted for that money as follows:

- $119.4 million for payroll to employees, most of whom are Cherokee;
- $167.2 million for operating expenses, with preference for spending the money with businesses owned by and employing Cherokees;
- $20.4 million for gaming compact fees with the state, with the money earmarked for public education and jobs in the horse racing industry;
- $77.9 million for creating hundreds of new jobs for Cherokees in local communities; and
- $33.7 million for services for Cherokee elders, youth and communities.[14]

Those phenomenal numbers continue to rise. Between October 2007 and October 2008, revenues generated from Cherokee casinos and other businesses, paired with casino earnings, garnered some $441.2 million. Even amidst a global recession, and with ongoing construction on casino premises, the tribe continues to thrive economically. The Cherokees are by no means alone in this regard.[15]

Among Oklahoma's largest casinos[16] are the following:

- River Spirit Casino, Muscogee (Creek) Nation, Tulsa;
- WinStar World Casino, Chickasaw Nation, Thackerville;
- Firelake Casino, Citizen Potawatomi Nation, Shawnee;
- Choctaw Casino, Choctaw Nation, Durant;
- Riverwind Casino, Chickasaw Nation, Norman;
- Hard Rock Hotel & Casino Tulsa (formerly, the Cherokee Casino), Cherokee Nation, Catoosa; and
- Downstream Casino, Quapaw Tribe of Oklahoma, Oklahoma-Kansas-Missouri border.

Critics charge that some tribes, the Cherokees among them, use portions of these growing revenue streams to fund anti-Freedmen lobbying efforts. Tribal influence-peddling is not illegal. While both houses of Congress have specific regulations governing gifts that members and staffers may accept, the regulations admit exceptions. Congress carved out one such exception for federally recognized Native-American tribes.[17]

Opponents paint the Freedmen as mere gold diggers,[18] interlopers with no legitimate claim to tribal membership. Newly acquired Indian wealth, Freedmen defenders argue, has triggered a drive to narrow the tribal canvas by purging Freedmen from tribal rosters.

A few smaller tribes allocate gaming revenues *per capita* and, arguably, they have initiated disenrollment stratagems as a way of boosting individual incomes. Those adversely affected often have no redress. Tribal assertions of sovereign immunity, coupled with the lack of available avenues to vindicate the litany of civil rights codified in the Indian Civil Rights Act, make challenges to disenrollment overwhelming.[19]

The sea change in the Indian income stream began in 1988 with the passage of The Indian Gaming Regulatory Act.[20] That statutory framework authorized three classes of gaming, with an attendant regulatory scheme for each. Ostensibly, the legal scheme attempts to utilize gaming—fair and corruption-free—as a means of promoting tribal economic development and self-sufficiency.[21]

The Indian Gaming Regulatory Act directs Indian tribes to use gaming revenues for five general purposes: (1) funding tribal government services (e.g., police and fire protection); (2) promoting tribal general welfare; (3) promoting tribal economic development; (4) making charitable contributions; and (5) funding local government agencies.

In Oklahoma, tribal gaming continues to grow despite the state's decidedly socially conservative bent. In 2008, Oklahoma tribes spent more than $1 billion on casino expansions. The Osage, Chickasaw, Choctaw, Muscogee (Creek), Cherokee, and Quapaw tribes capitalized on already extraordinary gaming successes.[22] It appears, at least in Oklahoma, that gaming poses less of a moral dilemma if it is facilitated by Indians.[23]

Of Oklahoma's thirty-seven federally recognized tribes who are eligible for gaming, thirty-three have inked compacts (i.e., agreements) with the State of Oklahoma. John Berrey, Chairman of the

Quapaw Nation, headquartered just east of Quapaw, Oklahoma, remarked that tribal gaming is "changing the whole face of the state."[24] No doubt thousands of other Oklahomans share that observation.

Thanks to a meteoric rise in Indian casino gaming, Oklahoma ranks among the top states in terms of gambling revenue. This is all the more remarkable given the fact that Oklahoma, both in terms of its population and the size of its overall economy, ranks in the second tier of states (twenty-eighth in population; twenty-ninth in size of overall economy).[25] The State of Oklahoma raked in about $105 million from gambling compacts with Native American tribes in 2009. That figure represented a twenty-three percent increase over the previous fiscal year. Top tribal contributors to the state coffers included: Chickasaw Nation ($28.7 million); Choctaw Nation ($21.5 million); Cherokee Nation ($12.1 million); and Muscogee (Creek) Nation ($6.1 million). The state uses a portion of its gaming compact fees to fund initiatives for problem gamblers. The rest is earmarked for education.[26] Commenting on the State of Oklahoma's share of 2010 tribal gaming revenues,[27] some $120 million, a *Tulsa World* editorial noted: "The exponential growth in tribal gaming—Oklahoma is second only to California in the amount generated—has meant a lot to the state....[W]ithout a doubt[,] tribal gaming is here to stay...."[28]

In a 2007 speech, Chickasaw Nation Governor (the equivalent of a "Chief") Bill Anoatubby credited gaming operations with enriching the business and social service programs of his tribe. Praising "self-sufficiency" and "self-governance," Governor Anoatubby noted the operating budget of the 38,000-member, Ada, Oklahoma-based, tribe went from $11 million to $330 million during the twenty-year span from 1987-2007. This infusion of funds lessened tribal dependency on the federal government.

Remarkably, the federal funding/tribal funding ratio now sits at 20%/80%, largely on account of gaming revenues. That is, the federal government provides 20% of tribal funding and the tribe itself provides 80%. In prior years, a more common ratio for most tribes was 80%/20%, the reverse ratio, with the federal government subsidizing most tribal expenses.[29]

Ernest L. Stevens, Jr., Oneida Nation of Wisconsin, Chairman of the National Indian Gaming Association, summarized the importance of Indian gaming and its far-reaching impact:

Indian gaming is a sovereign right inherent in tribal governments, a government akin to that of the federal government and the states, which choose their own destiny in gaming. It was developed from small operations run by dedicated tribal members and their visionary foresight[,] and [it] has grown into resorts, hotels, and facilities that compete or partner with some of the most successful names in the resort and gaming industry.

The work we accomplish in this industry brings many benefits to communities nationwide, tribal and non-tribal. With 4.1 million American Indians in the United States, roughly 1.5 percent of the nation's population, our responsibility to Indian Country is great. [I]ndian gaming fuels tribal governments supporting those 4.1 million Americans, as well as neighboring governments and communities. We are proud of the success ... and anxious to reinforce that success for generations to come.[30]

Indian casinos raked in $25 billion in 2006,[31] outstripping gaming revenues tallied in the world's gambling Mecca: Las Vegas, Nevada. Indeed, one casino, the Foxwoods Resort Casino, which is operated by the Mashantucket Pequots in Ledyard, Connecticut, takes in some $1.6 billion annually.[32]

Gambling proponents argue that the infusion of Indian gaming funds helps alleviate some of the chronic socioeconomic problems facing Native Americans nationally—poverty and unemployment, violent crime victimization, health care issues, inadequate housing, and educational deficits.[33] Similar ills plague the African-American community.[34] Gaming revenues to date, however, have not profoundly affected many of the socioeconomic challenges facing Native Americans.

A number of startling statistics leap off the pages of a January 2010 United Nations report written by independent experts and produced by the Secretariat of the United Nations Permanent Forum on Indigenous Issues. The document, entitled *State of the World's Indigenous Peoples*, noted:

- Among Native Americans, the average income amounts to less than half the average for the United States overall.
- Almost a quarter of Native Americans and Alaska Natives live under the poverty line in the United States, as compared with the rate for the total population, around 12.5%.
- Native Americans and Alaska Natives have higher death rates than other Americans from a number of causes: tuberculosis

(600% higher); alcoholism (510% higher); motor vehicle crashes (229% higher); diabetes (189% higher); unintentional injuries (152% higher); homicide (61% higher); and suicide (62% higher).
- The unemployment rate in the United States declined from 6.5% to 5.9% between 1994 and 2003. During the same period, the unemployment rate among Native Americans and Alaska Natives increased from 11.7% to 15.1%.
- Sexual violence disproportionately affects Native-American women, who are 2.5 times more likely to be raped or sexually violated than females in the United States in general.[35]

Despite these deep-seated social problems, gaming cheerleaders continue to tout the ability of the lucrative pastime to shatter socioeconomic barriers, spark economic development, and spawn employment growth. Detractors point to gaming-related woes such as addiction.[36] Some characterize gaming as a form of regressive taxation.[37] Too often, gambling opponents note, these ills are borne by unsuspecting communities.

In one sense, the general experience with legalized gambling is a variation on the old folk tale about the man who invited a snake to share his living room. The snake bites him, and when the man complains, the snake replies, "You knew I was a snake when you invited me in." With states starved for cash and legislatures unwilling to tax their constituents directly, revenues from gambling are seen as a painless alternative. Except that, as has become increasingly clear, that is a relative assessment. In 1999, the National Gambling Impact Study Commission found 7.6 million Americans could be classified as "problem gamblers" or "pathological gamblers," with all that entails as regards family breakdown and personal bankruptcy. The town of Ledyard, Connecticut, where Foxwoods is located, estimated that it spent nearly $2 million on casino-related issues such as traffic control and law enforcement in a single year.

"The tragic thing about this industry," says Massachusetts State Senator Susan Tucker of Andover, a Democrat who opposed the expansion of gambling in the Commonwealth, "is that it doesn't pay the true costs of its operation. The state has to pick up those."[38]

Despite the real and perceived "evils" associated with gaming, the revenues it spawns make it difficult to suppress. In 2004, gaming revenues from Indian casinos in Oklahoma exceeded one billion dollars. Such exponentially increasing revenue generating capacity cannot help but influence the psychological, political, and economic dynamics of the benefited tribes.

The Freedmen controversy—the legitimacy of Freedmen claims to tribal rights and benefits—takes on yet another dimension when viewed in the context of this relative economic boon. To some, the Freedmen represent a potential drain on resources meant for "real Indians."

Former Cherokee Deputy Chief John Ketcher asserted, "I think [the Freedmen] want some of the goodies that are coming our way."[39] Former Cherokee Principal Chief Chad Smith[40] intimated similar suspicions about the motivations of those same Freedmen. Chief Smith claimed the Freedmen had been "paid off" under the allotment system; they had not done anything to help build up the Cherokee Nation; and they did not deserve the benefits of tribal membership. He further suggested that an Indian nation should be composed of Indians, suggesting some purebred standard once held sway.[41]

Others question the motivations of the Cherokees themselves, arguing that economic and political opportunism are at the root of the Cherokee Freedmen imbroglio: "[T]he history of the Cherokee Nation since reconstruction indicates that each time major financial or political opportunities have arisen, 'native Cherokees' have striven to distinguish themselves as a social subset of the common citizenry and accrue to themselves control of these opportunities to realize their vision of the Nation."[42] The question of motivation, then, is a double-edged sword.

That matter of motivation arises in yet another, related, context. The relative gold mine tapped into via gaming opened up opportunities for the exertion of political influence.

In a move that came as a surprise even to the Cherokee Tribal Council, the business arm of the Cherokee Nation, Cherokee Nation Businesses, contributed $50,000 to the inauguration fund of President-elect Barack Obama in 2008.[43] This substantial sum, the maximum allowable under applicable law, was the largest donation from any Oklahoma entity to that fund. In light of the challenge to Freedmen citizenship, one can scarcely avoid questioning the motivation(s) underlying this generous donation.

The Oklahoma-based Cherokee Nation has also contributed to the political campaigns of those opposing Freedmen allies. For example, the tribe gave to the campaign of California Democrat Felton Newell, the primary opponent of vocal Freedmen advocate and United States Representative Diane Watson, who represented California's 33rd Congressional District. On November 18, 2009, the tribe's Executive Finance Subcommittee authorized a $2,400 campaign donation to Newell and a $5,000 contribution to a political action committee called "New Leadership PAC for Newell."[44]

As with other tribes, the Cherokee Nation's new-found sources of revenue, gaming among them, have built political muscle. The Cherokee Nation has shown a willingness to flex that muscle in face-offs with Freedmen who are intent on preserving tribal membership.

Beyond gaming, a less commonly discussed economic behemoth lurks in Indian Country: tobacco sales. Like swelling gaming revenue, tobacco sales account for a sizeable portion of some tribal revenue streams.[45]

The United States Supreme Court affirmed tribes' rights to sell tobacco on Indian land to tribesmen on a tax-free basis (i.e., without paying applicable state taxes).[46] States such as Oregon have entered into cigarette tax agreements with tribes. Under the Oregon agreement, tribes agree that all cigarette sales, including those to tribal members on Indian land, are subject to Oregon's cigarette tax. The State of Oregon agrees to remit tax refunds to the tribes, based on tribal rolls and *per capita* cigarette consumption. In the end, the tribes retain their tax breaks and the State of Oregon gets its share, systematically, of cigarette tax revenue from taxable tribal sales.[47]

In Oklahoma, the state government negotiates compacts with various tribes that govern cigarette taxation. These compacts grant the tribes advantageous tax rates on cigarette sales. Tribe-operated "smoke shops" make sales to tribal citizens and non-citizens alike. Because of the tax advantage, these shops price cigarettes lower than their competitors in the regular retail market. Price-driven consumers flock to these economically superior alternatives, and the tribes generate significant revenue.[48]

The Internet represents the new frontier in tobacco sales by tribes and tribal members. Indian-owned Web sites selling cigarettes take advantage of the favorable tax position tribes have with respect to sales to tribesmen. Sales and excise taxes are not added to the on-line prices of cigarettes.[49]

Tobacco sales generate millions of dollars in revenue for tribes and individual Indians. Such sales, however, raise moral and ethical concerns for some. Such concerns center around one question: Are tobacco revenues justified in light of the negative health impacts and spillover social costs associated with cigarette smoking?[50]

For the foreseeable future, gaming and tobacco revenues will continue to fuel tribal economic engines. The question is: Whose tank will get filled? Will the Freedmen be among the fortunate drivers?

By some accounts, there are as many as 25,000 prospective Freedmen in America's largest Indian tribe, the Cherokee Nation.[51] Cherokees boast a total population in excess of 300,000, or more than fifteen percent of all Native Americans.[52] Even in the unlikely event that all of the eligible Freedmen signed up for all the available services within the Cherokee Nation, they would represent less than ten percent of the outlays. (Some Freedmen already receive services.) Moreover, new enlistees in the tribe would proportionately increase the level of any federal or state funding opportunities apportioned on a pro rata basis.

As Freedmen activist Marilyn Vann points out, the battle against the Freedmen in the Cherokee Nation is a costly one financed, at least in part, by surging gaming and tobacco revenues: "Now persons in top leadership positions [in the Cherokee Nation] have available funds to mount lawsuits, engage in political/lobbying campaigns, advertise, and spread false propaganda about the Freedmen and to write a false history of the tribe, omitting the contributions and rights of persons of African descent."[53]

As for the Freedmen as Johnny-come-lately gold diggers, Cherokee activist and "Freedmen Fighter" David Cornsilk notes:

> What the opposition forgets is the fact that the majority of the Cherokee Nation population was enrolled AFTER gaming came to the tribe. Why are they here and why weren't they here when we had little or nothing? [T]he Freedmen have participated in every election in the Cherokee Nation since statehood right up to their expulsion in 1983. They are not newcomers. Further, the battle for their citizenship rights began in 1983, almost ten years prior to the opening of the first bingo parlor owned by the Cherokee Nation.[54]

Apart from its legal and moral implications, the decision to disenfranchise the Cherokee Freedmen raises weighty pragmatic issues. A balancing of the relatively modest financial impact of Freedmen inclusion against the potentially severe economic, political, and social fallout from Freedmen exclusion may suggest a different course for the Cherokee Nation. Under the circumstances, exclusion seems at best imprudent, and at worst self-destructive. Could there be some motivation beyond sheer economics at work?

Are gaming and tobacco revenues, this newfound wealth among Native American tribes, fueling part of the disenfranchisement debate? Some, certainly some among the Freedmen, think so.

Apartheid in Indian Country?

INDIAN GAMING: LONG-TERM CONTRIBUTION TRENDS

Election Cycle	Total Contributions	Contributions from Individuals	Contributions from PACs	Soft Money Contributions	Donations to Democrats	Donations to Republicans	% to Dems	% to Repubs
2008*	$ 8,627,759	$ 8,478,019	$ 149,740	N/A	$ 6,467,628	$ 2,157,581	75%	25%
2006*	7,656,244	1,401,180	6,255,064	N/A	4,757,217	2,859,173	62%	37%
2004*	7,400,115	1,650,500	5,749,615	N/A	4,968,608	2,431,507	67%	33%
2002	6,816,546	803,877	3,555,038	$2,457,631	4,522,165	2,294,381	66%	34%
2000	3,187,487	851,974	62,565	2,272,948	2,507,730	672,608	79%	21%
1998	1,623,074	342,846	91,128	1,189,100	976,094	646,980	60%	40%
1996	2,033,799	373,496	114,782	1,545,521	1,723,398	310,151	85%	15%
1994	705,200	169,250	28,950	507,000	574,250	130,950	81%	19%
1992	164,471	50,300	0	114,171	133,450	31,021	81%	19%
1990	6,400	6,400	0	N/A	6,400	0	100%	0%
Total	$38,221,095	$14,127,842	$16,006,882	$8,086,371	$26,636,940	$11,534,352	70%	30%

*These figures do not include donations of "Levin" funds to state and local party committees. Levin funds were created by the Bipartisan Campaign Reform Act of 2002.

METHODOLOGY: The numbers on this page are based on contributions of $200 or more from PACs and individuals to federal candidates and from PAC, soft money and individual donors to political parties, as reported to the Federal Election Commission. While election cycles are shown in charts as 1996, 1998, 2000, etc. they actually represent two-year periods. For example, the 2002 election cycle runs from January 1, 2001, to December 31, 2002.

NOTE: Soft money contributions to the national parties were not publicly disclosed until the 1991-92 election cycle, and these were banned by the Bipartisan Campaign Finance Reform Act following the 2002 elections.

Source: Center for Responsive Politics, http://www.opensecrets.org/industries/indus.php?ind=g6550.

NATIONAL INDIAN GAMING COMMISSION TRIBAL GAMING REVENUES

Gaming Revenue Range	Number of Operations	Revenues (in thousands)	Percentage of Operations	Percentage of Revenues	Mean (in thousands)	Median (in thousands)
Gaming operations with fiscal years ending in 2005						
$250 million and over	21	9,738,744	5.4	43.0	463,750	379,129
$100 million to $250 million	39	6,209,904	10.0	27.4	159,228	145,771
$50 million to $100 million	43	2,897,277	11.0	12.8	67,379	63,518
$25 million to $50 million	58	2,019,555	14.8	8.9	34,820	33,116
$10 million to $25 million	75	1,268,546	19.2	5.6	16,914	16,383
$3 million to $10 million	68	411,773	17.4	1.8	6,055	5,474
Under $3 million	87	83,776	22.3	0.4	963	483
Total	391	22,629,575				
Gaming operations with fiscal years ending in 2004						
$250 million and over	15	7,200,911	4.0	37.0	480,061	376,449
$100 million to $250 million	40	6,277,698	10.7	32.2	156,942	155,160
$50 million to $100 million	33	2,240,010	8.8	11.5	67,879	67,233
$25 million to $50 million	60	2,144,496	16.0	11.0	35,742	33,391
$10 million to $25 million	71	1,180,438	18.9	6.1	16,626	16,035
$3 million to $10 million	58	354,050	15.5	1.8	6,104	6,040
Under $3 million	98	81,531	26.1	0.4	832	530
Total	375	19,479,134				
Gaming operations with fiscal years ending in 2003						
$250 million and over	11	5,381,204	3.1	32.0	489,200	343,230
$100 million to $250 million	32	5,333,377	8.9	31.7	166,668	163,916
$50 million to $100 million	35	2,459,698	9.7	14.6	70,277	65,416
$25 million to $50 million	57	2,040,711	15.9	12.1	35,802	35,219
$10 million to $25 million	69	1,170,169	19.2	7.0	16,959	16,741
$3 million to $10 million	57	350,398	15.9	2.1	6,147	5,819
Under $3 million	98	90,825	27.3	0.5	927	522
Total	359	16,826,382				

Gaming Revenue Range	Number of Operations	Revenues (in thousands)	Percentage of Operations	Percentage of Revenues	Mean (in thousands)	Median (in thousands)
Gaming operations with fiscal years ending in 2002						
$250 million and over	10	4,640,064	2.9	31.5	464,006	302,298
$100 million and over	31	4,870,596	8.9	33.1	157,116	150,174
$50 million to $100 million	24	1,694,606	6.9	11.5	70,609	68,225
$25 million to $50 million	55	1,978,519	15.8	13.4	35,973	38,984
$10 million to $25 million	65	1,067,513	18.6	7.3	16,423	16,570
$3 million to $10 million	63	386,399	18.1	2.6	6,133	5,373
Under $3 million	101	79,965	28.9	0.5	800	469
Total	349	14,717,662				
Gaming operations with fiscal years ending in 2001						
$100 million and over	39	8,398,523	11.8	65.5	215,347	158,836
$50 million to $100 million	19	1,415,755	5.8	11.0	74,513	79,083
$25 million to $50 million	43	1,528,611	13.0	11.9	35,549	34,264
$10 million to $25 million	58	997,546	17.6	7.8	17,199	16,328
$3 million to $10 million	57	385,654	17.3	3.0	6,766	7,292
Under $3 million	114	96,257	34.5	0.8	844	575
Total	330	12,822,346				
Gaming operations with fiscal years ending in 2000						
$100 million and over	31	6,606,284	10.0	60.3	213,106	141,684
$50 million to $100 million	24	1,693,510	7.7	15.5	70,563	73,314
$25 million to $50 million	41	1,360,777	13.2	12.4	33,190	29,944
$10 million to $25 million	50	856,464	16.1	7.8	17,129	17,335
$3 million to $10 million	55	350,110	17.7	3.2	6,366	6,250
Under $3 million	110	91,545	35.4	0.8	832	365
Total	311	10,958,690				

Source: Compiled from gaming operation audit reports received and entered by the NIGC through 6/29/06.

CHAPTER VII

Fighting for the Franchise: The African-American Struggle for Tribal Rights

> *Throughout history, it has been the inaction of those who could have acted; the indifference of those who should have known better; the silence of the voice of justice when it mattered most that has made it possible for evil to triumph.*
> —HAILE SELASSIE

A. In The Cherokee Nation

The word Cherokee, an Anglicized form of "Tsalagi" (spelled a host of different ways), means "cave people." A variant of the word first appears as "Chalaque" in a 1557 Portuguese narrative of explorer Hernando de Soto's expedition.[1] The Cherokee, prior to removal to Oklahoma, were woodlands dwellers in the Appalachians and other parts of the South. Today, the Cherokee Nation makes its tribal headquarters in Tahlequah, Oklahoma.[2]

As previously noted, slavery gained a foothold in Cherokee culture. It is that legacy of human bondage that haunts even today.

The struggle between the Cherokee Freedmen and their Nation—the Cherokee Nation[3]—looms largely beneath the radar. Most Americans, even those committed to human and civil rights, know little about the controversy. Why? Perhaps because of the complex and uncomfortable web of blood, race, color, and culture issues that lie at the heart of this identity crisis.

> The Cherokee [F]reedmen continue to be one of the most marginalized groups in Native North America, and their story has never received the attention it deserves, in part because many people would prefer that it remain buried.
>
> . . . .
>
> At the center of this story is an absence, an exclusion, a silence where the Cherokee freedmen might have been. The reason for this absence is clear: When Cherokee citizens conflate blood, color, race, and culture to demarcate their sociopolitical community, they often exclude multiracial individuals of Cherokee and African ancestry, who are treated in both discourse and practice in qualitatively different ways from multiracial individuals with Cherokee and White ancestry.[4]

The case of Tulsan Reuben Gant, Chief Executive Officer of the Greenwood Chamber of Commerce and a former professional football player, presents an example of the conflation of blood, color, race, and culture referenced above. Gant is the grandson of Ethel Georgeanne Howell, who appears on the Cherokee Freedmen Roll. Howell, despite her listing on the Freedmen Roll, was one-half Cherokee. Her husband, Richard Gant, was of African ancestry. Because Gant, the male head of the household, was black, the Dawes Commission agents designated everyone in the household as such. The Cherokee blood running through Ethel Georgeanne Howell's veins disappeared as a matter of official record. Reuben Gant, with both treaty and blood-based connections to the Cherokee Nation, risks official severance from the tribe should the move to disenfranchise the Freedmen succeed.

Gant's consternation at the Cherokee expulsion effort has nothing to do with the "goodies" that Cherokee citizenship could bring. His interest, he insists, is in his ancestry—his family history: "I cannot thoroughly learn my history if some of it is denied."[5]

Cutting to the quick of the Freedmen controversy requires stripping away layers of misinformation. A searching look at the unvarnished history of our nation—national introspection—with particular focus on American slavery and its manifold legacies, is the *sine qua non* of such an undertaking. An internal, historical examination, however painful, must be undertaken if we are to understand the foundations of what some see as an identity crisis in Indian Country.

Emblematic of the perceived predicament is the disenfranchisement of the Cherokee Freedmen. The Cherokees have drawn the ire not only of the Cherokee Freedmen, but also of other Freedmen, African Americans, and civil rights advocates generally.[6]

"No other citizens in this country are required to subsidize their own mistreatment."[7] So charges a widely circulated and endorsed petition drawn by Verdie Triplett. Triplett is a black Indian, but not a Cherokee.

At a July 26, 2008, forum hosted by the Congressional Black Caucus, actor and activist Danny Glover bemoaned the Cherokees' disenfranchisement decision and its far-reaching implications for Freedmen. Citing longstanding relations between African Americans and Native Americans, including his own Choctaw heritage, Glover stressed the possible precedential value of the Cherokees' decision for other tribes.[8]

The Cherokee Nation controversy, Glover suggested, demands our attention. Understanding the history of the relationship between African Americans and Native Americans is the first step. The Cherokee Nation/Cherokee Freedmen flashpoint is a particularly compelling vessel for this historical journey.

As previously noted, Cherokee encounters with Africans date back centuries. In the 1500s, enslaved Africans accompanied Spanish explorers such as Hernando de Soto (1540) and Juan Pardo (1567) when they passed through.[9] Enslaved Africans and Indian bondsmen developed relationships as they worked alongside one another doing the bidding of white settlers. Indians in general seemed to appreciate what the Africans had to offer.

> It is generally agreed that the Southeastern Indians at first welcomed runaway slaves because they had important skills which were helpful to the Indians; e.g., they could speak English and thus serve as interpreters and negotiators with whites; they knew how to repair guns and traps, to shoe horses, to improve agricultural methods, to spin and weave, to make butter, to build houses, barns and wagons.[10]

Later, Cherokees came to understand the economic opportunity attendant to the capture and handover of fugitive slaves, for which they obtained valuables such as guns.[11] In time, a small fraction of the tribe profited greatly at the expense of the Africans they enslaved.

"Mixed-blood" Cherokees became especially enamored of the

"peculiar institution." By way of example, in the state of Georgia in 1835, 776 enslaved Africans resided within the Cherokee Nation. Of that number, 69 belonged to full-blood Cherokees, 70 to Cherokee women, and 637 to mixed-blood Cherokees. Mixed-blood Cherokees held a whopping 82% of the total number of Africans enslaved by tribal members.[12]

Some Cherokees attempted to mimic the Southern plantation economy, utilizing slave labor to create economic wealth. Some scholars credit the Cherokees with great compassion toward their African charges, especially in relation to the brutality heaped upon chattel slaves by the Southern white plantation owners who oversaw them.[13] Others, however, urge that Cherokee benevolence toward the Africans they enslaved is largely a myth.[14]

John Ross, the legendary Principal Chief of the Cherokee Nation at a pivotal time in its history, was a wealthy, mixed-blood slave owner who could not speak his native tongue. Chief Ross, like many other Cherokees, brought the Africans whom he enslaved with him to Oklahoma along the Trail of Tears forced migration. A Christian and a Freemason,[15] he gave not even a passing thought to manumission. Once in Oklahoma, Chief Ross expanded his wealth and moved, with family and enslaved Africans in tow, to a Park Hill, Oklahoma, mansion known as "Rose Cottage."[16]

A small number of Africans lived among the Cherokees as free persons after removal. Indeed, one accounting lists only seventeen such free Africans in 1860.[17] The number of black slaves living within the Oklahoma Cherokee Nation burgeoned between removal and the dawn of the Civil War. Still, only a scant two percent of the Cherokee population engaged in the practice of slavery.[18]

The Cherokees, of their own accord, became the first to manumit enslaved Africans during the Civil War. In February of 1863, Cherokees loyal to the Union repudiated the Cherokee alliance with the Confederacy, emancipated the enslaved Africans among them, and abolished the institution of slavery. The actual signatories of the Cherokee "emancipation proclamation" held few, if any, Africans in bondage. Large slaveholders within the Nation remained loyal to the Confederacy, and treated the law that foreswore slavery as a mere nullity.[19] The post-Civil War Treaty of 1866 ended slavery within the Cherokee Nation.

Scholars suggest the Cherokees had few qualms about, and experienced no guilt around, slavery as an institution. Few questioned its morality or legitimacy. No abolitionist movement or "underground railroad" blossomed within the Cherokee Nation.[20] The explanation for this seeming ambivalence toward slavery may be cultural or anthropological: "[In terms on Southeastern Indians][,] only people with kin relations within a larger clan network...were considered human. ... In fact, the opposition between slavery and freedom is peculiar to Europeans; for many other peoples, the opposite of slavery is kinship."[21]

Cherokee irresoluteness on the issue of slavery helped propagate the institution. The number of enslaved Africans living within the Cherokee Nation rose precipitously from the beginning of the nineteenth century to its end.[22]

Year	Cherokee Population (rounded)	Slaves of Cherokees (number)	Slaves of Cherokees (as percentage of Cherokee population)
1809	12,000	583	4.85
1825	14,000	1,277	9.12
1835	15,000	1,592	10.61
1860	17,000	4,000	23.52

Many of those emancipated remained as tribal members within the Native-American communities in which they had been enslaved. The post-Civil War Treaty of 1866, with its provision for land allotments, gave Cherokee Freedmen a leg up on newly-freed African Americans in the other parts of the country.

> [T]he treaty ... extend[ed] all the privileges of Cherokee citizenship, including an allotment of land, to the Nation's [F]reedmen. ... The Cherokee concept of communal ownership enabled the [F]reedmen to obtain land that former slaves of white southerners never received. But the elevation of [F]reedmen to the status of property holder in the Nation did not extirpate the racism of many Cherokees. ... At least the land provided for Cherokee [F]reedmen under the treaty of 1866 enabled them to be somewhat independent of their former masters and allowed them a retreat from the violence so common in the outside world.[23] [footnote omitted]

Many Cherokee Freedmen became enmeshed in Cherokee life. They voted in elections, attended Cherokee stomp dances, learned Cherokee traditions and folklore, and served on the tribal council. This rich history of tribal acculturation on the part of the Cherokee Freedmen goes largely unheralded. Ignorance of the past perhaps partially explains the plight of the Freedmen in the present.

On March 3, 2007, a small fraction of the voting-eligible Cherokee Nation of Oklahoma population approved an amendment to the Cherokee Constitution. As amended, the Constitution limits citizenship to those with census notations of a link to an Indian ancestor listed on the Dawes "Blood Rolls." As outlined previously, these are lists of persons with documented Native-American ancestry listed by federal government census agents representing the Dawes Commission. The decision to amend the Cherokee Nation Constitution resulted in the rooting out of some 2,800 Cherokee Freedmen.

As noted earlier, the federal government created a separate registration list for the Freedmen, the "Freedmen Roll," that did not record the degree, if any, of Indian blood.[24] Thus these Freedmen, given the way the federal agents compiled and maintained the Indian rosters in question, generally cannot prove the requisite blood ties.

In stark contrast, some Cherokees listed on the now sacrosanct Blood Rolls had only a 1/320 blood quantum. That amounts to a scant 0.003125.[25] The federal government thus went out of its way to be *inclusive* of whites with any trace of Indian blood and *exclusive* of anyone on any side of the racial divide who had a trace of African blood.

Links to a listing on the Freedmen Roll instead of the Blood Roll, under the amended Cherokee Nation Constitution, entail substantive, substantial consequences. For Cherokee Freedmen, it will mean disenfranchisement if the amendment to the Cherokee Constitution is ultimately sustained by reviewing courts. As of this writing, the status of the Cherokee Freedmen rests in the hands of a federal judge in Tulsa, Oklahoma. Freedmen disenfranchisement means not only the loss of voting rights, but also the surrender of access to tribal benefits such as health care, housing, and scholarship assistance for higher education.

Cherokee tribal leaders frequently invoke "sovereignty" as a justification for the constitutional amendment and the contentious vote that approved it. In September of 2007, Principal Chief Chad

Smith, while visiting Washington, D.C. to meet with Congressional representatives, asserted, "[T]he last thing that we have [left] is the right, the unmolested right, to determine who our citizens, our members, are."[26]

This, of course, is reminiscent of the "states rights" arguments of Southern obstructionists during the height of the twentieth century Civil Rights Movement. In the end, the sovereign right to "segregation now, segregation forever"[27] collapsed.

Dismissing claims of racism, Principal Chief Chad Smith, whose roots in the Cherokee Nation run deep,[28] famously remarked: "The Cherokee Nation simply wants to be an Indian tribe composed of Indians."[29] That bold, yet simple-sounding, aspiration—to be an Indian tribe composed of Indians—gets to heart of the matter: What does it mean to be Indian in a *political*, as opposed to a racial/ethnic, sense?

Principal Chief Smith argues that to be Cherokee is to be a person with a demonstrable Cherokee ancestor.[30] The Cherokee Nation, itself, however, long ago took a different tack, deciding to be more inclusive.

The Cherokee Nation continues to struggle with the legacy of human bondage. Former Principal Chief of the Cherokee Nation Joe Byrd noted that the Freedmen walked side by side with the Cherokees into Oklahoma in the nineteenth century, and Freedmen have long been considered part of the tribe. Byrd blames the Cherokee Nation's change in attitude toward the Freedmen on insensitivity to, and even conscious disregard of, history.[31]

Likewise, David Cornsilk, Cherokee activist and supporter of Freedmen rights, speaking to Freedmen as part of a 2004 Muskogee panel, took the Cherokee Nation to task for its treatment of the Freedmen: "We have never acknowledged our role in it [i.e., human bondage], and we have shunned the descendants of the people we held in slavery."[32] Others echo Cornsilk's bluntness:

> In what looks suspiciously like racism, Cherokees have been giving the cold shoulder to American blacks whose ancestors were once enslaved by that tribe, but were granted the privileges of tribal membership ... by an 1866 treaty. But while the "full-blood" Cherokee accept blacks related by blood, they are opposed to accepting those who are not, treaty or no treaty. It is a sickening spectacle, this un-American business of claiming privileges by blood, even to the extent of ignoring treaty obligations. And, of course,

since American citizenship is not based on blood, the only truly native Americans are those who were born here and (not "or") subject to the jurisdiction of the Constitution and the laws.[33]

Despite widespread criticism, the Cherokee Nation officially stands by Freedmen exclusion. By contrast, individual Cherokee citizens are among those who have condemned Freedmen disenfranchisement.

Other tribes have also been embroiled in parallel controversies over the rights of their Freedmen, especially the Seminole and Muscogee (Creek) Nations. Faced with the loss of federal government recognition, and concomitant funding, the Seminole Nation conceded the issue of Freedmen citizenship in 2004. The Muscogee (Creek) Nation continues to fight full acknowledgment of its Freedmen.

The Cherokee disenfranchisement vote in 2007 proved to be the straw that broke the camel's back. The race consciousness of the Cherokee Nation's move, though roundly denied by the Nation itself, became self-evident to many observers.

By 2007, The Freedmen of the Five Civilized Tribes, the Congressional Black Caucus, the National Association for the Advancement of Colored People, and myriad other organizations and individuals had endorsed the withholding of federal funds from the Cherokee Nation until eventually it restored the full citizenship rights of the Freedmen.[34] This backlash thrust the issue into the national spotlight.

On June 21, 2007, Congresswoman Diane Watson, D-California, and twenty-three of her legislative colleagues introduced a bill that would go further and sever federal ties and federal authorizations to the Cherokee Nation pending the restoration of Freedmen rights.[35] Representative Watson, dismissing Principal Chief Smith's sovereignty claim, noted: "[T]he sovereign right to discriminate is no right at all."[36]

The Watson bill, if passed, will prohibit the Cherokee Nation from receiving federal funds. It also will disallow the tribe's participation in its lucrative Indian gaming operations.

Principal Chief Smith acknowledged that the draconian measures contained in the Watson bill, if implemented, would deal more than a glancing blow to a tribal heavyweight.[37] Labeling the bill a "scorched earth" approach, Principal Chief Smith said it would "eradicate the legal existence of the tribe."[38] He would prefer that the courts referee and resolve the matter.[39]

Federal lawmakers made clear their expectation that the Freedmen retain their citizenship rights, one way or another. On a voice vote on September 6, 2007, members of the United States House of Representatives voted to deny housing benefits to the Cherokee Nation until the tribe recognizes the Freedmen as tribal citizens. The implementation of the measure was subsequently delayed until such time as the court battle over Freedmen citizenship has been resolved.

The author of the housing amendment that would result in the denial of funding to the Cherokee Nation, Mel Watt, D-North Carolina, is of African and Indian ancestry. Offering the amendment pained him deeply: "I am not offering the amendment [to the bill reauthorizing a tribal housing program] proudly, unfortunately, but because of circumstances that have arisen."[40]

Principal Chief Smith conceded that the public image of the Cherokee Nation has been bruised by the Freedmen controversy. That image suffers even more because of the Principal Chief's off-hand comments, remarks that minimize the Freedmen's posture and plight. "I think, historically, nationally, we had sort of a Pocahontas kind of image in the public," opined Principal Chief Smith. "Everybody had a great-grandmother who was a Cherokee princess."[41]

Such flippant comments attenuate legitimate questions of kinship and culture. This kind of language can minimize, even trivialize, the core issues of personhood, identity, and belonging that lie at the heart of the Freedmen claims.

The extirpation of Cherokee Freedmen from the tribe by popular vote in early 2007, while couched in terms of "tribal sovereignty," may be something else. Award-winning journalist Kenneth J. Cooper, an African American with Cherokee Freedmen roots, offers a disturbing alternative perspective:

> This may seem a small matter of tribal politics. It's bigger than that. Just like the dispute over admitting the black descendants of Thomas Jefferson's family into the association of his white descendants, the Cherokee referendum reflects a national failure to resolve the central trauma in American history: slavery, which in the 21st century still orders relations, inflames emotions and colors attitudes.[42]

Likewise, David Cornsilk, an unquestioned Cherokee by blood, scratched beneath the surface of the controversy, where he found uncomfortable and inconvenient truths:

> Chad Smith fears that if the Freedmen descendants are permitted to vote in June 07 general election, they will form a voting bloc against him. Chad Smith knows that the Dawes Commission Rolls is not a "Cherokees by blood" roll. He uses deceptive terminology to motivate Cherokees who know little or nothing of their history to turn against members of our own tribe.
> Smith knows that the 1900s Dawes Commission was steeped in racism and this virulent form of hatred prompted them to classify Cherokee Indians with [N]egro ancestry as Freedmen, not permitting them to record their Cherokee blood degrees.
> Smith plays the Cherokee people like a fiddle as he foments racial bigotry that should have died 100 years ago, or at least after the 1960s. He plays on the racial biases of Indian country, knowing that the white Cherokee, in his/her never-ending desire to "appear more NDN" ["NDN" means "Indian"] will swallow his "NDN blood" ploy hook[,] line and sinker when the real motive is to eliminate voters who might be opposed to his policies.
> One of the main proponents of the drive to eliminate the Freedmen is a Cherokee Nation councilwoman with a blood degree of 1/256. The president of the Freedmen Association is 1/8, but cannot get a CDIB [Certificate of Degree of Indian Blood] card because the Dawes Commission, while aware of the blood, did not permit it to be recorded. If we are to throw out the less connected individual, it should the former, yet that is not what Smith proposes.
> And finally, this controversy, which was initiated by Smith himself, begs the question of when can a people, once made citizens of a nation, finally rest. The Freedmen were made citizens of the Cherokee Nation 140 years ago by a treaty with the United States and amendment to our Constitution. What right does any Cherokee have to look at their fellow man and say "I have the right to destroy your heritage and steal away your rights."
> I[,] for one, if this question appears on a ballot, will vote according to the Cherokee way of thinking. I will vote with a good mind, following our sacred White-Path and doing what is right. I will practice the true meaning of the Cherokee ethos known in our language as Ga-du-gi, wherein my vote will be to preserve the rights of others, not take them away. Noted Cherokee humorist and favorite Oklahoma son Will Rogers once said, "We will never be truly

civilized until we learn to respect the rights of others." I will take these things to the polls with me and say with my vote [that] the Freedmen must stay.[43]

David Cornsilk describes his motivation for supporting the Freedmen citizenship as primarily political. Embracing the Freedmen would extend the Cherokee Nation's power base and silence many of its critics.[44] Morality aside, in Cornsilk's view, honoring the commitment to the Freedmen made in the Treaty of 1866 makes eminent, practical sense.

Aware of the high stakes attendant to the Freedmen controversy, the Cherokee Nation has begun to reach out to the African-American community to deflect charges of racism. The Cherokees paired with the Area Council for Community Action (ACCA) in Tulsa on a genealogy project. The initiative seeks to assist persons with genealogical research and guidance in gathering the information necessary to become Cherokee citizens.

ACCA President Pleas Thompson applauded the project, but he did not ignore the Freedmen controversy. He noted: "We realize that the Cherokee Nation requires citizens to have an Indian ancestor on the Dawes Roll, but we also know there may be many African Americans who are eligible for citizenship but have not enrolled, for whatever reason. This partnership will help eligible people of any race to find the documentation they need to show an Indian ancestor on the rolls and become a citizen of the Cherokee Nation."[45]

The ACCA genealogy project, salutary though it may be, might yield only a handful of new black Cherokees. That, though, is small consolation for the hundreds of Freedmen to whom the Cherokee Nation promised citizenship, but whom it now seeks to expel.

The story of the Cherokee Freedmen, extending back for centuries, warrants a genealogical project. Cherokee people with African blood have been members of the Cherokee Nation on some basis since the first people with African blood came into the Cherokee homelands in the southeastern United States.

Former Principal Chief of the Cherokee Nation Wilma Mankiller reflected on the uncomfortable legacy of African slavery among the Cherokees:

> During the 1700s, if not before, our people also came to value the possession of slaves and to participate in the terrible commerce,

introduced into the tribe by English traders who intermarried with our women. The Cherokees' black slaves were taken as the spoils of war or were captured runaways. The British government also presented slaves to influential tribal leaders, calling them "king's gifts." During the late eighteenth century, a growing number of the Cherokee elite—mimicking the English colonists—bought and sold slaves for their own use a field workers and servants. By 1790, the Cherokee elite had definitely adopted black slavery, although the practice never permeated the entire Cherokee Nation.[46]

. . . .

In the 1850s, the Cherokee Nation enjoyed an era of revitalization throughout their domain in Indian Territory. Cherokee wealth, particularly among the mixed-blood aristocracy, also increased because of successful farms and livestock operations, which were kept running in some instances by the continued and quite despicable use of black slaves. I have tried to find some comfort in the knowledge that only a tiny fraction of Cherokee families owned slaves, but I cannot. The truth is that the practice of slavery will forever cast a shadow on the great Cherokee Nation. It is no wonder that during that same time, the role of women in the Cherokee Nation was also diminished.[47]

Free black non-citizens, usually the descendants of Cherokee men and women with African blood, constituted the other contingent of black persons living among the Cherokee. Children of Cherokee women tribal members became tribal citizens regardless of the race of the father. The Cherokee Constitutions of 1827 and 1839 formalized this matrilineal tradition.

After 1850, key developments transformed the relationship between the Cherokee Nation and her darker denizens. Pivotal moments in the tumultuous relationship between the Cherokee Nation and persons of African descent include the following:[48]

Key Points in Cherokee Freedmen History

- In 1863, the Cherokee government, by acts of its tribal council, outlawed slavery.[49]
- The Cherokee Nation, pursuant to the Treaty of 1866, agreed to extend tribal rights to the Freedmen.
- After the execution of the Treaty of 1866, the Cherokee Nation amended its 1839 Constitution to extend citizenship to the Freedmen as a matter of *tribal* law. The tribe also entered into

individual treaties with both the Delaware and the Shawnee Indian tribes, adopting both tribes as citizens of the Cherokee Nation.
- The Cherokee Nation Supreme Court entertained several citizenship cases in the 1870s. The Court never endorsed the denial of citizenship to the Freedmen as a class. While the Court rejected individual Freedmen for failure to meet residency or timing requirements, it also admitted many other Freedmen as citizens of the Cherokee Nation.
- In the late 1800s, the Cherokee Nation conducted several censuses pursuant to Cherokee tribal law. Those censuses included native Cherokee, Freedmen, adopted whites, and adopted Indians, including the Shawnee and Delaware people. The Cherokee Nation's own censuses did not list blood degrees, which appeared later on the Dawes Rolls.
- In 1895, the United States Court of Claims ruled, in *Whitmore v. Cherokee Nation*,[50] that Cherokee Freedmen have the same rights as "native" Cherokees. Therefore, Freedmen were entitled to a share of payments from the sale of Cherokee lands. The decision in *Whitmore* rests on the Treaty of 1866 and amendments to the 1839 Cherokee Constitution.
- The Dawes Rolls included Cherokee Freedmen. As a result, Cherokee Freemen received allotments as citizens of the Cherokee Nation. Such allotments, conveyed by the Cherokee Nation and signed by its Principal Chief, came about as a result of a 1902 Agreement.
- In 1906, the United States Supreme Court heard a challenge concerning the allotment of Cherokee lands. In *Redbird v. United States*,[51] the Supreme Court held that intermarried whites married after 1875 were not entitled to the same citizenship rights as Cherokees by blood, Shawnee Indians, Delaware Indians, and Freedmen.
- An opinion by the Bureau of Indian Affairs dated October 1, 1941,[52] affirms the tribal membership status of the Freedmen: "[T]he membership rights of the Freedmen in the Five Civilized Tribes have been fixed by Treaties which are the equivalent of statutes, and by formal tribal action in pursuance of these treaties...."
- In 1962, Congress passed legislation ordering payments to the Cherokee Nation via individuals listed on the Dawes Rolls for prior taking of Cherokee lands.[53] Cherokee Freedmen, like the others listed on the Dawes Rolls, received payments.
- During the interim between the compilation of the Dawes Rolls

and the adoption of the 1975 Cherokee Nation Constitution,[54] neither the federal nor the tribal government passed a law altering Cherokee citizenship.
- Freedmen voted in the referendum wherein voters adopted the 1975 Cherokee Nation Constitution. That Constitution: (1) affirms the supremacy of federal law; (2) incorporates by reference relevant portions of the Civil Rights Act of 1964; (3) states members of the Cherokee Nation must be citizens as proven by reference to the Dawes Rolls ("Rolls" is used in the plural, and therefore, by implication, includes both the "Blood Roll" and the "Freedmen Roll"); (4) mandates federal approval of federally-required enactments of the tribal government; and (5) contains election provisions, including the limitation of tribal council membership to Cherokees by blood, but does not otherwise limit voting rights.[55]
- Article III of the 1975 Cherokee Nation Constitution includes, as members of the Cherokee Nation, those individuals classified as citizens pursuant to the Dawes Rolls. That definition embraces the Freedmen, as the word "Rolls" once again appears in the plural.

Despite this extensive history of Freedmen inclusion in Cherokee life—debate rages over Cherokee Freedmen citizenship. Why, in recent years, the push for Freedmen excision?

The modern drive for Freedmen excision from the tribe began in the 1970s. In 1971, the federal government authorized the Cherokee Nation to re-establish its own government. The Cherokee people, including some Freedmen, approved a new Constitution in 1975. Cherokee Freedmen voted in subsequent tribal elections in 1975 and 1979.

As previously noted, the Cherokee Nation accorded Dawes Commission enrollees and their descendants Cherokee citizenship pursuant to the 1975 Cherokee Nation Constitution (ratified in 1976). That document subjected the tribe to all of the laws of the United States and required federal executive branch imprimatur for amendments to the existing Constitution or the adoption of new Constitutions.

Between 1970 and 1980, the Cherokee Nation grew lighter—whiter. It simultaneously increased its numbers by welcoming individuals with lesser Cherokee ancestry (i.e., less Cherokee blood quantum) and, through outright rejection, reduced the number of its black citizens, the Freedmen.

When the Cherokee Nation reorganized its government between 1970 and 1976, the resulting changes in blood legislation had important implications for the [F]reedmen and for race relations within the tribe. During that period, the [F]reedmen were quietly disenfranchised and denied their rights to citizenship, at the same time these rights were extended to tribal members with minimal Cherokee blood. In December of 1977, the one-fourth blood quantum limitation for Indian Health Services was successfully challenged by the tribe. New economic incentives, such as free health care, lured many people to return to the tribal fold, particularly those who through a gradual process of acculturation and intermarriage had long since passed into the surrounding communities of Oklahoma.[56]

Efforts that excluded the Freedmen continued—even intensified—into the 1980s and beyond. In 1983, Cherokee Principal Chief Ross Swimmer instituted rules that effectively disenfranchised Cherokee Freedmen. These rules seemed to represent a sharp philosophical shift.

Almost a decade earlier, Principal Chief Swimmer advocated on behalf of Freedmen inclusion. He urged the extension of medical care to the Cherokee Freedmen in a letter to the Indian Health Service.[57] The letter stated:

> I have been advised by the local Health Service unit that the BIA does not recognize enrolled Freedmen for benefits and that this is carried over to IHS [Indian Health Service]. . . . The IHS says they cannot participate...because the people are Freedmen instead of Indians. It would appear that since the government had us include Freedmen on our rolls[,] they should be entitled to similar benefits of other enrolled Indians. I can understand the blood-quantum problem, but again it would appear that the Freedmen would be taken as a class and would have the same status as 1/4 blood.[58]

The Swimmer letter acknowledged the political nature of the obligations of the Cherokee Nation with respect to Cherokee Freemen mandated by the Treaty of 1866. It sought to avoid the issue of race with a presumptive blood quantum—a sort of legal fiction—for Cherokee Freedmen as a class. The letter avoided any attempt to validate what other evidence suggests: At least some of the Cherokee Freedmen are, in fact, Cherokee by blood.

Chief Swimmer's 1983 rules for the Cherokee Nation registration committee required applicants for tribal membership to hold a valid CDIB card "which represents that the applicant has proven through legal documentation to at least one direct lineal ancestor who is listed with a blood degree from the Final Rolls of Citizens and Freedmen of the Five Civilized Tribes/Cherokee Nation."[59] Because the Freedmen Roll did not reflect blood degrees, the CDIB requirement, as applied to the Freedmen, proved virtually insurmountable.

Proponents of Freedmen citizenship cried foul, asserting that a retributive political motive had prompted Chief Swimmer's about-face. Some Freedmen had supported Swimmer's election opponent, Deputy Chief Perry Wheeler. For this reason, some believed, Chief Swimmer sought to punish all Freedmen.

Cherokee citizen John Cornsilk, the father of Freedmen advocate David Cornsilk, is 7/8 Cherokee. He protested the CDIB requirement, asserting that tribal leaders "colluded and drew up a new set of rules that said only people that could produce one of those cards could be a member. What the Cherokee Nation of Oklahoma has been doing in regard to disenfranchising the Freedmen is all totally illegal."[60]

Controversy notwithstanding, Chief Swimmer triumphed in the election and thereafter embarked on a successful career in Indian affairs. Swimmer, an attorney, served as stints as Assistant Secretary of Indians Affairs at the Bureau of Indian Affairs and as Director of the Office of Indian Trust Transition. He also became a sought-after consultant on Indian land and business development. As Chief Swimmer's stock rose, the stock of the Freedmen experienced a concomitant decline.

Although the Freedmen were Dawes enrollees, received funds resulting from tribal land sales under the United States Supreme Court ruling in *Whitmore v. Cherokee Nation*,[61] and previously voted in Cherokee Nation elections, Cherokee Nation officials banned them at the polls. They did not, according to poll workers, have the right to vote in the Cherokee Nation.

Today, Principal Chief Swimmer admits some ambivalence with respect to the Freedmen citizenship issue. He believes, philosophically, some amount of Cherokee blood should be required for citizenship in the Cherokee Nation. As a practical matter, however, he sees the present conflict with the Freedmen as largely untenable.

When I put the first constitution since 1906 to a vote in 1976, I understood that [F]reedmen were included as citizens, but they could not hold elective office. Later, in the 1980s, I underst[oo]d they were denied the right to register for membership because they could not provide a certificate of Indian blood. I do not recall if that was ever challenged before the Cherokee tribunal, although my last election was challenged by Perry Wheeler alleging that I denied [F]reedmen the right to vote. That case was decided years later on the general principle that it was a Cherokee matter, not [a] federal court [matter].

. . . .

My bottom line is that I believe the Cherokees have a right to require that one must be a blood descendant, no matter how small, in order to be a citizen. However, as a practical matter, I do not think it was worth the battle the Tribe is going through to stand on this principle.[62]

Principal Chief Wilma Mankiller, successor to Principal Chief Ross Swimmer, and the first female Principal Chief of the Cherokee Nation, further entrenched the Cherokee registration requirement, disenfranchising most Freedmen. On March 12, 1988, Mankiller approved Resolution 21-88 which, in effect, formalized the CDIB registration requirement. The Resolution, formally entitled "Supporting the Guidelines: Rules and Regulations of the Cherokee Registration Committee," reads, in pertinent part:

> WHEREAS, the Cherokee Nation of Oklahoma has the sovereign right to determine its own membership; and
> WHEREAS, the Constitution of the Cherokee Nation of Oklahoma empowers the Cherokee Registration Committee to consider the qualifications and to determine the eligibility requirements for those applying to have their names entered in the Cherokee Register; and
> WHEREAS, the Cherokee Registration Committee has developed revisions to the 1978 "Guidelines: Rules and Regulations of the Cherokee Registration Committee." These revisions have also had the input of the Principal Chief, the Tribal Council through the Tribal Council Registration Committee, and the Tribunal of the Cherokee Nation of Oklahoma—clearly desiring these revisions to be in line with the philosophy and vision of the Executive, Legislative, and Judicial branches of the Cherokee Nation of Oklahoma; to be in line with the Constitution of the Cherokee

Nation of Oklahoma; and to be in the best interest of all Cherokee Tribal Members; and
NOW THEREFORE BE IT RESOLVED BY THE CHEROKEE NATION, it supports and ratifies the "Guidelines: Rules and Regulations of the Cherokee Registration Committee. . . ."[63]

On September 12, 1992, the Cherokee Tribal Council strengthened still further the Cherokee registration restrictions, by morphing the referenced Resolution into a law. The legislation, "Act Relating to the Process of Enrolling as a Member of the Cherokee Nation," echoed former Principal Chief Swimmer's rules and Principal Chief Mankiller's Resolution regarding tribal citizenship. The law, in Section 6, states explicitly "Tribal Membership is derived only through proof of Cherokee blood based on the final rolls." The term "final rolls" is defined in Section 4, part (c) of the law, which reads:

(c) Base Roll means a specific list of individuals used for determining tribal membership. One must prove back directly to an individual who is listed by blood on a base roll. The base roll as used herein means those final rolls otherwise known as the Dawes Commission Rolls or the Final Rolls. The Final Rolls were closed in 1907. Those Final Rolls by blood used for membership purposes are (1) Cherokees by Blood, (2) Cherokee Minors by Blood, and (3) Delaware Cherokees.[64]

The Mankiller-era law thus conditioned tribal membership on the ability to acquire a CDIB which, as discussed earlier, provided documentary proof of the holder's blood ties to the tribe (i.e., based on his/her listing or the listing of a direct ancestor on the Dawes "Blood Rolls").[65] The law erected an insuperable barrier to recognized tribal membership for most Freedmen. Disenfranchisement loomed.

In most cases, Freedmen claims to membership emanate from the Treaty of 1866. In cases where the Freedmen had blood ties to a tribe, those ties were often to be found "off line." They frequently could not prove them with reference to the Dawes Blood Rolls, since the blood quantum of the Freedmen was, as a matter of course, not listed.

Paradoxically, Principal Chief Mankiller, an early (and perhaps unwitting) architect of the move toward Freedmen disenfranchisement, has long acknowledged the unequal treatment of black Indians vis-à-vis "white" Indians.[66] Indeed, she gained a reputation as a champion of human rights generally, and received the Presidential Medal of Freedom in 1998.

Chief Mankiller's actions cemented the Cherokee Freedmen descendants' disenfranchisement from the Cherokee Nation. Her new tribal law imposed citizenship restrictions more severe than those of the Cherokee Nation Constitution. Article III, Section 1, of the 1975 Constitution required only that all members of the Cherokee Nation must be citizens as proven by reference to the Dawes Commission Rolls. According to the Dawes Rolls, Freedmen were citizens in fact. Still, the Cherokee Nation continued the practice of only granting citizenship to those it deemed Indians by blood.

The exclusion of Freedmen from tribal membership continued even in the face of express reservations on the part of the Bureau of Indian Affairs. BIA Muskogee officials Dennis Springwater and Joe Parker met with tribal officials in 1983 and emphasized that the 1975 Cherokee Constitution, as well as the Treaty of 1866, granted citizenship to the Cherokee Freedmen and their descendants.[67] The press took note of these matters, especially after several Freedmen filed a lawsuit against the Cherokee Nation and the BIA in 1984.

The Baltimore Sun reported on July 29, 1984, that then Deputy Chief Wilma Mankiller argued against Cherokee Freedmen enfranchisement. Tribal membership, Mankiller remarked, should be for "people with Cherokee blood."[68]

Such rhetoric, intended or not, reinforced stereotypes and promoted disinformation. It encouraged the Cherokee people and the general public to believe: (1) The Freedmen have no legitimate claim to Cherokee citizenship, which they do under the Treaty of 1866; and (2) Freedmen lacked "Cherokee blood" by virtue of their listing on the Freedmen Roll by Dawes Commission agents, while that listing actually signaled the presence of "African blood" rather than the absence of "Indian blood."

Sentiments such as those expressed at that time by Chief Mankiller had the effect of reinforcing the unspoken rule of hypodescent.[69] For much of this country's history, branding a child "black" consigned him/her to a subclass—to inferior social, economic, and political status vis-à-vis white persons. Remnants of the rule of hypodescent remain with us.

Hypodescent served a critical role in our broader, racialized society. Under its tenets, race is fixed at birth; race is immutable. It is a powerful determinant of who and what we are. The offspring of a white woman and a black man is, under the rule of hypodescent, inexorably black in terms of racial classification—even a pale-skinned, fair-haired and blue-eyed child.[70]

This "one drop rule" has its roots in racism: The presumption is that African blood infests and contaminates all other blood. As such, those in whose veins it runs need to be isolated from others—quarantined for the greater good of society.

> [The] power of a drop of "Indian blood"—if not more than a drop—is to enhance, ennoble, naturalize, and legitimate.[71] Conversely, "black blood" becomes a contaminating force that delegitimizes the claims of black Indian individuals and families to Indian communities and nations. A revamped "one drop" rule has permeated some discourses regarding Indian sovereignty. As a result, the historical stigma of "one drop" of "black blood" serves to erase any imagined or real drops of "Indian blood" and, by extension, any claims to "Indianness."[72]

Some believe the notion of hypodescent is part and parcel of the Cherokee Freedmen dispute. The Cherokee Freedmen certainly do, and they have mounted a spate of challenges to that unstated, but liberally applied, principle.

On July 7, 1983, Reverend Roger H. Nero, a Freedmen advocate, and several other original Freedmen enrollees attempted to vote in a Cherokee Nation election. Tribal poll workers turned away the Freedmen. Reverend Nero first filed a complaint with the Civil Rights Division of the United States Department of Justice. Then, on June 18, 1984, he and other Freedmen lodged a class action lawsuit against tribal officials, the federal government, and federal government officials claiming racial discrimination. The multi-million-dollar suit sought to declare the subject election a nullity. In the end, the Freedmen lost the case on jurisdictional grounds. The ruling courts never reached the merits of the case.[73]

More than a decade passed. Then, in 1998, the Cherokee Nation Judicial Appeals Tribunal (the Cherokee Nation Supreme Court) heard a citizenship case involving Bernice Riggs, a descendant of Cherokee Freedmen.[74] In 2001, the Justices upheld Mrs. Riggs' claim to Cherokee blood based on testimony and records. However, the Justices found Mrs. Riggs' Cherokee ancestor, a man named Rogers, was deceased at the time of the Dawes enrollment process and, for that reason, went unlisted. Had Rogers been alive to register on the Dawes Roll, Mrs. Riggs would have been able to become a Cherokee citizen based on his degree of Cherokee blood.

The Dawes Commission listed Rogers' descendents as Freedmen. Mrs. Riggs did not have an ancestor with a Dawes Final Roll number from whom she could obtain a CDIB card. In the end, the Justices determined the Cherokee Nation is a sovereign nation and could grant membership to whomever it wished.

Perversely, individuals with Caucasian mothers and dead Cherokee fathers were not excluded from enrollment on the Dawes Blood Rolls. As such, the descendants of those individuals may be or become citizens of the modern Cherokee Nation.

In 1999, the Cherokee Nation prepared a new Constitution to submit for BIA approval. The BIA, under Kevin Gover, found it flawed, and thereby rejected it, on two grounds: (1) the Cherokee Nation refused to allow Cherokee Freedmen to vote on the new Constitution; and (2) the new Constitution did not allow Cherokee Freedmen to hold office.

According to the official tribal newspaper, the *Cherokee Phoenix*, tribal leaders attempted unsuccessfully to persuade President Bill Clinton to approve the Constitution. He balked. Leaders then decided to request that the BIA remove the requirement of federal government approval for Constitutional amendments and new Constitutions.

Subsequently, the BIA modified its stance. In 2003, BIA head Neal McCaleb entertained a request to allow a referendum by Cherokee voters on a Constitutional amendment removing the necessity of federal approval for a new Cherokee Nation Constitution.

In a March 15, 2003, letter, Mr. McCaleb stated the Cherokee Nation could remove the federal approval clause from its existing Constitution so long as the Freedmen were entitled to vote in the election. Later, in an April 23, 2003, memorandum, Mr. McCaleb denied signing or authorizing his signature on the March 15, 2003, letter. He suggested the Freedmen could be barred from voting in the election under consideration.[75]

The Cherokee Nation, under Principal Chief Chad Smith, held various meetings around the Cherokee Nation, encouraging people to approve both the referendum and the proposed Constitution. The proposed Constitution contained no provision for federal approval of amendments. It did not explicitly subject the Cherokee Nation to the laws of the United States.

In May 2003, the Cherokee Nation entertained a referendum regarding the Constitutional amendment and, in July 2003, held a vote on the proposed new Constitution. Both passed. Descendants of Cherokee Freedmen who tried to participate as voters were not given voting cards or absentee ballots. Instead, they were provided with "challenged ballots" at the polls if they tried to vote in person.

In June 2003, several descendants of Cherokee Freedmen, through their attorneys, contacted the Department of the Interior, challenging the 2003 elections predicated upon the rights of the Freedmen pursuant to: (1) the 1866 Treaty; (2) the 1975 Cherokee Nation Constitution; and (3) judicial precedent, *Seminole Nation of Oklahoma v. Norton*,[76] wherein Judge Kolar-Kotelly upheld the Treaty of 1866 for the Seminole Freedmen and their voting and membership rights in the Seminole Nation.

Several prominent Cherokee Nation citizens, including Deputy Chief Hastings Shade, wrote to the BIA questioning the validity of an election in which the Cherokee Nation disenfranchised its Freedmen. Principal Chief Smith accused the BIA of having an antisovereign bias with respect to the Cherokee Nation.

In late July 2003, the Muskogee BIA director penned a letter in which he temporarily recognized Chad Smith as Principal Chief of the Cherokee Nation, but withheld approval of the Constitutional amendment, citing the *Seminole Nation* cases. Days later, another letter, written by the same Muskogee BIA official, recognized Chief Smith as Principal Chief, but still did not approve the Constitutional amendment.

Led by Marilyn Vann, descendants of Cherokee Freedmen filed suit in the District of Columbia in 2003, seeking to enforce the Treaty of 1866 and the Thirteenth Amendment against certain federal officials, the Cherokee Nation, and Principal Chief Chad Smith. *Vann v. Kempthorne*,[77] a lawsuit seeking Freedmen citizenship rights in the Cherokee Nation, clarified key issues related to Indian sovereignty and individual Indian civil rights.

The United States Court of Appeals for the District of Columbia rendered a decision on July 29, 2008, upholding the sovereignty of the Cherokee Nation. The Court applied the doctrine of "sovereign immunity"—an aspect of sovereignty that deems a sovereign protected from suit absent its consent—to protect the Cherokee Nation from suit by the Freedmen. The same Court, however, left open the possibility the officers of the Cherokee Nation may be held accountable for the Freedmen's disenfranchisement claims. The Court ordered the lower federal court to determine whether such liability on the part of Cherokee Nation officers may be pursued absent the Cherokee Nation itself as a party to the lawsuit.

The Court's decision, praised by both sides of the case for striking a balance between tribal sovereignty and individual Indian civil rights,[78] made clear that unfettered tribal sovereignty does not exist. Congress is the final arbiter of its breadth and depth.

> Indian tribes did not relinquish their status as sovereigns with the creation and expansion of the republic on the North American continent. The courts of the United States have long recognized that the tribes once were, and remain still, independent political societies.... That said, Congress may whittle away tribal sovereignty as it sees fit.
>
> . . . .
>
> As sovereigns, Indian tribes enjoy immunity against suits.... This immunity flows from a tribe's sovereign status in much the same way as it does for the States and for the federal government.... Congress's power to limit the scope of a tribe's sovereignty extends to tribal sovereign immunity.... But abrogation of tribal sovereign immunity requires an explicit and unequivocal statement to that effect.[79] (footnotes omitted)

The Court found nothing in the legal basis underlying the Freedmen's claim (i.e., the Thirteenth Amendment or the 1866 Treaty) that would constitute an express and unequivocal abrogation of tribal sovereign immunity. Thus, the Cherokee Nation could not be sued without its consent.[80] Tribal officers, on the other hand, may possibly be held accountable. The Court remanded the case to the lower federal court to determine whether a suit against such individuals could, "in equity and good conscience," proceed.[81]

In addition to the aforementioned *Vann* case, the Lucy Allen case also provided hope for the Freedmen's cause. Decades ago, census takers enrolled Ms. Allen's ancestors as Cherokee Freedmen despite clear evidence of Cherokee blood.

In the fall of 2004, Ms. Allen filed suit in the Cherokee Nation tribal court, the culmination of a quest for knowledge about her family's Cherokee connection begun in the 1970s. Then, in the early 1990s, she received a package from the National Archives that intensified her journey. The papers recounted her great grandfather's meeting with Dawes Commission agents.

On a Thursday in 1901, William Martin, a black farmer, engaged in this recorded exchange with a white Dawes Commission operative:

> **Operative**: "How old would you be?"
>
> **Martin**: "Something over 40, I judge."
>
> **Operative**: "What is your father's name?"
>
> **Martin**: "Joe Martin."
>
> **Operative** [to Martin's mother, also present for questioning]: "Was Joe Martin an Indian and a citizen of the Cherokee Nation?"
>
> **Martin's Mother** [a freed slave]: "Yes sir."[82]

Ms. Allen would soon discover her great-great grandfather was none other than Captain Joseph L. Martin, a Cherokee Confederate officer who owned a sprawling 100,000-acre ranch, on which a whopping 103 Africans lived in bondage. One of those enslaved Africans bore him a son, Ms. Allen's great grandfather, William Martin.[83]

While the 1880 authenticated Cherokee Nation Tribal Roll categorized Ms. Allen's ancestors as Cherokees (as opposed to "Adopted Coloreds"), the Dawes Commission Roll listed them as "Freedmen."

Ms. Allen challenged the right of the Cherokee Nation Tribal Council to strip citizenship from descendants of Dawes enrollees who are citizens based on the 1975 tribal Constitution. She emphasized the fact that such persons were denied the right to vote on those actions.

The disputed law[84] stated:

> A. Tribal membership is derived only through proof of Cherokee blood based on the Final Rolls.
> B. The Registrar will issue tribal membership to a person who can prove that he or she is an original enrollee listed on the Final Rolls by blood or who can prove to at least one direct ancestor listed by blood on the Final Rolls.

On March 7, 2006, the Judicial Appeals Tribunal of the Cherokee Nation issued its opinion in the pivotal case of *Lucy Allen v. Cherokee National Tribal Council, et al.*[85] The Tribunal declared unconstitutional legislation designed to limit Cherokee tribal membership to those who could demonstrate their "Cherokee by blood" status.

The Tribunal distinguished prior decisions that dismissed similar claims on sovereign immunity grounds.

> [The] Cherokee Nation asks this Court to follow the United States Supreme Court's decision in *Santa Clara v. Martinez* [436 U.S. 49 (1978)] and dismiss this case because the Cherokee Nation is immune from suit. If this case were filed against the Cherokee Nation in a federal or state court, Santa Clara would certainly require dismissal. In fact, when other Cherokee Freedmen have asked the federal courts to enforce their rights under the 1975 Constitution, the federal courts have properly dismissed those lawsuits [citing *Nero v. Cherokee Nation of Oklahoma*, 892 F.2d 1457 (10th Cir. 1989)]. Article VII of the 1975 Constitution, however, created this Court to "hear and resolve any disagreements" arising under the "constitution or any enactments of the Council." This case involves a direct conflict between the language of the constitution and legislation passed by the Council. The Cherokee JAT is the only proper forum.[86] (footnotes omitted)

The Tribunal invalidated the law because it prescribed tribal membership criteria more restrictive than required in Article III of the 1975 Cherokee Nation Constitution. The Tribunal opined on Cherokee citizenship and its abrogation:

> The Cherokee citizenry has the ultimate authority to define tribal citizenship. When they adopted the 1975 Constitution, they did not limit membership to people who possess Cherokee blood. Instead, they extended membership to all the people who were "citizens" of the Cherokee Nation as listed on the Dawes Commission Rolls.
>
> The Constitution could be amended to require that all tribal members possess Cherokee blood. The people could also choose to set a minimum Cherokee blood quantum [footnote omitted, citing the blood requirement imposed by the people of the United Keetoowah Band and the Eastern Band of Cherokee Indians]. However, if the Cherokee people wish to limit tribal

citizenship, and such limitation would terminate the pre-existing citizenship of even one Cherokee citizen, then it must be done in the open. It cannot be accomplished through silence.

The Council lacks the power to redefine tribal citizenship absent a Constitutional amendment. The Council is empowered to enact enrollment procedures, but those laws must be consistent with the 1975 Constitution. The current legislation is contrary to the plain language of the 1975 Constitution.[87]

The Tribunal pointed out the 1975 Constitution includes as Cherokee citizens those who are Cherokee by blood, other Indians (specifically, adopted Shawnee and Delaware Indians), and Freedmen. Cherokee tribal censuses that predated the Dawes Commission Rolls included native Cherokees, Freedmen, intermarried whites, and Indians of other tribes. The Cherokee Nation recognized all these groups as citizens.

Some consider the *Allen* case to be a *Brown v. Board*[88] parallel. Indeed, Cherokee Judicial Appeals Tribunal Justice Stacy L. Leeds, who wrote the majority opinion in *Allen*, has a connection to that storied desegregation case.

Leeds, now Dean and Professor of Law at the University of Arkansas School of Law in Fayetteville, Arkansas, is the only woman and youngest person ever to serve as a judge on the Judicial Appeals Tribunal of the Cherokee Nation. She received a Fletcher Fellowship in 2008 for her advocacy on behalf of the Freedmen. The Fletcher Fellowship program, a charitable initiative created in 2004 and named for Alphonse Fletcher, Sr., commemorates the 50th anniversary of *Brown v. Board*.[89]

Since the ruling of the Judicial Appeals Tribunal of the Cherokee Nation, the tribe's highest court, more than 1,500 Freedmen have enrolled in the Cherokee Nation. The fate of those new enrollees is, as previously indicated, uncertain.

Following the Tribunal ruling, some Cherokee citizens circulated a referendum petition. Principal Chief Chad Smith called a special election for February 2007 to consider changing the Constitution so as to limit citizenship to those of Indian ancestry based on the Dawes Blood Rolls.

The stance of Cherokee Principal Chief Chad Smith blindsided many African Americans in Oklahoma and beyond. Indeed, two African American legislators from Tulsa, Senator Judy Eason

McIntyre and Representative Jabar Shumate, wrote a searing open letter to the Chief:

An Open Letter to Chad Smith, Principal Chief of the Cherokee Nation of Oklahoma

It is with considerable dismay and no small amount of anger that we respond to your opposition to membership in the Cherokee Nation of person[s] who were segregated from the larger tribal population by the Dawes Commission in 1906 because of perceived—but mostly erroneous—racial affiliation. Cherokee people—your people—were one culture—one society, until those with any identifiable black genetic heritage were relegated to second-class status by being listed on the Freedmen Rolls. All Cherokee people, those who were phenotypically black, as well as those of you with mixed genetic heritage but of fairer complexion, were denied the lands and rights promised to all by treaty. Only the former were denied their birthright.

The amendment to the Cherokee Constitution [you propose] is no less racist-based than the cultural dichotomy created by the actions of the Dawes Commission, which for too long has divided the people of the Cherokee Nation. That cultural divide lasted for nearly a full century and has just now been bridged by the decision of the highest Court of the Cherokee Nation.

Your proposal for a constitutional amendment has created a great deal of concern among those of our constituency who will be directly impacted should the amendment succeed, as well as those whose sense of fairness has been offended. As you know, in our official capacity we have been consistent supporters of the Cherokee Nation and issues . . . affecting the same[.] In particular, just last year Sen. Eason McIntyre took the unpopular but uncompromising stance against the usage of Indian images as sports mascots. Likewise, although we clearly recognize and deeply respect the sovereignty of the Cherokee Nation, we will fully utilize our offices to help ensure that our [constituents] whose ancestors [were] enrolled as Cherokee Freedmen are not again disenfranchised based on racism and misinformation.

In closing, we sincerely hope that this positive relationship [will] continue. It is not too late to repair some of the damage that your political posturing has created. Therefore, [we] urge you to accept with good grace the decision of your own highest court, which in [our] opinion does no more than recognize and rectify an injustice of long standing. Although it may be unpopular with those who now hold citizenship and who have perhaps grown complacent concerning the implied racism, it is a decision long overdue—one whose time has come.

Signed: Senator Judy Eason McIntyre
Signed: Representative Jabar Shumate[90]

Senator Judy Eason McIntyre, co-writer of the open letter, spoke as a recognized Native American ally. She has been a vocal supporter of Native American issues in Oklahoma. In 2009 and, previously, in 2005, she shepherded legislation that would prohibit public schools from using sports team mascot names considered derogatory by Indians. Working with the Tulsa Indian Coalition Against Racism (TICAR), Senator McIntyre and her allies sought to remove offensive school nicknames like "Redskins" and "Savages."[91]

Despite the urgings of Senator McIntyre and Representative Shumate, the Cherokee Nation pressed on with its Freedmen removal initiative. The Cherokee Nation reelected Principal Chief Chad Smith on March 3, 2007. Smith proclaimed neutrality on the merits of the election as regards Freedmen citizenship.[92]

On the ballot in this special election was an Amendment to the Constitution of the Cherokee Nation mandating the removal of all Freedmen and non-Indian descendants of "intermarried whites" from the tribal rolls. The Amendment read:

> Notwithstanding any provisions of the Cherokee Nation Constitution approved on October 2, 1975, and the Cherokee Nation Constitution ratified by the people on July 26, 2003, upon passage of this Amendment, thereafter, citizenship of the Cherokee Nation shall be limited to those originally enrolled on, or descendants of those enrolled on, the Final Rolls of the Cherokee Nation, commonly referred to as the Dawes Rolls, for those listed as Cherokees by blood, Delaware Cherokees pursuant to Article II of the Delaware Agreement dated the 8th day of May, 1867, and the Shawnee Cherokees pursuant to Article III of the Shawnee Agreement date[d] the 9th day of June, 1869.[93]

A miniscule portion of eligible voters cast some 8,700 ballots in a fourteen-county district. A majority of a minority of Cherokee Nation voters, by a 77% affirmative vote, passed the amendment. Note the amendment did not adversely affect the "adopted"

Shawnee and Delaware Indians, who, though possessed of "Indian blood," would not be *Cherokee* (i.e., as a matter of ethnic identity) absent their adoption via the Treaty of 1866.[94]

Cherokee tribal councilor Taylor Keen, with understated prescience, foreshadowed the Pandora's Box effect of the balloting: "With this vote, the Cherokee Nation will start into motion the violation of the 1866 treaty, a severing of the nation's legal continuum with the United States, and perhaps our very precious sovereignty as a federally recognized tribe." Choices. Consequences.[95]

Freedmen advocate Jonathan Velie put those consequences in stark relief just after the controversial disenfranchisement vote occurred. "The United States, when posed with the same situation with the Seminoles [in 2000] . . . ultimately cut off most federal programmes [and] determined that the Seminoles, without this relationship with the government, were not authorised to conduct gaming."[96] The Seminoles relented under the incredible financial pressure, allowing the Freedmen back into the fold.

Other Native Americans have likewise lamented the obstinacy of the Cherokee Nation on the question of the Freedmen. Louis Gray, President of TICAR, is one such individual. TICAR, with alliances inside the Cherokee Nation and within the African American community, took no official position. Rather, the group offered to mediate the dispute. Chief Smith rejected the offer.[97]

The TICAR website prominently features an apropos quote by Leonard Peltier, self-described great-grandfather, artist, writer, & indigenous rights activist and citizen of the Anishinabe and Dakota/Lakota Nations.[98] Peltier urges: "Never cease in the fight for peace, justice, and equality for all people. Be persistent in all that you do and don't allow anyone to sway you from your conscience."[99] The matter of Freedmen citizenship, certainly viewed from the perspective of the Freedmen and their allies and supporters, is a matter of conscience.

Gray personally supports the cause of the Freedmen. Caught between the proverbial rock and hard place, he struggles with the status quo:

> I remain frustrated. Racism is racism. [M]y position has damaged my relationship with many Cherokees[.] I only want to see the Cherokees find a sensible way to settle this once and for all. This has damaged Indian relations with many Black folk all over the country. More than anything, the whole affair is tragic and unfair.[100]

For many, those three words, "racism is racism," lie at the heart of the Freedmen controversy. Recent data show Native Americans as leading victims of hate crimes and subtle racism. Given that, some are surprised by a perceived lack of empathy from the leadership of the Cherokee Nation on the Freedmen issue.[101] For more than a few observers, Freedmen disenfranchisement, denationalization, or expulsion by any other name reflects, at least in part, a lack of historical grounding and a failure to appreciate the broad sweep of institutional racism.

Jon Velie likewise puts the issue of racism within the Cherokee Nation at the forefront of the Freedmen controversy: "This is something happening within our society that we cannot stand for. We cannot have second class citizens. We cannot have Jim Crow again. We cannot allow apartheid within the geographical area of the United States of America."[102] Velie characterizes the expulsion of the Freedmen from the Cherokee Nation as "the most significant civil rights violation of the century and an unprecedented attack on treaty rights for tribes."[103]

Velie, who is Jewish, became enmeshed in the Freedmen citizenship imbroglio a mere month after passing his bar examination. He met Sylvia Davis, a Seminole Freedmen who had been denied participation in a special settlement fund established for the Seminole Nation. He felt an injustice had been done, so he approached the Chief and Assistant Chief of the Seminole Nation on Davis' behalf. In that meeting, "the N-word was dropped." Velie was stunned.[104] Since then, he has been fully engaged in the fight for Freedmen citizenship, mostly notably within the Cherokee Nation.

A fierce and unrelenting advocate, Velie articulated what is at stake for the Freedmen at a 2010 gathering in Bartlesville, Oklahoma sponsored by the Descendants of Freedmen of the Five Civilized Tribes. Billed as the "First Annual Treaty Celebration Banquet," the assembly drew Freedmen from a variety of tribes and from various states.

"This is about identity," Velie declared. "This is about stripping away [Freedmen] identity." He wondered aloud how different Freedmen disenfranchisement really is from The Nuremberg Laws of 1935,[105] anti-Semitic laws in Nazi Germany introduced at the annual Nazi Party rally in Nuremberg.

The first law, "The Law for the Protection of German Blood and German Honor," prohibited marriages and extra-marital intercourse between "Jews" and "Germans." It also forbade the employment of German women under the age of forty-five in Jewish households. The second law, "The Reich Citizenship Law," stripped Jews of their German citizenship and created a legal distinction between "Reich citizens" and "nationals." In practical effect, The Nuremberg Laws formalized the unofficial and particular measures taken by the German government against Jews up to 1935. German leaders noted The Nuremberg Laws were consistent with the Nazi Party imperative that Jews be deprived of their rights as citizens.[106]

"Take back your birthright. Be proud of your tribe," Velie exhorted. He warned tribal adversaries have a wealth advantage, but insisted the Freedmen fight is winnable: even if not in a court, then in the court of public opinion. Justice, he intimated, will prevail, one way or the other.[107]

Members of the Congressional Black Caucus share Velie's grave concerns about the motives behind Freedmen disenfranchisement. They cried foul in the immediate wake of the Cherokee Nation's disenfranchisement vote. Voicing dismay and outrage, the Congressional Black Caucus demanded the federal government look into the tribal election.

In a letter to the Bureau of Indian Affairs, Caucus members questioned the "validity, legality, as well as the morality" of the March 2007 expurgation. Representative Diane Watson (D-California) articulated the sentiments of the group: "The black descendant Cherokees can trace their Native American heritage back in many cases for more than a century. They are legally a part of the Cherokee Nation through history, precedent, blood and treaty obligations.[108]

The New York Times, in a June 8, 2007, editorial, excoriated the Cherokee Nation for its actions.

> Many members of Congress were rightly outraged by the Cherokee Nation's decision earlier this year to revoke the tribal membership of about 2,800 descendants of slaves once owned by the tribe. The tribe's leaders have since tried to avoid any punishment by restoring partial rights to some black members. Congress should disregard that ruse and move ahead with legislation that would force the Cherokee to comply with their treaty obligations and court decisions that guarantee black members full citizenship rights, including the right to vote and hold tribal office.

. . . .

It is shameful that the Cherokee have to be pressured into restoring the rights of their own black citizens. But that clearly is what is needed.[109]

The Cherokee tribal memberships of numerous Freedmen, including Marilyn Vann, hang in the balance. Her connection with her Cherokee roots will be severed in critical respects if the vote is sustained.

"I've always considered myself a Cherokee Native American with African blood," says Vann, a petroleum engineer from Oklahoma City who claims Cherokee, Chickasaw, and African American ancestry. Ms. Vann contends being listed on the Freedmen Roll ignores her Indian ancestry.

Stunned when the Cherokee Nation rejected her tribal citizenship application in 2001, Ms. Vann reapplied after the tribal court ruling in 2006. At long last, she is an acknowledged, albeit provisional, citizen of the Cherokee Nation.

Ms. Vann's motive for seeking affirmation of her Cherokee heritage is simple: "[I wanted to] have a voice in the affairs of the tribe," she says. "I did not come to my tribe to get something," she continued.

Some Freedmen opponents, Cherokees and otherwise, claim the Freedmen are motivated principally by money—especially newfound gaming revenues. The Cherokee Nation, however, does not pay profits from its lucrative gaming industry to its members on a *per capita* basis. Rather, such gambling profits fund the government, social services, and job creation. Cherokee Freedmen, even if successful on their citizenship claims, would not reap the individual bonanzas some imagined.

Vann believes the tribe fears the Freedmen's voting power. Daniel Littlefield, director of the Sequoyah Research Center at the University of Arkansas at Little Rock, an archive for contemporary Native American issues, offers a more troublesome explanation for the posture of the Cherokee Nation: racism.[110]

A public meeting featuring Representative Diane Watson, author of the tribal de-funding bill, was held in Tulsa on August 20, 2007. Most in the crowd supported the cause of the Freedmen. A handful of speakers from the Cherokee Nation, however, made interesting assertions.

One woman claimed the United States has violated countless

treaties with the Cherokee Nation. Therefore, she urged, how could the Cherokee Nation now be held to account under the Treaty of 1866? No one seemed persuaded by her argument.

The audience member's premise about the federal government's infidelity as regards treaties with Native Americans resonated. Many Americans, and perhaps most Native Americans, concur in her assessment. Yet the speaker's conclusion did not follow. Each treaty represents a separate and independent exchange of commitments. Moreover, African Americans, of all people, cannot be blamed for the historic misdeeds against Native Americans on the part of the United States. African Americans had virtually no official political power—and certainly no *executive* political power—when the federal government executed various treaties with Native-American tribes. What sense does it make, then, to punish the African-American beneficiaries of the Treaty of 1866 for past breaches by whites with respect to wholly different treaties? What logic supports discarding persons who have been acknowledged as tribal citizens—as family—for more than a century?

Other voices echoed Principal Chief Smith's "Indian nation for Indians" argument. It is, rhetorically, a perfect pronouncement. But again, it merely begs the cardinal question: Who is Indian?

Beyond the "Indianness" question looms yet another: Is the Cherokee Nation a racial group or is it a political unit? Recall that under the Treaty of 1866, the Cherokees adopted the Shawnee and Delaware tribes. These are Native Americans, to be sure, but not *Cherokees*. The Cherokees also adopted some whites. The Cherokee Nation has heretofore been, and remains, a political entity as opposed to a racial identity.

Many prominent Cherokees—Cherokees whose Indian pedigree is seldom questioned—admit to as much or more European ancestry as Cherokee blood. Curiously, the "Indian nation for the Indians" argument seems to arise only with respect to black Indians, not white ones.

> This "blood"-based sense of Cherokee identity fits well with the race science of the nineteenth century and with the philosophy and public policy of assimilation which guided the Dawes Commission in its work of tribal enrollment and allotment of land. The resulting Dawes Rolls established race-based categorizations of complex social and biological identities of both Native Americans and African Americans. When, as now, the Cherokee

Nation turns to the Dawes Rolls as its exclusive authority for citizenship, it is perpetuating those categorizations and their race-value significations by embedding them in the very body of the Nation.[111]

Yet another speaker at that 2007 Tulsa meeting opined the Cherokees signed the Treaty of 1866—the legal commitment binding the Cherokees to accept the Freedmen as citizens—under duress. While duress may be a tantalizing argument, there is a clear absence of any hint of duress in the language of the Treaty itself. Article 9 of the Treaty states, in pertinent part:

> The Cherokee Nation having, **voluntarily**, in February, eighteen hundred and sixty-three, by an act of the national council, forever abolished slavery, hereby covenant and agree that never hereafter shall either slavery or involuntary servitude exist in their nation. . . . They further agree that all freedmen who have been **liberated by voluntary act of their former owners or by law**, as well as all free colored persons who were in the country at the commencement of the rebellion, and are now residents therein . . . shall have all the rights of native Cherokees. . . . [emphasis added][112]

That same year, the Cherokee Nation amended its own 1839 Constitution to give effect to the Treaty of 1866:

> All native born Cherokees, all Indians and whites legally members of the Nation by adoption and all [F]reedmen who have been liberated by voluntary act of their former owners or by law, as well as freed colored persons who were in the country at the commencement of the rebellion, and are now residents therein, or who may return within six months from the 19th day of July, 1866, and their descendants, who reside within the limits of the Cherokee Nation, shall be taken and deemed to be citizens of the Cherokee Nation.[113]

If indeed some *sub rosa* level of duress sufficient to vitiate the Treaty of 1866 existed at the time of its execution: Why would the Cherokee Nation so amend its Constitution? Why should not all post-war agreements be subject to question as the products of alleged undue influence?

This much seems axiomatic: The vanquished always occupy an inferior bargaining position vis-à-vis the victors. Moreover, as a matter of equity, the doctrine of *laches*—the law's insistence that claims be raised in a timely fashion—also comes into play. The duress argument comes more than a century after the execution of the Treaty of 1866.

In 2009, the Cherokee Nation issued a position paper on its Freedmen stance.[114] That document claims that Congress, via the Five Tribes Act,[115] modified Article IX of the Treaty of 1866 so as to limit the class of persons defined as Freedmen.[116] This "limited class of Freedmen," the Cherokee Nation urges, included only those residing in the Cherokee Nation as of February 11, 1867—six months from the date of the promulgation of the Treaty of 1866, i.e., August 11, 1866.[117]

The Nation's claim rests on early twentieth century Congressional Acts and court decisions relating to those acts that dealt with Indian allotment issues, not Freedmen citizenship per se. It bears noting that Congress and the courts offered precious little solicitude for the rights of African Americans during this era of unparalleled racial tumult.

Institutional racism notwithstanding, substantial evidence exists that the Freedmen did not, in fact, constitute a limited class. For example, the Dawes Rolls for the Cherokee Nation included Freedmen minors who, by definition, could not have been alive and residing within the Cherokee Nation on February 11, 1867. Moreover, Congress later authorized a number of distributions to Freedmen who were not yet born on February 11, 1867.[118]

While Congress is unquestionably possessed of plenary power[119] over Indian affairs,[120] it is likewise true that treaty abrogation is not to be taken lightly. Indeed, the United States Supreme Court set the bar high for a finding of treaty abrogation: "What is essential is clear evidence that Congress actually considered the conflict between its intended action on one hand and Indian treaty rights on the other, and chose to resolve that conflict by abrogating the treaty."[121] That Congress ever intended in the early twentieth century to abrogate the Treaty of 1866—to deny Freedmen and their descendants the citizenship rights for which Congress had itself bargained—is by no means clear.[122]

The Cherokee Nation itself stands to lose as much as, or more than, the Freedmen by virtue of reneging on the Treaty of 1866:

[T]he group with the most at stake in this contest is not the [F]reedmen but the citizens of the Cherokee Nation, who shape their own fate as they decide the [F]reedmen's. If they formally choose to exclude the [F]reedmen, then their own blood policies might be turned against them at some future date, giving the Cherokee Nation a painful lesson in racial politics—the same one they have been teaching the [F]reedmen for over a century.[123]

On January 14, 2011, Judge John Cripps of the District Court of the Cherokee Nation overturned the 2007 Amendment to the Constitution of the Cherokee Nation, the amendment that disenfranchised the Freedmen. He restored tribal citizenship to about 2,800 Freedmen who had been removed from the Cherokee Nation by that enactment. Judge Cripps wrote:

> The Cherokee Nation's entry into the . . . Treaty of 1866 was an agreement which, to this date, has not been modified or abrogated by any action heretofore taken either through Constitutional change or Amendment thereto and the Nation is still bound by such provisions. The Cherokee Constitutional Amendment of March 3, 2007, by virtue of the provisions of the Treaty of 1866, and subsequent actions taken in furtherance thereof, are hereby determined to be voided as a matter of law.[124]

One of the newly-enfranchised Cherokee Freedmen, Howard Riley, reflected on his strong sense of Cherokee identity: "Being recognized by the tribe doesn't change the fact that we are [F]reedmen by birth. We always considered ourselves part of the tribe, regardless of being kicked out or not."[125]

Within days, the Cherokee Nation appealed Judge Cripps's ruling. Diane Hammons, Cherokee Nation Attorney General, noted in a news release: "A constitutional case of this magnitude should be decided by the Cherokee Nation's highest court."[126] Freedmen activist Marilyn Vann reacted to news of the appeal with defiant resignation: "The [F]reedmen people, again, we have to continue the fight. We just have to continue to fight until justice is done."[127] Ralph Keen, Jr., who represents some of the Freedmen in the Cherokee Nation tribal courts, emphasized that the fight is much more than academic. At stake are Freedmen voting rights, as well as entitlements to such tribal benefits as health care, housing assistance, and college scholarships.[128]

In *Cherokee Nation Registrar v. Raymond Nash*,[129] an August 22, 2011, decision, the Supreme Court of the Cherokee Nation reversed and vacated the January 14, 2011, decision by Cherokee Nation District Court Judge John Cripps. The Court also lifted all previous orders and injunctions by Judge Cripps, in effect immediately terminating the tribal citizenship of some 2,800 Cherokee Freedmen. In practical effect, the ruling, if it stands, means that these Freedmen will lose not only the franchise, but also access to health care, housing, and other services provided by the Cherokee Nation.

The ruling came at a pivotal moment in Cherokee history. The Court's decision to uphold Cherokee Freedmen termination rendered the Freedmen ineligible to vote in the September 24, 2011, election for Principal Chief of the Cherokee Nation, a Cherokee Nation Supreme Court-ordered "re-do" of a too-close-to-call contest between rivals Chad Smith, incumbent Principal Chief, and Bill John Baker, a Tahlequah businessman, just weeks prior. The vast majority of the Freedmen favored Baker over Smith.[130] As noted previously, legal maneuvering in the *Vann* federal case temporarily restored Freedmen citizenship, and thus allowed Freedmen to vote in the election.

The Cherokee Nation Supreme Court is the successor of the Cherokee Nation Judicial Appeals Tribunal,[131] the Court that rendered the 2006 decision enfranchising the Freedmen. Marilyn Vann assailed the decision to dismantle the Judicial Appeals Tribunal as a political ploy to ensconce Principal Chief Smith in his position of power:

> [I]n 2006, [Chief Smith] dismantled the [Judicial Appeals Tribunal] and established this Supreme Court in its place and selected new judges. It is obvious this decision is the tool he is using to regain his position as Chief and deliver the blow to eliminate my citizenship and [the citizenship of] other Cherokees who have held this status since 1866. Despite Federal and Tribal Court rulings stating the Freedmen enjoy all the rights of Cherokee citizenship, [t]he Smith administration has kept out 90% of the Freedmen.[132]

Among the salient holdings of the Supreme Court of the Cherokee Nation were: (1) The Cherokee Courts lack jurisdiction to overturn the duly approved March 3, 2007, referendum that amended the Cherokee Constitution so as to exclude the Freedmen (the Court hailed the referendum as "[t]he latest sovereign ex-

pression of the Cherokee people concerning the Freedmen.[133] . . .";
(2) An 1866 amendment to the Cherokee Constitution, *not the Treaty of 1866*, extended citizenship to the Freedmen in the first instance;[134] (3) The Freedmen lack standing to bring suit under the Treaty of 1866, such standing being properly vested in the United States government, the other sovereign party to the Treaty;[135] and (4) Freedmen disenfranchisement does not violate the Thirteenth Amendment to the United States Constitution as a badge or incident of slavery, because some individuals who are Freedmen are able to trace ancestors to the Dawes "Cherokees by Blood" rolls and are thus still citizenship-eligible.[136]

Freedmen and their advocates wasted no time in reacting to the crushing decision. Attorney Jon Velie, who represented plaintiff Marilyn Vann in her federal court case, found the Cherokee Supreme Court's assertion that the Treaty of 1866 did not confer citizenship rights on the Freedmen particularly troubling. Velie noted:

> This language conflicts with the undisturbed line of Federal Court cases from 1895 through now. The Cherokee Nation simply has no interest in protecting sovereign concerns that have been taken away by the United States. The Thirteenth Amendment and the 1866 Treaty whittled away the Tribes' sovereignty with regard to slavery and left it powerless to discriminate against the Freedmen.[137]

Kenneth J. Cooper likewise took umbrage at the Cherokee Nation Supreme Court's reading of history:

> The four-judge majority appears to ignore the historical context of the 1866 treaty, which compelled the Cherokee Nation to do exactly what the Confederate states had to do to get readmitted to the union—free the slaves and grant them citizenship and equal rights. The opinion's suggestion that the former slaves had protection under federal law makes no sense. At the time, Cherokee Freedmen were not U.S. citizens, nor were Cherokees by blood. And what category of persons in any other sovereign nation has all the rights of citizens, yet are not citizens?[138]

Marilyn Vann, president of the Five Civilized Tribes Association, lamented, "It is a dark day for the Cherokee Nation, for Indian

Country and for mankind."[139] Tria Robinson posted the next day on a Cherokee Freedmen Descendants cite:

> This decision breaks my heart. I am Choctaw and Cherokee Freedman and this affects me [and] my children. It seems the CNO [Cherokee Nation of Oklahoma] disregards us and kicks us to the side again. We are [their] sisters and brothers. I can't comprehend how they took our tribal community away from us. CNO leaders spend tribal [money] on themselves and [their] friends. I don't want tribal [money]. I don't want handouts. I just want my community and tribal ties! This hurts. To feel unwanted. . . .[140]

Soon thereafter, Robert Warrior opined:

> The moral case against the Cherokees is straightforward. As a duly constituted nation in the nineteenth century, they legally embraced and promoted African slavery, a position they maintained after Removal to Indian Territory in the 1830s. The vast majority of Cherokees could not afford slaves, as was also the case throughout the American South, and historians of Cherokee slavery have demonstrated that some aspects of the Cherokee social world gave a different, less negative character to being enslaved by wealthy Cherokees rather than wealthy whites. Make no mistake, though. No one is on record as having volunteered to become a Cherokee slave. History records plenty of Cherokee slaves attempting to escape to freedom, as well as Cherokee slave revolts. The institution of slavery was for Cherokees, as it has been for all people who practice it, morally and politically corruptive, and many citizens of this Native slaving nation knew it.
>
> . . . .
>
> In spite of being egged on and provoked by the legislated racism of the Cherokee Nation, the vast majority of Freedmen descendants have reacted with impressive dignity befitting their proud history. . . . It remains for more people, including Native American writers, scholars, and artists, not to mention elected leaders, presidents, and chiefs, to stand up and be counted on the right moral side of this questions. . . .[141]

Now that the highest court in the Cherokee Nation has ruled on the matter of Freedmen disenfranchisement, the Freedmen must look elsewhere for vindication of their rights. Freedmen attorney Ralph Keen, Jr., noted: "Because the Cherokee Nation justice system has failed them, the Cherokee freedmen have no option [but] to resort to the federal courts or the halls of Congress for the vindication of their rights."[142] Kenneth J. Cooper urged executive intervention: "When the Seminole expelled its [F]reedmen during the Clinton administration, the Bureau of Indian Affairs in 2000 suspended federal funding to the tribe until those rights were restored. It is time for Obama and his administration to take a stand."[143] As noted previously, a decision in the *Nash* case, pending in Tulsa federal court, will provide at least a temporary resolution of the Freedmen dilemma. Some action at the federal level, whether it emanates from the executive, legislative or judicial branch, will ultimately determine whether the Freedmen are in or out.

The Cherokee Nation does not stand alone in its efforts to circumvent the Treaty of 1866. The Muscogee (Creek) Nation, too, finds itself in a parallel quandary, with Freedmen citizenship twisting perilously in the wind.

B. In the Muscogee (Creek) Nation

The British called the Muscogee (Creek) people "Ochese Creek Indians" after the Ocmulgee River tributary in Georgia, the location of a number of tribal towns at the beginning of trading relations between them. The Muscogee, the recognized name of the people, are not a tribe. Rather, they are a confederacy of more than 100 "tribal towns" united under the umbrella of a single government. The Muscogee (Creek) Nation is headquartered in Okmulgee, Oklahoma.[144]

Oklahoma historian Angie Debo pointed out the Muscogee (Creek) people largely rejected the institution of chattel slavery—people as property. Where slavery did exist among the tribe, it generally took on a character unparalleled in the greater society.

> Except on the plantations of a few mixed (white and red) bloods, slavery rested very lightly upon the [Muscogee (Creek)] Negroes. The easygoing Indians found the possession of slaves a great convenience, but they saw little reason to adopt the white man's ruthless system of exploiting and degrading them.[145]

Other scholars concur with Debo. David A. Chang, a University of Minnesota historian who focuses on race and ethnicity, with emphasis on the histories of American Indian and Native Hawaiian people, notes:

> [The] Creek form of slavery....was certainly a form of domination, but it seems to have been permissive in comparison with Anglo-American slavery of the period and was neither heritable nor permanent. In fact, prior to the end of the eighteenth century, most enslaved people regained their freedom. They often married Creeks and became integrated into Creek towns and clans.[146] [footnotes omitted]

The acceptance of chattel slavery among a minority of Muscogee (Creek) people emerged during the mid-eighteenth century, amid the larger context of tensions over private versus communal property. As Chang pointed out:

> In the nineteenth century, the communal ownership of lands and the inclusion of people of African descent were established facts among the loose confederacy of *talwas* (towns) that the English knew as the Creeks. After about 1760, however, a small minority of Creek people came to embrace not only property in general but property in land and black chattel slaves in particular. They accumulated wealth and wanted the power that would secure it. With the encouragement of the American authorities, they built the beginnings of a national state: a national council and a police force to protect the new order of property. But the majority of Creeks rejected the accumulation of private wealth, racial slavery, and the creation of a coercive state. They favored instead communal town agriculture, the dispersal of wealth, and a town and clan governance.[147] [footnote omitted]

The confederacy of Native American groups called "Creek" came to be dominated by a collective known conventionally as the "Muscogee" or "Muskogee." The language of the people bore the same name. Those sharing linguistic roots—Muskhogean linguistic stock—with the Muscogee include the Oconee (a group related to the Seminoles), Choctaw, Chickasaw, and the Yamasee.[148]

In addition to a common base language, the Muscogee (Creek) people share a common ancestry with the Choctaws and the Chickasaws. H. B. Cushman, the son of Choctaw missionaries, spent years observing Choctaw life firsthand. In his well-known 1899 book, *History of the Choctaw, Chickasaw and Natchez Indians*, Cushman noted: "According to an ancient tradition of the Choctaws, the ancient Choctaws, Chickasaws, and Muscogee (now, Creeks) were once the same people. This claim is bolstered by the fact that today, many pure Choctaw words remain part of the Muscogee (Creek) language."[149] Indeed, some authorities believe the Choctaws and Chickasaws followed the Cherokees and Muscogee (Creek) to what is now the United States from early origins in Mexico.[150]

Ancestors of the Muscogee (Creek) people built spectacular earthen pyramids. These pyramids became central to tribal ceremonial complexes. Eventually, the Muscogee (Creek) constructed expansive towns within the broad river valleys of the modern states of Alabama, Georgia, Florida, and South Carolina. The Muscogee (Creek) Nation, long inclusive of people of assorted ancestry, emerged as a series of "tribal towns" bound together by a unitary government.[151]

As an "open society," the Muscogee (Creek) regularly acquired citizens through adoption and intermarriage. Adoptees became full-fledged tribal members, with all the appurtenant rights, duties, and protections. Indeed, as an 1893 Department of the Interior report points out, adopted Africans living among the Muscogee (Creek) Nation excelled:

> The Creek Nation is an alert and active one, which is largely due to the [N]egro element which fairly controls it. . . . In any of The Five Tribes where the [N]egroes have a fair chance there is a perceptible progress due to them.
>
> . . . .
>
> The [N]egroes are among the earnest workers in The Five Tribes. The Creek Nation affords the best example of [N]egro progress. The principal chief, virtually a [N]egro, comes of a famous family in Creek annals. His name is Lequest Choteau Perryman. He was born in the Creek Nation, Indian [T]erritory, March 1, 1833; educated at Tallahassee Mission of the same nation, enlisted in the Union army in Kansas [in] November 1862, and was mustered out as sergeant major of the first regiment Indian Home Guards [in] 1863. He served as district judge of the Coweta [D]istrict, Mus[c]ogee Nation, [for] six years; was elected to the council and served 13 years. He was elected principal chief and inaugurated [on] December 3, 1887, for the term of four years.[152]

One group affiliated with the Muscogee (Creek) consisted exclusively of persons of African ancestry. This collective, called the Yamassee, became "one of a small number of isolated tribes of dark complexion," made up of "immigrants from Africa prior of the European discovery of America."[153]

Because the Muscogee (Creek) identified themselves nationalistically, not racially, they considered people of divergent cultural and racial backgrounds "full-bloods." The American ideal—*E pluribus unum*: Out of many cultures and colors, Americans are one—is a contemporary analogue to this politically-based system of identification and affiliation.

Throughout the period of contact with Europeans, most of the Muscogee (Creek) population occupied two geographical areas. The English called the Muscogee peoples living in towns on the Coosa and the Tallapoosa Rivers "Upper Creeks," and those living to the southeast, along the Chattahoochee and Flint Rivers "Lower Creeks."[154]

Because of their proximity to the English, the Lower Creek towns engaged in substantial intermarriage with the Europeans. This culture crossing led to a dilution of traditional political and social practices and institutions. The Lower Creeks emulated Southern custom, practice, and, notably, prejudice. They often looked askance at persons of African descent. Also, they assimilated into white society and cultivated literacy in English. Not infrequently, Lower Creeks could "pass" for white.

The Upper Creek towns, by contrast, remained largely unaffected by European influences. They maintained traditional political and social practices, as well as culturally distinct institutions.[155] Unlike the Lower Creeks, the Upper Creeks often intermarried with persons of African descent. They tended to be darker in complexion, and often they spoke no English.

The fissure between the Upper and Lower Creeks increasingly turned on issues of race. Clashes proved inevitable. The Lower Creeks at one time sought to expel the Africans from the Muscogee (Creek) Nation. Years later, they signed a Civil War treaty with the Confederacy to preserve their interest in African slavery.

The Muscogee (Creek) people soon came to realize peaceable coexistence with Europeans Americans would come, if at all, on terms other than their own. They resisted the westward push set in motion by the federal government in the early nineteenth century.[156]

208   Apartheid in Indian Country?

On March 27, 1814, General Andrew Jackson and an army of 3,300 men attacked 1,000 Upper Creek warriors, led by Chief William Weatherford (a.k.a., Red Eagle), on the Tallapoosa River near present-day Alexander City, Alabama, in the east central part of the state. More than 800 Upper Creeks died defending their homeland in the deadliest single battle in history for Native Americans. This conflict, known as the Battle of Horseshoe Bend, is generally considered part of the War of 1812. The Upper Creeks allied themselves with the British in that battle.

The Muscogee (Creek) tribe went to war at the urging of Shawnee Chief Tecumseh. Tecumseh, a leading ally of the British, sought to build a pan-Indian resistance to American expansion. The British hoped to create a large, neutral Indian state that would provide a buffer against American expansionists.

Horseshoe Bend became the major battle of the Creek War (1813-1814). General Jackson saw the conflict as an opportunity to clear Alabama for white settlement. Some 600 Cherokee, Choctaw and Lower Creek Indians fought as Jackson troops. Eventually, on August 9, 1814, Andrew Jackson forced the Creeks to sign the Treaty of Fort Jackson (a.k.a., the Treaty with the Creeks, 1814) at Fort Jackson near Wetumpka, Alabama.

On the other side were the traditionalist "Red Stick" Creek Indians. They fought under the command of Chief Menawa, known as "Great Warrior," who was considered the military leader of his people. After the Creek War, Menawa continued to oppose the encroachment on Muscogee (Creek) lands. On April 30, 1825, he led the party that assassinated Chief William McIntosh, signatory of the February 12, 1825, Treaty of Indian Springs. That instrument authorized the relocation of the Muscogee (Creek) people west of the Mississippi River to a promised equivalent parcel of land along the Arkansas River.

Ultimately, the Muscogee (Creek) Nation ceded 23 million acres—half of Alabama and part of southern Georgia—to the United States government.[157] Andrew Jackson became a war hero and, later, the seventh President of the United States of America (1829-1837).

Between 1834 and 1837, the United States forcibly removed the Muscogee (Creek) from their traditional homelands (Alabama, Georgia, South Carolina, and Florida) and sent them to live in what is now Oklahoma. People of African descent, both free and enslaved, suffered the pain of removal right along with their Muscogee (Creek) kin.[158]

One Muscogee (Creek) Indian who embarked on that dark journey was named Samuel Carr. Many years later, his great-great-great-grandson, Gary Lee, a reporter for the *Washington Post*, would recreate an automobile version of the trek. With his sister, Lilla, Gary Lee tried to follow Samuel Carr's footsteps from Montgomery, Alabama, all the way to Oklahoma. Lee, a fifth-generation Oklahoman with an African-American mother and a father of mixed Muscogee (Creek) and African ancestry, grew up with stories about the infamous path to Oklahoma.

Along the way, Lee encountered a variety of Native Americans from several tribes. He took time to experience Indian culture with them. He learned that there had been at least a dozen "Trail of Tears" routes. Duane King, a highly regarded scholar of Indian culture, explained: "In a sense, the trail started at the home of every Indian yanked from their [*sic*] houses throughout the South, and it ended wherever they put down stakes and made a new home."[159]

Lee ended his journey in his hometown of Tulsa, more fully appreciating his history, his family, and himself:

> I [brought] my own journey to a close with a stroll down Cheyenne, a street in Tulsa. I started at one end, where a ceremonial oak tree, planted by Creeks when they first arrived from the East, towers near the banks of the Arkansas River. I ended two miles north, in the wooden two-story house where I was raised and where my parents have lived for more than three decades.
>
> As a result of the trip, I think I know myself better. I understand a few things about my father, too—his lifelong aversion to travel, his stubborn insistence on holding his ground to the bitter end of an argument. These characteristics may be in his historical memory.[160]

Such profound ties between the African-American and Native-American people of Oklahoma are not at all uncommon. Persons of African descent living among the Muscogee (Creek) built the first church established in Oklahoma: Fountain Baptist Church (a.k.a., Ebenezer Baptist Church). Erected in 1832, in the "Point" between the Arkansas and Verdigris Rivers, in what became Marshalltown, one of Oklahoma's all-black towns, the church still holds regular services.[161]

Individuals of African extraction rank among the luminaries of Muscogee (Creek) history. Two such individuals, Harry Island and Cow Tom, merit particular attention. These men negotiated on behalf of, and interpreted for, the Muscogee (Creek) Nation, proving themselves indispensable ambassadors by virtue of their English literacy and business acumen.

Harry Island (1812–August 15, 1872), Cow Tom's friend and a citizen of the Muscogee (Creek) Nation, embraced Muscogee (Creek) culture. He knew the customs. He spoke the language. He was one with the people.

Island served as one of the official United States interpreters for the Muscogee (Creek) Nation, and he is listed as an official witness to the execution of the Treaty of 1866. Island also took part in many official post-Civil War hearings, always looking out for the interests of the Freedmen.

In March of 1867, government payments to those Muscogee (Creek) who remained loyal to the Union in the Civil War began. Harry Island is widely credited with ensuring that the Muscogee (Creek) Freedmen received their share of these benefits.

Some even claim Harry Island "tricked" the Muscogee (Creek) by negotiating benefits for Freedmen during the course of his dealings with federal authorities. In *The Road to Disappearance: A History of the Muscogee (Creek) Indians*,[162] noted Oklahoma historian Angie Debo described Harry Island as a "shrewd Creek Negro who served as interpreter and apparently looked after the interest of his race."

Cow Tom,[163] Harry Island's contemporary, colleague, and friend, epitomized the sophistication, ingenuity, and savvy of the African leaders within the Muscogee (Creek) Nation. Born into slavery circa 1810, Cow Tom "belonged" to an Upper Creek leader from Alabama named Yargee. Chief Yargee, head of the Upper Creeks, had little interest in mixing with whites, but interacted freely with persons of African extraction.

As a young man, Cow Tom tended Yargee's cattle, a position of significant responsibility and stature. Yargee began using the appellation "Cow Tom," a pragmatic moniker created to distinguish, functionally, this particular Tom from other men with that name.

When the United States government enforced its brutal dictate evicting the Five Tribes from the Southeast, Cow Tom and his family accompanied Yargee on the journey. Cow Tom grew close to

Yargee—so close, in fact, that he became an invaluable ally and confidant as well as a precious and prized asset.

Unlike Chief Yargee, Cow Tom spoke both Muscogee (Creek) and English. Before removal, Yargee earned some $300 a year leasing Tom out to the United States Army for services as an interpreter.

Cow Tom surpassed his black counterparts in the interpreting and translation business. His adroitness at interpretation and his human relations skills earned the admiration and respect of famed General Thomas Jessup.[164] Cow Tom realized it would be advantageous to persons of African ancestry who lived among the Muscogee (Creek) to follow them westward. He used his influence with the military to help ensure the safety of several hundred Africans who migrated to Indian Territory with the tribe.

After arrival in Indian Territory, Chief Yargee's dependence on Cow Tom only grew. Cow Tom became principal negotiator and interpreter for the Chief, who still knew no English and had little or no interest in learning the language.[165]

As a result of his linguistic facility and negotiation acumen, Cow Tom acquired enough money to purchase freedom for himself and his family. As a free man, he earned substantial sums for his services as an interpreter. With this newly acquired wealth, he purchased land and livestock in his own right.

After the Confederate defeat in the Civil War, the Lower Creeks battled unsuccessfully against the presence of Africans among the tribe. The Upper Creeks, by contrast, remained loyal to those Africans. Cow Tom thrived.

While many black Indians fled to Kansas during the Civil War, Cow Tom remained in Indian Territory, largely sheltered from the conflict. After the pivotal Battle of Honey Springs near Rentiesville, Oklahoma, in July 1863, many of the Confederate-aligned Lower Creeks settled nearby. Cow Tom moved his family to Fort Gibson, Oklahoma, to escape the race-based wrath of these defeated, and sometimes hostile, Lower Creeks.

At Fort Gibson Cow Tom became a de facto chief. Because of his fluency in both English and the tribal language, he served as a liaison between the United States military and the Muscogee (Creek) Nation.

The Muscogee (Creek) tribesmen who migrated to Kansas during the Civil War also needed a cultural liaison. There, Cow Tom's friend, Harry Island, emerged as a valued interpreter.

As the Muscogee (Creek) Nation reassembled after the Civil War, Oktars-sars-har-jo, known as "Chief Sands," appointed Cow Tom as an official chief. Harry Island worked nearby as the official interpreter for the United States Army.

In 1866, the federal government ordered leaders of the Five Civilized Tribes to Fort Smith, Arkansas, to negotiate the official Civil War peace treaties. The Muscogee (Creek) Nation stood alone in the utilization of persons of African ancestry in official negotiating roles.

After the Civil War, Cow Tom's concerns about the Confederate-aligned Lower Creeks grew. This group reasserted its authority under the direction of Sam Checote, a preacher and enlistee in the Confederate Army who became the first elected Muscogee (Creek) chief after the Civil War.[166]

Cow Tom and others decided to take action. They set out to protect the rights of the Freedmen against anticipated encroachment attempts by Confederate-aligned "mixed bloods."

Cow Tom, Ketch Barnett, and Harry Island surreptitiously traveled to Washington, D.C., to fight for the rights of the Muscogee (Creek) Freedmen. They sought to ensure that any post-Civil War concessions to the Muscogee (Creek) Nation (i.e., land allotments and other governmental perquisites) would not bypass the Africans in the tribe.

A Lower Creek faction followed Cow Tom and company to Washington, D.C. These Lower Creeks, fearing that persons of African ancestry would dilute funding destined for the Muskogee (Creek) Nation, argued, unsuccessfully, against integration of Freedmen into the Nation. The execution of the Treaty of 1866 came despite the vocal protestations of the Eurocentric Lower Creeks.

In a letter dated March 18, 1866, a Lower Creek partisan purported to speak for the tribe against citizenship for Freedmen:

> We are determined to protect the interests of the Negroes who were among us before the war. . . . But we believe that our ancient care and kindness ought to be a sure guarant[ee] that their interests and welfare will be safe in our municipal jurisdiction. We never have, and have not now, any disposition to injure or tyrannize over them. Still, we can never recognize them as our equals. We are honest and candid in this declaration. . . . It is, we conceive, contrary to nature and nature's laws. The antipathies of race among

Indians are strong, if not stronger than they are among the whites. The government of the United States is very strong; we are very weak; it can, and may, force us to things repugnant to our nature; but it cannot change our honest convictions and faith any more than it can change the skin of the Ethiopian or the spots of the leopard.[167]

In the end, the United States government negotiated and signed a new treaty with the Muscogee (Creek) Nation. The Treaty of 1866, facilitated in part by Cow Tom,[168] a Treaty signatory, took two bold steps toward the empowerment of persons of African ancestry in the tribe. It: (i) outlawed slavery in the Muscogee (Creek) Nation; and (ii) granted tribal rights to persons of African ancestry formerly enslaved by members of the Muscogee (Creek) Nation. The Treaty of 1866, signed with the Muscogee (Creek) Nation on June 14, 1866,[169] became the foundational document establishing the jurisdiction of the modern Muscogee (Creek) Nation.[170]

Article II of the Treaty of 1866 with the Muscogee (Creek) provides that people of African descent, free or formerly enslaved, who are living among the Muscogee (Creek) will be adopted as full citizens.

> The Creeks hereby covenant and agree that henceforth neither slavery nor involuntary servitude, otherwise than in the punishment of crimes, whereof the parties shall have been duly convicted in accordance with laws applicable to all members of said tribe, shall ever exist in said nation; and inasmuch as there are among the Creeks many persons of African descent, who have no interest in the soil, it is stipulated that hereafter these persons lawfully residing in said Creek country under their laws and usages, or who have been thus residing in said country, and may return within one year from the ratification of this treaty, and their descendants and such others of the same race as may be permitted by the laws of the said nation to settle within the limits of the jurisdiction of the Creek Nation as citizens [thereof,] shall have and enjoy all the rights and privileges of native citizens, including an equal interest in the soil and national funds, and the laws of the said nation shall be equally binding upon and give equal protection to all such persons, and all others, whatsoever race or color, who may be adopted as citizens or members of said tribe.[171]

Having helped secure for the Freedmen a measure of true freedom, Cow Tom eventually retired to farm and family life. He maintained a cattle business and became the patriarch of one of Oklahoma's premier African-American families. Cow Tom died in 1874. He is buried in Cane Creek Cemetery in Boynton, Oklahoma, a small town in Muskogee County, about forty miles southeast of Tulsa. His legacy lives.

Cow Tom is the grandfather of Muskogee oil tycoon Jake Simmons, Jr.[172] Simmons's father, Jake Simmons, Sr., blue-eyed and fair-haired when young, could "pass" for a Muscogee (Creek) Indian. He selected as his wife a jet-black woman named Rose Jefferson. According to family members, the elder Simmons chose Jefferson because of her education, financial wherewithal, and near-pure African roots, which included no legacy of slavery and no badge of inferiority that often accompanied that legacy.[173]

Simmons's kin also included the Perryman family. Angie Debo acknowledged the African roots of the Perryman family without "naming names":

> [T]he ablest and most prominent mixed-blood family in the nation had received a noticeable strain of negro blood in its early history. The members of this family ignored this admixture without attempting to deny it and associated themselves with the white-and-Indian Creeks; and so great was the respect felt for their character and ability that they were freely accepted even by this proud and aristocratic group. But except for this one numerous family the negro-Indian admixture was confined to the "full bloods."[174] (footnote omitted)

Members of the prominent Perryman family served on the General Council of Indian Territory, an inter-tribal body with authority emanating from the Treaty of 1866. Minutes of the September 27, 1870, meeting list the General Council representatives, including: George Washington Stidham, Pleasant Porter, John R. Moore, Legus C. Perryman, George Washington Grayson, Joseph M. Perryman, and Sandford Perryman from the Muscogee (Creek) Nation; and William Potter Ross, Riley Keys, and Allen Ross from the Cherokee Nation. Representatives from the Ottawa, Quapaw, Seneca, Wyandotte, Confederate Peoria, and Sac and Fox tribes also attended.[175]

Moses (Mose) Perryman, an early Oklahoma settler, operated a thriving plantation that was run on the labor of enslaved Africans. Mary Grayson recalled what it was like to labor under the yoke of old man Perryman:

> I am what colored people call a "native." That means that I didn't come into the Indian country from somewhere in the Old South, after the War, like so many Negroes did, but I was born here in the old Creek Nation, and my master was a Creek Indian. That was eighty[-]three years ago, so I am told.
>
> . . . .
>
> Mose Perryman was my master and he was a cousin to Legus Perryman, who was a big man in the Tribe, he was a lot younger than Mose, and laughed at Mose for buying my mammy, but he got fooled, because my mammy got married to Mose's slave boy Jacob, the way the slaves was married them days, and went ahead and had ten children for Mr. Mose.
>
> . . . .
>
> Mose Perryman had a lot of land broke in all up and down the Arkansas [R]iver along there. . . . The land was very rich, and the Creeks who got to settle there were lucky. They always had big crops.
>
> . . . .
>
> [A]ll the Negroes I knew who belonged to Creeks always had plenty of clothes and lots to eat and we all lived in good log cabins we built. We worked the farm and tended to the horses and cattle and hogs.[176]

Jim Samuels, one of the enslaved Africans who toiled on Mose's vast land holdings, subsequently acquired part of that same property as a Freedmen allotment:

> Jim Samuels was a slave of Mose Perryman previous to the [C]ivil [W]ar, and after the [W]ar and the slaves were made free, Jim Samuels resided in the immediate vicinity and when allotments were eventually made to the [F]reedmen, the land upon which the [Samuels Cemetery, a.k.a., Mose Perryman Graveyard] is situated, and part of the old Mose Perryman claim[,] happened to be Jim Samuels['] allotment.[177]

Jane (Burgess), the daughter of Moses Perryman by his wife, Molly, enrolled with the Dawes Commission, and was assigned card number 373 on the "Blood Roll" as a full-blood. Her sister, Louisa (Wilson), born of the same mother and father, enrolled, too. Federal Dawes agents placed Louisa on the Freedmen Roll, card number F. 854. Two sisters, born of the same parents, wound up with different Dawes outcomes, without rhyme or reason, and in defiance of logic. Such was the precision with which Dawes agents accounted for, or, in the case of persons whose physiognomy appeared to be of African ancestry, discounted Indian ancestry.

Legus C. Perryman, Mose's nephew, enrolled with the Dawes Commission on October 7, 1899, in Tulsa. Legus C. had been a prosecuting attorney and judge in the Coweta district, as well as a member of the Creek Nation House of Warriors (a body similar to the United States House of Representatives). The father of Legus C., Lewis Perryman, became a city father of Tulsa.

In 1836, the Lochapoka clan of the Muscogee (Creek) Indians spread ashes from their sacred ceremonial fires in Alabama under a tree in Tulsa. That tree, the "Council Oak Tree" today located near 18th Street and South Cheyenne Avenue, stands among Tulsa's premier landmarks. It is a reminder of the forced removal to and new birth in Oklahoma endured by the tribe.[178] The story of the christening of the Council Oak Tree speaks to continuity—to survival.

The Upper (Muscogee) Creeks carried a pot of ashes and a burning brand from their Tulwa Town, Alabama, council fires on their trek from Alabama to Indian Territory. Throughout the journey, tribesmen employed the burning brand from the previous night's fire to ignite the campfire at the close of that day's march.

Upon arrival, the marchers chose a spot atop a hill overlooking the Arkansas River crowned with a mighty oak. From that vantage, they viewed the plains to the south and the east. A ceremonial scattering of the ashes on the ground surrounding the base of the chosen tree—the Council Oak Tree—followed. Through this ritual of continuity, the western council fire in Indian Territory burned from the embers of homeland fires in Alabama.[179]

Tulsa boasts other connections to Muscogee (Creek) history in general, and to the prominent Perryman family in particular. Tulsa's celebrated Brookside neighborhood acknowledges its Perryman roots:

> [The] Brookside area began as a part of the Creek Indian land just south of Tulsa. This land was granted to the Creek Nation in 1824.

They were removed from Alabama to Indian Territory in about 1836. The name for Tulsa is said to be derived from the Creek language and was called Tulsey Town. The mixed[-]blood Creek Nation Perryman family was one of the first families to settle in this area and operated the first post office in 1882 at the home of George Perryman near what is now 41st & Trenton. (A marker stands at this site today.)[180]

On September 6, 1887, tribal citizens elected Legus C. Perryman Principal Chief of the Muscogee (Creek) Nation.[181] During the federal allotment enrollment process, Dawes agents assigned Legus C. roll number 910. Despite his mixed ancestry, the agents listed him as a Creek full-blood on the Blood Roll. Once again, such was the arbitrary and capricious nature of the Dawes enrollment process, particularly on matters of "race."[182]

Progeny of the "mixed-blood Creek Nation Perryman family" still reside in Tulsa.[183] In fact, longtime Tulsa resident Monetta Trepp, a "by blood" Muscogee (Creek), is the great-great-granddaughter of Lewis Perryman, widely considered a Tulsa founding father. Her grandfather, Moses S. Perryman, was the son of George Beecher Perryman, Lewis's son. Lewis arrived from Alabama in the Creek Nation in 1828. He and his offspring figured prominently in Tulsa history as landowners, ranchers, and merchants.

> Creek law allowed him as much land as he could use and when the Dawes Commission broke the common Indian lands into one hundred sixty acre allotments, there were enough Perrymans by that time to keep a good share of the family's holdings together. For some years the Perryman ranch remained as the only vestige of the huge cattle operations that the mixed-bloods ran in the Creek Nation during the [18]70s and [18]80s.[184]

Today Monetta Trepp owns the historic Perryman Wrangler Ranch, which sits on part of Moses's original allotment. Located in the town of Jenks, just outside Tulsa, the Perryman Ranch was the first ranch established in the Tulsa area prior to Oklahoma statehood in 1907. Of the original 250,000 acres operated by the Perryman family, 200 acres remain with the family.

Trepp does not like the way the Freedmen issue has played out, particularly in the Cherokee Nation. She thinks it unfair to deny citizenship to the Freedmen in light of the Treaty of 1866. Trepp cites

218   Apartheid in Indian Country?

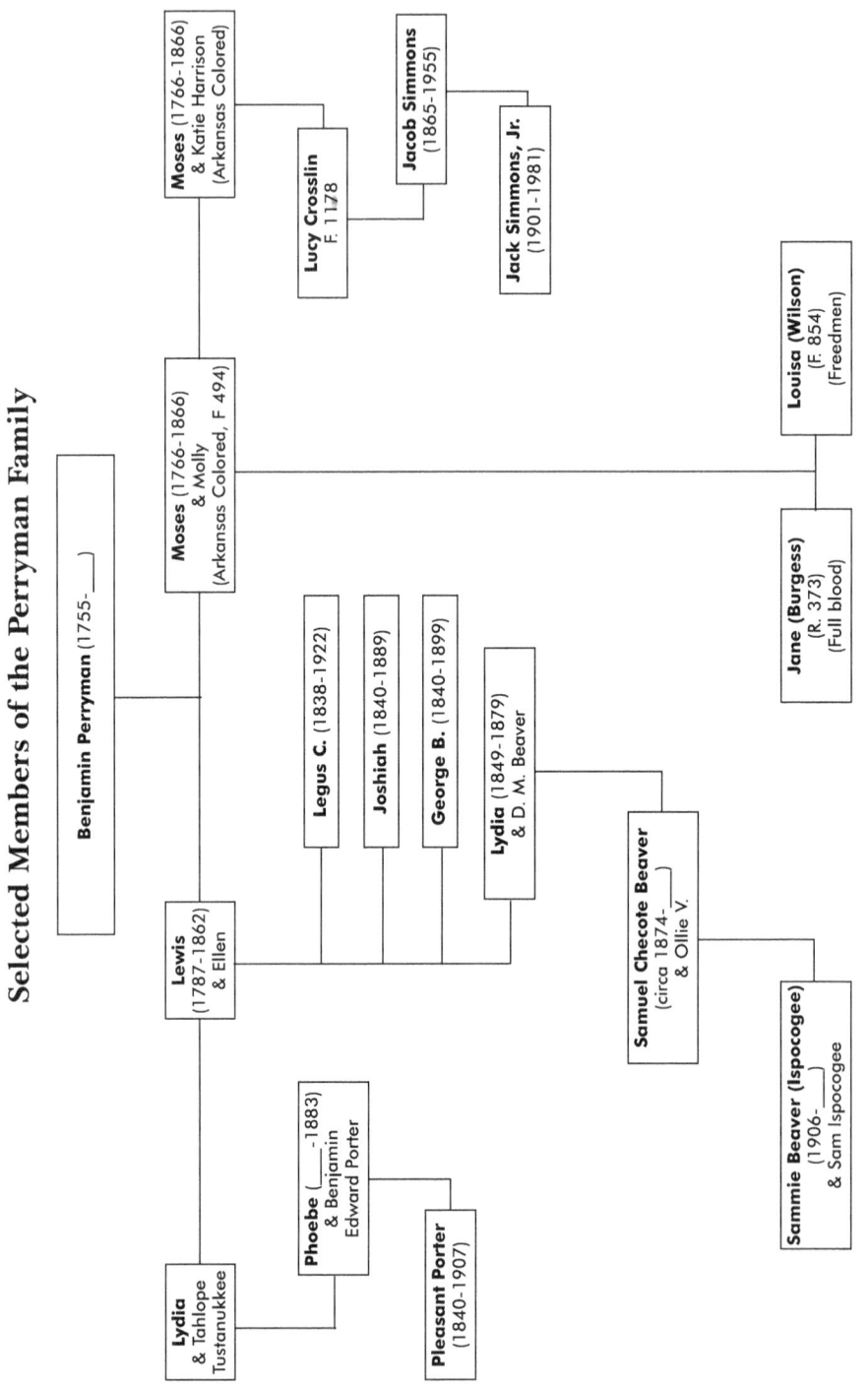

Selected Members of the Perryman Family

- Benjamin Perryman (1755-)
  - Moses (1766-1866) & Katie Harrison (Arkansas Colored)
    - Lucy Crosslin (F. 1178)
    - Jacob Simmons (1865-1955)
      - Jack Simmons, Jr. (1901-1981)
  - Moses (1766-1866) & Molly (Arkansas Colored, F 494)
  - Lewis (1787-1862) & Ellen
    - Legus C. (1838-1922)
    - Joshiah (1840-1889)
    - George B. (1840-1899)
    - Lydia (1849-1879) & D. M. Beaver
      - Samuel Checote Beaver (circa 1874-) & Ollie V.
        - Sammie Beaver (Ispocogee) (1906-) & Sam Ispocogee
        - Jane (Burgess) (R. 373) (Full blood)
        - Louisa (Wilson) (F. 854) (Freedmen)
    - Lydia & Tahlope Tustanukkee
    - Phoebe (-1883) & Benjamin Edward Porter
      - Pleasant Porter (1840-1907)

F = listed on the Muscogee (Creek) National Freedmen Roll. R = listed on the Muscogee (Creek) Nation Blood Roll. The numbers listed correspond to the registrar's Dawes Roll card number.

Fighting for the Franchise 219

Perryman Family

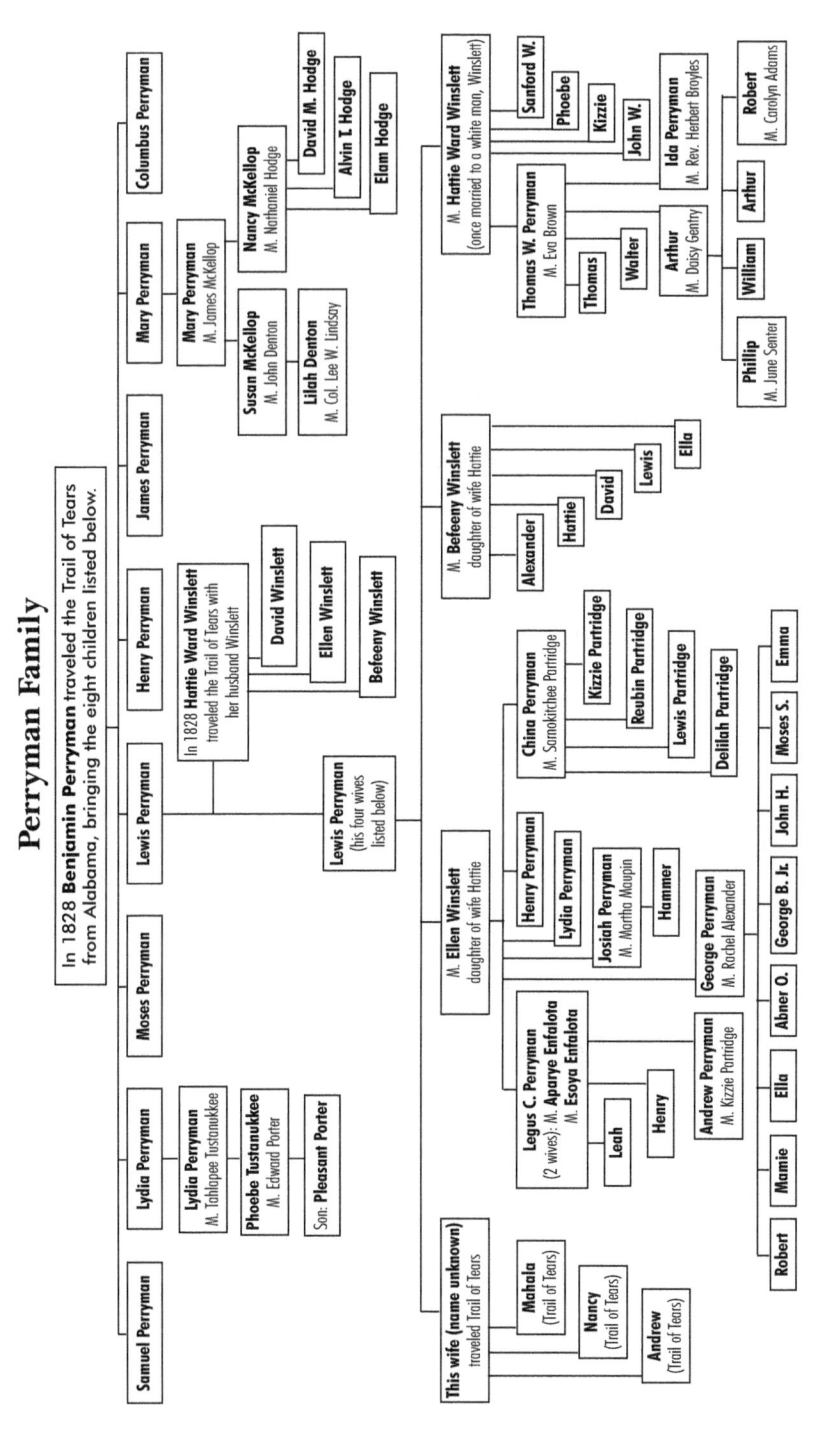

In 1828 **Benjamin Perryman** traveled the Trail of Tears from Alabama, bringing the eight children listed below.

- **Samuel Perryman**
- **Lydia Perryman**
  - **Lydia Perryman** M. Tahlopee Tustanukkee
  - **Phoebe Tustanukkee** M. Edward Porter
    - Son: **Pleasant Porter**
- **Moses Perryman**
- **Lewis Perryman** (his four wives listed below)
  - This wife (name unknown) traveled Trail of Tears
    - Mahala (Trail of Tears)
    - Nancy (Trail of Tears)
    - Andrew (Trail of Tears)
  - M. Ellen Winslett daughter of wife Hattie
    - **Legus C. Perryman** (2 wives); M. Aparye Enfalota; M. Esoya Enfalota
      - Leah
      - Henry
    - **Henry Perryman**
    - **Lydia Perryman**
    - **Josiah Perryman** M. Martha Moupin
      - Hammer
    - **George Perryman** M. Rachel Alexander
    - **Andrew Perryman** M. Kizzie Partridge
      - Robert
      - Mamie
      - Ella
      - Abner O.
      - George B. Jr.
      - John H.
      - Moses S.
      - Emma
    - **China Perryman** M. Somokitchee Partridge
      - Kizzie Partridge
      - Reubin Partridge
      - Lewis Partridge
      - Delilah Partridge
  - M. Befeeny Winslett daughter of wife Hattie
    - Alexander
    - Hattie
    - David
    - Lewis
    - Ella
  - M. Hattie Ward Winslett (once married to a white man, Winslett)
    - **Thomas W. Perryman** M. Eva Brown
      - Thomas
      - Walter
      - Arthur M. Daisy Gentry
        - Phillip M. June Senter
        - William
        - Arthur
      - Sanford W.
      - Phoebe
      - Kizzie
      - John W.
    - **Ida Perryman** M. Rev. Herbert Broyles
      - Robert M. Carolyn Adams
- **Henry Perryman**
  - In 1828 **Hattie Ward Winslett** traveled the Trail of Tears with her husband Winslett
    - David Winslett
    - Ellen Winslett
    - Befeeny Winslett
- **James Perryman**
- **Mary Perryman**
  - **Mary Perryman** M. James McKellop
    - **Nancy McKellop** M. Nathaniel Hodge
      - David M. Hodge
      - Alvin T. Hodge
      - Elam Hodge
    - **Susan McKellop** M. John Denton
    - **Lilah Denton** M. Col. Lee W. Lindsay
- **Columbus Perryman**

Source: Nina Lane Dunn, *Tulsa's Magic Roots* (Tulsa, OK: N.L.D. Corp. 1979), 53.

the sacrifices made by the Freedmen who accompanied the Five Civilized Tribes during their forced westward migrations as warrant for their inclusion.[185]

The notion of African inclusion on various tribal rosters is nothing new within the Muscogee (Creek) Nation. Between 1866 and 1906, the Muscogee (Creek) Nation created numerous citizen rolls. All of them included persons of African ancestry. Moreover, during that same period, persons of African ancestry participated fully in the political, economic, educational, social, and cultural life of the Muscogee (Creek) Nation.

After the signing of the Treaty of 1866, Muscogee (Creek) citizens lived in relative calm as a nation until the allotment era of 1898-1906. Persons of African descent played an integral role in the Muscogee (Creek) Nation, serving in pivotal and prominent positions throughout.

This relative peace within the Muscogee (Creek) Nation for persons of African descent was, in some respects, remarkable. Such tranquility could not be found generally in the United States during this period, the heyday of "Black Codes," lynchings, other forms of domestic terrorism, and the dawn of nationwide "race riots."

The 1894 United States Department of Interior census bulletin characterized the Muscogee (Creek) Nation as a place "alert and active . . . largely due to the [N]egro element which fairly controls it[,]" and a place that "affords the best example of [N]egro progress." The bulletin continued: "The principal chief, virtually a Negro, comes of a famous family in [Muscogee (Creek)] annals. His name is Lequest Choteau Perryman."[186]

The Curtis Act[187] in 1898 shattered the relative harmony within which the diverse and intermarried members of the Muscogee (Creek) Nation had lived during the nineteenth century. The Curtis Act facilitated the destruction of the tribal government and the disintegration of common lands through the application of the allotment procedure developed by the Dawes Commission.

The allotment system wiped out communal land ownership. In its stead, the federal government parceled out 160-acre individual plots to each Muscogee (Creek) citizen. Congress empowered the Dawes Commission[188] to find, identify, and enroll all members of the Muscogee (Creek) Nation who were eligible for an allotment.

Pleasant Porter (Creek name, Talof Harjo), Principal Chief of the Muscogee (Creek) Nation from 1899 to 1907, presided over the dissolution of the tribe. By most accounts, Porter, the grandson of Lydia Perryman, performed this solemn task admirably. His name appears on allotment documents in and around Tulsa, which sits in the heart of the Muscogee (Creek) Nation.

Principal Chief Porter earned the confidence of his people through a mix of military and public service. During the Civil War, Porter rode with the 1st Creek Mounted Volunteers, a Confederate unit. In 1870, he served as Superintendent of Schools in the Muscogee (Creek) Nation. By 1883, Porter had become a commander of the Creek Light Horsemen, tribal law enforcement officers. Throughout his life, he relished the role of statesmen, often acting as the Muscogee (Creek) delegate to the United States Congress.

Pleasant Porter presided over the Sequoyah Statehood Convention in 1905 as its president. That Convention culminated in a failed attempt to persuade the federal government to grant statehood to Indian Territory—to carve out a "red state" much like African Americans had lobbied for a "black state" years earlier.

Porter was a Presbyterian and thirty-third degree Mason. Toward the end of his life, he and his business partners chartered the Indian Central Railway, a line that would run from Ponca City to Muskogee to McAlester. However, this 1906 venture never came to fruition. On September 3, 1907, while in Vinita, Pleasant Porter, the Muscogee (Creek) leader and facilitator of the government-imposed allotment process, suffered a stroke and died.[189]

Again, as was the case with the Cherokees, the Dawes Commission, the body charged with executing tribal dissolution through the allotment process, created two lists of tribal members eligible for allotment: (1) the "Creek Roll," purportedly composed of Muscogee (Creek) citizens with Muscogee (Creek) blood; and (2) the "Freedmen Roll," ostensibly a roll of those citizens who were formerly enslaved Africans and devoid of any Muscogee (Creek) blood. The mere compilation of the Muscogee (Creek) Freedmen Roll sparked controversy.

Among the Muscogee (Creeks), opposition to Freedmen citizenship mounted after the Civil War. With authority conferred by the Treaty of 1866, the federal government held fast on the issue of Freedmen enrollment. Tribal officials and the Dawes Commission locked horns.

Beyond the foundational issue of Freedmen acceptance, tribal leaders feared an influx of opportunists who were not Muscogee (Creek) Freedmen, but rather "State Negroes"—persons of African descent with no Native-American ties. "State Negroes" consisted principally of "Negroes" who migrated to Indian Territory from the South in search of economic uplift and political rights. The identity of the formerly enslaved Africans among the tribe became a bone of contention.

In 1867, a Muscogee (Creek) agent at Fort Gibson, J. W. Dunn, prepared a roll (the "Dunn Roll") of 1,774 persons of African ancestry whom he believed to be entitled to citizenship. Dunn arranged his compilation by tribal town. He further divided the tribal towns by family groups. The Dunn Roll, certified by Dunn and acknowledged by the Freedmen in June of 1869, is a receipt roll for a per capita payment of $17.34 made under Article 3 of the Treaty of 1866 for ceded lands in Alabama.[190]

Tribal officials contended many names on the Dunn Roll were late returnees, and thus ineligible for citizenship. Others, they felt, were "State Negroes."

Muscogee (Creek) full-bloods charged that officials of the three "colored towns"—Arkansas Colored, Canadian Colored, and North Fork—regularly colluded to include on the citizenship rolls the names of ineligible people of African ancestry. On August 4, 1896, federal officials asked the Muscogee (Creek) National Council to establish a Special Census Commission to make a census of the "colored citizens."

Chief Justice T. J. Adams of the Muscogee (Creek) Supreme Court decided the matter on August 5, 1896. He held, essentially, that while the Muscogee (Creek) National Council could *recognize* any person entitled to citizenship, it had no power to *grant* citizenship. Justice Adams reasoned that a grant of citizenship would vest a person with property rights at the expense of existing citizens.

Justice Adams' decision, if upheld, would have struck almost three thousand Freedmen from the rolls. The Freedmen fought it successfully.

The Commissioner of Indian Affairs sent the Dawes Commission a copy of the Dunn Roll on May 2, 1899. The Dawes Commission used the Dunn Roll as its basis for determining eligibility.[191]

In 1896, during the era of the Dawes Commission, the rule of hypodescent[192]—the prevailing public policy—applied. As previously indicated, an individual with even a scintilla of "black blood" would officially be classified as "black, "Negro," or "colored." For example, an individual with 7/8 "Indian blood" and 1/8 "black blood" would automatically be categorized as "black" for purposes of racially restrictive and oppressive social and legal determinations.[193]

Even assuming the necessity and appropriateness of these blood quantum determinations, it is important to recall why the Dawes Commission did what it did. The stated purpose of the Dawes Commission's blood degree determination was not to determine the "Indianness" of an individual registrant. Rather, the Dawes Commission used blood degree to determine whether an enrollee would be allowed to sell his/her allotment of land. Blood quantum related to land allotment decisions, not citizenship determinations.

As with the Cherokees, the Dawes Commission enrolled Muscogee (Creek)s of African descent, particularly those of darker hues, on the Freedmen Roll, irrespective of enslavement ancestry or the presence of Muscogee (Creek) blood. Moreover, Dawes agents arbitrarily transferred individuals from the Muscogee (Creek) Roll to the Freedmen Roll during the enrollment process. Dawes Commission expert Ken Carter notes that "in cases of mixed Freedmen and Indian parents, which was common among the [Muscogee (Creek)] . . . the applicant was always enrolled as a 'Freedmen.'"[194]

The Dawes Commission separated families. It enrolled full siblings and gave them different blood degree values. It enrolled members of a single family on different rolls.

In 1979, the Muscogee (Creek) Nation adopted its current Constitution. The Constitution provides that "[p]ersons eligible for citizenship in the Muscogee (Creek) Nation shall consist of Muscogee (Creek) Indians by blood whose names appear on the final rolls . . . and persons who are lineal descendants of those Muscogee (Creek) Indians by blood whose names appear on the final rolls. . . ."[195]

Soon after the adoption of that Constitution, the Muscogee (Creek) Nation National Council enacted the Nation's first Citizenship Code under the new Constitution. The 1981 Muscogee (Creek) Nation Citizenship Code remained substantially the same for almost twenty years.

Under the Muscogee (Creek) Nation Citizenship Code, persons who had a direct lineal ancestor on the Freedman Roll prepared pursuant to the Act of April 26, 1906, were eligible for citizenship in the Muscogee (Creek) Nation. The Citizenship Code allowed such individuals to show an ancestor with Muscogee (Creek) Indian blood using numerous pre-1906 Muscogee (Creek) Nation rolls, request a hearing on the matter, and appeal an adverse citizenship determination.

In August of 2001, the Muscogee (Creek) Nation enacted a new rule, NCA 01-135. The rule effectively disenfranchised the Freedmen—even those who could prove an Indian blood connection to the tribe through documentation beyond the Dawes Blood Roll. The Dawes Blood Roll became the sole touchstone for Muscogee (Creek) Indian citizenship. The Muscogee (Creek) Nation amended this rule in May of 2002 with the enactment of NCA 02-078, which was intended as a correction to the prior rule. The new rule, a proverbial nail in the coffin, fully and finally disenfranchised persons of African ancestry.

The hurdles to Freedmen citizenship erected by the Muscogee (Creek) Nation with respect to those of African ancestry among them parallel those extant in the Seminole Nation years before and the Cherokee Nation currently. The legal posture of the Seminole Freedmen, in particular, provides strong precedent for ensuring the citizenship rights of Muscogee (Creek) Freedmen in that: (i) the Seminole Treaty of 1866 and the Muscogee (Creek) Treaty of 1866 contain identical language and meaning as regards the citizenship rights of Freedmen; and (ii) Freedmen citizenship rights pursuant to the Seminole Treaty of 1866 have not been abrogated, according to the Department of the Interior and the federal courts.

Two sovereign governments signed the Muscogee (Creek) Treaty of 1866 on April 14, 1866. Both the Muscogee (Creek) Nation and the United States of America recognized and relied upon this solemn commitment. So, too, did the Freedmen. Congress has yet to abrogate the Treaty, and has given no indication of an inclination to do so in the future. Thus it would seem the citizenship rights of those protected by Article II of the Treaty remain valid and protected by the supreme law of the land, the Constitution of the United States of America.

As with the Cherokee Nation, The Muscogee (Creek) Nation's efforts to separate out its Freedmen trace back to the race-based conduct of the Dawes Commission. People of mixed African and Muscogee (Creek) descent still struggle to prove they belong and that they, too, are entitled to the basic benefits of citizenship.

To many observers, it appears the leadership of the Muscogee (Creek) Nation has chosen to rely upon a biased enrollment process to make decisions affecting the core of peoples' lives—who they are and where they belong. Indeed, some in the leadership of the Muscogee (Creek) Nation proclaim the Freedmen possess no Muscogee (Creek) blood.[196] Such assertions fly in the face of historic Muscogee (Creek) documents, United States history, and legal and scholarly research.

Recall Cow Tom, the celebrated Freedmen who served as an interpreter, translator, and ambassador for the Muscogee (Creek) Nation in the Civil War era. Cow Tom's great-great-great-grandson, Damario Solomon-Simmons, is a Tulsa lawyer. He represented the Freedmen in litigation against the Muscogee (Creek) Nation over citizenship rights. Solomon-Simmons emphasized the illogic inherent in the not-infrequent Dawes Commission practice of dividing family members by assigning some to the Freedmen Roll while placing others on the Blood Roll, simply based on overt physical characteristics.

Important trials for membership in the Muscogee (Creek) Nation on behalf of Freedmen Ron Graham and Fred Johnson wrapped up in September 2005. The cases posed a key issue: whether descendants of Muscogee (Creek) citizens whom the Dawes Commission enrolled as Freedmen may qualify for membership in the Nation as "Muscogee (Creek) by blood" through evidence of blood quantum from sources other than the Dawes Rolls.[197]

Ron Graham, an African American of Muscogee (Creek) descent, appealed in 2007 to the Muscogee (Creek) Nation tribal court from a decision by the Muscogee (Creek) Nation Citizenship Board (the Citizenship Board) denying him citizenship. His claims rested on the alleged deprivation of: (i) the right to equal protection under the Muscogee (Creek) Constitution or the Indian Civil Rights Act of 1968, or both; (ii) the right to due process under the Muscogee (Creek) Constitution or the Indian Civil Rights Act of 1968, or both; and/or (iii) the right to citizenship under the Muscogee (Creek) Treaty of 1866.

Graham based his contention for citizenship eligibility on the Treaty of 1866, the Muscogee (Creek) Nation Constitution, and the Muscogee (Creek) Nation Citizenship Code as it existed prior to the amendments added in 2001 and 2002. He argued that the amendments to the Citizenship Code in 2001 and 2002 were unconstitutional and, as such, void *ab initio* (from the beginning).[198]

Graham's Muscogee (Creek) ancestry seems unmistakable. A look at his family history aids in understanding his posture within the Muscogee (Creek) Nation. It also reveals the inconsistencies and errors plaguing a blood-based citizenship requirement dependent upon the Dawes Rolls. What emerges from the Graham saga is a tale told in black and red.

Graham's parents instilled a powerful dose of Native pride. From as far back as he can remember, Graham recalls hearing about his Indian roots—roots embedded, on his father's side, in the Muscogee (Creek) Nation. Graham grew up considering himself both Native American and African American.

Graham's father, Theodore "Blue" Graham, an original Dawes enrollee pursuant to a 1906 law, spoke the tribal language fluently, participated as a ceremonial grounds leader at Arbeka Stomp Grounds, and participated in the Muscogee (Creek) Nation as a full citizen. Hardly a pretender or "wannabe," Blue immersed himself in Muscogee (Creek) culture.

Growing up, Graham believed himself to be a tribal citizen. He reasoned that since his father and other paternal ancestors held citizenship status within the Muscogee (Creek) Nation, he, too, was automatically a citizen. From observation and experience, Graham learned to turn to the Bureau of Indian Affairs office in Muskogee, Oklahoma, for assistance with citizenship matters such as identification cards. After all, when Muscogee (Creek) Nation citizens such as his father needed help on those fronts, they turned to the Muskogee BIA.

Graham's father died in 1979. That death spurred Graham to seek to reconnect with his father's heritage and begin family research in an effort to reclaim his own Indian heritage.

In 1983, Graham embarked upon his journey to become an official member of the Muscogee (Creek) Nation. He traveled to the Nation's headquarters in Okmulgee, Oklahoma. Upon arrival, he inquired about the application procedure for citizenship. Staff directed him to the Okmulgee BIA office.

Upon his attempt to enroll, officials informed Graham that he needed a direct lineal ancestor who was enrolled as a Muscogee (Creek) on the Dawes Roll. Graham confidently gave the name of his father, whom he knew to be an original Dawes enrollee.

Subsequently, BIA staff informed Graham that he was a Freedmen descendant. As such, he could not be considered for

Muscogee (Creek) citizenship. According to these officials, Freedmen, former slaves of the Muscogee (Creek) Nation, did not possess any "real Indian blood."

Graham left abruptly. Dejected and humiliated, he returned home.

In 1984, Graham began researching his family history. He located his father's Dawes enrollment card and other documents. He then returned to the BIA office in Okmulgee and presented his documentation. Again, staff informed Graham that his father appeared on the Freedmen Roll, and therefore lacked the requisite Muscogee (Creek) blood.

In 1986, Graham attempted to enroll into the Muscogee (Creek) Nation yet again. This time, staff informed him for the first time that enrollment in the Muscogee (Creek) Nation required he prove his lineal ancestor had a "blood degree." Encouraged by this nuanced response, Graham pressed on.

In the summer of 1987, Graham learned of a significant enrollment in the Muscogee (Creek) Nation, that of his paternal first cousin, Elmer Payne. Payne held a Muscogee (Creek) card bearing the number 37604, issued by the Okmulgee BIA office. Payne's enrollment card listed his blood degree as one-eighth (1/8). He enrolled through his mother, Sissy Graham, the full sister of Ron Graham's father.

Perplexed, Ron Graham went to the BIA and asked how his first cousin, Elmer Payne, could successfully enroll in the Muscogee (Creek) Nation when he could not. After all, he explained, both were direct blood relatives of an Indian-by-blood, Sissy Graham—Elmer Payne, her son, and Ron Graham, her nephew (the son of her brother).

Despite this evidence, the BIA rebuffed Graham's complaint, asserting that Graham would not be eligible for citizenship unless he could show an official blood quantum of Muscogee (Creek) Indian blood from his father.

In 1991, Graham made yet another pilgrimage to the BIA. For the fifth time, he attempted to enroll as a citizen of the Muscogee (Creek) Nation. He completed the requisite application. He never got a response.

In 1993, Graham located documents showing blood quantum levels for members of his paternal family, including: (i) a document showing his paternal great-grandfather, Joe Hutton, was at least one-fourth Native American; and (ii) a Proof of Death & Heirship document prepared by the superintendent for the Five Civilized Tribes for his paternal grandmother, Creasy Graham (the daughter of Joe Hutton), that listed his father's degree of Muscogee (Creek) Blood as one-eighth.

As a result of the newly discovered information, Graham wrote BIA Superintendent for the Okmulgee Field Office Jimmy Gibson in 1993. He requested a meeting to share additional information about his lineage and further his quest for citizenship in the Muscogee (Creek) Nation.

On July 17, 1994, Graham met with Gibson. He filled out what he believed to be a citizenship application given to him by BIA staff. Gibson told Graham he would investigate the matter.

Graham received a letter dated March 17, 1995, from Gibson stating that the application submitted on July 17, 1995, together with all related documents, would be duly processed by the Muscogee (Creek) Nation. Graham received a subsequent letter, dated March 19, 1995, from the Muscogee (Creek) Nation's Citizenship Board. That correspondence notified Graham that his application had been rejected because he did not demonstrate that he had an ancestor on the Muscogee (Creek) Roll.

In 1996, Graham made yet another pilgrimage to the Okmulgee office of the BIA, seeking to enroll. Staff informed him the BIA would no longer issue enrollment cards, and he would have to obtain a citizenship application from the Muscogee (Creek) Nation Citizenship Office. Graham pursued the matter further, only to be told, as a Freedmen descendant, that citizenship would not be possible.

In 1998, Graham morphed into a professional genealogist, specializing in persons of African–Native American descent. Having researched numerous cases like his own, he began to understand some of the more curious aspects of the Dawes Commission enrollment process. He collected dozens of documented cases, including those where: (i) Muscogee (Creek) citizens with listed blood degrees who were transferred to the Freedmen Roll, which Roll did not list blood degrees; (ii) full brothers and sisters whom Dawes agents enrolled with different blood quanta; (iii) entire families split up by Dawes agents, with some enrolled on the "Creek Roll" and others on the "Freedmen Roll"; (iv) the routine enrollment of registrants by Dawes agents who relied on the rule of hypodescent; and (v) the frequent enrollment of persons under names other than their given names.

In 1998, Graham again filed a citizenship application with the Muscogee (Creek) Nation Citizenship Board. He never received a response. Again in 2001, Graham filed another citizenship application, and again rejection followed.

In 2002, Graham submitted a final, complete, formal application for citizenship to the Muscogee (Creek) Nation Citizenship Office. In his effort to prove eligibility for citizenship, Graham offered the following documented facts: (i) his father, Theodore (Blue) Graham, was listed on the final rolls of the Muscogee (Creek) Nation pursuant to the Act of April 26, 1906, as Muscogee (Creek) Freedmen New Born #671; and (ii) the Proof of Death & Heirship document prepared by the Office of the Superintendent for the Five Civilized Tribes for his grandmother, Creasy Graham, identified his father as one-eighth Muscogee (Creek).

The Muscogee (Creek) Nation Citizenship Board denied Graham's application in a letter dated August 12, 2003. That body reasoned that Graham's lineal ancestor with documented Muscogee (Creek) Indian blood appeared on the Freedman Roll. The appearance of that solitary ancestor on the Freedmen Roll negated his claim to "by blood" status.

In his application, Graham also laid claim to Muscogee (Creek) ancestry on his maternal side. He learned that his great-great grandmother, Rose McGilbray, was a full-blood Muscogee (Creek) citizen, listed on Roll #673, who was fluent only in the tribal language. McGilbrary and Graham's great-great-great-grandmother, Hoktee, Roll #667, were murdered on the same day, soon after receiving land allotments. His great-grandmother, Rachael Corbray, the daughter of Rose McGilbray, was enrolled on the Freedmen Roll erroneously. Graham listed his great-great-grandmother, Rose McGilbray.

On January 10, 2003, Graham received a letter from the Citizenship Office explaining the rejection of his application for citizenship. The letter also explained his right to appeal the decision. Graham did appeal, but again he was unsuccessful. He is now Founder and President of the Muscogee Creek Indian Freedmen Band and a sought-after genealogist on Freedmen lineage.[199]

Unlike Graham, Eli Grayson has Indian authenticated, direct ancestors on the Muscogee (Creek) Nation "Blood Roll"—eight of them, the closest being his grandmother, Fannie (Nero) Grayson. Fannie Nero married Eli Grayson, Eli's father's father. Others in the

Grayson line include Mary Sarwanoge ("Sarwanoge" means "Shawnee"), Mary's mother, Fannie Sarwanoge, and Fannie's father, the famous Muscogee (Creek) medicine man, Jackson Lewis. With this pedigree, Eli Grayson avoids the hurdles that litter the paths of persons of African ancestry listed solely on the Freedmen Roll.

Grayson, President of the California Muscogee (Creek) Association (the CMCA), considers himself mixed-race. The CMCA works to preserve Muscogee (Creek) history, tradition, and culture. The diverse group draws about 1,000 members to special events and some 200 for regular business meetings. Grayson, at the helm of CMCA since 2003, pushed the group to support Freedmen rights. After a spate of initial reluctance, the group now boasts Freedmen representation on its board and roundly embraces the Freedmen's fight for citizenship.[200]

Eli Grayson descends from a slave-holding family. Yet Grayson unabashedly supports Ron Graham and the other Freedmen. "It's not about Indian blood. They [the enslaved Africans] were being purchased 200 years ago by Creeks and Choctaws who sided with the Confederate states. And they lost."[201] Other African Indians are likewise supportive of the Freedmen.

Vanessa Adams-Harris, an enrolled Muscogee (Creek) of African ancestry, has come to realize the broader significance of the Freedmen citizenship controversy. Her views on the matter have evolved.

> At first I was confused because I could not understand why the Freedmen wanted to lay claim to being "Indian" if they did not have direct blood lineage, and it appeared as though the Indians were saying, "You're not Indian." At least that was what I was hearing. But I came to understand that it was not about being Indian for the Freedmen but about being included into a group which had a history of inclusivity for African Americans. These two cultures once accepted one another—they were part of one another's existence—but they were divided by a political system, a Eurocentric viewpoint of divide and conquer. Native Americans were interfered with by European explorers. Africans were interfered with by slave-traders, Europeans. Neither indigenous group had reason to be hostile toward the other on these North American shores, because they realized that both groups were indeed marginalized and enslaved by this European culture.
>
> Only small groups within the Five Civilized Tribes want to hold

on to a Eurocentric worldview which keeps the Freedmen on the outside of the tribe. There was a time when, if these two groups of indigenous people had come together, they would have posed a threat to the "natural" order of things. And this still holds true today. And maybe that speaks to the politicization of what it means to "be Indian" today. In reality, being Indian has nothing to do with keeping the Freedmen out. The Freedmen without blood ties are not saying, "We want to be Indian." They are saying, "We are a part of this tribe/culture, our ancestors were very much so a part of this tribe/culture and we want to honor their inclusivity of the tribe and culture, we want to remember their ways with the tribe/culture and by this acceptance we have not forgotten their commitment to tribal ways and acceptance of the others."
The impulse to exclude, then, runs counter to the Indian way. The Indian way is about the language, the culture, and the family and about respecting the culture and respecting those who honor and respect our culture. These Freedmen descendants, or at least many of them, have that respect for the Indian way, because it is very much like the African way. To deny the Freedmen only repeats the systemic cultural rejection foisted on Indians and Africans by Europeans. Why do we so often repeat the mistakes of the past—do unto others what has been done to us? Unless we break the cycle, we will never achieve reconciliation, and [we will] forever continue to fight our likenesses instead of seeing our inclusive natures.[202]

Other prominent Muscogee (Creek) citizens have also expressed concern over the plight of the Freedmen. Robert Trepp, an enrolled Muscogee (Creek) citizen, tribal activist, and sometime tribal consultant on governmental policy and research, offers unique insights into the Freedmen debate within the Muscogee (Creek) Nation. Robert Trepp is the son of Monetta Trepp, mentioned earlier, and a descendant of the prominent Muscogee (Creek) Perryman family.

According to Trepp, a number of tribe members think the Freedmen "sold out," literally, years ago. A number of enrolled Muscogee (Creek) citizens believe the Freedmen voted overwhelmingly for allotment, received their parcels, and then essentially abandoned the Muscogee (Creek) Nation for greener pastures. While the Freedmen overwhelmingly supported allotment, per Trepp, they played active roles in tribal politics and culture, even assumed leadership positions, both before and after the process of land division ended.

The political landscape at the time of allotment should be noted. Context is the key to understanding why those Freedmen who left Indian Territory after allotment may have done so.

The allotment period roughly parallels the dawn of Oklahoma statehood. A desire on the part of some Freedmen to "escape" from Oklahoma would seem to have been both rational and prudent, given Oklahoma's mimicry of the Old South in terms of her treatment of African Americans.

Trepp remains unclear as to the precise nature of the Freedmen conflict—whether it is based on political, social, or economic considerations—or some combination of the three. He readily admits, however, that the handling of the tribal enrollment process by the Dawes Commission poisoned the well with respect to the Freedmen.

Like so many others, Trepp asserts that the Dawes Commission process for assigning blood degrees left much to be desired. He cites the case of a Muscogee (Creek) family whose sons were enrolled as ¼ bloods while its daughters were enrolled as ¾ bloods. The sons thereby received unrestricted allotments. The daughters received restricted allotments on account of their high blood quantum and presumed disability. Recall that under white supremacist ideology, Indians were not fully civilized. The more Indian blood one possessed, the less civilized one was presumed to be. Moreover, under then-prevailing gender stereotypes, women were deemed less capable than men, and thus more in need of "protection."

For Trepp, the way forward on the Freedmen issue involves an approach that takes into consideration blood descent, but also looks to acculturation and physical proximity/presence in the Muscogee (Creek) Nation. His own cultural imprinting—a childhood rich with family oral histories, native traditions, and cultural functions—undoubtedly shaped his views on the matter.[203]

Ron Graham and Eli Grayson take a more definitive stance. Both men stressed that the denial of citizenship status for Freedmen and their descendents disregards: (i) the Muscogee (Creek) Nation Constitution, which protects the rights and privileges of all individual citizens of the Nation; and (ii) treaty rights and obligations, including those contained in the Treaty of 1866. "I don't have the right to determine Freedmen citizenship," Grayson insists. "That was decided by the Treaty of 1866, and the matter is closed."[204]

Like David Cornsilk of the Cherokee Nation, Eli Grayson contends that the Muscogee (Creek) Nation is a political entity, pure and simple. Race, he insists, is irrelevant, and the apparent movement toward "blood quantum" will be disastrous for the tribe. He holds that the Dawes Rolls should never have included blood quantum. There should have been a single roll of citizens.[205]

Grayson's own prominent Muscogee (Creek) family enslaved Africans, some of whom were blood relatives. He makes a strong moral case for Freedmen citizenship:

> I have to ask myself in the Indian way, in the native way[,] what's honorable about kicking out people who breast fed my grandmother and made their meals, and kept their farms and all of that? What's honorable about that? There's nothing honorable about that. That's what white people do. This is the same thing that Ross Barnett and George Wallace [did] in the 1960s.[206]

Arguably, safeguarding Freedmen citizenship protects the historical tribal interest of the Nation. Loyal Muscogee (Creek) Indians—including Ok-ta-has Harjo, Cow Mikko, and Cotch-chochee—stood firm in supporting Article II of the Treaty of 1866. Over the objections of Confederate-aligned Lower Creeks, they insisted it be included.

Daniel F. Littlefield, a leading authority on Native American history, noted:

> [T]the United States commission urged the loyal delegation to yield temporarily on the point [full citizenship for people of African descent within the Muscogee (Creek) Nation]. They [loyal delegation] refused: they held out firmly for their [F]reedmen, urging that when the brave old Opothleyoholo, resisting all the blandishments of the rebel emissaries, and of his Indian friends, stood out for the government, and led a large number of his people out of the country, fighting as they went, abandoning their hoes, they *promised* their slaves that if they would remain also faithful to the government they should be free as themselves. Under those circumstances the delegates declined to yield, but insisted that the sacred pledge should be fulfilled, declaring that they would sooner go home and fight and suffer again with their faithful friends than abandon the point.[207]

By rejecting its Treaty of 1866 obligations, the Muscogee (Creek) Nation may be jeopardizing other treaty rights and bilateral agreements (such as gambling compacts). Disavowing the Treaty of 1866 may signal to local, state, and federal officials that the Muscogee (Creek) Nation believes bilateral, negotiated provisions of any contract (or treaty) may be breached at the whim or convenience of the breaching party.

The Muscogee (Creek) Nation joins the Cherokee Nation and others among the Five Civilized Tribes in grappling with Freedmen citizenship issues. The controversy surrounding Freedmen tribal inclusion has come full circle in one of them, the Seminole Nation. The saga of the Seminole Freedmen offers important insights for the other tribes wrestling with what it means to be a citizen.

C. In the Seminole Nation

According to some, the word "Seminole," first applied to the tribe in about 1778, derives from the Muscogee (Creek) word "semino'le," meaning "runaway." The word signifies emigrants, and refers to those who left the main body to settle elsewhere. The Seminoles evolved from the Muscogee (Creek). The Seminole Nation is headquartered in Wewoka, Oklahoma.[208]

The Seminole Indians have maintained a close relationship with African Americans—perhaps closer than any of the members of the Five Civilized Tribes. Some Seminoles enslaved Africans, but other Africans lived among the Seminoles as free persons. Ties borne of bondage, blood, and belonging evolved.

> Frank Berry, living at 1614 [W]est Twenty-Second [S]treet, Jacksonville, Florida, claims to be a grandson of Osceola, last fighting chief of the Seminole tribe. Born in 1858 of a mother who was part of the human chattel belonging to one of the Hearnses of Alachua County in Florida, he served variously during his life as a State and Federal Government contractor, United States Marshal (1881), Registration Inspector (1879). Being only eight years of age when the Emancipation Proclamation was issued, he remembers little of his life as a slave. The master was kind in an impersonal way but made no provision for his [F]reedmen as did many other Southerners—usually in the form of land grants—although he gave them their freedom as soon as the proclamation was issued.[209]
>
> —Frank Berry, Seminole Freedmen
>   (from *Slave Narratives: A Folk History of Slavery in the United States*, Work Projects Administration, 1936)

Some authorities translate the word "Seminole" as "runaway," "separatist," or "pioneer."[210] Others, however, find that translation incomplete, if not misleading: "[T]he nucleus of the Seminole Nation was not merely a body of 'outcasts' as has been so often represented, but a distinct tribe, the Oconee, affiliated...with the Creeks, but always on the outer margin of the confederacy and to a considerable extent an independent body. . . ."[211] The Oconee occupied an area in Georgia along the Oconee River when encountered by late seventeenth-century European explorers.[212]

Bands of Muscogee (Creek) Indians from Georgia and Alabama migrated to Florida in the 1700s, because skirmishes with whites and other tribesmen had spurred a desire to seek a more peaceful abode.[213] Groups of Lower Creeks moved to Florida, some in an effort to get away from the dominance of Upper Creeks, and others in search of verdant fields in which to plant crops. Spain temporarily encouraged these migrations in order to help provide a buffer between Florida and the British colonies.

In addition to Muscogee (Creek), Seminoles included Yuchis, Yamasees, and a few aboriginal remnants. The Yamasee merit special mention. Encountered by early Spanish expeditions in a region they called "Guale"—the Georgia coast—the Yamasees belong to the Muskhogean linguistic family—the same family to which the Muscogee (Creek) belong. Many early observers noted the darker complexions of members of the Yamasee tribe vis-à-vis other Seminoles. Yamasees called their town chiefs "mico," just as their Muskhogean kin, the Muscogee (Creek), did.[214]

In the eighteenth century, explorers found the Yamasee living among various Native-American populations:

> In 1727 a tradition survived among the Cherokee that the Yamasee were formerly Cherokee driven out by the Tomahitans, i.e., the Yuchi. . . .
>
> In 1713 we are informed that the Chiaha who were then with the Creeks on Ocmulgee River, had had their homes formerly among the Yamasee.[215]

William Bartram, a naturalist, traveled through the American Southeast in the mid-to-late eighteenth century. Bartram chronicled both the natural and the native history of the region, examining flora and fauna and conducting detailed analyses of the Native

Americans who inhabited the area. Bartram took note of the enslaved Yamasees he encountered among the Muscogee (Creek).[216] Earlier in the century, the Yamasee War (1715) was fought, in part, over the enslavement of Indians by English traders.[217]

The population of Seminoles increased as Africans who escaped American chattel slavery found refuge in the tribal bosom. The Seminoles practiced slavery on a limited basis. By most accounts, slavery among the Seminoles lacked much of the cruelty associated with traditional American chattel slavery.

The Seminoles lived under Muscogee (Creek) law until the two tribes executed a treaty in 1856. That treaty established the Seminole Nation as a separate and distinct Indian nation.[218]

African Seminoles, in the Seminole language, became known either as "Maroons" or "Estelusti." The Seminoles designated as "Maroons" those free Africans or African fugitives who had lived among them. These Maroons, who were substantially acculturated, wore native turbans, tunics, and moccasins, and participated in battle alongside the Seminole. "Estelusti," by contrast, referred to new escapees from the bonds of slavery,[219] and now also refers to Freedmen generally, irrespective of tribal affiliation. For example, The Estelusti Foundation works to preserve Indian Territory Freedmen history.[220]

The Seminoles proved fierce in battle and resolute in spirit, resisting outside incursions by white settlers, which became more frequent by the turn of the nineteenth century. These unwelcome guests lusted after Indian lands and coveted the human chattel they once controlled.

In 1817, Seminole conflicts with white immigrants escalated into the first of three wars against the United States. Future United States President Andrew Jackson invaded then-Spanish Florida. Jackson vanquished the Seminoles, and Florida, ancestral homeland of the Seminoles, became a United States territory in 1821. In 1823, the Seminoles ceded lands in Florida to the United States.

After passage of the Indian Removal Act in 1830, the federal government attempted to relocate the Seminoles to Oklahoma. This precipitated yet another deadly conflict, the Second Seminole War. The Seminole defeated United States forces in early battles of the Second Seminole War, but federal troops captured Seminole leader Osceola on October 20, 1837. The troops used peace treaty talks as a ruse to ensnare the fabled chief, and the battle-weary Seminoles became the last of the southeastern tribes removed to Indian Territory.

By May 8, 1858, when the United States declared an end to hostilities in a Third Seminole War, more than 3,000 Seminoles had been moved west of the Mississippi River. Some 200 to 300 Seminoles remained in Florida, many of them hiding in the dense swamps.

After the Civil War, the Seminoles, too, came to terms with the federal government on the issue of the rights of the Africans living among them. Ace federal interpreters Cow Tom and Harry Island, together with Robert Johnson, all Freedmen, helped negotiate and are signatories to the Treaty of 1866 with the Seminoles. That pact provides, in pertinent part:

> ARTICLE 2. The Seminole Nation covenant[s] that henceforth in said nation slavery shall not exist, nor involuntary servitude, except for and in punishment of crime, whereof the offending party shall first have been duly convicted in accordance with law, applicable to all the members of said nation. And inasmuch as there are among the Seminoles many persons of African descent and blood, who have no interest or property in the soil, and no recognized civil rights[,] it is stipulated that hereafter these persons and their descendants, and such other of the same race as shall be permitted by said nation to settle there, shall have and enjoy all the rights of native citizens, and the laws of said nation shall be equally binding upon all persons of whatever race or color, who may be adopted as citizens or members of said tribe.[221]

Decades later, in 1906, the Dawes Commission created two authoritative membership rolls for the Seminole Nation. As it had with the Cherokee and the Muscogee (Creek) tribes, the Dawes Commission created a segregated registry for black tribal members. Agents enrolled black Seminoles on a separate "Freedmen Roll," and non-black Seminoles on the "Seminole Blood Roll." Again, as with other members of the Five Civilized Tribes, this duality in registrations would come back to torment those who landed on the Freedmen Roll and haunt the Seminole Nation as a whole.[222]

In 1950 and 1951, the Seminole Nation and the Seminoles still residing in Florida filed separate claims with the Indian Claims Commission seeking compensation for tribal lands in Florida ceded to the United States in 1823. Twenty-six years later, the Indian

Claims Commission ruled in favor of the Seminoles and awarded a $16 million judgment to "the Seminole Nation as it existed in Florida on September 18, 1823."[223] With interest, the judgment funds totaled approximately $56 million (the "Judgment Fund Award").

In 1990, Congress passed legislation that set forth criteria for the use and distribution of the Judgment Fund Award.[224] Although a report prepared by the BIA had recommended excluding the Freedmen from participating in the Judgment Fund Award,[225] the Congressional legislation specifically allocated approximately seventy-five percent of the Judgment Fund Award to the "Seminole Nation of Oklahoma,"[226] and authorized the tribe to prepare a distribution plan for the portion of the Judgment Fund Award allocated to it.[227] The Congressional reference to the "Seminole Nation of Oklahoma" deliberately sidestepped the issue of Freedmen status.

A tribal legislative body established by the Seminole Nation General Council prepared the distribution plan ("the Usage Plan"), which was narrowly approved by the Seminole Nation General Council, and then submitted to Congress. The Usage Plan became effective on May 15, 1991.[228]

After Congress accepted the Usage Plan, the Seminole Nation General Council established programs to be funded by the Judgment Fund Award, called the "Judgment Fund Programs." Tribal resolutions authorizing each Judgment Fund Program contained eligibility requirements for participation linked to an applicant's ability to trace his/her ancestry back to the Seminole Nation as it existed in 1823.

Seminoles determine heritage matrilineally (i.e., through the mother's bloodlines). An individual with an African mother and an Indian-by-blood father would not be considered Seminole; rather he/she would wind up on the Freedmen Roll with no listing of blood degree—presumptively, "non-Indian." Authorities often interposed this rule of *partus sequitur ventrem*, a Latin phrase meaning, literally, "that which is brought forth follows the womb," to deny tribal membership to black Indians.[229]

The Seminole Nation accepted CDIB (Certificate of Degree of Indian Blood) cards as proof an applicant seeking to participate in a Judgment Fund Program did in fact descend from a member of the tribe as it existed in 1823. Estelusti Seminoles—black Seminoles—did not achieve express citizenship recognition until

Fighting for the Franchise 239

the Seminoles signed the Treaty of 1866. Like its counterparts in the other Indian groups constituting the Five Civilized Tribes, the Seminole Freedmen Roll lacked any reference to blood degree. Most Estelusti, enrolled by Dawes agents on the Freedmen Roll, could not for that reason establish the requisite blood connection for CDIB eligibility. They were thus excluded from partaking in the benefits provided by the Judgment Fund Programs. The BIA, as trustee of the Judgment Fund Award, disbursed millions of dollars for programs unavailable to Estelusti Seminoles.

The consequences of that played out in real time, with real impact on real people. In the early 1990s, Sylvia Davis, an Estelusti Seminole from Shawnee, Oklahoma, filed an application with the tribe on behalf of her minor son, seeking to participate in one of the Judgment Fund Programs.

Davis traced her family roots back to late 1700s and early 1800s. She counted among her ancestors a Seminole chief, William Augustus Bowles, and a prominent Seminole warrior, Chief Billy Bowlegs. Davis even served on the Seminole Nation tribal council.[230]

The Seminole Nation denied Davis's application to receive $125 for clothing for her school-age son. The tribe's decision rested on Davis's inability to provide a copy of her son's CDIB card. According to the tribe, Davis could not prove that her son descended from a member of the Seminole Nation as it existed in Florida on September 18, 1823, a key eligibility requirement for participation in all Judgment Fund Programs. Davis filed suit in 1994.

In court, Davis argued that the tribe had no authority to exclude the Estelusti Seminoles from Judgment Fund Programs. She noted that Section 4 of the measure authorized the distribution provided:

> Any plan for the use and distribution of the funds allocated to the Seminole Nation of Oklahoma shall provide that not less than 80 per centum thereof shall be set aside and programmed to serve common tribal needs, educational requirements and such other purposes as the circumstances of the Seminole Nation of Oklahoma may determine.[231]

The elision of Estelusti Seminoles from use of the Judgment Fund Award, Davis contended, did not "serve common tribal needs." Davis alleged that the trustees of the Judgment Fund Award, defendants in the lawsuit, violated the law when they disbursed monies conditioned upon satisfaction of eligibility criteria that excluded substantially all Estelusti.

Davis further charged that the BIA violated its own policy by refusing to issue CDIBs to Estelusti Seminoles. She cited a written policy of the BIA expressly recognizing Estelusti Seminoles' entitlement to CDIB cards.

The district court dismissed Davis's complaint for failure to join an indispensable party, the Seminole Nation. Because of sovereign immunity, the tribe could not be sued without its consent. Despite further consideration by the courts, that dismissal withstood all challenges.[232]

The Seminole Nation subsequently refashioned its government. In the summer of 2000, voters passed several resolutions that, among other things, provided for: (i) the establishment of a court system; (ii) tax-collection by the tribe, and in a separate proposal, the exclusion of private, individually-owned Seminole Indian businesses on restricted and trust land; (iii) changing the 1886 treaty boundary; (iv) term limits for the chief and the assistant chief; (v) allowing member-initiated referenda; (vi) a one-eighth blood quantum for membership in the Seminole Nation; (vii) a new definition of tribal membership; and (viii) tribal council modifications to the Judgment Fund Plan.

This massive overhaul of the Seminole Nation government resulted in the ouster of the Estelusti Seminoles from the tribe. The BIA took umbrage, and cut off federal funds to the Seminole Nation. Faced with a shut-off of the federal spigot, the tribe weighed its options. It could have held fast to its decision to disenfranchise the Estelusti as a sovereign prerogative, but to do so would have reaped enormous financial costs. Therefore, succumbing to intense pressure, the Seminole Nation relented and restored the franchise to its Estelusti members. With that, the federal government restored tribal funding.

Two prominent federal cases emanated from the determination of the BIA to enforce the Treaty of 1866 on behalf of the Estelusti Seminoles, *Seminole Nation of Oklahoma v. Norton*[233] (2001) ("Seminole I") and *Seminole Nation of Oklahoma v. Norton*[234] (2002) ("Seminole II") Together, these cases stand for the following propositions: (i) the Treaty of 1866 ensured the tribal citizenship of the black Seminoles; and (ii) the BIA properly refused to recognize a Seminole Nation that disenfranchised her black citizens.

The Dawes Rolls still determine membership in the Seminole Nation, but both the Freedmen Roll and the Seminole Roll are given deference. Indeed, the Seminole Nation of Oklahoma Constitution provides that "membership . . . shall consist of all Seminole citizens whose names appear on the final rolls of the Seminole Nation of Oklahoma . . . and their descendants."[235]

A person who can trace his or her ancestry back to the Dawes Rolls will be deemed to be a member of the Seminole Nation. Notwithstanding the separate classification of the Estelusti Seminoles by the Dawes Commission, the Treaty of 1866 between the United States and the Seminole Nation mandated the inclusion of the Estelusti Seminoles as tribal members.[236]

The restoration of the franchise to the black Seminoles did not, however, resolve the issue of eligibility for federal tribal benefits pursuant to the Judgment Fund. Participation in Judgment Fund programs still requires both tribal membership and a determination that the applicant is descended from a member of the Seminole Nation as it existed in Florida on September 18, 1823.[237] The latter determination, based as it is on CDIB cards tied to the Dawes "Blood Rolls," is an insuperable obstacle for the vast majority of the Estelusti. Dawes agents placed black Seminoles on the Freedmen Roll irrespective of Native American ancestry, and without denoting Native blood quantum.

The predicament of the Estelusti Seminoles captured Congressional attention. Members of the Congressional Black Caucus lamented: "[T]he Seminole Nation does not permit its [F]reedmen access to federal tribal benefits but, in a cruel ironic twist, allows them to vote and hold office."[238]

Like the Cherokee, Muscogee (Creek), and Seminole Nations, the Choctaw Nation faces an identity crisis of its own as respects the Freedmen. Paralleling the experience of the other members of the Five Civilized Tribes, reliance on the Dawes land allotment enrollment system to prove entitlement to citizenship has proven to be fraught with peril.

D. In the Choctaw Nation

The word "Choctaw" is the Anglicized form of "Chahta," the tribe's name for itself. "Chahta" derives from the Muscogee (Creek) word "cate" (pronounced "cha-the"), meaning "red." The Choctaw Nation is headquartered in Durant, Oklahoma.[239]

As previously noted, the Choctaw and Chickasaw Nations share a common ancestry:

> The ancient traditional history of the Choctaws and Chickasaws claims for them a Mexican origin, and a migration from that country at some remote period in the past, under the leadership of two brothers, respectively named Chahtah and Chikasah[,] both noted and influential chiefs to their possessions east of the Mississippi. Adair, in his "American Indians," says: "The Choctaws and Chickasaws descended from a people called Chickemacaws, who were among the first inhabitants of the Mexican empire; and at an ancient period wandered east, with a tribe of Indians called Choccomaws; and finally crossed the Mississippi River, with a force of ten thousand warriors." It is reasonable to suppose that the name Choctaw has its derivation from Choccomaw, and Chickasaw, from Chickemacaw (both corrupted). . . .[240]

In the United States, the two nations held land together, maintained reciprocal citizenship rights, and intermarried. The federal government dealt with the Choctaws and Chickasaws jointly.[241]

A fancy for the enslavement of Africans proved to be another legacy the Choctaws shared with the Chickasaws and others among the Five Civilized Tribes. The Choctaws, and to an even greater extent, the Chickasaws, earned a reputation for harsh treatment of their Freedmen—the most severe among the Five Civilized Tribes.[242] That said, an aura of family sometimes enveloped relations between tribespersons and the Africans they enslaved during the pre-Civil War era.

> I was born on a farm near Doaksville, near Hugo, Oklahoma, befo' de Civil War. My parents belonged to an Indian family when I was jest a little child. After the Rebellion . . . I lived near the family of Governor Allen Wright for sixty years. I nussed all his chillun' and den later, long come dey's chillun' and I nussed dem, and I'se even nussed the great grand chillun'. After the War I was what you call a Freedman. De Indians had to give all dey slaves forty acres of land. I'se allus lived on dis land. . . .[243]
>
> —FRANCES BANKS, Choctaw Freedman
> (from *The Slave Narratives of Indian Territory*)

The Choctaws became acquainted with Africans in their native homeland of Mississippi and adopted the Eurocentric practice of slavery. Enslaved Africans accompanied Choctaw Indians on their pilgrimage to Oklahoma in the 1830s. Slavery continued in the Choctaw Nation until 1866, when the Choctaws negotiated and signed the Treaty of 1866 with the federal government. Though that pact ended slavery within the Choctaw Nation, it would be much later—1883—before the Choctaw Nation accepted the Freedmen as tribal citizens.[244] It would be even later before forty-acre Freedmen land allotments described in the Treaty of 1866 would be forthcoming.[245]

The Choctaw and Chickasaw Treaty of 1866 offered two options not available to other tribes: (1) within two years, give the Freedmen citizenship and forty acres of land and receive $300,000 from the federal government in exchange for western lands held by the Choctaw and Chickasaw Nations; or (2) allow removal and resettlement of the willing Freedmen on western Choctaw and Chickasaw lands, with the assistance of the U.S. Army, and with per capita payments of $100 to each Freedmen so removed (the per capita payments to come out of the $300,000 to be paid in exchange for the lands ceded by the tribes). The $300,000 was to be held in trust until the Choctaw and Chickasaw Nations decided on the fate of their Freedmen. The Treaty provided, in pertinent part:

ARTICLE 2.
The Choctaws and Chickasaws hereby covenant and agree that henceforth neither slavery nor involuntary servitude, otherwise than in punishment of crime whereof the parties shall have been duly convicted, in accordance with laws applicable to all members of the particular nation, shall ever exist in said nations.

ARTICLE 3.
The Choctaws and Chickasaws, in consideration of the sum of three hundred thousand dollars, hereby cede to the United States the territory west of the 98° west longitude, known as the leased district, provided that the said sum shall be invested and held by the United States, at an interest not less than five per cent, in trust for the said nations, until the legislatures of the Choctaw and Chickasaw Nations respectively shall have made such laws, rules, and regulations as may be necessary to give all persons of African descent, resident in the said nation at the date of the treaty of Fort Smith, and their descendants, heretofore held in slavery among

said nations, all the rights, privileges, and immunities, including the right of suffrage, of citizens of said nations, except in the annuities, moneys, and public domain claimed by, or belonging to, said nations respectively; and also to give to such persons who were residents as aforesaid, and their descendants, forty acres each of the land of said nations on the same terms as the Choctaws and Chickasaws, to be selected on the survey of said land, after the Choctaws and Chickasaws and Kansas Indians have made their selections as herein provided; and immediately on the enactment of such laws, rules, and regulations, the said sum of three hundred thousand dollars shall be paid to the said Choctaw and Chickasaw Nations in the proportion of three-fourths to the former and one-fourth to the latter, less such sum, at the rate of one hundred dollars per capita, as shall be sufficient to pay such persons of African descent before referred to as within ninety days after the passage of such laws, rules, and regulations shall elect to remove and actually remove from the said nations respectively. And should the said laws, rules, and regulations not be made by the legislatures of the said nations respectively, within two years from the ratification of this treaty, then the said sum of three hundred thousand dollars shall cease to be held in trust for the said Choctaw and Chickasaw Nations, and be held for the use and benefit of such of said persons of African descent as the United States shall remove from the said Territory in such manner as the United States shall deem proper—the United States agreeing, within ninety days from the expiration of the said two years, to remove from said nations all such persons of African descent as may be willing to remove; those remaining or returning after having been removed from said nations to have no benefit of said sum of three hundred thousand dollars, or any part thereof, but shall be upon the same footing as other citizens of the United States in the said nations.[246]

Not all persons of African ancestry lived among the Choctaws as bondservants. "Free" Africans also shared space with the tribesmen. The saga of the Beams family, the descendants of William Beams, a white man from the old Choctaw Nation in Mississippi, and his paramour, Nelly, an enslaved African, is illustrative.

Beams, a widower, had four children by his Choctaw wife before her death. He purchased Nelly, a so-called mulatto—half black and half white—and the son she bore by a former master. Beams fathered an additional eight children by Nelly.

Ultimately, Beams manumitted Nelly and her descendants. Nelly and her brood held "free" status within the Choctaw Nation at the time of removal. Their half-Choctaw siblings challenged that status, and sought to sell them for profit. The Choctaw Nation, however, affirmed the free status of these "black Beams" and thwarted the proposed sale.[247]

Decades later, other persons of African ancestry living among the Choctaw Nation gained freedom. The Treaty of 1866 ultimately gave the Freedmen citizenship, and thereby the legal right to remain within the Choctaw Nation. Most Freedmen stayed after the collapse of slavery, though many in the Choctaw Nation actively sought their removal. As previously noted, the Choctaw Nation formally adopted the Freedmen as citizens in 1883 after much discussion, debate, and political wrangling. Soon thereafter, the Choctaw Nation took the first official census of its black residents. The tribe recorded names, ages, names of former Choctaw slave owners, and the amount of personal property amassed by each family.

Prominent Choctaw Freedmen included Henry Crittendon, a leading educator at the time of the establishment of the Choctaw Freedmen Oak Hill Industrial Academy. Built near Valliant, Oklahoma, in the far southeastern corner of the state, the Presbyterian Board of Missions started the facility in 1869 as a boarding school for children of Choctaw Freedmen. In 1912, it was renamed "Elliot Academy." Other well-known Choctaw Freedmen included Rufus Cannon and Squire Hall, a marshal and a deputy sheriff, respectively.[248] Wallis Willis, a Choctaw Freedmen, wrote the spiritual *Swing Low, Sweet Chariot*.[249]

Choctaw Freedmen engaged in all aspects of Choctaw life for decades. Despite this, the modern Choctaw Nation, like others of the Five Civilized Tribes, continues to rebuff its Freedmen.

Angela Walton-Raji, a Washington, D.C.-area genealogist focused on African-Native research, grew up in Fort Smith, Arkansas, a border town once the hub of the western Arkansas/eastern Oklahoma region. Walton-Raji's great-grandmother, Sallie Walton, was born into slavery in 1863 in the Choctaw Nation, Indian Territory. Sallie Walton died in 1961. Walton-Raji, a young child in 1961, came to know her great-grandmother and her Choctaw roots well through direct interaction and family oral history. She bemoans the fact that the history of the Choctaw Freedmen—people like Sallie Walton—goes largely unheralded. These were people, she noted, who accompanied the Choctaws to present-day Oklahoma in the early 1830s; people with deep ties, some by affinity, some by blood, to the Choctaw natives; people whom the Choctaws themselves regarded as essential to their survival in the new world into which they were thrust.[250]

Historical neglect is one thing. Repudiation by the tribe itself is quite another. The Choctaw Nation, like several other of the Five Civilized Tribes, has taken steps to disenfranchise its Freedmen.

In 1983, the Choctaw Nation of Oklahoma adopted a new constitution limiting membership to "all Choctaw Indians by blood whose names appear on the final rolls of the Choctaw Nation approved pursuant to Section 2 of the Act of April 26, 1906, (34 Stat. 136) and their lineal descendants."[251] By referencing the Dawes Commission "Blood Rolls" for tribal inclusion, the tribe removed virtually all Choctaw Freedmen from membership. This provision, found in Section 1 of Article II of the Constitution of the Choctaw Nation of Oklahoma, ratified by Choctaw voters on July 9, 1983, remains in effect.[252] The Choctaw Freedmen, reluctantly and belatedly embraced by the tribe, have now been shunned—disenfranchised.

Verdie Triplett, who initiated a petition in support of the Cherokee Freedmen, is a lifelong resident of Fort Coffee, a majority-black hamlet in Eastern Oklahoma with fewer than 500 residents. Many families in Fort Coffee live on land allotments received by Freedmen of the Choctaw Nation and handed down through generations.

Triplett is a Choctaw descendant by blood to the Darneal line of the Choctaw Nation. He is also a direct descendant of Freedmen from the Chickasaw Nation. Triplett, an oil and gas driller and cattle rancher, boasts a profound interest in local history and heritage.

Triplett's grandmother, Ardena Darneal, was the daughter of a Choctaw Indian, Silas Darneal. Ms. Darneal's mother, Fanny Parks, was born into freedom in about 1867. Ms. Darneal's grandmother, Hettie Reynolds Lucas, was enslaved by a man named Levi Reynolds. Ms. Darneal was a year old in 1898, the year in which her name appeared on the Chickasaw Freedmen Roll. Her Dawes enrollment card explicitly notes: "Separated from Silas Darneal[,] a Choctaw Indian."[253]

Despite this ancestry, Triplett, upon application for citizenship in the Choctaw Nation, met with swift denial. The Nation told Triplett the Dawes Rolls are fixed and final. Despite his ancestor's notation of Indian ancestry, she, Ardena Darneal, appeared on the

Freedmen Roll. Choctaw citizenship requires the presence of an ancestor on the Choctaw Blood Roll.

Undeterred, Triplett continues his quest to cement the Native-American portion of his genealogical foundation. He refuses to surrender any of his Native-American ancestry.

Discovering his own rich, multicultural history stimulated Triplett's interest in genealogy and cultural preservation and spurred him to cultivate similar enthusiasm among his neighbors. He encouraged his neighbors to look deeper into their own roots; to organize and to discover, commemorate, and protect the unique and valuable contributions of the persons of African ancestry who inhabited Indian Territory.

In December 2006, Triplett convened a meeting to organize the Choctaw-Chickasaw Freedmen Association of Oklahoma. In March 2007, Triplett organized the drive that led to a petition seeking a Congressional inquiry into the disenfranchisement of the Cherokee Freedmen. Supporters presented a petition to the members of the Congressional Black Caucus in the spring of 2007.

The Choctaw-Chickasaw Freedmen Association of Oklahoma works with the local community to research, document, and celebrate the unique history, heritage and legacy of the Freedmen of the Choctaw and Chickasaw Nations. The group stands in solidarity with the Freedmen of other tribes among the Five Civilized Tribes who face similar issues and share related concerns.[254]

The Triplett-initiated petition highlighted an inter-tribal Freedmen awakening. The continuing confrontation over citizenship in the Cherokee Nation may be the current flashpoint, but the Freedmen affiliated with the other members of the Five Civilized Tribes, Verdie Triplett among them, see their own identity dilemma reflected in the plight of the Cherokee Freedmen.

An announcement for the August 2009 convention of the Choctaw Chickasaw Freedmen Association captures the frustration borne of years of struggle simply to belong.

> This historic heritage conference and reunion will bring back families that were once Oklahoma based families, to celebrate a unique and richly dynamic legacy. Our goal is to establish our right to replant ourselves on the historical landscape of our ancestors, and to promote scholarly efforts of this incredible history and story of survival.
>
> This conference and reunion will also be the launching of a re-

source institute and give birth to an initiative to preserve the history of the Freedmen of the Five Tribes and to affiliate our efforts with established historical preservation facilities.

We hope to launch an oral history project to preserve these African-American families that were part of Indian Territory, and part of the Choctaw and Chickasaw communities of the 19th and 20th centuries. The African presence in Indian Territory has been largely erased through elimination, omission and neglect. But a group of dedicated researchers[,] [has] determined to preserve what was almost completely gone—and this is an effort to restore the legacy of a proud African-American and African-Native American history. We celebrate our survival in what was once a hostile land, and we re-implant our legacy upon the soil where our ancestors contributed to the survival of Choctaw, Chickasaw, and the people of the state of Oklahoma.

We are Oklahomans. We are of documented Choctaw & Chickasaw descent. We are proudly African descended people. We are coming home!![255]

The "back stories" of the Choctaw and Chickasaw people intertwine and intersect, and likely spring from a common fount. While the particulars of the origin stories for the two groups differ, credible authorities believe, as previously indicated, that the Choctaws and Chickasaws share common ancestors and heritage.[256] That said, an examination of the status of the Freedmen among the Chickasaws follows.

E. In the Chickasaw Nation

The word "Chickasaw," the Anglicized version of the tribe's name for itself, "Chikasha," means, roughly, "he who walked ahead." Chickasaw traditional lore portrays its people as "the people of one fire." The Chickasaw Nation, historically linked to the Choctaw Nation, is headquartered in Ada, Oklahoma.[257]

As noted earlier, the family of the man whom some consider the dean of African-American history, the late Dr. John Hope Franklin, traces strands of its roots back to the Chickasaw Nation. Like the other four of the Five Civilized Tribes, the Chickasaws' centuries-old relations with persons of African descent mix the bitter with the sweet. As those interactions illustrate, the ties that bind sometimes enslave, too.

> I sho' remembers all about slavery times[,] for I was a grown woman, married and had one baby, when de War done broke out. That was a sorry time for some poor black folks but I guess Master Frank Colbert's [Negroes] was about as well off as the best of [']em. I can recollect things that happened way back better than I can things that happen now. Funny[,] ain't it?
> Frank Colbert, a full-blood Choctaw Indian, was my owner. He owned my mother but I don't remember much about my father. He died when I was a little youngun. My Mistress' name was Julie Colbert. She and master Frank was de best folks that ever lived. All the [Negroes] loved master Frank and knowed jest what he wanted done and they tried their best to do it, too.[258]
>
>> —KIZIAH LOVE, Chickasaw Freedman, 93, the former chattel slave of Benjamin Franklin Colbert (Frank Colbert), was interviewed in August 1937. Colbert owned and operated the Colbert Ferry & Stagecoach Station, a stop along the Butterfield Trail. (Kiziah Love: Chickasaw Freedman Card No. 1001)

Despite Kiziah Love's cheerful, optimistic reflections on her working experiences under Choctaw slave-masters, politics was another matter. "[D]uring the time [the Freedmen] lived in the Chickasaw Nation they had no citizenship; they were literally a people without a country."[259] It would be decades later before citizenship for the Chickasaw Freedmen became firmly established. Ultimately, more than forty years after the end of the Civil War, a homeland of record emerged as Oklahoma and Indian Territories melded into the State of Oklahoma and the forty-sixth state entered the Union.[260]

Despite the actions of the other members of the Five Civilized Tribes, the Chickasaw Nation spurned its Freedmen, refusing to adopt them as citizens pursuant to the Treaty of 1866. Unlike the Choctaws, who resisted Freedmen citizenship initially, the Chickasaws never acquiesced. Post-Civil War treatment of Chickasaw Freedmen proved especially oppressive.[261] After considerable debate and various changes in position on the "The Negro Question," an October 22, 1885, act of the legislature of the Chickasaw Nation settled the matter:

> That the Chickasaw people hereby refuse to accept or adopt the Freedmen as citizens of the Chickasaw Nation upon any terms or conditions whatever and respectfully request the Governor of our Nation to notify the Department at Washington of the action of the legislature in the premises.[262]

The federal government initially insisted the Choctaws and Chickasaws jointly assent to the Treaty of 1866, which required the tribes to adopt their Freedmen within two years or face the prospect that federal authorities would remove those Freedmen. Most of the Freedmen wished to remain within the Chickasaw Nation, despite misgivings about their continued welfare among the Chickasaws, particularly the Chickasaw "mixed-bloods."

Freedmen numbers exploded after the Civil War, in part propelled by the numerous intermarriages with "State Negroes," African Americans who lived outside Indian Country. These State Negroes, oppressed elsewhere, flocked to the relative freedom and economic opportunity within the borders of Indian Country.[263] Chickasaw leaders feared reaching the tipping point—the point at which a critical mass of Freedmen might wrest political control from tribal powerbrokers. Suspicion and mistrust mounted. In Freedmen hands, what would be the fate of the Chickasaw Nation?

The federal government, despite its fiduciary responsibility, declined to protect Freedmen rights in the Chickasaw Nation. Federal officials abdicated the special trust relationship the United States government crafted with respect to its dealings with Native American groups. The trust relationship evolved through treaty-making and legislation, ultimately becoming ensconced in law (i.e., in the so-called "Marshall Trilogy" of United States Supreme Court cases discussed previously).

Though pressed by the United States government, the Chickasaw Nation never amended its constitution or revised tribal laws to include the Freedmen. Instead, the Chickasaws called the federal government's bluff. Rather than extend the Freedmen citizenship, the Chickasaw Nation asked the United States to remove the emancipated Freedmen from its midst. The government balked. Had it acceded to the request of the Chickasaws, the government would have had to find land on which to settle the removed Freedmen. One logical location—perhaps the only logical location—was Oklahoma's unassigned lands. As a practical matter, however, whites had begun clamoring for the opening of those lands for their own resettlement. As the Chickasaws surmised, and the federal government subsequently demonstrated, removal of the Freedmen was a hollow threat inconsistent with political realities.

The federal government's failure to make good on Freedmen removal had dire consequences:

> When the Chickasaws emancipated their slaves under the Treaty of 1866, they were given the option of adopting their former slaves as citizens of the Nation. If they did not, the United States agreed to remove the blacks from the Chickasaw country. The Chickasaws failed to adopt the freedmen, and the United States did not keep the treaty agreement. Thus the freedmen lived in the Chickasaw Nation for over forty years without civil rights or protection of law.[264]

The Freedmen remained within the Chickasaw Nation "in grinding poverty . . . without civil rights, the right to vote, and, for the most part, educational privileges."[265]

Even the 11th United States Secretary of the Interior, Columbus Delano, decried the appalling situation that faced the Chickasaw Freedmen. Delano (June 4, 1809–October 23, 1896) was a lawyer and a statesman and a member of the prominent Delano family. He served in the United States House of Representatives, became an Ohio delegate to the Republican National Convention in 1860, and supported Abraham Lincoln's nomination as President. Delano subsequently served in the Ohio House of Representatives and was appointed Commissioner of Internal Revenue in March 1869, a position he held until November 1, 1870, when President Ulysses S. Grant appointed him Secretary of the Interior.

The graft and corruption that enveloped the Grant administration became especially rampant in the Bureau of Indian Affairs during Delano's tenure, and it ultimately swallowed him up. Evidence emerged that Delano's son, John Delano, had been given partnerships in surveying contracts over which the Interior Department had control. Delano resigned his post on October 19, 1875.[266]

Despite the organizational tumult that surrounded him, Delano displayed flashes of compassion and empathy. The Choctaw and Chickasaw Freedmen became unlikely beneficiaries.

In a May 2, 1874, letter to William A. Buckingham, Chairman of the United States Senate Committee on Indian Affairs, Secretary

Delano argued the case of the Choctaw and Chickasaw Freedmen with passion and candor.

> Neither the Choctaw nor the Chickasaw Nation has secured to said persons of African descent the rights, privileges, and immunities, including the right of suffrage provided for in the treaty [the Treaty of 1866]. The United States has not removed any of the said persons of African descent, because such persons are so identified by marriage and custom with said nations as to be unwilling to break up their homes and go elsewhere.
>
> . . . .
>
> [The bill under consideration] provides that the persons of African descent before alluded to shall have all the rights, privileges, and immunities, including the right of suffrage, of citizens of said nations, respectively, and in the annuities, moneys, and public domain claimed by [o]r belonging to said nations, respectively. Is this wrong? The Choctaw and Chickasaw Nations are under treaty obligations to secure [these things] to these people. They ought to have done so long since. Their failure to do so is a great wrong and a great injustice, which should be speedily corrected.
>
> If you look at the manner in which the Choctaw and Chickasaw Nations acquired their property, and if you consider that the improvements made thereon have been made by the labor of the African people in as large, if not a larger proportion, than by the labor of the native Choctaws and Chickasaws, you will see that there is not any injustice in giving to these persons of African descent, made free and made citizens, equal rights in all respects with the native Choctaw and Chickasaw people.
>
> A failure to pass this bill will leave the treaty of 1866 unexecuted; will continue the Africans among the Choctaws and Chickasaws in their present unjust and disastrous situation, will preserve the strife, animosity, and disturbance incident to these relations, and therefore I cannot too earnestly or too urgently recommend the passage of the bill referred to, or some equivalent measure, during the present session of Congress.[267]

The Chickasaw Freedmen, Africans disowned by their mother nation, fought for recognition. Long after the conclusion of the Civil War, the fate of the enslaved Africans in the Chickasaw Nation remained uncertain.

The Chickasaw Nation did not want them. The United States

apparently did not want them, either. The Freedmen, neither citizens of the Chickasaw Nation nor citizens of the United States of America, languished for decades as people without a nationality.[268]

During this interim period, the Freedmen persevered through segregation and discrimination inside the tribe. They performed valuable services for the Chickasaw Nation, such as acting as interpreters. Indeed, "[i]n 1878, it was reported that all of the estimated 2,300 Chickasaw Freedmen could speak the language."[269]

The Freedmen formed the Chickasaw Freedmen Association. That group pressed the Dawes Commission to honor their status as members of the Chickasaw Nation.

> First, they asked for rights, privileges, and immunities equal to those of the Chickasaw citizens, including suffrage, equal educational privileges, equal protection under the law, and equal shares in the moneys and public domain of the Nation. Second, they claimed indemnification for damage, loss, and injury sustained since 1866 as a result of being denied their rights as citizens. Third, they asked that, once their rights were secured, the Chickasaw lands be surveyed and allotted in severalty, at least to the [F]reedmen. . . .[270]

In 1882, Chickasaw Freedmen leaders King Blue[271] and Isaac Alexander penned a poignant appeal to Congress for a resolution of the citizenship status of their brothers and sisters, the Chickasaw Freedmen. That entreaty, in part, reads as follows:

> **THE MEMORIAL OF THE CHICKASAW FREEDMEN**
>
> To the Honorable the Senate and House of Representatives of the United States of America:
> The undersigned, your memorialists, respectfully show that they are residents of the Chickasaw nation, and are "persons of African descent" and were born and bred in the said nation.
> They have such interests there as inspire them with an earnest desire to remain residents, and to become citizens of the Nation. There they have families, wives, and children, and property; in fact everything that is dear to them is there; and they would consider it a great hardship to be forced to leave their firesides and to seek new homes.
> Your memorialists represent not only themselves, but also that class of persons known in the nation as "persons of African descent" of which class there are about three thousand individuals.

We and they have ever been loyal to the Government of the United States, and expect ever so to remain.

. . . .

From the terms and language of [the 3rd article of the Treaty between the Choctaw and Chickasaw Nations and the United States, of April 1866], it is quite evident that the leading desire and intention of the Government of the United States was the complete enfranchisement of the "persons of African descent" in the said nations. . . .

The Chickasaw Indians have, up to this time, neglected and refused to pass the "laws, rules and regulations" enumerated in the said clause of the treaty. In 1877, after the lapse of eleven years from the date of said treaty, the Legislature of the Chickasaw Nation passed [An Act Confirming The Treaty of 1866].

This act reflects the settled design and purpose of the Chickasaw Nation not to enfranchise the said "person of African descent" named in said treaty. They have refused and neglected, and still refuse and neglect to pass such laws. Besides the evidence of the settled purpose of the Chickasaws, as found in this statute, we are enabled to state as a fact that on several occasions during pending elections, applications have been made at the polls of voting, to be allowed to vote, by persons of "African descent" yet these applications though made by some of the oldest and most respectable of such persons—persons born and bred in the nation—have been invariably rejected.

. . . .

For many and grave reasons we do not elect to remove [ourselves from the Chickasaw Nation]. As natives, we are attached to the localities of our birth and childhood; as men, we are attached to the people among whom we have been born and bred; we like the Chickasaws, as friends; and we know by the experience of the past that we can live with them in the future in the close union of sincere fraternity and brotherly love. It is for these and other grave considerations that we do earnestly desire to be [F]reedmen in fact as well as in theory; for without the elective franchise—a free vote—there can be no real liberty. As things now exist so far as the persons of African descent in the nations are concerned the word [F]reedmen is a sham.

. . . .

In the fourth article of said treaty of 1866, it was stipulated on the part of the nations, "*That all laws shall be equal in their operation upon Choctaws, Chickasaws and Negroes, and that no distinction affecting the latter shall at any time be made; and that they shall be treated with kindness and protected against injury."*

In the seventh article of said treaty "The Choctaws and Chickasaws agree to such legislation as Congress and the President of the United States may deem necessary for the better administration of justice and the protection of the rights of person and property within the Indian Territory. Provided, however, such legislation shall not in any wise interfere with or annul their present tribal organization or their respective legislatures and judiciaries, or the rights, laws privileges and customs of the Choctaw and Chickasaw nations, respectively."

Therefore, we pray that the Congress pass such an act as will place us on a footing with the persons, other than the Chickasaws, as are referred to in the following seventh clause of the general provisions of the constitution of the Chickasaw Nation. That is to say:

Section 7: All persons, other than Chickasaws, who have become citizens of this nation, by marriage or adoption, and have been confirmed in all their rights as such, by former conventions and all such persons as aforesaid, who have become citizens by adoption by the legislature, or by intermarriage with the Chickasaws, since the adoption of the constitution of August 18, AD 1856, shall be entitled to all the rights, privileges and immunities of native citizens. All who may hereafter become citizens, either by marriage or adoption, shall be entitled to all the privileges of native born citizens, without being eligible to the office of governor.[272]

Later, the Chickasaw and the Choctaw Nations negotiated jointly with the Dawes Commission. The process yielded the Atoka Agreement, signed April 23, 1897, in Atoka, Choctaw Nation, Indian Territory. That pact provided, *inter alia*, for allotment in severalty of tribal lands. The contemplated apportionment scheme included the Freedmen, who would be awarded smaller allotments. The Atoka Agreement provided that mineral-rich parcels would be withheld from the allotment, and then sold or leased for the benefit of the tribes. The Agreement further stipulated that the governments of the respective tribes would terminate on March 4, 1908.

The federal government incorporated the Atoka Agreement, ratified in a joint election of the Chickasaw and Choctaw Nations on August 24, 1898, into the Curtis Act (1898).[273] That Act is known for abolishing the tribal governments of the Five Civilized Tribes and placing tribal affairs under federal control.[274]

Chickasaw Freedmen enrolled during the Dawes Commission census process. They received allotments. They did not, however, gain citizenship rights despite court challenges.[275]

In 1907, hundreds of African Indians filed suit, claiming discrimination in the Chickasaw and Choctaw Nations. The legal matter became known as "Equity Case 7071" (*a.k.a., Bettie Ligon v. Douglas H. Johnson, Breen McCurtain, and James Garfield, Secretary of the Interior*)[276] At the heart of the matter was the Freedmen argument that the Dawes Commission knowingly and willfully ignored evidence and testimony that could have resulted in the transfer of up to 2,000 individuals from the Freedmen Rolls to the "Blood Rolls" as *Chahta Iusa* (black Choctaw) and *Chika Iusa* (black Chickasaw).[277]

> While it was generally claimed that the Chickasaws were racially pure, miscegenation was apparently common and probably widespread. . . . In the first decade of the twentieth century there were many [F]reedmen claimants to Chickasaw blood. . . . Bettie Ligon alleged that she was the daughter of Bob Love, a Chickasaw, and a "mixed breed slave woman named Margaret Ann Wilson. . . ." In 1907 two thousand persons claimed to have Indian blood. Granted, these claims were made in an effort to obtain a greater share in the wealth of the Chickasaw Nation, which was then being dissolved. But most of them no doubt had merit.[278]

An article appeared in the *Indian Citizen*, a newspaper published in Atoka, Oklahoma, on April 18, 1907. The piece, entitled "Choctaw and Chickasaw Freedmen Seek Enrollment," captured the essence of the claims made and remedy sought by Bettie Ligon and her co-plaintiffs.

> The suit filed in the United States court at Ardmore Saturday evening involving property worth probably $15,000,000, attracts attention as one of the most gigantic pieces of litigation in the history of Indian Territory.
>
> The plaintiffs are Choctaw and Chickasaw [F]reedmen, that is, negroes or persons born of negro mothers and fathers. They are called [F]reedmen, where recognized by the government as such as were each allotted forty acres of land [as opposed to a full allotment for "blood" Indians of 320 acres of land], for which they have received their allotment certificates or patents.
>
> There are about 1,500 of them and after their names had been placed on the [F]reedmen rolls they made application to the sec-

retary of the interior to be transferred to the tribal rolls. The secretary held that even were it legal to so transfer them that the allotments had been made, the rolls closed and the whole affair ended.

Then they appealed to [C]ongress and as the last session sought to have the Indian appropriations bill so amended as to allow the transfer.

The matter was fought out before the [S]enate committee on Indian affairs of the Choctaw and Chickasaw Indians.

The claim of these [F]reedmen to a right to be placed on the tribal rolls, not as [F]reedmen, but as Choctaw and Chickasaw Indians, appears to rest on the constructions of the word "descendants" as used in the treaty.

. . . .

[T]he rolls were closed absolutely on March 4th [1907] and were never to be reopened for any purpose. To open them would result in unsettling titles and work irreparable injury to every citizen of the two nations.[279]

Equity Case 7071 thus involved much more than a question of who is an "Indian," or even who has "Indian blood." It homed in on the primacy of matrilineal descent and the inescapability of the rule of hypodescent. Opponents of the Freedmen argued: "The most that can be contended in favor of the persons [seeking relief] is that they are the illegitimate progeny of [F]reedmen women (negro women who were the slaves of Choctaw or Chickasaw Indians or the descendants of such) by Indian men."[280] Webster Ballinger, representing the claimants, offered an alternative view when he appeared before the Select Committee on the United States Senate to Investigate Affairs in the Indian Territory in 1907.

Ballinger noted that the claimants "acquired their citizenship in the Choctaw and Chickasaw nations by descent from recognized citizens by blood thereof, by birth in the nations, and by uninterrupted and continuous residence there and allegiance thereto."[281] They simply sought remedial legislation to correct inapposite placement of their names on the Freedmen Roll, a roll devoid of reference to the Indian ancestry they possessed.

In a January 23, 1907, hearing before the Committee on Indian Affairs on the Choctaw and Chickasaw Indians, Attorney Ballinger and his co-counsel, Albert J. Lee, urged an amendment to a pending Indian appropriations bill. The specific language of the proposed amendment fairly captured the "descent dilemma" at the heart, at least ostensibly, of the Choctaw and Chickasaw Freedmen dispute:

> That the Secretary of the Interior is hereby authorized and directed to transfer from the Choctaw and Chickasaw [F]reedmen rolls to the rolls of citizens by blood of said nations, the name of a person who is of Indian blood or descent on either his or her mother's or father's side as shown by either the tribal rolls, the records prepared by and in the custody of the Commissioner to the Five Civilized Tribes or the Department of the Interior, or by any governmental records in the possession of any bureau, division, or commission, or any of the departments of the Government, or any of the courts of Indian Territory, and persons having rights conferred by this act shall be entitled to establish only by evidence their descent from persons of Indian blood and recognized members of the tribes, as appears from any such record: *Provided further*, That nothing herein shall be construed so as to permit the filing of any original application for the enrollment of any person not heretofore, and the time of the passage of this act, enrolled as a [F]reedman of either the Choctaw or Chickasaw nations, or who has an undetermined application for such enrollment now pending, it being the purpose of this act to provide only for a correction of the enrollment of persons of Choctaw or Chickasaw Indian blood who have been enrolled as [F]reedmen of said nation, and no limitation of time within which to file original applications, or to perfect appeals, heretofore fixed by law, shall be construed as a bar to rights conferred by this act; and any person so transferred may contest any allotment heretofore made to which he or she had a superior right at the time of his or her erroneous enrollment; *Provided, however*, That such contest shall be instituted within ninety days from the date of such transfer and that patent has not issued for such allotment.[282]

Equity Case 7071 also turned on economics. To recognize the Freedmen as "blood Indians" based on their demonstrated ancestry would be to affirm their entitlement to additional land—land at the time wanted not just by other Indians, but by American industry and industrialists, too.

The matter commonly known as "Equity Case 7071" bounced from court to court largely on jurisdictional issues. It found its way to the federal legislature. Yet Equity Case 7071 never reached a resolution that would satisfy the petitioners, the longsuffering Chickasaw and Choctaw Freedmen.

Terry J. Ligon, the great-grandson of Bettie Ligon, a named plaintiff in Equity Case 7071, continues the fight for Freedmen recognition and rights. He helped create and now directs the Choctaw-Chickasaw Freedmen Project, and he is a founding member of the African-American Genealogical Society of Northern California and the creator of the Estelusti Foundation. A professional artist, Ligon began conducting extensive research on the history and genealogy of his Choctaw and Chickasaw Freedmen ancestors in 1989. Equity Case 7071 fascinates him.

Ligon's passion for Freedmen rights and his disdain for perceived inequity and injustice are palpable. He calls into question the whole notion of "Indian blood" as mere hypocrisy. African Americans with Indian ancestry, he notes, were often summarily rejected by the tribes:

> During the period of enrollment there was a concerted effort to deny anyone with Negro blood rights and privileges of citizenship. If your maternal ancestor was of African descent, the tribes routinely ignored any and all contributions by a father who was Choctaw or Cherokee or Chickasaw and so on. The tribal leaders offer up a disingenuous argument based on the slenderest of historical reeds, a flawed document called the Dawes Rolls.[283]

A 1901 Congressional Act provided citizenship to Indians in the Five Civilized Tribes.[284] Oklahoma statehood made United States citizens of the Chickasaw Freedmen. Years later, Congress passed the Indian Citizenship Act of 1924 (a.k.a., the "Snyder Act") to provide full citizenship to all other Indians not already having citizenship status. That law, in pertinent part, states:

> "[A]ll non citizen Indians born within the territorial limits of the United States be, and they are hereby, declared to be citizens of the United States: Provided that the granting of such citizenship shall not in any manner impair or otherwise affect the right of any Indian to tribal or other property."[285]

The woes of the Freedmen did not end with United States citizenship. Conditions for the Chickasaw Freedmen during the initial years after citizenship proved "[i]n many respects . . . worse than

260   Apartheid in Indian Country?

[they] had been during the forty years they were a people without a country."[286] These were, after all, particularly oppressive times in America for people of African descent.

Today, the Chickasaw Nation, pursuant to its Constitution, defines as citizens "all Chickasaw Indians by blood whose names appear on the final rolls of the Chickasaw Nation . . . and their lineal descendants." Freedmen are thus effectively excluded from tribal citizenship.[287]

CERTIFICATE OF DEGREE OF INDIAN BLOOD ("CDIB")

BUREAU OF INDIAN AFFAIRS
CERTIFICATE OF DEGREE OF INDIAN OR ALASKA NATIVE BLOOD
INSTRUCTIONS

All portions of the Request for Certificate of Degree of Indian or Alaska Native Blood (CDIB) must be completed. You must show your relationship to an individual Indian listed on an Indian census roll, tribal base roll, Indian judgment fund distribution roll (Roll) that includes Indian blood degrees, or other document prepared and approved by the Secretary of the Interior (Secretary), or his/her authorized representative.

- Your degree of Indian blood is computed from ancestors of Indian blood who were listed on a Roll or other document acceptable to the Secretary, or his/her authorized representative.
- You must give the maiden names of all women listed on the Request for CDIB, unless they were enrolled by their married names.
- A certified copy of a birth certificate or other official documentation is required to establish your relationship to a parent(s) listed on Roll or other document acceptable to the Secretary.
- If your parent is not listed on a Roll or other document acceptable to the Secretary, a certified copy of your parent's birth or death certificate, or other official documentation is required to establish your parent's relationship to someone listed on such Roll. If your grandparent(s) were not listed on such Roll, a certified copy of the birth or death certificate or other official documentation for each grandparent who was the child of an enrolled member of a federally recognized Indian tribe is required.
- Certified copies of birth certificates, delayed birth certificates, and death certificates may be obtained from the State Department of Health or Bureau of Vital Statistics in the State where the person was born or died, or from a tribal office of Vital Statistic. The Indian tribe must have a duly adopted tribal ordinance concerning the issuance of such documents.
- In cases of adoption, the degree of Indian blood of the natural (birth) parent must be proven.
- Your request and supporting documents should be sent to the Agency from whom you receive services.
- Incomplete requests will be returned with a request for further information. No action will be taken until the request is complete.

Fighting for the Franchise 261

OMB Control #1076-0153
Expiration Date: July 31, 2011
Page 2

NOTICES AND CERTIFICATION

NOTICE OF APPEAL RIGHTS

- When you receive your CDIB, you must review it for the correct name spelling, birth dates, and blood degrees. If you believe that there are any mistakes on the DCIB, you must give a written request for corrections and provide supporting documentation to the issuing officer.

- If you are denied a CDIB, you will be given a written determination with an explanation for the denial and a copy of the appeal procedures contained in 25 CFR Part 62.

NOTICE OF PAPERWORK REDUCTION ACT

The information collection requirement this request have been approved by the Office of Management and Budget under the Paperwork Reduction Act of 1995, 44 U.S.C. 3507(d) and assigned clearance number 1076-0153. The agency may not conduct or sponsor, and a person is not required to respond to, a collection of information unless it displays a currently valid OMB control number. Information is collected when individuals seek certification that they possess sufficient Indian blood to receive Federal program services based upon their status as American Indians or Alaska Natives. The information collected will be used to assist in determining eligibility of the individual to receive Federal program services. The information is supplied by a respondent to obtain a Certificate of Degree of Indian or Alaska Native Blood. It is estimated that responding to the request will take an average of 1.5 hours to complete. This includes the amount of time it takes to gather the information and fill out the form. If you wish to make comments on the form, please send them to the Information Collection Clearance Officer, Bureau of Indian Affairs, 625 Herndon Parkway, Herndon, Virginia 20170. Note: comments, names and addresses of commentators are available for public review during regular business hours. If you wish us to withhold this information, you must state this prominently at the beginning of your comment. We will honor your request to the extent allowable by law. In compliance with the Paperwork Reduction Act of 1995, as amended, the collection has been reviewed by the Office of Management and Budget, and assigned a number and expiration date. The number and expiration date are at the top right corner of the form.

NOTICE OF PRIVACY ACT STATEMENT

This information is collected as provided pursuant to the Privacy Act, 5 U.S.C. 552a. The Bureau of Indian Affairs will not disclose any record containing such information without the written consent of the respondent unless the requestor uses the information to perform assigned duties. The primary use of this information is to certify that an individual possession Indian blood to receive Federal program services. Examples of others who may request the information are U.S. Department of Justice or in a proceeding before a court or adjudicative body; Federal, state, local, or foreign law enforcement agency; Members of Congress; Department of Treasury to effect payment; a Federal agency for collecting a debt; and other Federal agencies to detect and eliminate fraud.

NOTICE OF EFFECTS OF NON-DISCLOSURE

Disclosure of the information on this CDIB request is voluntary. However, proof of Indian blood is required to receive certain Federal program services.

NOTICE OF STATEMENTS AND SUBMISSIONS

Falsification or misrepresentation of information provided on this request is punishable under Federal Law 18 U.S.C. 1001. Conviction may result in a fine and/or imprisonment of not more than 5 years.

Source: OMB Control #1076-0153; Expiration Date: July 31, 2011, available at http://www.bia.gov/idc/groups/public/documents/text/idc-001805.pdf, last viewed March 4, 2010.

I request a CDIB and certify that I have read the instructions, and above notices about my request for a CDIB. I further certify that the information which I have provided with this request to the Bureau of Indian Affairs is true and correct.

_____   _____
(Requester's signature)   (date)

262   Apartheid in Indian Country?

OMB Control #1076-0153
Expiration Date: July 31, 2011
Page 2

BUREAU OF INDIAN AFFAIRS
REQUEST FOR CERTIFICATE OF DEGREE OF INDIAN OR ALASKA NATIVE BLOOD

Requester's Name (list all names by which Requester is or has been known)	Requestee's Address (including zip code)	Date Received by Bureau of Indian Affairs
Requester's Date of Birth Requester's Place of Birth Is Requester Adopted? ☐ Yes ☐ No Are Requester's Parents Adopted? ☐ Yes ☐ No If Yes, list natural (birth) parents (if known) Tribe(s) with which Requester is enrolled Roll No.	Father's Name Tribe Roll No. DOB Deceased ☐ Yes ☐ No Year ____ Mother's Name Tribe Roll No. DOB Deceased ☐ Yes ☐ No Year ____	Paternal Grandfather's Name Tribe Roll No. DOB Deceased Year ____ Tribe Roll No. DOB Deceased Year ____ Paternal Grandmother's Name Tribe Roll No. DOB Deceased Year ____ Maternal Grandfather's Name Tribe Roll No. DOB Deceased Year ____ Maternal Grandmother's Name Tribe Roll No. DOB Deceased Year ____	Paternal Great Grandfather's Name Tribe Roll No. DOB Deceased Year ____ Paternal Great Grandmother's Name Tribe Roll No. DOB Deceased Year ____ Paternal Great Grandfather's Name Tribe Roll No. DOB Deceased Year ____ Paternal Great Grandmother's Name Tribe Roll No. DOB Deceased Year ____ Maternal Great Grandfather's Name Tribe Roll No. DOB Deceased Year ____ Maternal Great Grandmother's Name Tribe Roll No. DOB Deceased Year ____ Maternal Great Grandfather's Name Tribe Roll No. DOB Deceased Year ____ Maternal Great Grandmother's Name Tribe Roll No. DOB Deceased Year ____

Conclusion

Remember that all through history the way of truth and love has always won. There have been tyrants and murderers, and for a time they seem invincible, but in the end, they always fall—think of it, ALWAYS."
—Mahatma Gandhi

Much of the discussion about Freedmen rights minimizes Freedmen connections to the Five Civilized Tribes, including their contributions to, participation in, and leadership among, tribal governments. For some, Freedmen disenfranchisement conjures up the words of abolitionist and statesman Frederick Douglass:

> Power concedes nothing without demand. It never did and it never will. Find out just what any people will quietly submit to and you have found the exact measure of injustice and wrong which will be imposed upon them, and these will continue till they are resisted with either words or blows, or with both.[1]

Some find it particularly troubling to witness struggles from within—the violence of exclusion that is sometimes intra-familial, and other times minority-on-minority. Hurt people *hurt people*. Perhaps that is part of the legacy of slavery and the remnants of Jim Crow.

Measuring the distance between the person one is and the person one aspires to be is difficult. It is, however, a necessary step for each of us if indeed we are to move forward. Noted historian Howard Zinn, writing about race and racism in the South in the 1960s, said it well:

> In effective psychotherapy, the patient is at first disturbed by self-recognition, then grateful for the disclosure. It is the first step toward transformation, and . . . this nation, with its huge potential for good, needs to take another look in the mirror. We owe this to ourselves, and to our children.[2]

For most people, that look in the proverbial mirror would yield startling and ambiguous images. Most people are more than they think they are.

Racial/ethnic purity is rare; in fact, it is virtually non-existent. Why should persons not be able—even encouraged—to claim all of who and what they are? The history of the Freedmen, accurately told, is rich in images of slavery, subjugation, and segregation, but it also reveals scenes of interracial conciliation, cooperation, and collaboration. Historic relationships between African Americans and Native Americans bear that out.[3]

As Marilyn Vann lamented, "History books teach people nothing about the relationship between African Americans and Native Americans. Few people know anything about persons of African descent who were tribal leaders, crossed the Trail of Tears, and much more. School curricula ignore these things."[4]

Ms. Vann and many others see education—an inclusive, accurate historical education—as a top priority. The rationale is simple: So long as we remain ignorant of where our paths have crossed, we will be unable to chart a new course together.

Americans—Native, black, white, brown, and yellow, Christian, Jew, Muslim, Agnostic, and otherwise—stand on common ground. Ostensibly divergent paths invariably and inevitably intersect. Beneath the surface, Americans' roots intermesh and intertwine, and severing them comes at a high cost.

The business of undoing a centuries-old legacy of race-based distinctions demands much of this and future generations.[5] Race-based distinctions may have subsided, but they continue. Despite the persistence of race, increasing numbers of people view institutional and individual actions that help perpetuate race-based disparities as morally bankrupt, economically unsound, and fundamentally un-American.

President Bill Clinton, long interested in America's tortured history around, and fascination with, race, eloquently articulated the task ahead:

> Today I ask the American people to join me in a great national effort to perfect the promise of America for this new time as we seek to build our more perfect union.... That is the unfinished work of our time, to lift the burden of race and redeem the promise of America.[6]

The scourge of African chattel slavery will forever be part of the American consciousness. Those dark days serve as reminders of the depravity to which the country is capable of sinking. Just as it was within America's capacity to close the institution of slavery, we are likewise capable of unshackling ourselves from its remaining vestiges.

The Founding Fathers gave Americans a blueprint from which to build a structurally sound democracy, able to embrace and nurture all its citizens. The engineers of our democracy designed a set of ideals which, intended or not, have proven broad enough to envelop all of us. Nonetheless, the issues of race have presented our nation with perhaps her greatest challenge and, ironically, our most profound opportunity:

> During more than two centuries, in the hands of the people, a great democracy continues under construction. At the same time, the "we" [in "we the people"] has changed considerably, from white men, propertied, educated, and privileged, to today's vastly broader and more diverse multiracial population. The people who are today's custodians of the great legacy of democracy are as varied as the nation is: men and women, rich and poor, from every walk of life and with family trees rooted in every nation on earth— all sharing the responsibilities of citizenship.
>
> . . . .
>
> The struggle of "we the people" to bring black Americans from slavery to the portals of freedom within the framework of the Constitution is, by far, the greatest proof that the Constitution is, indeed, a living document.[7]

"Race," though a social construct of dubious biological significance, has a profound impact on American life. It has been used to empower and to subjugate, to enrich and to impoverish, to anoint and to annihilate.[8] Indeed, one cannot understand American history without first learning about race, both conceptually and as manifest in American life over time.

The way forward begins with a look back. We have to consider how issues of power and privilege have shaped our intergroup and interpersonal relations. As Americans, we need to examine the often unequal relationship between the dominant white culture and Native Americans. We have to look at the adoption by some Native Americans of that same sense of "otherness" with respect to persons of African descent. This classic vicious cycle of dominance by proxy of race is evident not just in our American history, but in world history as well (e.g., the Nazis in the 1930s and 1940s, and the Serbs in the 1900s and early 2000s).

There is a need for a "post-race" view, a worldview that acknowledges the psychosocial realities of race, but does not attach determinative status to them. Sociologist Dr. Calvin C. Moore sees salutary signs of movement toward a post-racial society, but he cautions that the achievement of that ideal looms somewhere beyond a distant horizon.[9]

S. A. Ray, J.D., Ph.D., a Cherokee scholar, has urged the Cherokee Nation to move beyond race in defining what it means to be Cherokee. According to Dr. Ray:

> If Cherokee [N]ation identity is to escape its continued construction upon the effects of a spurious race science, Cherokees must be attentive to their "official" genealogy's structural and historical affiliation with that false god, and re-imagine criteria of citizenship based not on "Indian blood" but on new, non-racialized understandings of and appreciation for Cherokee ancestry. [footnote omitted][10]

. . . .

> Cherokees must reclaim ancestry from biology and articulate a new political relationship to their individual and collective pasts, one which does not use law to deploy categories based on colonialist racial ideologies to exclude potential citizens.
>
> To decide the question of the Freedmen's descendants' status ... Cherokee citizens, including Freedmen's descendants, should engage in a searching dialogue on political and social identity, one that expressly includes race.[11]

Dr. Ray suggests:

> [A] good [citizenship] criterion should serve the practical function of distinguishing [tribal] members from non-members while re-

maining flexible to changing circumstances; it must respond to an overarching ... vision of the tribe's purpose in the world, and it must be attuned to how the inheritance of colonialism may be at work in the tribe.[12]

Dr. Ray further urges a citizenship formula that considers: (i) kinship and cultural affinity; (ii) the values of practicality, i.e., effectiveness at discerning members and non-members; (iii) spirituality, i.e., fidelity to Native American tribal spirituality in all of its manifestations; and (iv) historical integrity, i.e., factoring into the equation the history of American colonialism.[13]

Dr. Ray thus suggests a more fluid framework for determining citizenship among the various Native American tribes. His analysis suggests some relevant, practical considerations in analyzing tribal citizenship. Areas of inquiry might include the prospective citizen's: level and types of tribal activities; tribal language facility; familiarity with and adherence to Native customs/traditions; extent of historical and family engagement in tribal culture; and concept of what it means to be a tribal member (i.e., self-definition of "Indianness" within the context of the tribe under consideration).

The latter criterion—looking honestly at American colonialism—seems to have gained a modicum of traction in Congress, at least as regards the Native-American experience. On May 6, 2004, Senator Sam Brownback of Kansas introduced legislation titled "A joint resolution to acknowledge a long history of official depredations and ill-conceived policies by the United States [g]overnment regarding Indian Tribes and offer an apology to all Native [p]eoples on behalf of the United States." The Senate Joint Resolution speaks eloquently to the perverse relationship between Native Americans and the United States government. It recounts the initial promise of collaboration and cooperation that too quickly descended into confrontation and confinement. On behalf of the United States, the joint resolution accepts culpability and offers contrition:[14]

> The United States, acting through Congress—
> (1) recognizes the special legal and political relationship the Indian Tribes have with the United States and the solemn covenant with the land we share;
> (2) commends and honors the Native Peoples for the thousands of years that they have stewarded and protected this land;
> (3) acknowledges years of official depredations, ill-conceived

policies, and the breaking of covenants by the United States Government regarding Indian Tribes;

(4) apologizes on behalf of the people of the United States to all Native Peoples for the many instances of violence, maltreatment, and neglect inflicted on Native Peoples by citizens of the United States;

(5) expresses its regret for the ramifications of former offenses and its commitment to build on the positive relationships of the past and present to move toward a brighter future where all the people of this land live reconciled as brothers and sisters, and harmoniously steward and protect this land together;

(6) urges the President to acknowledge the offenses of the United States against Indian Tribes in the history of the United States in order to bring healing to this land by providing a proper foundation for reconciliation between the United States and Indian Tribes; and

(7) commends the State governments that have begun reconciliation efforts with recognized Indian Tribes located in their boundaries and encourages all State governments similarly to work toward reconciling relationships with Indian Tribes within their boundaries.

The Brownback resolution offered at least the beginnings of a route to federal government/Native American reconciliation—*rapprochement*. Only by acknowledging the past, however difficult, will the bonds of respect and trust grow stronger.[15]

That notion of *rapprochement*—of reconciliation—around race-drilled fissures in our nation's historic infrastructure should be extended. If the goal is to move into an enlightened period of post-racialism, then we must acknowledge the need for repair and begin laying tracks that connect all Americans. Moving forward sometimes requires a step backward:

> This is the burden of history. And to start the healing process, there needs to be a "walk through history"—a taking of an inventory of hurts—carried out together by the winners and the losers or the aggressors and their victims, or their descendents, to rediscover what happened in the past which keeps alive so much anger and resentment in the present.[16]

In a number of communities, this process has begun. In Tulsa, Oklahoma, for example, the John Hope Franklin Center for

Reconciliation[17] is working to transform society's divisions into social harmony through the serious study and work of reconciliation. As part of that effort, the organization has, among other things: (1) hosted symposia that have brought together academicians and practitioners to study historic events around which reconciliation is needed and offer insights into "best practices" that foster hope and healing; (2) embarked upon a documentary project focused on historical memory that will capture how the story of the 1921 Tulsa Race Riot has been told in families inter-generationally; (3) surveyed racial attitudes in the Tulsa community; (4) worked toward a more inclusive history curriculum for Tulsa Public Schools; and (5) opened a community park dedicated to Dr. John Hope Franklin.

In Richmond, Virginia, the nonprofit "Hope in the Cities"[18] has been instrumental in building trust in the community through honest conversation on race, reconciliation, and responsibility. The ultimate aim of the organization is to create just and inclusive communities through reconciliation among racial, ethnic, and religious groups. That mammoth task requires both personal and institutional change, involving: (1) Honest conversations: Creating models of sustained community dialogue involving all sectors and leading to new and unexpected partnerships; (2) Acceptance of personal responsibility: moving beyond blame and personal pain to constructive action; and (3) Public acts of acknowledgment and reconciliation: breaking cycles of guilt or anger to reach understanding and healing.

Outside Atlanta, Georgia, citizens established the biracial Moore's Ford Memorial Committee in 1997 to commemorate an infamous, unsolved lynching of two black couples. The quadruple slaying occurred on the Moore's Ford Bridge that spans the Appalachee River, some 60 miles east of Atlanta, on July 25, 1946. The Moore's Ford Committee continues to work toward racial reconciliation. Committee members have conducted a number of activities, including: (i) restoration of cemeteries where the victims were buried; (ii) erection of tombstones at the previously unmarked graves; (iii) facilitation of educational sessions; (iv) establishment of scholarships in the names of the lynching victims; (v) sponsorship of a biracial memorial service on the anniversary of the attack; and, in concert with the Georgia Historical Society (vi) placement of a state historical marker near the site of the Moore's Ford Bridge lynchings.

Reconciliation requires sustained effort and continuous dialogue. It is not work for the fainthearted. These communities, through individual commitments and bold leadership, have accepted the challenge full-on.

Rob Corcoran, national director of Initiatives of Change USA (IofC) and founder of IofC's flagship program, Hope in the Cities, in Richmond, Virginia, identified seven key criteria for community reconciliation in his book, *Trustbuilding: An Honest Conversation on Race, Reconciliation, and Responsibility*:

- Listening carefully and respectfully to one another and to the whole community;
- Bringing people together, not in confrontation but in trust, to tackle the most urgent needs of the community;
- Searching for solutions, focusing on what is right rather than who is right;
- Building lasting relationships outside individual comfort zones;
- Honoring each person, appealing to the best qualities in everyone, and refusing to stereotype the other group;
- Holding ourselves, our communities, and our institutions accountable in areas where change is needed; and
- Recognizing that the energy for fundamental change requires a moral and spiritual transformation in the human spirit.[19]

Beyond large-scale community initiatives, change will come through the countless and seemingly small things individuals do to foster reconciliation. One example of a person's taking the initiative is Sanford R. "Sandy" Cardin, President of the Charles and Lynn Schusterman Family Foundation headquartered in Tulsa, Oklahoma. Sandy, a personal friend of the author, regularly hosts Shabbat salons, dinner parties for diverse configurations of invited guests, on Shabbat, the Jewish Sabbath. These informal assemblages on Friday evenings are filled with food, fun, and fellowship.

Guests arrive over the span of thirty to forty-five minutes. Introductions and polite banter follow as each new person arrives. Strands of conversation continue or begin as new faces find their places. The chatter continues until dinner, which is always exceptional, is served.

As an immediate prelude to dinner, guests learn experientially about the rudiments of Shabbat ritual. Questions are asked and answered. Dinner, served up with heaping helpings of unscripted conversation, follows. Sandy, the consummate host, sometimes doubles as moderator and, less frequently, provocateur. A stimulating exchange invariably results. Not infrequently, the colloquy turns to the hard stuff: race, religion, and politics.

This confab happens in a context of absolute safety, and this leads to open and honest dialogue (and sometimes, debate). The depth and richness of the discussions builds new and strengthen existing relationships. This, in turn, generates the impetus for improved community relations overall. Such small steps matter.

The task of moving toward post-racialism, of reconciliation, is no doubt daunting but, as with all things, it begins at the micro level. It begins individually, with each of us. It begins with our moments of choice. Our future will be the sum of those individually considered determinations.

So what can we do as individuals to move beyond the parochialism of race? While there is no magic pill, some small, practical, individual steps include the following:

- **Expand your horizons and your mind**. Learn about your racial, ethnic, and cultural heritage and that of others. Examine your history and that of the world around you.[20]
- **Know and be true to yourself**. Through introspection, get in touch with your feelings, preconceptions, and stereotypes. Do the work necessary to confront your own fears and reduce your biases.
- **Reach out to, and share with, others**. Step outside your comfort zone. Connect with "the other"—people from backgrounds and circumstances different from your own.
- **Listen actively; think critically**. Record mental snapshots of what others say about their diversity and inclusion-related experiences. Use this information as you work on diversity and inclusion in your own life.
- **Engage constructively**. Take part in meaningful, ongoing dialogue about race. Support organizations and causes that further diversity and inclusion.
- **Be longsuffering**. Making headway on matters of race invariably involves experiencing some level of discomfort around a sensitive topic. Progress, not finality, is the goal. Make a long-term commitment to the process of racial healing.

In the end, our racial, ethnic, and tribal affiliations must yield to a higher calling: shared humanity. As statesman Frederick Douglass noted in the late nineteenth century:

> I do now and always have attached more importance to manhood than to mere kinship or identity with one variety of the human family. Race, in the popular sense, is narrow; humanity is broad. The one is special, the other is universal. The one is transient; the other is permanent.[21]

Douglass's vision of the inexorable interdependence of all people—the "human family"—parallels the notion of shared humanity. Where it really matters, self-interest and mutual interest align. We stand, as a nation, on common ground.

"One America in the 21st Century: The President's Initiative on Race," President Bill Clinton's late 1990s effort to foster dialogue and spur action on issues of race, spoke to Americans' unity of interest:

> Some common values and aspirations that Americans share became evident as we traveled throughout the Nation. We all share common values—a thirst for freedom, the desire for equal opportunity, a belief in fairness, and the need for essential justice. We all possess common aspirations—a decent and affordable home, a good education, a fulfilling job, financial and personal security, adequate and available health care, and healthy and educated children whose dreams for a bright future are a vision of reality, not a mirage. We all feel the same emotions—joy at the birth of a child, sadness at the death of a loved one, love for our family, fear of conditions beyond our control, anger at people who disrespect us, hope for the future, and frustration at the daily barriers we encounter. We all should aspire to the vision of an America in which we honor and respect the differences that make each of us unique and celebrate the common threads that bind us together.[22]

America's forty-fourth president, Barack Obama, likewise emphasized our shared space rather than our real or imagined differences in his inaugural address. America's first African-American President urged:

> [W]e know that our patchwork heritage is a strength, not a weakness. We are a nation of Christians and Muslims, Jews and Hindus—and non-believers. We are shaped by every language and

culture, drawn from every end of this Earth; and because we have tasted the bitter swill of civil war and segregation, and emerged from that dark chapter stronger and more united, we cannot help but believe that the old hatreds shall someday pass; that the lines of tribe shall soon dissolve; that as the world grows smaller, our common humanity shall reveal itself; and that America must play its role in ushering in a new era of peace.[23]

A "post-race" America (i.e., an America in which race no longer hobbles anyone) is but an ideal, but so, too, are freedom, justice, and equality. We progress when we inch closer and closer to that distant marker. Lofty aspirations, eternal vigilance, unwavering commitment—these are the foundational elements of the journey.

The quest of the Freedmen to reclaim roots within the Five Civilized Tribes represents movement along the path toward the "post-race" or "race-neutral" society so many embrace, in word if not in deed. In the end, it is not our differences, but the difference our differences make, that matters. So it is with the Freedmen. With thoughtfulness, commitment, and constructive engagement, it is possible both to salvage sovereignty and respect rights.

At the 2011 John Hope Franklin Center for Reconciliation Symposium, Cherokee Nation Principal Chief Chad Smith seemed to signal a future opportunity for, and an interest in, rapprochement. Speaking at a luncheon "Point/Counterpoint" on the status of the Freedmen in the Five Civilized Tribes, Chief Smith noted: "The real question is the day after [i.e., the day after the Freedmen's legal claims have run their course in the legal arena]. How do we proceed to reconcile our communities, to reconcile our pasts, to deal with productive, constructive ways for us to build our future?"[24] Indeed, that is the question, and there is no better time than the present to begin addressing it.

Appendix A

Having Their Say: The Freedmen Respond to Detractors

> Nothing worth doing is completed in our lifetime,
> Therefore, we are saved by hope.
> Nothing true or beautiful or good makes complete sense in any immediate context of history;
> Therefore, we are saved by faith.
> Nothing we do, however virtuous, can be accomplished alone.
> Therefore, we are saved by love.
> No virtuous act is quite as virtuous from the standpoint of our friend or foe as from our own;
> Therefore, we are saved by the final form of love[,] which is forgiveness.
> —REINHOLD NIEBUHR

Freedmen, committed to their individual and collective re-empowerment, have spent countless hours engaged in genealogical research and wide-ranging educational efforts. The need for identification runs deep. Some Freedmen, seeking empirical proof of blood ties to Native-American tribes, have even turned to genetic testing.[1]

Like a Southern black church, Freedmen gatherings often include a "love offering"—donations to the cause. Money, organization, and political currency are required in waging battle against well-funded Indian nations over Freedmen rights. Acknowledged deficiencies in these areas delayed Freedmen challenges to some initial salvos in the citizenship battles (e.g., changes in rules within the Cherokee Nation in the 1980s).[2] Finally, the Freedmen and their allies stand ready to wage war over citizenship rights. What the Freedmen lack in resources, they more than make up for in passion.

The Freedmen argue that misconceptions, myths, and threadbare theories underlie tribal disenfranchisement efforts. As such, they have addressed eight key propositions—"myths," in Freedmen parlance—they feel affect the dynamics of their relationships with the Five Civilized Tribes.

The Freedmen have chosen to meet their detractors head-on, answering criticisms and accusations squarely. By addressing these eight points, the Freedmen seek to stake claim to a threatened identity, allay fears about opportunism, and highlight perceived civil and human rights violations long overlooked. The eight "myths," and the Freedmen's response to each, follow.

PROPOSITION 1: Freedmen seek only money and benefits from their Native-American affiliation. They do not aid in the advancement of tribal culture.

First, the Freedmen's principal claim of entitlement is a claim *of belonging*, not *to benefits*. The Freedmen, a number of whom are professionals, would fail to qualify for many of the income-based benefits available to Native-American tribal members (e.g., housing, Indian Health Services), even if they were otherwise eligible.

Second, even assuming, *arguendo*, the truth of this "gold digger" proposition, the Freedmen would by no means be the first and only opportunists seeking to take economic advantage of recognized Indian status. A number of "white Indians" lay claim to Indian heritage in order to reap social and economic benefits, with little complaint from the tribes. Why, then, do the tribes single out "black Indians" as the only culprits in this perceived "faux Indian" ruse?

The Freedmen seek no more than that to which they are entitled. Far from mere gold diggers, many are already actively engaged in Indian life, whether attending cultural activities, learning tribal languages, or immersing themselves in native tradition and ritual.

Some Freedmen have even written books about their tribal ancestry and history. For example, Bob Curry, an enrolled Chickasaw of African ancestry, wrote *Chickasaw Rolls*.[3]

PROPOSITION 2: Freedmen and their descendants do not possess Indian blood.

Approximately one-third of the original Chickasaw Freedmen went to court to be transferred from the Freedmen rolls to the "Chickasaw by blood rolls" [as discussed previously in connection with "Equity Case 7071]. Affidavits, witnesses, parents' marriage licenses, Dawes Commission census cards, and other relevant documentation corroborated these claims of tribal blood connections. The Chickasaw Freedmen marshaled their evidence and trumpeted their claim to "Indian blood." Despite this impressive showing, their pleas fell on deaf ears. The Chickasaw Freedmen saga demonstrates the resistance of the tribes even to reasonable efforts on the part of the Freedmen to prove blood connections. Reliance solely on the race-based Dawes Rolls, in the face of such overwhelming supplementary data documenting Indian blood ties, defies logic and smacks of anti-black prejudice.

PROPOSITION 3: Freedmen have no desire to be classified as Indians by blood.

Choctaw and Chickasaw Freedmen received allotments of 40 acres, while Choctaws and Chickasaws "by blood" received 320 acres. The Chickasaw Nation did not consider Freedmen citizens, and therefore felt no obligation to educate them. In fact, education for Chickasaw Freedmen was almost non-existent until Oklahoma gained statehood in 1907.

Given the choice, any reasonable person would have claimed Indian blood. The Dawes Commission, however, made that choice for the Freedmen of the Five Civilized Tribes, enrolling them on the "Freedmen Roll" instead of the "Blood Roll." The Freedmen, often undereducated, lacking English proficiency, and unfamiliar with the legal system, neither understood how to challenge their suspect classification nor appreciated the longstanding consequences of their failure to do so. Only in recent years have the Freedmen fully grasped the life-altering capacity of their categorization and the imperative that it be challenged. Given the relative powerlessness of persons of African ancestry, even through much of the twentieth century, any such challenge would likely have been, until relatively recently, futile.

PROPOSITION 4: The added enrollment of Freedmen will wreak financial havoc on the tribes.

The enrollment of Seminole Freedmen in the Seminole Nation following a Freedmen citizenship struggle early in the twenty-first century did not imperil the financial viability of the tribe. Indeed, surveys indicate: (i) the average individual of African descent has a higher income than the average non-African Indian; and (ii) newly enrolled Freedmen are less likely to use the needs-based tribal services than their non-African counterparts. Moreover, the federal government pegs tribal funding to membership numbers. Larger tribes like the Cherokees receive a greater proportional share of federal funds for programs and service than do smaller tribes like the Shawnee. Added enrollment thus translates into increased federal funding.

PROPOSITION 5: The Final Rolls of the Dawes Commission constitute accurate listings of the blood quantum of members of the Five Civilized Tribes.

The Final Rolls of the Dawes Commission recorded the Indian blood of non-African tribal members only. Even then, the Dawes Commission more than once listed full brothers and sisters as having different degrees of Indian blood. Tribal citizens enrolled as Freedmen may or may not have had Indian blood. Dawes Commission bureaucrats simply ignored the blood degree of persons perceived to be of African ancestry, presumptively assuming them to be "non-Indian" and segregating them on a census roster that did not reference Indian ancestry.

Proposition 6: Freedmen are merely "wannabe" Indians.

Freedmen treaty rights, ancestral connections, and cultural ties to the Five Civilized Tribes make them much more than Indian "wannabes."[4] The labor of enslaved Africans benefited the tribes enormously. While most Indians did not enslave persons of African descent, some of those who did rose to the uppermost ranks of tribal government. For example, William Potter Ross, a member of the slaveholding Ross family, became a Cherokee Chief after the Civil War. Ross, a mixed blood "white Indian," claimed longtime Cherokee Chief John Ross as a relative. W. P. Ross and the Cherokee Nation he led benefited from the institution of slavery. Freedmen blood, sweat, and tears contributed mightily to the Five Civilized Tribes.

Proposition 7: Freedmen "Buffalo Soldiers" oppressed other citizens of the Five Civilized Tribes after the Civil War.

After the Revolutionary War, the United States government forbade free persons of African descent from serving as armed military troops. For that reason, no black soldiers participated in the infamous "Trails of Tears" during the 1830s. During and after the Civil War, black soldiers served voluntarily in the military. These troops mostly consisted of "State Negroes," black citizens of the United States, as opposed to the black Indians affiliated with the Five Civilized Tribes. The military offered a steady paycheck.

Freedmen, by contrast, realized more social and economic opportunities than State Negroes. They could work the land in common with other Indian citizens and pursue education, training, and employment. Free of the yoke of Southern oppression, Freedmen engaged in entrepreneurship and political pursuits often foreclosed to State Negroes.

White-led "Buffalo Soldiers," segregated black infantry and cavalry units, gained notoriety. Commanders dispatched the Buffalo Soldiers, about ten percent of the military, to search for Plains Indian leaders and to guard the Five Civilized Tribes against Plains Indian incursions.

Black troops did not participate in the infamous massacres of indigenous people, e.g., General George Armstrong Custer's onslaught at the Battle of the Washita in 1868 and the 7th Cavalry's slaying of unarmed Lakota Sioux Indian women and children at Wounded Knee in 1890. Still, apocryphal tales of widespread Indian mistreatment at the hands of Freedmen-turned-soldiers linger.

Proposition 8: Freedmen sold their right to citizenship in the Five Civilized Tribes.

In 1885, fewer than 100 Choctaw Freedmen took cash payments in exchange for the surrender of their Choctaw citizenship. The majority of Choctaw Freedmen elected to remain citizens of the Choctaw Nation.[5] Beyond that exceptional case, the Freedmen of the Five Civilized Tribes never relinquished their claims to citizenship; they never "sold out."

Appendix B

The Voice of a Freedmen Advocate: Marilyn Vann in Her Own Words

Marilyn Vann, a petroleum engineer from Oklahoma City, Oklahoma, claims African and Cherokee ancestry. She is the President of the Descendants of the Freedmen of the Five Civilized Tribes Association and Band Chief of the Freedmen Band of the Cherokee Nation. Ms. Vann is a vocal and prominent advocate for the citizenship rights of Cherokee Freedmen—persons of African descent (and sometimes mixed African and Cherokee blood lines) who were guaranteed citizenship status by the Cherokee Nation in an 1866 treaty with the United States of America.

An early twentieth century federal Indian census taken by agents of the Dawes Commission recorded data on persons living among the Cherokee Nation for purposes of land allotment. These agents registered persons of discernible African ancestry on a segregated Freedmen Roll. The same census takers listed persons living among the tribes who exhibited no evidence of African ancestry on a Blood Roll. Unlike the Freedmen Roll, the Blood Roll documented each registrant's percentage of Indian blood or "blood quantum." The modern-day Cherokee Nation of Oklahoma uses these segregation-era allotment rolls to make citizenship decisions on the basis of "Indian blood."

Over the last several years, the Cherokee Nation has squandered millions to remove from its tribal citizenship roster a small number of "Freedmen"—persons of African ancestry with historic ties to the tribe and federally protected legal rights to tribal membership. The Freedmen descended from enslaved Africans who trekked the Trail of Tears, some shackled, others carrying baggage, while their Cherokee owners—sometimes their own fathers or brothers—rode in wagons or on horseback. The Treaty of 1866 guaranteed the Freedmen citizenship in the Cherokee Nation.

Spurred on by tribal leaders, the Cherokee Nation minimizes the scope of the harm to persons of African descent wrought by the disenfranchisement of those to whom it promised citizenship. The Nation ignores the contributions of Freedmen to Cherokee life and culture, while inflating the economic burden Freedmen citizenship might exact on the tribe.

The Cherokee Nation claims that 1,500 or so persons of African ancestry who currently maintain citizenship in the Cherokee Nation would not be affected by the pending disenrollment actions. These persons presumably have ties to the Dawes Commission "Blood Roll." Whether or not that claim is accurate, some 22,000 persons of African ancestry have been, or will be, adversely affected by Cherokee Nation disenfranchisement efforts. There are many more Freedmen than the relative few African Americans linked to the Cherokee "Blood Roll."

The Cherokee Nation stresses its right to do as it wishes—its sovereign prerogative—as regards tribal citizenship. But sovereignty implies a willingness to live up to such agreements as the Treaty of 1866. That pact promised the Freedmen tribal citizenship. Sovereignty includes the acceptance of responsibility for tribal minorities—particularly persons whose ancestors tribal members enslaved, and whose kin tribal members turned to for nurturance and sustenance again and again. Sovereignty means stepping up as a *political* entity, as opposed to a racial or ethnic group, to follow the law—to protect Freedmen rights.

The Cherokee Nation cautions against Congressional intervention and incursions upon tribal sovereignty. But the people's representatives are legally and morally obliged to step up and step in to protect the civil and human rights of the Freedmen.

The Cherokee Nation seeks to denationalize the Freedmen. Just as chattel slavery was morally repugnant in the first instance, the disenfranchisement of the Freedmen magnifies the original sin. The United States government should not continue to fund the Cherokee Nation while the Cherokee Nation refuses to honor its commitment to the Freedmen under the Treaty of 1866. Congress, the guardian of taxpayers' dollars, is not obligated to provide federal funds to Indian tribes who refuse to comply with federal law. Federal law is supreme.

What rationale could explain the disrespect accorded the Freedmen? The Cherokee Nation asserts that the Freedmen are not culturally Cherokees. It argues that tribal self-rule (i.e., sovereignty) trumps the legal rights promised to the Freedmen by the tribe itself.

There is no cultural or residency test for Cherokee tribal membership. From the standpoint of the federal government, being an "Indian" is not a matter of race, but rather a matter of law. Native-American tribes constitute political entities, not racial groups.

That said, even if racial/cultural components are relevant, "white Indians" face no cultural affinity litmus test like that sought to be applied to the Freedmen. People who have never visited the Cherokee Nation, who lack United States citizenship, and who reside in foreign countries—these are all people who have sought and obtained Cherokee citizenship status. Many of these individuals and their ancestors identify primarily as "Caucasians," and only recently stumbled upon the fact they have an ancestor registered on the Cherokee Blood Roll.

Questions of acculturation cut both ways. Few persons now registered with the Cherokee Nation follow traditional religions or speak the Cherokee language. Neither former Cherokee Principal Chief Chad Smith, a vocal advocate for Freedmen disenfranchisement, nor the members of the Cherokee Nation Tribal Council during his tenure, speak the native tongue.

By contrast, a number of Cherokee Freedmen attend Cherokee language classes, participate in Cherokee organizations (including the Cherokee Historical Society), attend Cherokee holiday events, and work at Indian Health Services. Some Freedmen previously worked for the Bureau of Indian Affairs, and many Freedmen, including the officers and directors of the Descendants of Freedmen of the Five Civilized Tribes Association, have lived in or near the Cherokee Nation jurisdictional area for most of their lives.

Former Cherokee tribal attorney general Julian Fite told the *Southwest Times Record* in Fort Smith, Arkansas, on August 16, 2003, that the Freedmen had never voted in the history of the tribe. That kind of reckless and inaccurate comment demonstrates a lack of knowledge about the history of the Cherokee Nation, the legal rights of the Freedmen, and the significant contributions of the Freedmen to the Cherokee Nation. Calculated misinformation deceives the general public and does dishonor to the entire Cherokee Nation. The Cherokee cultural competency and civic engagement of numerous Freedmen matches or surpasses that of many non-Freedmen Cherokees, including some of the leadership and authorities within the Cherokee Nation.

Former Cherokee Principal Chief Chad Smith has contributed to the disinformation about the Cherokee Freedmen by making unsubstantiated and irresponsible claims. For example, Chief Smith erroneously claims that a 1902 Act of Congress barred the Freedmen from receiving additional tribal benefits.

He has also urged Congress to leave Freedmen issues to the tribal courts. But Chief Smith himself has tapped federal forums when such courts suit his needs. Moreover, he has criticized or contradicted the tribal court rulings adverse to his interests. Chief Smith apparently does not respect the very tribal courts he would foist upon the Freedmen.

Given the federal role in Indian affairs, Congress must not ignore the present controversy. The Cherokee Nation typically receives 80% of its operating budget from federal coffers. Its leaders realize the significance of the Freedmen controversy at the federal level. In some contexts, the

Cherokee Nation argues that Freedmen issues should be left to the courts. In others, it pushes for Congressional resolution. One thing is clear: Freedmen issues must be addressed at the federal level—soon.

The Freedmen are regular people—widows, policemen, decorated veterans, ministers. They are "everyman" and "everywoman." The Freedmen seek merely to stake claim to their identity, and to reaffirm their political and economic rights under the Treaty of 1866—rights validated by countless courts through the years.

Cherokee Nation leaders claim that Congress, and particularly the Congressional Black Caucus, opposes tribal sovereignty. That assertion seeks to divert attention from the core injustice of Freedmen disenfranchisement. The Cherokee Nation voluntarily entered into the Treaty of 1866, pursuant to which the tribe agreed to grant the Freedmen citizenship. It is time to honor that commitment. It is reasonable to expect at least that if the Cherokee Nation expects the federal spigot to remain open.

The United States government accepted responsibility for its enslaved and conquered peoples (African Americans; Native Americans), as evidenced by its grants of citizenship to and, ultimately, by its enfranchisement of, these groups. The Cherokee Nation should likewise accept its responsibility and treaty obligations to the descendants of the persons whom it enslaved.

Sovereignty requires responsibility. The United States government expected South Africa and other nations to live up to their responsibilities regarding the persons whom they conquered and enslaved. Our government should expect no less of the Native-American governments with whom it maintains a special relationship.

Imagine the outrage if the governor of one of our Southern states, say Mississippi, designed and implemented a movement to denationalize all African Americans living within the confines of that state. That scenario is not unlike the present condition of the Freedmen. Neither can be tolerated. Just as we would rightly condemn the actions of the governmor of Mississippi in the proposed hypothetical, so, too, should we reject the actions of the Cherokee Nation with respect to Freedmen disenfranchisement.

The Cherokee Nation should not be subsidized by American taxpayers in its efforts to denationalize the descendants of the Africans it once enslaved. Justice demands that the federal government act to enforce existing laws and treaties by barring federal expenditures until the Cherokee Nation complies with the Treaty of 1866 and its promise of citizenship to the Freedmen.

Appendix C

The Cherokee Nation Perspective on the Freedmen

History of Freedmen Descendants: Timeline

1975

To rejuvenate the Cherokee Nation after decades of U.S. policy to terminate Indian nations, and to return to its roots as an Indian tribe made up of Indians, the Cherokee people approved a new Constitution defining citizenship as being open only to descendants of Indians who were original enrollees on the Dawes Rolls, the federally authorized census of the Cherokee people taken in 1906. To become a citizen, the Cherokee people decided that one must trace one lineal Indian ancestor (specifically, Cherokee, Shawnee or Delaware) listed on the Dawes Rolls. Descendants of original enrollees in non-Indian categories on the Dawes Rolls (the Freedmen and Intermarried Whites categories) would not be eligible for citizenship.

1988

The 10th Circuit Court of Appeals ruled in *Nero v. Cherokee Nation* that Cherokees could decide their own citizenship requirements and thus exclude Freedmen descendants. The facts involved with this case are similar to the facts in the *Vann v. Kempthorne* case.

2001

The Cherokee Nation Supreme Court (the Nation's highest court) ruled that Freedmen descendants were properly excluded through the 1975 Constitution.

2003

The Cherokee people approved another Constitution, knowing the 2001 Cherokee Nation Supreme Court decision said that descendants of original enrollees under the Freedmen and Intermarried Whites categories of the Dawes Rolls would be excluded from citizenship in the 1975

Constitution. This led to the filing of *Vann v. Kempthorne* by six Freedmen descendants against the U.S. Department of the Interior in U.S. District Court in Washington, D.C.

March 2006

The Cherokee Nation Supreme Court ruled in the *Lucy Allen* case that language in the 1975 and 2003 Constitutions was not clear enough to exclude descendants of original enrollees in non-Indian categories on the Dawes Rolls. To limit citizenship to descendants of Indians on the Dawes Rolls, the Court ruled that the exclusionary language must be explicit.

The Cherokee Nation began granting citizenship with full social services (including health care, education and housing assistance) and the right to vote to descendants of Freedmen and Intermarried Whites.

2006

Three thousand Cherokee citizens signed a citizen-organized petition calling for a Cherokee people's referendum on a new Constitutional amendment that, per the *Lucy Allen* decision, would explicitly limit citizenship in the Nation to descendants of Indians on the Dawes Blood Rolls.

December 19, 2006

The U.S. District Court, in the *Vann v. Kempthorne* litigation, ruled that the sovereign immunity of the Cherokee Nation had been abrogated and, as a result of that abrogation, the Cherokee Nation could be named as a defendant in the lawsuit. The Cherokee Nation immediately appealed the decision to the D.C. Circuit Court of Appeals.

March 3, 2007

The proposed amendment to the Cherokee Nation Constitution was approved by 77 percent of those voting on the matter. To be eligible for Cherokee citizenship under the amendment, a prospective citizen must be able to trace his/her Cherokee heritage back to a Cherokee, Shawnee, or Delaware ancestor on the Dawes Blood Rolls. Proponents of the measure held that Cherokee Nation citizenship is colorblind, having nothing to do with race and everything to do with one's "Indianness."

As a result of the adoption of the Constitutional amendment, 2,867 Freedmen and nine Intermarried Whites descendants who had become citizens in March 2006 (after the *Lucy Allen* decision) were dis-enrolled after being citizens for less than one year.

May 14, 2007

After the amendment's passage, more than 300 dis-enrolled Freedmen descendants have filed challenges to the March 2007 amendment in Cherokee Nation District Court since its passage. The tribal court issued an order reinstating the 2,867 Freedmen descendants and nine Intermarried Whites to citizenship, with full social services assistance and the right to vote through the duration of the litigation. Proposed by the plaintiffs, [the tribal court's] order had the full support of the Cherokee Nation Attorney General.

May 17, 2007
The Cherokee Nation District Court issued another order, specifically reopening voter registration for the Freedmen descendants who were reinstated pending the litigation.

June 23, 2007
The Cherokee Nation held its June General Election for Principal Chief, Deputy Chief and Tribal Council officers. Previously, the Bureau of Indian Affairs (BIA) approved the Nation's election procedures. Registered Freedmen descendants voted in the election. A new Constitutional amendment revoking federal government oversight of Cherokee Nation Constitutional amendments was approved by 67 percent of those voting, and later approved by the BIA.

June-September 2007
Despite the fact that litigation over Freedmen citizenship status continued in tribal and federal courts (both U.S. District and Appeals Courts in Washington, D.C.), members of the House introduced a bill to terminate the Cherokee Nation and cut all its federal funding (H.R. 2824) and an amendment to prohibit federal housing funds assistance until and unless the Nation permanently reinstates the Freedmen and extended citizenship for this group's own living descendants (attached to H.R. 2786). In FY 2008 alone, that would have meant $300 million in federal funding overall. Oklahoma Congressman Dan Boren attached a measure to prohibit H.R. 2786's funding cut until the tribal court resolved the litigation.

February 2008
The U.S. District Court in Washington, D.C., stayed the *Vann* litigation at the trial level until the D.C. Circuit Court of Appeals decided the appeal of the December 2006 opinion that first captured the Nation in the *Vann* litigation.

May 6, 2008
Oral arguments were held in the *Vann* case at the D.C. Circuit Court of Appeals.

Source: Cherokee Nation website (adapted): http://freedmen.cherokee.org/Historyof FreedmenDescendants/tabid/724/Default.aspx (last visited September 15, 2010)

Appendix D

A Conversation with David Cornsilk[1]

Prompted by the author's questions, Cherokee activist and "Freedmen Fighter" David Cornsilk discusses his work in behalf of the Cherokee Freedmen.

What is the single most critical point about the Freedmen controversy you would like to communicate?

That our Cherokee ancestors made a promise and it is up to us to honor that promise. We must keep our word because it is a sacred trust handed to us for safekeeping. If we cannot be trusted to hold to our word, what is our worth?

How much a part of your life has the Freedmen controversy become?

I don't think it's measurable. The Freedmen issue has taken up a lot of my time and resources, but it has also opened up new friendships, relationships, opportunities and knowledge. Those are things that cannot be measured.

Do you have any regrets associated with your work on the Freedmen controversy?

Sometimes I have regrets. At the end of the day, I am still an Indian and see most things through the veil of race and culture. But such provincial views are not in the best interest of the Cherokee Nation as a whole, any more than they were for the whites of Alabama in the 1950s and 1960s.

Have you experienced backlash from the Cherokee Nation because of your work on the Freedmen issue? If so, please describe those experiences.

The Cherokee Nation is the whole Nation, not just the people who govern. I have experienced some individuals who are opposed to the Freedmen and [who] have blamed me for the controversy, but nothing where I felt my life was in danger. Most Cherokees who take the time to understand the issues, learn the history, and apply a doctrine of fairness, actually come around to an acceptance of the Freedmen. Unfortunately, the battle is "one person at a time." Compared to the enemies of the Freedmen, Freedmen advocates and allies have few resources.

What motivates you to continue this pursuit?
I am motivated by a sense of equal application of justice. Perhaps best compared to the Golden Rule, I would not want my rights attacked simply because I am different from the majority. And I am taken back to the words of Bernice Riggs. When she was denied citizenship in the Cherokee Nation, she said, with tears in her eyes, "Why are they doing this to me?" She truly did not understand how a people she loved and respected, the Cherokees, could shun her because of the color of her skin.

How has the response of African Americans in general been toward your work on this issue?
Most have been very supportive. I have not encountered any negative responses. Most who are black with no connection lean toward indifference. The only negative remark I have ever heard from a black person is that the Freedmen should stop trying to "race jump" and get over the "anything but black" self-hatred. I work with a number of non-Freedmen blacks and they are very supportive. One lady introduced me to her family as "the guy who's watching out for the colored folk."

What about the issue of Native-American sovereignty? Doesn't the Freedmen challenge threaten that core concept?
The Chief of the Cherokee Nation has attempted to make this a sovereignty issue. It is not. Indigenous sovereignty is the right to self-governance that remains after Congress or treaties have taken most of it away. The Cherokee Nation, by treaty, bargained away its sovereign right to determine citizenship for the Freedmen. While that right still exists for all other classes of Cherokee citizens, it is no longer a right of the Cherokee Nation. Thus, an affirmative judgment for the Freedmen would have no impact whatsoever on tribal sovereignty, and particularly not for other tribes, because the Freedmen issue is so narrow, applying only to the Five Civilized Tribes.

Are there risks associated with a federal judicial resolution of the Freedmen controversy?
There is always a risk that a judge will go too far with a ruling. And any time indigenous rights are reviewed by the federal courts, the end result, more often than not, is adverse to tribal rights. However, this issue

is very narrow and it hinges upon an interpretation of a treaty right that applies to only one tribe, at the least, and five tribes at most. There are actually only two resolutions to this controversy that will have lasting effect on the rights of the Freedmen. That is a federal court ruling or congressional action, both of which are pending. As we have seen from [Chief] Chad Smith's actions, a ruling by the tribal court is meaningless to him and he will do whatever he can to overturn, go around, under or over a tribal court ruling.

From your standpoint, what would "victory" for the Cherokee Freedmen look like?

Victory for the Freedmen would be open enrollment and a restoration of rights "EQUAL" to Native Cherokees.

How might the Cherokee Nation "save face" on this issue? That is, how might things work out so as to achieve a "win-win" result?

Because the Cherokee Nation leadership has set itself up in absolute opposition to Freedmen citizenship, there is no win/win per se. The only option for the Freedmen is to be enrolled or be rejected. There is not, and never should be, any middle ground. I believe a win for the Freedmen, which means unquestioned citizenship, would be a win for the Cherokee Nation, because it would mean that the Treaty of 1866 is extant and its provisions favorable to the Cherokee Nation are enforceable. And further, the minority of Freedmen who have no Cherokee blood ancestry could become a wall of defense against the enemies of tribes who would have our Nations declared "race-based organizations" prohibited by the U.S. Constitution. If the Cherokee Nation has non-Indian members, it cannot be considered a race-based organization.

What actions would constitute "leadership" on the Freedmen issue on the part of the Cherokee Nation?

Leadership is a difficult thing to define. George Wallace could be described as a leader, even though he was leading deluded, ignorant racists into a federal brick wall. Good leadership would have accepted the ruling of the Court in the *Allen* case [*Allen v. Cherokee Nation Tribal Council* in the Cherokee Nation Supreme Court, 2006] and just gotten on with the business of governing. The current administration runs on superego and does not have the ability to do an about-face.

What does the current leadership of the Cherokee Nation and/or the Cherokee Nation itself stand to gain by continuing to battle the Freedmen over citizenship rights?

In my opinion, there is nothing to gain by continuing the fight. The fact that there is nothing to gain, and yet the tribal leadership continues to refuse to change its position, shows that the current leadership is ego-driven.

How much does race have to do with the Freedmen citizenship crisis in the Cherokee Nation?
There are two factors at play in the current Freedmen controversy. The first and foremost is race. [The Freedmen] are different from the majority of Cherokees who, by the way, are predominately white. Their appearance alone, due to the racist nature of eastern Oklahoma residents, both white and Indian, makes them easy targets. The second issue, which drove the Chief and his cronies on the Council to push for quick expulsion of the Freedmen, is a fear of their vote.

Is the matter of race in the context of the Freedmen issue, and generally within the Cherokee Nation, addressed in any focused, systematic way?
It's really kind of funny to read the responses of the Chief to the accusations of racism. He cries that the issue is not rooted in racism, yet he then says that everyone in the tribe must be Indian according to his definition. That is little different from the racist cries of the Wallace supporters in Alabama, who wanted Alabama only for the white man.

What do you want from the Cherokee Nation?
I want only to have an honest government that serves all of its constituents and does not segregate one group for maltreatment.

How well do you think the Native Americans in general understand the historical relationship between African Americans and Native Americans?
Most Cherokees are totally ignorant of their personal family connections in the Cherokee Nation. That they would reach out beyond their own comfort zones to explore relations with people they view as foreign is well beyond my expectations. The bottom line is where most Cherokees must be brought. What does the law say, and how is it applied? Only by enforcing the Treaty of 1866, just as it was necessary to enforce the desegregation laws in the Deep South, will the Cherokee Nation begin to move beyond the issues of race. This is the first time in modern history we have had to take a full accounting of our adopted racist views.

How well do you think the average Oklahoman (or the average American, for that matter) understands the historical relationship between African Americans and Native Americans?

I find that non-Cherokees tend to understand the issue much better than the average Cherokee. I attribute that to the fact that white America faced these issues nearly two generations ago. Cherokees are only now coming to full acceptance of our role in slavery, what adoption and/or naturalization really means, and why we became so racist after statehood.

Do present Oklahoma and American history curricula address the historical relationship between African Americans and Native Americans and, if so, to what extent?

The only information I have seen presented in curricula is a mere factoid of red-over-black slavery. Nothing is addressed regarding the relationships, citizenship, or anything else that might give a truer picture of life in the Five Tribes prior to and after the U.S. Civil War. Following statehood, the Freedmen became nearly invisible. It is just since the *Riggs* decision that the Freedmen began to make their voices heard. This seems odd to most white-Cherokees because they are culturally white and accustomed to people speaking out. [In *Riggs v. Ummerteskee*, a 2001 case in the Cherokee Nation Supreme Court, the Court acknowledged Ms. Riggs' blood connection to the Cherokee Nation, but found her ineligible for a CDIB because she had no Indian ancestor on the Dawes Blood Rolls.] This is not odd to the Indian-Cherokees because it is a norm among our people to withdraw when confronted with controversy. In this sense, the Freedmen have been more like Indian-Cherokees because they have been virtually silent as their rights were eroded. But no people can be pushed too far, and the Reverend Roger Nero took up the battle for the Freedmen. Bernice Riggs followed Reverend Nero. Marilyn Vann followed Bernice Riggs. Lucy Allen followed Marilyn Vann. But even as the Cherokee Freedmen fight for their rights in the courts, they do not make a display of their efforts by large public protests and media events.

Has the recent economic prosperity borne of gambling and tobacco revenues played a significant role in the Freedmen controversy?

Opponents of the Freedmen use tribal gambling and tobacco revenues to fund opposition efforts and to paint the Freedmen as gold diggers. What the opposition forgets is that a majority of the Cherokee Nation population was enrolled AFTER gaming came to the tribe. Why are they here and why weren't they here when we had little or nothing? And the Freedmen have participated in every election in the Cherokee Nation since statehood, right up to their first expulsion in 1983. They are not newcomers. Further, the battle for their citizenship rights began in 1983, almost ten years prior to the opening of the first bingo parlor owned by the Cherokee Nation.

Appendix E

Epochs and Signposts in Native American History

EPOCHS

Pre-European Period (Prior to 1492): Indian people lived in organized societies with their own forms of government, lifestyles, and languages, long before contact with Europeans.

Colonial Period (1492-1828): The movement to North America grew from a trickle of newcomers to a flood of people who left Europe en masse, primarily to: (i) escape political oppression of the ruling parties; (ii) find religious freedom; and (iii) avoid the economic difficulties plaguing England.

- **Early Colonists**: Settlers acquired Indian lands through "discovery" (simply locating land and laying claim to it), transfer from the English crown, and treaty-making with the Indians. Treaties—agreements between and among sovereign powers—settled borders, provided access to resources, resolved land and military disputes, and otherwise created order and stability. Treaties became a formal means by which the colonists and the Indians engaged civilly. Colonists settled primarily on the East Coast. The English government forbade encroachment west of the Appalachians in order to maintain peace with various Indian tribes and discourage any alliance between them and France.
- **Post-Revolutionary War**: Following the American Revolutionary War (1775-1783), the United States government continued to follow the Spanish and British models of making treaties with the Native-American tribes. Negotiated on a government-to-government basis, these treaties sought to establish peace and territorial boundaries and to regulate trade and extradition of criminals. The first such treaty, made in 1778, was between the United States and the Delaware Indians. Beginning in 1790, the Indian Intercourse Acts granted the United States government the sole authority to regulate interactions between Indians and non-Indians.

- **The United States Constitution**: Article I, Section 8, clause 3 of the United States Constitution authorizes Congress: "To regulate Commerce with foreign Nations, among the several States, and with Indian Tribes."
- **The Marshall Trilogy**: In 1823, Chief Justice Marshall of the United States Supreme Court delivered an opinion in the first of three key federal Indian law cases. These cases, which affirmed tribal sovereignty and established doctrine of federal trust responsibility, are known as the "Marshall Trilogy," and they form the foundation for current Indian sovereignty jurisprudence. The Marshall Trilogy includes:

  —*Johnson v McIntosh*, 21 U.S. 543 (1823): The High Court held that through doctrine "discovery," the United States acquired the exclusive right to extinguish the original title of possession of tribal lands. The federal government thus held such lands in trust, with the original tribal inhabitants having only a possessory interest. The case involved competing claims to the same lands acquired from the same Indian tribe by different means. The Court ruled that Indian nations could only convey ownership to the United States, and not individuals. This approach restrained unauthorized encroachment (i.e., not approved by the federal government) into Indian territories and confirmed federal control of Indian affairs.

  —*Cherokee Nation v. Georgia*, 30 U.S. 1 (1831): Chief Justice John Marshall, writing for the majority of the United States Supreme Court, addressed the issue of whether the Court had original jurisdiction to hear a case filed by a tribe against a state. Under Article III of the United States Constitution, such jurisdiction only existed in cases between a state and another state or between a state and a foreign nation and its citizens. The Court held the Cherokee Nation was a "domestic dependent nation," not a sovereign state or foreign nation. The Court, though sympathetic to the Cherokee Nation's concerns, stated that it simply did not have original jurisdiction to resolve the dispute.

  —*Worcester v. Georgia*, 31 U.S. 515 (1832): Missionaries living among the Cherokees appealed their conviction in Georgia courts for not having received licenses from the Governor of Georgia to enter Cherokee country. Justice Marshall declared the Georgia convictions void, holding that Cherokee sovereignty rendered the laws of the State of Georgia of no force and effect within the confines of Cherokee country.

- **Bureau of Indian Affairs**: The Continental Congress created the precursor to the Bureau of Indian Affairs in 1775, and charged the agency with managing the affairs of the tribes. This fulfilled the federal government's self-determined role as overseer of Indian affairs. In 1789, the federal government assigned Indian affairs to the Department of War, and in 1824, the government created the Bureau of Indian Affairs to administer funds for the "civilization" of Indians and to adjudicate claims between Indians and whites. In 1849, Congress ordered Indian affairs transferred to the newly created Department of Interior. The mission of the Bureau of Indian Affairs ("BIA") has shifted dramatically over time, from serving as a direct provider of services, to functioning as a technical specialist, to working with tribal managers in protecting and managing trust resources.

Removal and Relocation Period (1828-1871): As the United States population burgeoned and the demand for land on the East Coast increased, the federal government forced the Indian tribes living in the east to vacate. In 1835, the federal government forced the Cherokees, some 17,000 in number, out of their ancestral lands at gunpoint. The brutal march from northern Georgia to present-day Oklahoma became known as the "Trail of Tears." The forced migration killed an estimated 4,000 Cherokee people, including Africans, some enslaved, some free, living among the emigrating Cherokee population. In addition, during this period The Railroad Enabling Act (1866) appropriated Indian land for railway use and The Indian Appropriation Act (1871) nullified treaties and made Indians wards of the state.

- **Moving Tribes West:** The American government forced nearly all the eastern tribes to move from areas with desirable, fertile soil to the less desirable, semi-arid center of the country—known at the time as the "Great American Desert." Consequently, today few Indian tribes call the East Coast home. The removal policy gave way in the 1850s to an official policy of confining Indians to reservations rather than relocating them beyond the rapidly expanding frontier.
- **Treaties Ceding Lands:** Throughout this period, the federal government entered into hundreds of treaties with Indians, many with tribes in the northern plains, for their lands. This further restricted reservation boundaries. Some of these treaties contained provisions allowing the tribes to retain hunting, fishing, and gathering rights on the ceded lands. These treaty rights remain valid and enforceable today.
- **Violating Treaties:** The United States never ratified some of its treaties with Native-American tribes. Some came as a result of bribery. Others were executed by only a small part of the signatory tribes. The federal government failed to fulfill the terms of many treaties. The states regularly violated the treaty rights of Indians, too, often with impunity. By 1871, treaty-making had come to an end. In lieu of treaties,

the federal government began to negotiate agreements later enacted into law by Congress.

Allotment and Attempted Assimilation Period (1871-1928): During this period: (i) the federal government seized more Indian lands for white settlement; (ii) federal law expanded into internal tribal affairs; (iii) the use of boarding schools for the education and "civilization" of Indian children emerged; and (iv) the United States allocated reserved tribal lands, parceling such lands out for individual Indian ownership.

- **General Allotment Act—the "Dawes Act" (1887)**: The Dawes Act sought to break up tribes by breaking up the communal ownership of Native American tribal land and assimilating tribal members into what was thought to be mainstream America, i.e., white society. Specifically, the Dawes Act: (i) enabled the President to allot small parcels of tribal lands to individual Indians; (ii) authorized the federal government to hold land in trust for 25 years or more to prevent transfer of the land; (iii) authorized the United States to sell any lands remaining left after the completion of the allotment process; (iv) subjected allottees to state civil and criminal jurisdiction; and (v) extended United States citizenship to allottees.
- **The Curtis Act (1898)**: The Curtis Act dissolved tribal governments and required citizens of the abolished nations to submit to the allotment process. The Curtis Act extended the policy of allotment to the Five Civilized Tribes.
- **Congressional Extension of Citizenship to Indians in Indian Territory (1901)**: An Act of Congress extended United States citizenship to the Indians in "Indian Territory"—Oklahoma.
- **The Burke Act (1906)**: The Burke Act initiated the so-called "forced patent" period. The government issued thousands of patents that discontinued federal guardianship of Indian lands. If an Indian possessing a land allotment was certified "competent," then the government would give him the title to the land. Upon transfer of title, the land became subject to taxation. In practice, local Indian agents deemed many Indians "competent" and the allotted lands were taken out of trust without the knowledge of the Indians so adjudged. The land would then be sold several years later to cover delinquent taxes.
- **"Surplus" Land**: Under the original Dawes Act, the heads of household and minors received 160 and 40 acres each, respectively. This was soon changed to reduce the amount of acreage. Of the 138 million acres in Indian or tribal lands in 1887, only 48 million acres remained by 1934. Most of the loss resulted from "surplus land"—land remaining after individual allotments to Indian households. The federal gov-

ernment sold some of the surplus lands and made payments to the tribes. The federal government opened up other parcels for homesteading.
- **Removing Children from Their Families**: Federal Indian policy called for the removal of children from their homes and, in many cases, enrollment in government-run boarding schools far away from their families. This policy disrupted Native-American culture in myriad ways.
- **Destroying Tribal Traditions**: Federal policy during this period attempted to mold Indian children into clones of their so-called "civilized" white American brothers and sisters by destroying their traditions. Native-American culture suffered immeasurably.
- **The Indian Citizenship Act of 1924 (aka, the "Snyder Act")**: The Snyder Act granted full United States citizenship to those of America's indigenous peoples (Native Americans or, in the Act itself, "Indians") who had not theretofore attained citizenship. President Calvin Coolidge signed the Act into law on June 2, 1924. (The 14th Amendment to the United States Constitution provides: "All persons born or naturalized in the United States, *and subject to the jurisdiction thereof*, are citizens of the United States and of the state wherein they reside." The italicized clause excludes certain indigenous persons.)
- **Granting U.S. Citizenship to Indians**: In 1924, the United States recognized Native-American valor in World War I. After vigorous lobbying efforts, the remaining Native-American "non-citizens" were granted United States citizenship. A 1928 government-requested survey of conditions on Indian reservations in twenty-six states, the "Merriam Report," signaled the close of the Allotment and Attempted Assimilation Period. The Merriam Report deemed the policies of this period a failure.

Reorganization Period (1928-1945): This short, but progressive, period ended allotments and began restoring Indian lands. The federal government created programs and projects for health facilities, irrigation works, roads, homes and schools to help restore Indian economic and cultural life.

- **The Lea Act (1928)**: The Lea Act uncovered lost treaties. It restored federal support of Indian land claim filings. Among the lost documents uncovered were 18 treaties the Senate blocked in 1850. Those treaties would have set aside more than 7.5 million acres of land for Indian settlement.
- **The Indian Reorganization Act (1934)**: The Indian Reorganization Act (IRA), sometimes called the "Indian New Deal," was the centerpiece of this era. Instead of forcing Indian people to forsake their tra-

ditions for new lives on farms or in cities, the IRA recognized their right to exist as separate cultures. The Act contemplated chartered tribal governments with constitutions and bylaws based on a federal template. This structure differed markedly from the traditional government structures of the tribes. This period became the first time in American Indian history during which tribal councils gained formal recognition.

- **The Oklahoma Indian Welfare Act of 1936 (the "OIWA")**: The OIWA, a federal law, extended the IRA to tribes in Oklahoma. The IRA was designed to return some form of tribal government to various Native- American tribes. The OIWA extended the law so as to include those tribes within the boundaries of Oklahoma. Highlights of the OIWA included: (i) The Secretary of the Interior is authorized to obtain good lands (including Indian lands) to be held in trust for the Indians; (ii) Where Indian lands are sold, the Secretary of the Interior must show preference to obtain those lands for use by Native Americans; and (iii) Any tribe residing within the state of Oklahoma has the right to self-determination, including the right to draft its own bylaws.

Termination and Relocation Period (1945-1965): Termination basically ended what the federal government previously endorsed: (i) trust relationships between federal and tribal governments; and (ii) self-government of the tribes. The Indian Claims Commission Act (1946) created a body to reconcile cases of fraud and negligence by the United States in land transactions with Indian Nations. The three-person commission had only one remedy at its disposal: money for land. It was not empowered to take back lands illegally settled by whites and then owned by their descendants.

- **Termination Policies and Results**: More than 100 tribes were terminated during this period. The federal government simply no longer recognized them as Indian nations and ended federal supervision and control over Indians. The tribes lost their governmental authority, and state criminal laws were imposed on many tribes. Additionally, millions of acres of valuable natural resource land were taken through tax forfeiture sales.
- **Relocation Program**: The Bureau of Indian Affairs started a relocation program that granted money to Indians to move to selected sites to find work—yet another attempt to absorb Indians into mainstream society and eliminate these distinct indigenous cultures. The program succeeded in urbanizing Indians. Some forty percent of the Indian population still resides in cities.

Self-Determination Period (1965-Present): The abuses of the Termination and Relocation Period led to reforms. The federal government expanded the powers of tribal self-government and restored the recognition of tribes. In a special message to Congress in 1968, President Lyndon B. Johnson articulated his still-popular principles for tribal relations: "The greatest hope for Indian progress lies in the emergence of Indian leadership and initiative in solving Indian problems. And we must assure the Indian people that it is our desire and intention that the special relationship between the Indian and his government grow and flourish. For the first among us must not be the last." (President Lyndon Baines Johnson, Special Message to the Congress on the Problems of the American Indian: The Forgotten American, March 6, 1968) A number of modern-era laws promote President Johnson's goal of Indian self-determination.

- **Indian Civil Rights Act (1968)**: The Indian Civil Rights Act established civil rights for all people under tribal government jurisdiction and authorized the federal government to enforce these rights.
- **Indian Self-determination and Education Assistance Act (1975)**: The Indian Self-determination and Education Assistance Act recognized federal trust responsibility and directed the Bureau of Indian Affairs and Indian Health Services to contract with the tribes for programs that these agencies administer (e.g., education, health, and human services initiatives).
- **American Indian Religious Freedom Act (1978)**: The American Indian Religious Freedom Act preserves the rights of American Indians to practice traditional religious beliefs.
- **The Indian Gaming Regulatory Act (1988)**: The Indian Gaming Regulatory Act established the jurisdictional framework that currently governs Indian gaming. The stated purposes of the act include: (i) providing a legislative basis for the operation and regulation of Indian gaming; (ii) protecting gaming as a means of generating revenue for the tribes; (iii) encouraging economic development of the tribes; and (iv) protecting the enterprises from negative influences (e.g., organized crime).
- **Native[-]American Graves Protection and Repatriation Act (1990)**: The Native[-]American Graves Protection and Repatriation Act requires notification and return of human remains and cultural items to the tribes. The law also regulates the excavation of land where Indian remains or property are located.
- **Native[-]American Languages Act ("NALA") (1990)**: The Native[-]American Languages Act, intended to facilitate efforts to preserve indigenous languages, recognized the language rights of American Indians, Alaska Natives, Native Hawaiians, and Pacific Islanders.

NALA did not authorize any new programs for Native Americans and did not provide additional funding for existing ones.
- Tribal Amendments to the National Historic Preservation Act (NAGPRA") (1992): The Tribal Amendments to the National Historic Preservation Act, amendments to the National Historic Preservation Act, provided for expanded participation by Indian tribes in the national preservation program, particularly regarding resources on tribal lands.
- **Executive Order #13007 on Native-American Sacred Sites (1996)**: Executive Order #13007 on Native-American Sacred Sites requires each executive branch agency with statutory or administrative responsibility for the management of federal lands implement procedures to ensure reasonable notice is provided of proposed actions or land management policies that may restrict future access to or ceremonial use of, or adversely affect the physical integrity of, sacred sites.
- **Executive Order #13175 on Consultation and Coordination with Tribal Governments (2000)**: Executive Order #13175 on Consultation and Coordination with Tribal Governments is a measure designed to establish regular and meaningful consultation and collaboration with tribal officials in the development of federal policies that have tribal implications; strengthen the United States government-to-government relationships with Indian tribes; and reduce the imposition of unfunded mandates upon Indian tribes.

In addition to laws, one federal government agency's policy directive on certain dealings with Native American tribes further illustrates the present emphasis on Indian self-determination:

- **FEMA Tribal Policy (1998)**: Federal agencies, including the Federal Emergency Management Agency (FEMA), acknowledged their support for the independence and government-to-government relationships with the tribes through policy statements and removal of barriers to participation in national programs.

Signposts

The 16th Century
1541: Conquistador Francisco Vásquez de Coronado explored what is now the American Southwest for Spain. Spanish explorer Hernando de Soto trekked into Oklahoma, also in 1541.

The 17th Century
1673: Representing colonial power France, Father Jacques Marquette, a Jesuit missionary, and Louis Joliet, a fur trader, undertook an expedition to explore the unsettled territory in North America from the Great Lakes region to the Gulf of Mexico. They traveled down the Mississippi River documenting the area for French and Canadian officials.

The 18th Century
1719: French explorers Jean-Baptiste Bénard de la Harpe and Claude Charles du Tisné embarked upon separate trade excursions into Oklahoma.
1776: The Declaration of Independence was signed on July 4, 1776.

The 19th Century
1803: The United States acquired most of Oklahoma from France in the 1803 Louisiana Purchase.
1812: The War of 1812, fought between the United States and Great Britain, lasted from June 1812 to the spring of 1815, although the parties executed a peace treaty in Europe in December 1814 that officially ended the war. The War of 1812 stemmed from the United States' frustration over: (i) the failure of the British to withdraw from American territory along the Great Lakes; (ii) British backing of the Indians on America's frontiers; and (iii) unwillingness on the part of Great Britain to sign commercial agreements favorable to the United States. Land fighting occurred principally along the Canadian border, in the Chesapeake Bay region, and along the Gulf of Mexico. Extensive action also took place at sea. In the end, British withdrawal from American soil deprived Indian nations of a sovereign and powerful ally. Future treaties between Indian nations and the United States government would become, in many respects, unilateral instruments to advance western expansion of the United States.
1819: The Adams-Onís Treaty with Spain defined Oklahoma as the southwestern boundary of the United States.
1823: The United States Supreme Court held in *Johnson v. McIntosh* that, through the doctrine of "discovery," the United States acquired the exclusive right to extinguish the original title of possession of tribal lands. The federal government thus held such lands in trust, with the original tribal inhabitants having only a possessory interest.

1824: Fort Gibson became the first fort to be established in Oklahoma.

1830: Congress passed the Indian Removal Act, initiating the systematic, forced relocation of Native Americans in the eastern U.S. to lands west of the Mississippi River in order to free up land for additional white settlement.

1831: Chief Justice John Marshall, writing for the majority of the United State Supreme Court, delivered the opinion in *Cherokee Nation v. Georgia*. The Court held that it lacked original jurisdiction to hear a case filed by the Cherokee Nation against the State of Georgia. Under Article III of the United States Constitution, such jurisdiction only existed in cases between a state and another state or between a state and a foreign nation and its citizens.

1832: In *Worcester v. Georgia*, the United States Supreme Court found the Cherokee Nation to be a distinct and independent community that the State of Georgia had no right to enter except upon consent of the Cherokee people.

1830s-1840s: The United States government forced the Cherokee, Chickasaw, Choctaw, Muscogee (Creek) and Seminole tribes to cede their lands in the eastern U.S. and move westward. The federal government ultimately relocated the Five Civilized Tribes to Oklahoma, "Indian Territory." Thousands of Native Americans lost their lives on the bloody marches—referred to by some as the "Trail of Tears"—to Oklahoma. In addition to Native American casualties, scores of African Americans, some slaves, some free, perished on these forced migrations.

1834: Land in what is now Oklahoma was set aside as Indian Territory.

1842: Most of the remaining Seminole Indians from Florida completed the move to Oklahoma.

1845: The western panhandle region of the State of Oklahoma became United States territory with the annexation of Texas.

1860s: After the Civil War, Native-American tribes, many of which had brokered alliances with the Confederacy, suffered the consequences of that alignment. The Five Civilized Tribes officially sided with the Confederacy, and they faced the prospect of economic ruin and land forfeiture.

1870s: An additional 25 tribes were moved to Oklahoma to reside on federal lands.

1870–1872: The first railroad to cross Oklahoma was built.

1889: The federal government opened land in Indian Territory to general settlement via land runs, lotteries, and auctions. At high noon on April 22, a cannon boom signaled the start of the first land run, which opened the so-called "Unassigned Lands" for settlement.

1890: On May 2, the federal government split Indian Territory in half. The western half became "Oklahoma Territory," while the eastern half maintained the "Indian Territory" moniker.

1891: On September 21, the federal government opened the Sac and Fox, Pottawatomie-Shawnee Lands, located just east of the original land run site.

1892: On April 19, the federal government opened the Cheyenne and Arapaho lands in western Oklahoma.

1893: On September 16, federal authorities hosted the largest and most spectacular run in northern Oklahoma, the opening of the Cherokee Strip.

1893: Congress established the Dawes Commission to work for the negation of tribal title to lands held by the Five Civilized Tribes. James Mooney prepared a Native-American exhibit for the World's Fair in Chicago.

1895: On May 23, the federal government held the Kickapoo Land Run in central Oklahoma.

1898: The Curtis Act abolished tribal courts and laws, but allowed Native-American nations to retain mineral rights to their lands. The Act extended the allotment policy to the Five Civilized Tribes in Indian Territory. The Dawes Commission began to enroll persons living among the tribes on tribal rolls.

The 20th Century

1901: Congress conferred United States citizenship on all Native Americans residing in Indian Territory.

1907: On November 16, Indian Territory and Oklahoma Territory combined to create a new state, Oklahoma. Oklahoma became the forty-sixth state to join the Union.

1924: Congress passed the Indian Citizenship Act, granting voting rights and United States citizenship to all Native Americans born in the country's territorial limits, although indigenous Americans were still considered to be outside the protection of the Bill of Rights. Indians did not receive the right to vote in all states until 1948.

1930s: The State of Oklahoma experienced the devastating impact of severe drought and soil erosion as part of the "Dust Bowl." The dust storms characteristic of this period caused major ecological and agricultural damage.

1937: The federal government completed the end-to-end paving of Route 66, an early component of the U.S. Highway System that connected Chicago and Los Angeles. Also known as "The Mother Road," "The Main Street of America," and "The Will Rogers Highway," Route 66 ran through Missouri, Kansas, Oklahoma, Texas, New Mexico, and Arizona in addition to Illinois and California.

1968: The Indian Civil Rights Act established civil rights for all people under tribal government jurisdiction and authorized the federal government to enforce these rights.

1970: Congress passed the Principal Chiefs Act in an effort to restore tribal sovereignty and self-determination by placing electoral responsibility for tribal governance back in the hands of tribal members.

1975: The Indian Self-Determination and Education Assistance Act recognized the federal trust responsibility and directed the Bureau of Indian Affairs and Indian Health Services to contract with the tribes for programs these agencies administer (e.g., education, health, and human services initiatives).

1978: The American Indian Religious Freedom Act preserved the rights of American Indians to practice traditional religious beliefs.

1988: The Indian Gaming Regulatory Act ("IGRA") established the jurisdictional framework that currently governs Indian gaming. IGRA: (i) provides a legislative basis for the operation and regulation of Indian gaming; (ii) protects gaming as a means of generating revenue for the tribes; (iii) encourages economic development of the tribes; and (iv) protects the enterprises from negative influences (e.g., organized crime).

1990: The Native[-]American Graves Protection and Repatriation Act required notification and return of human remains and cultural items to the tribes and regulated the excavation of land where Indian remains or property are located.

1990: The Native[-]American Languages Act ("NALA"), a federal policy statement intended to facilitate efforts to preserve indigenous languages, recognized the language rights of American Indians, Alaska Natives, Native Hawaiians, and Pacific Islanders. NALA did not authorize any new programs for Native Americans and did not provide additional funding for existing ones.

1992: Amendments to the National Historic Preservation Act ("NHPA") provided for expanded participation by Indian tribes in the national preservation program, particularly regarding resources on tribal lands.

1996: Executive Order #13007 on Native-American Sacred Sites required that notice be accorded in advance of activities on sacred site. Specifically, Executive Order #13007 mandates that certain agencies with responsibility for the management of federal lands implement procedures to ensure that reasonable notice is provided of proposed actions or land management policies that may restrict future access to or ceremonial use of, or adversely affect the physical integrity of, sacred sites.

1998: Federal agencies, including FEMA acknowledged their support for the independence and government-to-government relationships with the tribes through policy statements and removal of barriers to participation in national programs.

2000: Executive Order #13175 on Consultation and Coordination with Tribal Governments required regular and meaningful consultation and collaboration with tribal officials in the development of federal policies that have tribal implications. It also strengthened the United States government-to-government relationships with Indian tribes and imposed a reduction in the imposition of unfunded mandates upon Indian tribes.

Adapted in part from "Oklahoma History Timeline: Important Dates, Events, and Milestones," http://www.e-referencedesk.com/resources/state-history-timeline/oklahoma.html; Wilma Mankiller and Michael Wallis, *Mankiller: A Chief and Her People* (New York, NY: St. Martin's Press, 1993); "Significant Acts: Federal Native American Policy," http://www.ecologycenter.org/tfs/pdf/2002summer/significantacts.pdf.

Appendix F

Federally Recognized Indian Tribes in Oklahoma

Following is an alphabetical listing of the 38 federally recognized Native American tribes in the State of Oklahoma. The names listed for each tribe are officially recognized by the Bureau of Indian Affairs and are the actual names used by the nation, tribe, band, or town referenced. An asterisk indicates the tribe operates a casino featuring class II (e.g., bingo) gaming and/or off-track betting.

Absentee–Shawnee Tribe of Oklahoma*
Alabama–Quassarte Tribal Town
Apache Tribe of Oklahoma
Caddo Nation of Oklahoma
Cherokee Nation*
Cheyenne–Arapaho Tribes of Oklahoma*
Chickasaw Nation*
Choctaw Nation of Oklahoma*
Citizen Potawatomi Nation*
Comanche Nation*
Delaware Nation (Western Oklahoma)*
Delaware Tribe of Indians (Eastern Oklahoma)
Eastern Shawnee Tribe of Oklahoma*
Fort Sill Apache Tribe of Oklahoma*
Iowa Tribe of Oklahoma*
Kaw Nation*
Kialegee Tribal Town
Kickapoo Tribe of Oklahoma*
Kiowa Indian Tribe of Oklahoma*
Miami Tribe of Oklahoma*
Modoc Tribe of Oklahoma*
Muscogee (Creek) Nation*
Osage Tribe*
Otoe–Missouria Tribe of Indians*

Ottawa Tribe of Oklahoma
Pawnee Nation of Oklahoma*
Peoria Tribe of Indians*
Ponca Tribe of Indians of Oklahoma*
Quapaw Tribe of Indians*
Sac & Fox Nation*
Seminole Nation of Oklahoma*
Seneca–Cayuga Tribe of Oklahoma*
Shawnee Tribe
Thlopthlocco Tribal Town*
Tonkawa Tribe of Indians of Oklahoma*
United Keetoowah Band of Cherokee Indians in Oklahoma*
Wichita and Affiliated Tribes (Wichita, Keechi, Waco, Tawakonie)
Wyandotte Nation*

Adapted from: Directory of Oklahoma Indian Tribes and Tribal Casinos, http://www.oklahomaresource.com/ (last viewed on June 23, 2009).

Appendix G

African-American Civil Rights in the United States

A TIMELINE*

1500

- The African slave trade included the "Middle Passage," the forcible movement of African people from Africa to the New World. Middle Passage refers specifically to the middle leg of the transatlantic trade triangle.

    Ships loaded with commercial goods departed Europe for African markets. Traders exchanged those goods for kidnapped Africans. Millions of Africans were imprisoned, enslaved, and transported across the Atlantic as slaves. Flesh merchants sold or traded the enslaved Africans as commodities for raw materials to be used in the European market, completing the triangular trade.

    Traders from the Americas and Caribbean received enslaved Africans. Various European, North American, and South American countries took part in the slave trade. Some 15% of the Africans captured for the slave trade died at sea. Mortality rates were considerably higher in Africa itself. Some two million African deaths were directly attributable to the Middle Passage voyages. Between 1500 and 1900, some four million Africans lost their lives as a direct consequence of the institution of slavery.

    The Middle Passage inalterably influenced the cultural and demographic landscapes of Africa and those countries that participated in the slave trade. Some also view the Middle Passage as a marker of the origin of a distinct African, or "black," social identity.

1619

- The first African slaves arrived in Jamestown, Virginia, in 1619. They were indentured to work for tobacco plantation owners for seven years. Single women from England were also brought over to help. The institution of hereditary lifetime servitude for persons of African ancestry soon developed.

1660s

- The practice of slavery became a legally recognized institution in British America. Colonial assemblies began to enact laws known as slave codes, which restricted the liberty of slaves and protected the institution of slavery.

1776

- The Declaration of Independence proclaimed that "All men are created equal," yet slavery remained legal in all thirteen of the newly-established states.

1777

- Vermont amended its constitution to ban slavery. Over the next 25 years, other Northern states emancipated their slaves and banned the institution: Pennsylvania, 1780; Massachusetts and New Hampshire, 1783; Connecticut and Rhode Island, 1784; New York, 1799; and New Jersey, 1804. Some state laws stipulated gradual emancipation.

1787

- The Northwest Ordinance banned slavery in the Northwest Territory (what became the states of Ohio, Indiana, Illinois, Michigan, and Wisconsin). The ordinance, together with state emancipation laws, created a free North.

1787-1788

- Drafted in 1787 and ratified in 1788, the United States Constitution did not expressly mention the institution of slavery, but addressed it indirectly in three places: (1) Congress was granted the authority to prohibit the importation of slaves after twenty years; (2) The "three-fifths" clause in Article I settled the debate over whether or not to count slaves for determining taxation and representation. [For those purposes, all free persons in the districts, including indentured servants, were to be counted. To that total was to be added the number of "three fifths of all other persons"—i.e., slaves.]; and (3) Article IV, Section 2 required a "person held to service or labor" in one state, who escaped to another state, "shall be delivered up on claim of the party to whom such service or labor shall be due." No enforcement mechanism was specified.

1793

- To enforce Article IV, Section 2, the U.S. Congress enacted the Fugitive

Slave Law. It allowed slave-owners to cross state lines to recapture their slaves, but required them to prove ownership subsequently in a court of law. In reaction, some Northern states passed personal liberty laws, granting the alleged fugitive slaves the rights to *habeas corpus*, jury trials, and testimony on their own behalf. These Northern state legislatures also passed anti-kidnapping laws, to punish slave-catchers who kidnapped free blacks instead of fugitive slaves.

1808

- In 1807, Congress banned the importation of slaves, effective January 1, 1808, the earliest date allowed by the Constitution. The internal slave trade continued in states where slavery remained legal.

1820-1821

- In the Missouri Compromise, Congress admitted the slave state of Missouri and the free state of Maine into the Union, and banned slavery north of the parallel 36° 30' north line of latitude in the Louisiana Territory.

1831

- In Boston, William Lloyd Garrison founded the abolitionist newspaper, *The Liberator*, signaling a dramatic shift in the antislavery movement. In the previous decades, it had centered in the South and favored a combination of compensated emancipation and colonization of freed slaves back to Africa. In the 1830s, the abolitionist movement became the dominant voice among antislavery advocates. Abolitionists demanded an immediate end to slavery, which they considered a moral evil, without compensation to slave-owners. In 1833, Garrison joined Arthur and Lewis Tappan in the establishment of the American Anti-Slavery Society, an abolitionist organization.

- Nat Turner, a literate slave who believed himself chosen as the Moses of his people, instigated a slave revolt in Virginia. He and his followers killed fifty-seven whites, but the revolt was ultimately unsuccessful. Some 200 enslaved Africans were killed. After an intense debate, the Virginia legislature narrowly rejected a bill to emancipate Virginia's slaves. The widespread fear of slave revolts, compounded by the rise of abolitionism, led legislatures across the South to increase the harshness of their slave codes. State and private censorship resulted in the suppression of expressions of anti-slavery sentiment throughout the South.

1842

- In *Prigg v. Pennsylvania*, the U.S. Supreme Court upheld the Fugitive

Slave Law of 1793, acknowledging a right on the part of slave-owners to retrieve their "property." In so doing, the court ruled Pennsylvania's anti-kidnapping law unconstitutional. At the same time, the Supreme Court declared that enforcement of the Fugitive Slave Law fell upon federal authorities. States therefore could not be compelled to participate. Between 1842 and 1850, nine Northern states passed new personal liberty laws, which forbade state officials from cooperating in the return of alleged fugitive slaves and barred the use of state facilities for that purpose.

1850

- Henry Clay introduced The Compromise of 1850 in Congress as an omnibus bill designed to settle disputes arising from the conclusion of the Mexican War. It passed after Stephen Douglas divided the bill into several parts: California entered the Union as a free state; the slave trade (but not slavery) was abolished in Washington D.C.; the fugitive slave law was strengthened; and the Utah and New Mexico Territories were opened to slavery on the basis of popular sovereignty (allowing territorial voters to decide the issue without federal interference).

1852

- *Uncle Tom's Cabin*, by Harriet Beecher Stowe, debuted. The novel depicted slavery as a horrible evil, but treated white Southerners sympathetically. The villain of the piece, cruel slave-overseer Simon Legree, was a transplanted New Englander. The South banned the book. The North made the book a bestseller.

1854

- The U.S. ministers to Britain, France, and Spain met in Ostend, Belgium. They drafted a policy recommendation to President Pierce, urging him to attempt again to purchase Cuba from Spain and, if Spain refused, to take the island by force. Leaked to the press, the "Ostend Manifesto" created controversy. Many speculated that Cuba, if purchased or taken by force, would become another slave state.

  In an attempt to spur population growth in the western territories in advance of a transcontinental railroad, Stephen Douglas introduced a bill to establish the territories of Kansas and Nebraska. In order to gain Southern support, the bill stipulated that slavery in the territories was to be decided by popular sovereignty. Thus the Kansas-Nebraska Act repealed the Missouri Compromise ban on slavery north of parallel 36° 30' north in the lands of the Louisiana Purchase.

1855-1856

- A miniature civil war—known as "Bleeding Kansas"—erupted in the

Kansas Territory over the issue of slavery. In May 1856, a pro-slavery group attacked the free-soil town of Lawrence, destroying and stealing property. In response to the "sack of Lawrence," radical abolitionist John Brown and his followers attacked a pro-slavery settlement at Pottawatomie Creek, killing five men. By the end of 1856, nearly 200 Kansans had been killed, and property worth $2 million had been damaged or destroyed.

1856

- Senator Charles Sumner delivered a stinging speech in the U.S. Senate, "The Crime against Kansas," in which he attacked both slavery and the South. Senator Sumner singled out his Senate colleague, Andrew Butler of South Carolina, for special criticism. In retaliation, Butler's nephew, Congressman Preston Brooks of South Carolina, attacked Sumner with a cane while the Massachusetts senator was seated at his desk on the floor of the Senate, inflicting injuries that caused Sumner to be absent from the Senate for four years.

1857

- The U.S. Supreme Court decided the *Dred Scott* case [*Dred Scott v. Sandford*, 60 U.S. (19 How.) 393 (1857)]. In the majority opinion, Chief Justice Roger Taney ruled that Scott, a slave, had no standing to sue. He pronounced black Americans, slave or free, non-citizens, with no civil rights protected by the U.S. Constitution. Finally, Chief Justice Taney concluded that neither the territorial governments nor the federal government could ban slavery in the territories. As such, the Northwest Ordinance and Missouri Compromise bans on slavery were unconstitutional.

1857-1858

- In the Kansas Territory, the rivalry between pro- and anti-slavery factions resulted in the establishment of two territorial legislatures, each claiming legitimacy. The pro-slavery legislature at Lecompton drafted a constitution making Kansas a slave state. Anti-slavery forces boycotted the popular referendum on the constitution, which passed and was sent to Congress. Senator Stephen Douglas considered the Lecompton Constitution a perversion of popular sovereignty, but President James Buchanan endorsed it. Congress sent the Lecompton Constitution back to Kansas for another referendum. This time, it was defeated overwhelmingly.

1858

- Illinois Republicans nominated Abraham Lincoln for the U.S. Senate. As part of his acceptance, Lincoln delivered his "House Divided" speech, in which he asserted that the nation could not endure permanently as half-slave and half-free. Incumbent Senator Stephen Douglas agreed to an unprecedented series of debates held in towns across the state. Although the Democrats won control of the state legislature and re-elected Douglas, Lincoln gained notoriety and became a contender for the 1860 presidential nomination.

1859

- John Brown, the radical abolitionist and veteran of "Bleeding Kansas," failed in his attempt to capture the federal arsenal at Harper's Ferry, Virginia (now West Virginia) and to use the weapons to foment a slave rebellion. Brown and his co-conspirators were hanged, becoming martyrs to the anti-slavery cause in the eyes of some abolitionists.

1865

- Congress ratified the Thirteenth Amendment, officially ending slavery in America.

    Amendment XIII (Ratified December 6, 1865): 1. Neither slavery nor involuntary servitude, except as a punishment for crime whereof the party shall have been duly convicted, shall exist within the United States, or any place subject to their jurisdiction. 2. Congress shall have power to enforce this article by appropriate legislation.

- "Reconstruction," the period from 1865 to 1877 during which the United States underwent a period of readjustment following the Civil War, began. The American South, vanquished in the Civil War, lay in ruin. African Americans worked to create an economic base, independent towns, and educational institutions. The demise of the South meant the collapse of the old social and economic order founded upon slavery. The eleven Confederate states needed to be restored to their positions in the Union and provided with loyal governments. The role of the emancipated slaves in Southern society begged for redefinition. Reconstruction ended as the political winds shifted and the federal government withdrew all federal troops from the South. White rule reemerged. African Americans lost many civil and political rights. Their economic position remained depressed. Hope for a post-slavery Southern reordering on social and economic fronts seemed doomed. The rise of the one-party solid South cloaked in white supremacist garb had begun.

1868

- Congress ratified the Fourteenth Amendment, granting citizenship to all persons born or naturalized in the United States.

Amendment XIV (Ratified July 9, 1868): Section 1—*All persons born or naturalized in the United States, and subject to the jurisdiction thereof, are citizens of the United States and of the State wherein they reside. No State shall make or enforce any law which shall abridge the privileges or immunities of citizens of the United States; nor shall any State deprive any person of life, liberty, or property, without due process of law; nor deny to any person within its jurisdiction the equal protection of the laws.* Section 2—*Representatives shall be apportioned among the several States according to their respective numbers counting the whole number of persons in each State, excluding Indians not taxed. But when the right to vote at any election for the choice of electors for President and Vice-President of the United States, Representatives in Congress, the Executive and Judicial officers of a State, or the members of the Legislature thereof, is denied to any of the male inhabitants of such State, being twenty-one years of age, and citizens of the United States, or in any way abridged, except for participation in rebellion, or other crime, the basis of representation therein shall be reduced in the proportion which the number of such male citizens shall bear to the whole number of male citizens twenty-one years of age in such State.* Section 3—*No person shall be a Senator or Representative in Congress, or elector of President and Vice-President, or hold any office, civil or military, under the United States, or under any State, who, having previously taken an oath, as a member of Congress, or as an officer of the United States, or as a member of any State legislature, or as an executive or judicial officer of any State, to support the Constitution of the United States, shall have engaged in insurrection or rebellion against the same, or given aid or comfort to the enemies thereof. But Congress may by a vote of two-thirds of each House, remove such disability.* Section 4—*The validity of the public debt of the United States, authorized by law, including debts incurred for payment of pensions and bounties for services in suppressing insurrection or rebellion, shall not be questioned. But neither the United States nor any State shall assume or pay any debt or obligation incurred in aid of insurrection or rebellion against the United States, or any claim for the loss or emancipation of any slave. But all such debts, obligations and claims shall be held illegal and void.* Section 5—*The Congress shall have power to enforce, by appropriate legislation, the provisions of this article.*

1870

- Congress ratified the Fifteenth Amendment, granting, theoretically, all citizens the right to vote.

Amendment XV (Ratified February 3, 1870): Section 1—The right of citizens of the United States to vote shall not be denied or abridged by the United States or by any State on account of race, color, or previous condition of servitude. Section 2—The Congress shall have power to enforce this article by appropriate legislation.

1877

- In the Compromise of 1877, Union troops exited from the South. Federal soldiers had enforced new antislavery laws during Reconstruction, and, by most accounts, the withdrawal of those federal troops doomed Reconstruction.

1881

- Educator and statesman Booker Taliaferro Washington (April 5, 1858 or 1859 – November 14, 1915) founded Tuskegee Institute in Alabama, a vocational school for African Americans. Washington, a staunch advocate of self-reliance, urged African Americans to concentrate on economic uplift rather than agitating for civil rights. The embrace of gradualism put Washington at odds with civil rights advocate and scholar Dr. W.E.B. Du Bois (February 23, 1868 – August 27, 1963), a Harvard-educated intellectual who urged immediate demands for political and civil rights.

1895

- Booker T. Washington delivered The Atlanta Cotton States and International Exposition Speech on September 11, 1895. The talk dealt with American race relations. Washington's philosophical rival, Dr. W.E.B. Du Bois, labeled the lecture the "Atlanta Compromise." Dr. Du Bois viewed Washington's remarks as embracing an enduring second-class citizenship for African Americans. Thus began the long intellectual rivalry between the politics of accommodation and those of agitation. Washington favored gradualism and a focus on economic uplift. Dr. Du Bois wanted—indeed, demanded—immediate social and political equality for African Americans.

1896

- In *Plessy v. Ferguson*, 163 U.S. 537 (1896), the United States Supreme Court upheld the concept of "separate but equal" public accommodations. The case involved railroad transport, but its implications were much broader. The decision endorsed state-mandated discrimination in public transportation under the "separate but equal" doctrine, which prevailed until its repudiation in the landmark *Brown v. Board of Education* decision [*Brown v. Board of Education*, 347 U.S. 483 (1954)].

1903

- Formed in 1903 on the site of Abigail Barnett McCormick's Freedmen's allotment, townsfolk incorporated the town of Boley in 1905. The town sits in central Oklahoma, in Okfuskee County, on Highway 62, 68 miles southwest of Tulsa. Booker T. Washington, visiting Boley in 1904, called it "[t]he most enterprising, and in many ways the most interesting of the Negro towns in the U.S." Boley represents a host of all-black communities formed largely between 1890 and 1910. Oklahoma led the nation in spawning these perceived islands of freedom and opportunity for oppressed African Americans. African Americans formed more black towns in Oklahoma than in any other state.

1905

- W.E.B. Du Bois and *Boston Guardian* co-founder Monroe Trotter, both Harvard University graduates, founded "The Niagara Movement," a forerunner of the National Association for the Advancement of Colored People (NAACP). Activists birthed the latter organization in 1909. The men presented a manifesto calling for "universal manhood suffrage" and the elimination of racial segregation at a meeting attended by civil rights activists. The moniker "The Niagara Movement" represented the "mighty current" of change the group wanted to affect and the natural landmark, Niagara Falls, located near where the first meeting took place in July of 1905. The Niagara Movement opposed racial segregation and disenfranchisement, as well as the accommodation and conciliation policies outlined in Booker T. Washington's "Atlanta Compromise" speech of 1895.

1909

- Founded February 12, 1909, the National Association for the Advancement of Colored People (NAACP) is the nation's oldest, largest and most widely recognized grassroots civil rights organization. Early on, the NAACP focused on challenging the Jim Crow laws prevalent throughout the South, succeeding only in a few early cases. A case in point is the NAACP's 1915 victory over Oklahoma's "grandfather clause," which exempted most white voters from stringent literacy requirements that effectively disenfranchised African Americans.

1910

- The National Urban League emerged to assist southern black emigrants seeking better fortunes in the North. The National Urban League remains vibrant today as a voluntary nonpartisan community service agency. It works to end racial segregation and discrimination in the

United States, especially toward African Americans, and to help economically and socially disadvantaged groups share equally in every aspect of American life.

1915

- In *Guinn v. United States* [*Guinn v. United States*, 238 U.S. 347 (1915)], the United States Supreme Court, in a case from Oklahoma, ruled against "grandfather clauses" used to deny persons of African ancestry the right to vote. Typical grandfather clauses provided an exemption from state property and literacy requirements to citizens, or descendants of citizens, who had the right to vote prior to 1866 or 1867. By design, these clauses, enacted in several southern states around 1890, disenfranchised persons of African ancestry who, by virtue of chattel slavery, did not meet their stipulations.

- *The Birth of a Nation* (a.k.a. *The Clansman*), director D. W. Griffith's silent film lionizing the Ku Klux Klan, became a Hollywood blockbuster. Considered innovative in both technical and narrative senses, the film set off a firestorm because of its sympathetic treatment of white supremacy.

1919

- James Weldon Johnson of the NAACP coined the term "Red Summer" to describe the summer and fall of 1919. Some 26 major "race riots" occurred throughout the United States. More aptly cast as assaults, incursions, or pogroms, these attacks on African-American communities were often influenced by economic uncertainty and political instability. They were precipitated primarily by racism. Bloody racial conflagrations erupted in several cities in both the American North and South, including Chicago, Illinois; Longview, Texas; Washington, D.C.; Omaha, Nebraska; and Elaine, Arkansas.

1921

- The worst of the so-called "race riots" in twentieth-century American history occurred in Tulsa, Oklahoma. The 1921 Tulsa Race Riot destroyed the nationally renowned African-American entrepreneurial community known locally as the "Greenwood District," and dubbed the "Negro Wall Street" by many. Authorities believe that as many as 300 people were killed, with hundreds more injured. Thousands were left homeless and destitute. Property damage ran into the millions of dollars. African-American Tulsa rebuilt the Greenwood District and, by 1942, the community boasted scores of black-owned and black-operated business establishments. The 1921 Tulsa Race Riot became yet another example of the widespread hostility toward African-American engagement and achievement that characterized this period in American history. More importantly, it became an example of African-American resilience and determination in the face of seemingly insurmountable odds.

1922

- Proposed by Representative L.C. Dyer of Missouri, the Dyer Anti-Lynching Bill would have made lynching a federal crime. The Dyer Bill was an attempt to reduce or eliminate the onslaught of lynchings in the United States in the aftermath of World War I. Lynching, a form of domestic terrorism and vigilantism, targeted persons for a supposed crime or social slight, often based on scant evidence and always without judicial process. A tool of White supremacy, lynching most often targeted African Americans. White mobs meted out summary "justice" with the intent not only of punishing the target, but also of sending a message to the group to which the target belonged. That message: Know your place and stay in it. President Warren G. Harding supported the Dyer Bill. The Bill passed the House of Representatives, but was defeated in the Senate on a filibuster.

1925

- Asa Philip Randolph organized the Brotherhood of Sleeping Car Porters, a landmark organization for labor, and particularly for African-American labor organizing. Randolph (April 15, 1889–May 16, 1979) became a prominent twentieth-century African-American civil rights leader.

1929

- The Reverend Dr. Martin Luther King, Jr. (January 15, 1929 – April 4, 1968) was born. King, an American clergyman and activist, became the preeminent leader of, and icon for, the African-American Civil Rights Movement. A Nobel Laureate, Dr. King remains a world-renowned human rights symbol.

1935

- Martin Luther King, Sr., father of the iconic Dr. Martin Luther King, Jr., led a protest against segregated elevators at the Fulton County, Georgia, Courthouse.
- Martin Luther King, Sr., and the Atlanta branch of the NAACP led a voter registration drive in anticipation of local school bond referendum.

1940

- Thurgood Marshall (July 2, 1908–January 24, 1993) and others founded

The NAACP Legal Defense and Educational Fund, Inc. (LDF) in 1940. Marshall went on to become a famed civil rights attorney, the first African American to serve as United States Solicitor General, and the first African American to sit on the United States Supreme Court. Although LDF's primary purpose was to provide legal assistance to poor African Americans, its body of work over the years has brought greater justice to all Americans.

1941

- A. Philip Randolph called for a march on Washington to protest race-based employment discrimination in the armed forces and war industry.

- On June 24, 1941, President Franklin D. Roosevelt issued Executive Order 8802, which forbade racial discrimination in defense industries and in government services, and which provided, in part:

  > *NOW, THEREFORE, by virtue of the authority vested in me by the Constitution and the statutes, and as a prerequisite to the successful conduct of our national defense production effort, I do hereby reaffirm the policy of the United States that there shall be no discrimination in the employment of workers in defense industries or government because of race, creed, color, or national origin, and I do hereby declare that it is the duty of employers and of labor organizations, in furtherance of said policy and of this order, to provide for the full and equitable participation of all workers in defense industries, without discrimination because of race, creed, color, or national origin[.]*

- Executive Order 8802 established the President's Committee on Fair Employment Practices.

1942

- James Farmer (January 20, 1920–July 9, 1999) founded The Congress for Racial Equality (CORE) in Chicago. CORE, a civil rights organization dedicated to the use of nonviolent direct action, sought to promote better race relations and end racial discrimination in the United States. It initially focused on activities directed toward the desegregation of public accommodations in Chicago. Later, CORE expanded its program of nonviolent sit-ins to the South and sponsored the Freedom Rides in 1961. The Freedom Rides, a series of bus rides throughout the South by interracial groups of CORE members and supporters, became a national sensation and, for many, a national disgrace. Racist mobs verbally abused and viciously beat the Freedom Riders on numerous occasions. Ultimately, CORE succeeded in ending segregation on interstate bus routes. CORE joined other organizations in sponsoring the 1963 March on Washington, at which Dr. Martin Luther King, Jr., delivered his signature "I Have A Dream" speech. After 1966, when James Farmer resigned from CORE, the organization concentrated more on black voter registration in the South and community problems. More recent CORE leaders have focused on African-American political and economic empowerment.

1944

- On April 25, 1944, Frederick D. Patterson, president of what is now Tuskegee University, Mary McLeod Bethune, and others incorporated The United Negro College Fund (UNCF). UNCF is a philanthropic organization that raises funds for college tuition on behalf of African-American students and general scholarship funds for thirty-nine private, historically black colleges and universities (referred to as HBCUs) in the United States.

1946

- African-American women formed the Women's Political Council (WPC) in Montgomery, Alabama. A civic organization for African-American professional women in Montgomery, WPC claimed as members numerous educators at Alabama State College or in the public schools of Montgomery. Some forty members attended the first organizational meeting. Mary Fair Burks, head of Alabama State's English department, served as the group's first president. For its first undertaking, WPC registered voters, a daunting task given the prevalence of literacy tests as barriers to African-American voting. All the WPC members eventually passed the tests. They then opened schools to help other African Americans complete registration forms and pass literacy tests. Later, WPC initiated the Montgomery Bus Boycott, a watershed event in the Civil Rights Movement.

- Primus King's legal challenge against the State of Georgia [*Chapman v. King*, 154 F.2d 460 (5th Cir. 1946), *cert. denied*, 327 U.S. 800 (1946)] removed legal barriers to black voting. The Fifth Circuit Court of Appeals struck down Georgia's all-white Democratic primary, declaring the "white primary" unconstitutional. White primaries—primary elections in the South in which non-White voters were prohibited from participating—existed in many Southern states after about 1890 and through the mid-1960s.

- In *Irene Morgan v. Commonwealth of Virginia*, [*Irene Morgan v. Commonwealth of Virginia*, 328 U.S. 373 (1946)], the United States Supreme Court banned segregation in interstate bus travel.

1947

- CORE and the Fellowship of Reconciliation sent the first "Freedom Riders" through the South to test compliance with the *Morgan v. Commonwealth* ruling. The Fellowship of Reconciliation consisted of a number of religious nonviolent organizations, particularly in English-speaking countries, linked together by affiliation to the International Fellowship of Reconciliation.

1948

- In 1948, the United States Supreme Court ruled in *Sipuel v. Board of Regents of the University of Oklahoma* [*Sipuel v. Board of Regents of the University of Oklahoma*, 332 U.S. 631 (1948)] that the State of Oklahoma must provide instruction for African Americans equal to that of whites. The case involved the desegregation of the University of Oklahoma Law School. Thurgood Marshall, in a forerunner to the *Brown v. Board of Education* [*Brown v. Board of Education*, 347 U.S. 483 (1954)], acted as the lead NAACP counsel on the case. Amos T. Hall, a Tulsa, Oklahoma, attorney and NAACP Tulsa branch president, served as co-counsel.

1950

- In *Sweatt v. Painter* [*Sweatt v. Painter*, 339 U.S. 629 (1950)], the United States Supreme Court ordered the University of Texas Law School to admit African-American students.

- *McLaurin v. Oklahoma* [*McLaurin v. Oklahoma*, 339 US 637 (1950)] abolished segregation in college classrooms, libraries, and cafeterias.

- *Henderson v. United States* [*Henderson v. United States*, 339 U.S. 816 (1950)]. prohibited dining car segregation on trains.

1953

- CORE began sit-ins in Baltimore, Maryland.
- The Baton Rouge, Louisiana, bus boycott began.

1954

- In *Brown v. Board of Education of Topeka, Kansas* [*Brown v. Board of Education*, 347 U.S. 483 (1954)], the United States Supreme Court declared racial segregation in public schools unconstitutional.

1955

- In August 1955, a fourteen-year-old African-American boy went to visit relatives near Money, Mississippi. The boy, Emmett Till, knew about racism and segregation, as he had experienced segregation in his hometown, Chicago. Unaccustomed to the extreme forms of racism he encountered in Mississippi, Emmett allegedly breached social mores by flirting with a white woman, Carolyn Bryant, in a local store. A few days later, two men barged into the cabin of Mose Wright, Emmett's uncle, in the middle of the night. Roy Bryant, the owner of the store and Carolyn's husband, and J. W. Milam, his brother-in-law, drove off with Emmett. Three days later, Emmett's lifeless, mutilated body turned up in the Tallahatchie River. Emmett's virtually unrecognizable corpse bore all manner of injuries: a gouged out eye; a crushed skull; a bullet-ridden torso. Emmett's mother, Mamie, held an open casket funeral in Chicago. The gruesomeness of Emmett's remains shocked the conscience of many Americans, but not the all-white jury that acquitted Roy Bryant and J. W. Milam of Emmett's murder. Bryant and Milam later confessed. The case galvanized the Civil Rights Movement.

- Authorities arrested seamstress Rosa Parks for refusing to give up her seat on a Montgomery, Alabama, bus. So began the Montgomery Bus Boycott, a political and social protest campaign that opposed the city's policy of racial segregation on its public transit system. Dr. Martin Luther King, Jr., helped lead the boycott. Because African Americans constituted a large percentage of people who used public transportation, the Montgomery public transit system lost substantial revenue during the boycott, which lasted from December 1, 1955, to December 20, 1956. In the end, the United States Supreme Court ruled Alabama and Montgomery laws requiring segregated buses were unconstitutional.

1956

- Montgomery, Alabama, authorities desegregated the local bus system.

1957

- The "Little Rock Nine" entered Central High School in Little Rock, Arkansas, escorted by 1,000 paratroopers under orders from President Dwight D. Eisenhower. This school desegregation showdown garnered international attention.

1958

- Clara Luper, educator and advisor for the Oklahoma City NAACP Youth Council, initiated the first known sit-in. On August 19, 1958, Luper and her Youth Council members entered the segregated Katz Drugstore in downtown Oklahoma City. They took seats and asked to be served. Two days later, Katz corporate management in Kansas City desegregated its lunch counters in three states. The Oklahoma City sit-in preceded the

February 1, 1960, Greensboro, North Carolina, event often credited with initiating the sit-in movement.

1960

- A February sit-in at the Woolworth's lunch counter in Greensboro, North Carolina, drew national attention to the "sit-in" as a tool of civil disobedience aimed at desegregating public eateries.

1961

- The "Freedom Rides" began. Busloads of volunteers of all races traveled across the country and through the Deep South in an effort to integrate bus terminals. [See 1942—discussion of CORE, above.]

1962

- On October 1, 1962, James Meredith (June 25, 1933–present) became the first black student at the University of Mississippi. He had been barred from entering on September 20, 1962. His enrollment, virulently opposed by segregationist Governor Ross Barnett, sparked riots on the Oxford, Mississippi, campus. U.S. President John F. Kennedy dispatched federal troops and United States Marshals to the University of Mississippi. At the end of the chaos, two people lay dead.

1963

- Martin Luther King, Jr., wrote his "Letter from Birmingham Jail." King had spent three days in solitary confinement after being arrested for participating in a protest march. That jail stint became his Muse for the acclaimed writing, which included the now-famous admonition: "Injustice anywhere is a threat to justice everywhere."

- Ku Klux Klan (KKK) bombs killed four little girls at the Sixteenth Street Baptist Church in Birmingham, Alabama. Founded by veterans of the Confederate Army in 1865, the KKK consists of several past and present secret domestic militant organizations in the United States. The KKK originated in the southern states, but eventually gained national scope. KKK members, known principally for advocating white supremacy and acting as a domestic terrorist organization, often hid their identities behind conical hats, masks and white robes. The KKK created a long record of terrorism, violence, mayhem, and lynching to intimidate, murder, and oppress African Americans, Jews, and, occasionally, other minorities (*e.g.*, Roman Catholics; labor union members).

- More than 30,000 people of all races gathered on the Mall in Washington on August 28 to protest civil inequities and hear Dr. Martin Luther King's famous "I Have a Dream" speech.

- Lee Harvey Oswald assassinated President John Fitzgerald Kennedy on November 22.

1964

- Malcolm X (May 19, 1925–February 21, 1965) delivered his speech, "The Ballot or the Bullet," at the Cory Methodist Church in Cleveland, Ohio. Malcolm X, born Malcolm Little, and also known as El-Hajj Malik El-Shabazz, was an African-American minister in the Nation of Islam, and later a Sunni Muslim. He became a celebrated orator, political firebrand, and human rights activist. His admirers saw him as a courageous advocate for the rights of African Americans, a man who indicted white America in the harshest terms for its crimes against African Americans. His detractors accused him of preaching racist violence. Some regard Malcolm X as one of the greatest and most influential African Americans in history.

- Congress passed the Civil Rights Act of 1964, guaranteeing African Americans' legal entitlement to equal access in public accommodations.

1965

- On February 21, 1965, members of the Nation of Islam assassinated black nationalist Malcolm X in Manhattan's Audubon Ballroom. Just a year prior, in 1964, Malcolm X had left the Nation of Islam after more than a decade of allegiance to become a Sunni Muslim.

- State troopers attacked civil rights protestors in Selma, Alabama, on "Bloody Sunday," spraying tear gas and wielding batons. Law enforcement officers assailed residents not participating in the demonstration, too. One person died.

- President Lyndon B. Johnson signed the Voting Rights Act of 1965 into law on August 5.

- The Watts Riots, lasting six days, left at least 34 people dead, 1,032 injured, and 3,952 arrested in the Watts neighborhood of Los Angeles, California. The riots began on August 11, 1965, when Lee Minikus, a California Highway Patrol motorcycle officer, pulled Marquette Frye over. Officer Minikus observed Frye driving erratically, and believed him to be intoxicated. Frye failed basic sobriety tests (e.g., walking in a straight line and touching his nose), so Minikus arrested him. The officer refused to let Frye's brother, Ronald, drive the car home. He radioed a call to have Frye's vehicle impounded. As events escalated, a crowd of onlookers steadily grew from dozens to hundreds. The mob became violent, throwing rocks and other objects while shouting at the police officers. A struggle ensued, resulting in the arrest of Marquette Frye,

Ronald Frye, and their mother. This incident inflamed pre-existing racial tensions, triggering the Watts implosion.

1967

- On June 13, 1967, President Lyndon Baines Johnson appointed Thurgood Marshall to the United States Supreme Court following the retirement of Justice Tom C. Clark. President Johnson realized the momentous nature of the appointment, noting it was "the right thing to do, the right time to do it, the right man and the right place." A 69-11 United States Senate vote confirmed Justice Marshall as Associate Justice of the United States Supreme Court on August 31, 1967.

1968

- On April 4, James Earl Ray assassinated the Reverend Dr. Martin Luther King, Jr., as King stood on the balcony of the Loraine Motel in Memphis, Tennessee. Authorities captured and arrested the triggerman, who was subsequently convicted of the murder and sentenced to 99 years in jail. Ray died in 1998.

- On June 5, Sirhan Bishara Sirhan, the son of a Palestinian Christian family, assassinated Presidential candidate and United States Senator Robert F. Kennedy at the Ambassador Hotel in Los Angeles, California.

1992

- The Los Angeles riots of 1992 erupted when a jury acquitted four police officers accused in the videotaped beating of black motorist Rodney King following a high-speed pursuit. Thousands of people in the Los Angeles area took part in the massive disturbance over a six-day period following the verdict. Widespread looting, assault, arson, and murder occurred. Property damage totaled $1 billion. Many of the crimes were racially motivated. When the dust settled, 53 people lay dead.

2005

- On June 13, 2005, in an unprecedented resolution, the United States Senate formally apologized for its failure to enact the Dyer Anti-Lynching Bill in 1922, as well as other anti-lynching bills.

2008

- In November, Americans elected Barack Obama, an African American, as the 44th President of the United States of America.

2009

- The United States Senate, on February 2, 2009, confirmed Eric Holder as the first African-American United States Attorney General.

---

*Adapted in part from: Amaela Wiley, "Timeline of the American Civil Rights Movement—Looking Back 50 Years after the Montgomery Bus Boycott" (AOL Research & Learn, 2006), http://reference.aol.com/nowyouknow/article?id=20050920113009990001; Borgna Brunner, "African-American History Timeline—A chronology of black history from the early slave trade through Affirmative Action," http://www.infoplease.com/spot/bhmtimeline.html; "Toward Racial Equality: Harper's Weekly Reports on Black America, 1857-1874," http://blackhistory.harpweek.com/2SlaveryTimeline.htm.

Appendix H

State of the Union Address:
President Andrew Jackson
(December 6, 1830)

President Andrew Jackson spoke candidly about Indian removal in his State of the Union Address on December 6, 1830. The following excerpt captures the tenor of the debate around removal.

Fellow Citizens of the Senate and of the House of Representatives:

. . . .

It gives me pleasure to announce to Congress that the benevolent policy of the Government, steadily pursued for nearly 30 years, in relation to the removal of the Indians beyond the white settlements is approaching to a happy consummation. Two important tribes have accepted the provision made for their removal at the last session of Congress, and it is believed that their example will induce the remaining tribes also to seek the same obvious advantages.

The consequences of a speedy removal will be important to the United States, to individual States, and to the Indians themselves. The pecuniary advantages which it promises to the Government are the least of its recommendations. It puts an end to all possible danger of collision between the authorities of the General and State Governments on account of the Indians. It will place a dense and civilized population in large tracts of country now occupied by a few savage hunters. By opening the whole territory between Tennessee on the north and Louisiana on the south to the settlement of the whites it will incalculably strengthen the southwest frontier and render the adjacent States strong enough to repel future invasions without remote aid. It will relieve the whole State of Mississippi and the western part of Alabama of Indian occupancy, and enable those States to advance rapidly in population, wealth, and power. It will separate the Indians from immediate contact with settlements of whites; free them from the power of the States; enable them to pursue happiness in their own way and under their own rude institutions; will retard the progress of decay, which is lessening their numbers, and perhaps cause them gradually, under the protection of the Government and through the influence of good counsels, to cast off their savage habits and become an interesting, civilized, and Christian community. These consequences, some of them so certain and the rest so probable, make the complete execution of the plan sanctioned by Congress at their last session an object of much solicitude.

Toward the aborigines of the country no one can indulge a more friendly feeling than myself, or would go further in attempting to reclaim them from their wandering habits and make them a happy, prosperous people. I have endeavored to impress upon them my own solemn convictions of the duties and powers of the General Government in relation to the State authorities. For the justice of the laws passed by the States within the scope of their reserved powers they are not responsible to this Government. As individuals we may entertain and express our opinions of their acts, but as a Government we have as little right to control them as we have to prescribe laws for other nations.

With a full understanding of the subject, the Choctaw and the Chickasaw tribes have with great unanimity determined to avail themselves of the liberal offers presented by the act of Congress, and have agreed to remove beyond the Mississippi River. Treaties have been made with them, which in due season will be submitted for consideration. In negotiating these treaties they were made to understand their true condition, and they have preferred maintaining their independence in the Western forests to submitting to the laws of the States in which they now reside. These treaties, being probably the last which will ever be made with them, are characterized by great liberality on the part of the Government. They give the Indians a liberal sum in consideration of their removal, and comfortable subsistence on their arrival at their new homes. If it be their real interest to maintain a separate existence, they will there be at liberty to do so without the inconveniences and vexations to which they would unavoidably have been subject in Alabama and Mississippi.

Humanity has often wept over the fate of the aborigines of this country, and Philanthropy has been long busily employed in devising means to avert it, but its progress has never for a moment been arrested, and one by one have many powerful tribes disappeared from the earth. To follow to the tomb the last of his race and to tread on the graves of extinct nations excite melancholy reflections. But true philanthropy reconciles the mind to these vicissitudes as it does to the extinction of one generation to make room for another. In the monuments and fortifications of an unknown people, spread over the extensive regions of the West, we behold the memorials of a once powerful race, which was exterminated or has disappeared to make room for the existing savage tribes. Nor is there any thing in this which, upon a comprehensive view of the general interests of the human race, is to be regretted. Philanthropy could not wish to see this continent restored to the condition in which it was found by our forefathers. What good man would prefer a country covered with forests and ranged by a few thousand savages to our extensive Republic, studded with cities, towns, and prosperous farms, embellished with all the improvements which art can devise or industry execute, occupied by more than 12,000,000 happy people, and filled with all the blessings of liberty, civilization, and religion?

The present policy of the Government is but a continuation of the same progressive change by a milder process. The tribes which occupied the countries now constituting the Eastern States were annihilated or have melted away to make room for the whites. The waves of population and civilization are rolling to the westward, and we now propose to acquire the countries occupied by the red men of the South and West by a fair exchange, and, at the expense of the United States, to send them to a land where their existence may be prolonged and perhaps made perpetual.

Doubtless it will be painful to leave the graves of their fathers; but what do they more than our ancestors did or than our children are now doing? To better their condition in an unknown land our forefathers left all that was dear in earthly objects. Our children by thousands yearly leave the land of their birth to seek new homes in distant regions. Does Humanity weep at these painful separations from every thing, animate and inanimate, with which the young heart has become entwined? Far from it. It is rather a source of joy that our country affords scope where our young population may range unconstrained in body or in mind, developing the power and faculties of man in their highest perfection.

These remove hundreds and almost thousands of miles at their own expense, purchase the lands they occupy, and support themselves at their new homes from the moment of their arrival. Can it be cruel in this Government when, by events which it cannot control, the Indian is made discontented in his ancient home to purchase his lands, to give him a new and extensive territory, to pay the expense of his removal, and support him a year in his new abode? How many thousands of our own people would gladly embrace the opportunity of removing to the West on such conditions! If the offers made to the Indians were extended to them, they would be hailed with gratitude and joy.

And is it supposed that the wandering savage has a stronger attachment to his home than the settled, civilized Christian? Is it more afflicting to him to leave the graves of his fathers than it is to our brothers and children? Rightly considered, the policy of the General Government toward the red man is not only liberal, but generous. He is unwilling to submit to the laws of the States and mingle with their population. To save him from this alternative, or perhaps utter annihilation, the General Government kindly offers him a new home, and proposes to pay the whole expense of his removal and settlement.

Jackson's address is available online at http://www.infoplease.com/t/hist/state-of-the-union/42.html (last viewed May 20, 2010).

Endnotes

Introduction

1. Jack D. Forbes, *Africans and Native Americans: the Language of Race and the Evolution of Red-Black Peoples*, 3rd ed. (Ubana, Illinois: University of Illinois Press, 1993); William Loren Katz, *Black Indians: A Hidden Heritage* (New York, New York: Atheneum Books, 1986).

2. Eminent Oklahoma historian Angie Debo captured the history of the Five Civilized Tribes from a Native-American perspective. That represented a significant challenge to traditional Eurocentric histories focused on land runs and white settlement. Even Debo, however, failed to explore the stories of the Freedmen, both free and enslaved, who lived among those Native Americans. In later life, Debo confided in her former student, historian Daniel F. Littlefield, Jr.: "I knew [the Freedmen] were there. I just didn't know their history. You write about them." Art T. Burton, *Black Gun, Silver Star—The Life and Legend of Frontier Marshal Bass Reeves* (Lincoln, Nebraska, and London, England: University of Nebraska Press, 2006), Foreword, xii.

3. Katz, *Black Indians*, 13-14.

4. Ibid.; see also David A. Chang. *Race, Nation, and the Politics of Landownership in Oklahoma, 1832-1929*. (Chapel Hill, North Carolina: The University of North Carolina Press, 2010). Discussion of land in Oklahoma as the basis of racial interactions and intersections.

5. Dr. Carter G. Woodson was an African-American historian, author, and journalist. He founded the Association of the Study of Negro Life and History. Dr. Woodson, the so-called "Father of Black History," is considered one of the first to conduct a scholarly effort to popularize the value of African-American history. He stressed the importance of a people—all people—having an awareness of, and appreciation for, their contributions to humanity. Dr. Woodson was a founder of the *Journal of Negro History*.

6. Carter G. Woodson. "The Relations of Negroes and Indians in Massachusetts," *Journal of Negro History* 5 (1920): 45.

7. Patrick Minges, *The Keetoowah Society and the Avocation of Religious Nationalism in the Cherokee Nation, 1855-1867* (New York, New York: Union Theological Seminary in the City of New York, 1994), Introduction, 1994, 1998; available online at http://www.us-data.org/us/minges/keetoodi.html.

8. See, e.g., the perspective of Professor Daniel Littlefield, http://www.freedmen 5tribes.com/pdf/cherokee/Professor%20Dan%20%20Littlefield%20on%20Freedme n%202006.pdf. Last visited February 9, 2009.

9. For extensive discussions of American Indian sovereignty, see, e.g., David E. Wilkins and K. Tsianina Lomawaima, *Uneven Ground: American Indian Sovereignty and Federal Law* (Norman, Oklahoma: University of Oklahoma Press, 2001); and David E. Wilkins, *American Indian Sovereignty and the U.S. Supreme Court: The Masking of Justice* (Austin, Texas: University of Texas Press, 1997). For more condensed and colloquial treatment of sovereignty, see Peter d'Errico, *American Indian Sovereignty: Now You See It, Now You Don't*. Text of inaugural lecture in the American Indian Civics Project at Humboldt State University in Arcata, California, delivered on October 24, 1997, http//www.umass.edu/legal/derrico/nowyouseeit.html. Last visited August 22, 2012.

10. United Nations Declaration on the Rights of Indigenous Peoples, adopted by General Assembly Resolutions 61/295 (September 13, 2007), http://www.un.org/esa/socdev/unpfii/en/drip.html. Of particular import on the issue of sovereignty are Articles 3–5, as follows:

> **Article 3**: Indigenous peoples have the right to self-determination. By virtue of that right they freely determine their political status and freely pursue their economic, social and cultural development.
>
> **Article 4**: Indigenous peoples, in exercising their right to self-determination, have the right to autonomy or self-government in matters relating to their internal and local affairs, as well as ways and means for financing their autonomous functions.
>
> **Article 5**: Indigenous peoples have the right to maintain and strengthen their distinct political, legal, economic, social and cultural institutions, while retaining their right to participate fully, if they so choose, in the political, economic, social and cultural life of the State.

11. Jim Myers. "Obama meets with tribal leaders on key issues of sovereignty," *Tulsa World* (December 17, 2010), www.tulsaworld.com, quoting the President: "The aspirations it affirms, including the respect for the institutions and rich cultures of native peoples, are ones we must always seek to fulfill."

12. d'Errico, *Now You See It, Now You Don't*, 4.

13. *United States v. Blackfeet Tribe*, 364 F. Supp. 192 (D. Mont. 1973).

14. Ibid., 194-195; Wilkins and Lomawaima, *Uneven Ground*; Wilkins, *American Indian Sovereignty*. For more condensed and colloquial treatment of sovereignty, see d'Errico, *Now You See It, Now You Don't*.

15. U.S. Constitution, Article VI; Wilkins and Lomawaima, *Uneven Ground*, 251:

> Treaties are constitutionally privileged as the supreme law of the land and are legally binding statements of federal and tribal intent and responsibilities. Treaty modifications or abrogation requires mutual consent; or if unilaterally undertaken, it requires explicit expression of intention. Since treaties are constitutionally acknowledged federal pledges, it is a federal mandate to defend treaties, the nations who signed them, and the provisions of treaties from attack or threat from others. . . .

16. *Morton v. Mancari*, 417 U.S. 535 (1974).

17. Ibid., 551-552.

18. The Bureau of Indian Affairs defines its mission as follows: "The Bureau of Indian Affairs' mission is to enhance the quality of life, to promote economic opportunity, and to carry out the responsibility to protect and improve the trust assets of American Indians, Indian tribes and Alaska Natives." See U.S. Department of the Interior, Bureau of Indian Affairs, Web site, http://www.bia.gov/WhoWeAre/BIA/index.htm. Last visited November 22, 2010.

19. *Morton v. Mancari*, 417 U.S. 535 (1974), 553; see also *United States v. Cohen*, 733 F.2d 128, 139 (D.C. Cir. 1984) (*en banc*); *United States v. Antelope*, 430 U.S. 641 (1977), 649 n. 11 "[The] Constitution itself provides support for legislation directed specifically at Indian tribes."

20. Ibid., n. 24.

21. "Jim Crow" was a character introduced in an 1832 song. Written and sung by "Daddy" Dan Rice in his minstrel show, Jim Crow morphed into a synonym for an African American. The term ultimately became the designation for strict racial segregation laws that reinforced the idea of black inferiority—a racial caste system. Some argue that Jim Crow, by design, pitted poor whites against their natural allies, blacks. By diverting focus away from class issues to "race" issues, poor and powerless whites felt alienated from blacks, from whom they were separated in all aspects of life on account of skin color. By contrast, these same poor and powerless whites felt solidarity with middle and upper class whites, with respect to whom social interaction knew few, if any, such restrictions. Feelings of white supremacy, of racial superiority, became the glue that bound all classes of whites together. Even economic self-interest could not loosen this seemingly impermeable bond. See, e.g., C. Vann Woodward, *The Strange Career of Jim Crow* (Oxford, England; Oxford University Press, 1955). Some modern observers see a new Jim Crowism afoot. This time, institutional racism, not particularistic legislation, is chief among the culprits. Evidence of the new racial caste system, in this view, abounds: soaring numbers of African Americans under "correctional control" (i.e., in jail/prison; on probation; on parole); swelling rolls of Africans Americans disenfranchised, often on account of felony convictions; dwindling numbers of African-American children born in two-parent households; and whole swaths of black males throughout America who have been branded "felons for life," and saddled with the consequences of that label (e.g., ineligibility for government benefits and full civic engagement). See, e.g., Michelle Alexander, *The New Jim Crow*, *The Nation*, http://www.npr.org/templates/story/story.php?storyId=124687663&sc=emaf. Last visited April 6, 2010.

22. Ivan Van Sertima, *They Came Before Columbus: The African Presence in Ancient America* (1st ed., New York, New York: Random House, 1976).

23. The self-descriptor "red," as applied to Native Americans, likely springs from two founts: (1) the desire of Native Americans to compare and contrast themselves with people who identified themselves as "white" and were often accompanied by enslaved Africans who were "black"; and (2) existential notions of human origin predating European contact somehow marked Native Americans as "red." See, e.g., Nancy Shoemaker, "How Indians Got To Be Red," *American Historical Review* 102 (June 1997), 624-644.

24. See, e.g., Rodney M. Baine, "Indian Slavery in Colonial Georgia," *Georgia Historical Quarterly* 1995 79(2), at 418-424; Christine Bolt, "The Anti-Slavery Origins of Concern for the American Indians," *Anti-Slavery Religion and Reform: Essays in Memory of Roger Ansley* (Folkestone, England: Dawson, 1980), 233-253.

25. George Washington Williams. *History of the Negro Race in American from 1619 to*

1880: Negroes as Slaves, as Soldiers, and as Citizens (New York; The Knickerbocker Press, 1882), 123-180; Patrick Minges. *Beneath the Underdog: Race, Religion, and the "Trail of Tears"* (Union Theological Seminary in the City of New York, 1994, 1998), 1-2.

26. Arguably, the racial hierarchy extant in the United States manifests itself around the globe. See, e.g., Martin Jacques, "The global hierarchy of race," *The Guardian*, September 20, 2003:

> [T]here is a global racial hierarchy that helps to shape the power and the prejudices of each race. At the top of this hierarchy are whites. . . . Whites are the only race that never suffers any kind of systemic racism anywhere in the world. And the impact of white racism has been far more profound and baneful than any other: it remains the only racism with global reach. . . . A race generally defers to those above it in the hierarchy and is contemptuous of those below it. . . . At the bottom of the pile, virtually everywhere it would seem, are those of African descent, the only exception in certain cases being the indigenous peoples.

27. Michael F. Doran, "Negro Slaves of the Five Civilized Tribes," *Annals of the Association of American Geographers* (1978): 335-350.

28. See National Congress of American Indians, 57th Annual Session, "Many Nations, One Family," November 12-17, 2000, St. Paul, Minnesota (comments of Dr. Daniel F. Littlefield, Jr., transcription of session entitled, "Exploring the Legacy and Future of Black/Indian Relations"; transcription published 2001 by The Kansas Institute of African-American and Native-American Family History with support from The Freedom Forum.

29. The Muscogee (Creek), Choctaw, and Chickasaw constitutions contain blood quantum requirements: The Constitution of the Muscogee (Creek) Nation provides "[p]ersons eligible for citizenship in the Muscogee (Creek) Nation shall consist of Muscogee (Creek) Indians by blood whose names appear on the final rolls . . . and persons who are lineal descendants of those Muscogee (Creek) Indians by blood whose names appear on the final rolls. . . ." Const. of the Muscogee (Creek) Nation, art. III, sec. 2; The Constitution of the Choctaw Nation provides that its membership consist of "Choctaw Indians by blood whose names appear on the final rolls of the Choctaw Nation . . . and their lineal descendants." Const. of the Choctaw Nation, art. II, sec. 1; and the Constitution of the Chickasaw Nation defines as citizens "all Chickasaw Indians by blood whose names appear on the final rolls of the Chickasaw Nation . . . and their lineal descendants." Const. of the Chickasaw Nation, art. II, sec. 1. Until 2007, the Constitution of the Cherokee Nation prescribed no blood quantum for trial citizenship: "[p]ersons eligible for citizenship in the Cherokee Nation must be original enrollees or descendants of original enrollees listed on the Dawes Commission Rolls. . . ." Const. of the Cherokee Nation, art. IV, sec. 1. On March 3, 2007, the Cherokee Nation of Oklahoma approved an amendment to the Cherokee Constitution. As amended, the Constitution limits citizenship to those with census notations of a link to an Indian ancestor listed on early twentieth-century federal government "Blood Rolls." The Constitution of the Seminole Nation contains no blood quantum requirement: "membership . . . shall consist of all Seminole citizens whose names appear on the final rolls of the Seminole Nation of Oklahoma . . . and their descendants." Const. of the Seminole Nation of Oklahoma, art. II.

30. R. David Edmunds, "Moving with the Seasons, Not Fixed in Stone—The Evolution of Native American Identity," 33-57 (Chapter 2), *Reflections on American Indian History: Honoring the Past, Building a Future.* Albert L. Hurtado, ed. (Norman, Oklahoma: University of Oklahoma Press, 2008), 38. Edmunds noted:

> [T]he concept of blood quantum is not a Native American one but was originated by the federal government. Blood quantums first appeared on removal lists when Indian agents enrolled the eastern tribes for removal to lands west of the Mississippi. Many of these newcomers to Indian Territory retained the blood quantum records during the territorial period, and the government then extended these criteria to other tribes who were allotted under the Dawes Act. Following the allotment period, the tribes' reliance on blood quantums became commonplace [footnote omitted].

31. Colin G. Calloway, "My Grandfather's Axe—Living with a Native American Past," 3-31 (Chapter 1), *Reflections on American Indian History: Honoring the Past, Building a Future.* Albert L. Hurtado, ed. (Norman, Oklahoma: University of Oklahoma Press, 2008), 23. Calloway observed:

> Indians having mixed ancestry, or even having no Indian ancestry, is not a new phenomenon. . . . Commitment to community and culture seem to have been much more important than "blood," which should not seem strange to anyone who has gone through the process of becoming a U.S. citizen—one need not have 'American' blood, but one must absolutely subscribe to the values the United States claims as its own.

32. See "Blood, race and sovereignty in Cherokee Freedmen dispute," Indianz.com (April 26, 2007), available at http://www.indianz.com/News/2007/002611.asp (comments from participants attending the 2007 Federal Bar Association Indian Law Conference).

33. See, e.g., the comments of Professor Daniel Littlefield, http://www.freedmen5tribes.com/pdf/cherokee/Professor%20Dan%20%20Littlefield%20on%20Freedmen%202006.pdf. Last visited February 9, 2009.

34. Ibid.

35. *The Cherokee Nation v. Nash et al.*, Case 4:09-cv-00052-TCK-PJC (N.D. Okla. 2010) (Document 48, Opinion and Order entered July 2, 2010).

36. *Vann et al. v. Salazar*, 1:03CV-1711-HHK (D.D.C. 2003) (originally filed August 2003).

37. See *Vann v. Kempthorne*, 467 F. Supp. 2d 56 (D.D.C. 2006); *Vann v. Kempthorne*, 534 F. 3d 741 (D.C. Cir. 2008).

38. "Northern District Federal Court of Oklahoma Sends Cherokee Freedmen Case (*Cherokee Nation vs. Nash et. al.*) To Washington, D.C. To Same Court As Cherokee Freedmen Federal Case (*Vann et al. v. Salazar*) Being Tried Since 2003." Press release from Marilyn Vann and Jonathan Velie, July 3, 2010.

39. *Raymond Nash v. Cherokee Nation Registrar*, Consolidated Cases No. CV-07-40, *et. al.* D.C., Cherokee Nation, January 14, 2011. Class action lawsuit on behalf of the Freedmen.

40. *Cherokee Nation Registrar v. Raymond Nash*, Case No. SC-2011-02 (Supreme Court of the Cherokee Nation, August 22, 2011).

41. *Vann v. Salazar*, Case No. 1:03-cv-01711-HHK (D.C.D.C. 2011) (Document 152-1, Order entered September 11, 2011).

42. *Vann v. Salazar*, Civil Action 03:1711-HHK (D.C.D.C. 2011) (Memorandum Opinion (Doc. No. 155) and Judgment (Doc. No. 156, September 20, 2011).

43. See, e.g., Robert J. Smith, "Cherokee lawsuit's focus on citizenship," *Arkansas Democrat Gazette*, NWAnews.com, February 16, 2009.

44. Letter to The Honorable Eric Holder, United States Attorney General, from United States Congress members Diane E. Watson, Barney Frank, John Lewis, John Conyers, Jr., Barbara Lee, and Sheila Jackson Lee, April 30, 2009.

45. Interview with Robert Littlejohn in Tulsa, Oklahoma, June 1, 2009.

46. Mr. Littlejohn's sense of and search for belonging, like that of other African-Native Americans, reveals much about our history. A collaborative effort between The National Museum of the American Indian and the National Museum of African-American History and Culture has generated an exhibition about the intersection of American Indian and African-American people and cultures called "IndiVisible: African-Native American Lives in the Americas." The exhibit addresses areas where issues of belonging overlap with concepts of race, culture, community, and creativity. See http://www.sites.si.edu.exhibitions/exhibits/indiVisible_African_Native_Lives/index.htm.

47. Interview with Robert Littlejohn in Tulsa, Oklahoma, June 1, 2009.

48. For Pulitzer Prize-winning journalist Kenneth J. Cooper, a Cherokee Freedmen, birthright is the overarching issue in the Freedmen disenfranchisement imbroglio. Cooper's views on the matter mirror those of many Freedmen. Conversation with Kenneth J. Cooper, Dinner in Honor of the Freedmen of the Five Civilized Tribes, Oklahoma City, Oklahoma, February 18, 2012.

49. Celia E. Naylor, *African Cherokees in Indian Territory: From Chattel to Citizens* (Chapel Hill, North Carolina: The University of North Carolina Press, 2008), 219.

50. Brian Klopotek. "Of Shadows and Doubts: Race, Indigeneity, and White Supremacy," p. 89, and Robert Keith Collins, "What is a Black Indian?: Misplaced Expectations and Lived Realities, Indivisible—African-Native American Lives in the Americas," p. 184. "[M]isplaced expectations about black and Indian mixed-bloods . . . demonstrate[] the fixity with which American race-making practices ascribe blackness. . . . Racial expectations have affected how black and Indian mixed-bloods have been understood and why some are motivated to forcefully assert their culturally specific or generic Native-American heritage, despite their 'black' appearance." [footnote omitted]. *Indivisible—African-Native American Lives in the Americas*, Gabrielle Tayac, gen. ed. (Washington, D.C., and New York, New York: National Museum of the American Indian, The Smithsonian Institution, 2009).

Chapter I: Pre-Removal, Removal, War and Treaties

1. For the full text of the Tecumseh speech, see, e.g., http://famousamericanindians4.homestead.com/Tecumseh.html. Last visited June 29, 2010.

2. Gregory A. Waselkov and Kathryn E. Holland Braund, eds., *William Bartram on the Southeastern Indians* (Lincoln, Nebraska: University of Nebraska Press, 1995), 197.

3. John R. Swanton, *Early History of the Creek Indians & Their Neighbors*

(Gainesville, Florida: University Press of Florida, 1998), 34-35. Originally published in 1922 by the Smithsonian Institution, Bureau of American Ethnology, Bulletin 73.

4. Ibid., 43, quoting Peter (D'Anghtera) Martyr, I and II De Orbe Novo (F. A. MacNutt, trans., New York, New York, 1912); see also Waselkov and Braund, *William Bartram on the Southeastern Indians*.

5. http://taltrust.org/de_soto.htm. Last visited May 13, 2009; see also Lawrence A. Clayton, Vernon J. Knight, and Edward C. Moore, eds., *The de Soto Chronicles: The Expedition of Hernando de Soto to North America in 1539-1543* (Tuscaloosa, Alabama: University of Alabama Press 1996); David Ewing Duncan, *Hernando de Soto: A Savage Quest in the Americas* (Norman, Oklahoma: University of Oklahoma Press, 1997).

6. Chang, *Race, Nation, and the Politics*, 23.

7. See, e.g., William S. Willis, Jr., "Divide and Rule: Red, White, and Black in the Southeast," *Journal of Negro History*, 48 (1963): 165; David Brion Davis, *The Problem of Slavery in Western Culture* (Ithaca, New York: Cornell University Press, 1966), 181.

8. See, e.g., George M. Fredrickson, *White Supremacy: A Comparative Study in American & South African History* (Oxford, England: Oxford University Press 1981).

9. See, e.g., Claudio Saunt, *Black, White, and Indian: Race and the Unmaking of an American Family* (New York, New York and Oxford, England: Oxford University Press, 2005). Exploring racial dynamics in the prominent Muscogee (Creek) Grayson family.

10. See Audrey Smedley, *Race in North America: Origin and Evolution of a Worldview* (Boulder, Colorado: Westview Press, 1999). Smedley urges that "race" necessarily implies inequity and hierarchy, and was used by the European settlers of the Americas to differentiate between and among the myriad demographic groups they encountered.

11. See generally, Alan Stoskopf and Margot Stern Strom, eds., *Race and Membership in American History: The Eugenics Movement* (Brookline, Massachusetts: Facing History and Ourselves National Foundation, Inc. 2002), 47-52; Alexander O. Boulton, "The American Paradox: Jeffersonian Equality and Racial Science," *American Quarterly*, 1995, 47(3): 467-492; Robert E. Bieder, "Scientific Attitudes Toward Indian Mixed-Bloods in Early Nineteenth-Century America," *Journal of Ethnic Studies*, 1980, 8(2): 17-30.

12. See, e.g., David Hurst Thomas, *Skull Wars: Kennewick Man, Archeology and the Battle for Native American Identity* (New York, New York: Basic Books, 2000); Stephen Jay Gould, *The Mismeasure of Man* (New York, New York: W. W. Norton & Company, 1981/1996).

13. Ibid.

14. Brian Klopotek, "Of Shadows and Doubts: Race, Indigeneity, and White Supremacy," *Indivisible—African-Native American Lives in the Americas*, Gabrielle Tayac, gen. ed.. (Washington, D.C. and New York, New York: National Museum of the American Indian, The Smithsonian Institution, 2009): 85-86.

15. Howard Zinn, *A People's History of the United States: 1492–Present* (New York, New York: HarperCollins Publishers, Twentieth Anniversary Edition, 1999), 54-55, referencing works by Gary B. Nash, including a seminal work now in its sixth edition, Gary B. Nash, *Red, White, and Black: The Peoples of Early North America* (Upper Saddle River, New Jersey: Prentice Hall, 2009), sixth edition. first published 1974.

16. Ronald N. Satz, *American Indian Policy in the Jacksonian Era* (Norman, Oklahoma: University of Oklahoma Press, 2002, originally published Lincoln, Nebraska: University of Nebraska Press, 1974), 2.

17. *Extra Census Bulletin: The Five Civilized Tribes In Indian Territory—The Cherokee, Chickasaw, Choctaw, Creek, and Seminole Nations* (Washington, D.C.: Department of the Interior, United States Census Printing Office, 1893).

18. Carla D. Pratt, *Loving Indian Style: Maintaining Racial Caste and Tribal Sovereignty Through Sexual Assimilation*, http://hosted.law.wisc.edu/lawreview/issues/2007-2/pratt.pdf, 427-428.

19. See W. David Baird, "Are the Five Tribes of Oklahoma "Real" Indians?" *The Western Historical Quarterly* (February 1990): 4-18. Baird suggested civilization policy and intermarriage changed the Five Civilized Tribes, but did not somehow render tribal members "less Indian." Indian identity turns mostly on the lived experience, not biological ancestry. Indeed, Baird noted that Muskogee [Creek] Indians often used the term "full blood" as descriptive of cultural qualities, not blood quantum.

20. Lani Guinier and Gerald Torres, *The Miner's Canary: Enlisting Race, Resisting Power, Transforming Democracy* (Cambridge, Massachusetts: Harvard University Press, 2002), 224-225.

21. See, e.g., Booker T. Washington's commentary on educational funding disparities, noting that whites receive the lion's share of funding, but special schools for Indians receive more funding than schools for African Americans. *The Booker T. Washington Papers*, 412, 13: 1914-15, (open book edition, Louis R. Harlan and Raymond W. Smock, eds., Susan Valenza and Sadie M. Harlan, asst. eds., Champaign, Illinois: University of Illinois Press, 1984), available at http://www.historycooperative.org/btw/Vol.13/html/11.html. Last visited May 18, 2009.

22. Tiya Miles, *Ties That Bind: The Story of an Afro-Cherokee Family in Slavery and Freedom* (Berkeley and Los Angeles, California: University of California Press, 2005), Introduction, 4-5.

23. See Lani Guinier and Gerald Torres, *The Miner's Canary: Enlisting Race, Resisting Power, Transforming Democracy* (2002), 225. Discussing elements of the "racial bribe."

24. Andrew Hacker, *Two Nations: Black and White, Separate, Hostile, Unequal* (New York, New York: Ballentine, 1992).

25. Bernard Vincent, "Slaveholding Indians: the Case of the Cherokee Nation," http://www.unive.it/media/allegato/dep/Ricerche/1_Vincent1.pdf. Last visited May 19, 2009.

26. See, e.g., David Pilgrim, "Purposeful Venom Revisited," *Journey Towards Nationalism: The Implications of Race and Racism*. Gerald Matthews, ed. (New York, New York: Farber, 1999). See also Hannibal B. Johnson, "To the Nth Power—The N Word Past & Present," *IncogNegro: Poetic Reflections on Race & Diversity in America* (Baltimore, Maryland: PublishAmerica, 2008), 20-23; Randall Kennedy, *Nigger: The Strange Career of a Troublesome Word* (New York, New York: Pantheon Books, 2002).

27. See, e.g., The Racial Slur Database, http://gyral.blackshell.com/names.html; Urban Dictionary, www.urbandictionary.com.

28. Angie Debo, *And Still the Waters Run: The Betrayal of the Five Civilized Tribes* (Princeton, NJ: Princeton University Press, Fourth Princeton Paperback Printing, 1991), ix. Originally published in 1940 by Princeton University Press.

29. Not all observers agree the Cherokees' treatment of Africans, particularly

enslaved Africans, differed markedly from that of the white man. See, e.g., Bernard Vincent, "Slaveholding Indians: the Case of the Cherokee Nation," http://www.unive.it/media/allegato/dep/Ricerche/1_Vincent1.pdf. last visited on May 19, 2009), 14. "[T]he so-called 'benevolence' of slaveholding Indians, and of Cherokee slavery in particular, is a myth. . . ."

30. Ronald N. Satz, *American Indian Policy in the Jacksonian Era* (Norman, Oklahoma: University of Oklahoma Press, 2002. Originally published Lincoln, Nebraska: University of Nebraska Press, 1974), 6.

31. See Appendix H.

32. See, e.g., Grant Foreman, *Indian Removal: The Emigration of the Five Civilized Tribes of Indians* (Norman, Oklahoma: University of Oklahoma Press, 1932).

33. See, e.g., Wyatt F. Jeltz, "The Relations of Negroes and Choctaw and Chickasaw Indians," *The Journal of Negro History* (vol. 33, no. 1, 24-37, January 1948): 26.

34. Donna L. Akers, "Removing the Heart of the Choctaw People: Indian Removal from a Native Perspective," *The American Indian Past and Present*, Roger L. Nichols, ed. (Norman, Oklahoma: University of Oklahoma Press, 6th ed., 2008), 127-140.

35. Ibid., 139.

36. Wilma Mankiller, "Reflections on Removal, 1993," in Theda Purdue and Michael D. Green, *The Cherokee Removal: A Brief History with Documents* (Boston, Massachusetts, and New York, New York: Bedford/St. Martin's, 2nd ed., 2005), 186.

37. Wilma Mankiller and Michael Wallis, *Mankiller: A Chief and Her People* (New York, New York: St. Martin' Press, 1993), 46; Mankiller, "Reflections on Removal, 1993," 184.

38. Muriel H. Wright, *Guide to the Indian Tribes of Oklahoma* (Norman, Oklahoma: University of Oklahoma Press, 1985). Produced with the help of the Oklahoma Tourism and Recreation Department and the office of the Oklahoma Indian Affairs Commission.

39. Indian Removal Act of 1830. Chapter CXLVIII, May 28, 1830.

40. See, e.g., http://www.ourdocuments.gov/doc.php?doc=25 [President Andrew Jackson's Message to Congress, "On Indian Removal," 1830].

41. *Cherokee Nation v. Georgia*, 30 U.S. 1. 1831.

42. *Worcester v. Georgia*, 31 U.S. 515. 1832.

43. *Cherokee Nation v. Georgia*, 30 U.S. 1. 1831.

44. *Worcester v. Georgia*, 31 U. S. 515. 1832.

45. Purdue and Green, *The Cherokee Removal*, 167.

46. See, e.g., Finger, *John R. Cherokee Americans: The Eastern Band of Cherokees in the 20th Century* (Lincoln, Nebraska: University of Nebraska Press, 1993); Mankiller, "Reflections on Removal, 1993," 185.

47. Michael Roethler, *Negro Slavery Among the Cherokee Indians, 1540-1866* (Ph.D. Dissertation, Fordham University, 1964), 150. Cited in Patrick Minges, *Beneath the Underdog: Race, Religion, and the 'Trail of Tears'* (New York, New York: Union Theological Seminary. 1994, 1998), 9.

48. George P. Rawick, *The American Slave: A Composite Autobiography* (Westport, Connecticut: Greenwood Press, 1972), 380-381. (Eliza Whitmire).

49. "Congressional Black Caucus Briefed on Cherokee Freedmen at 37th Annual Legislative Conference," *The Cherokee Observer*, vol. 16, no. 1, January 2008: 1, 7.

50. Chief Mankiller died on April 6, 2010, at age 64. Among those who commented on her life were the following:

- **President Barack Obama**: "As the Cherokee Nation's first female chief, she transformed the Nation-to-Nation relationship between the Cherokee Nation and the Federal Government, and served as an inspiration to women in Indian Country and across America."
- **President Bill Clinton and Secretary of State Hillary Clinton**: "[Wilma Mankiller]...exemplified the enduring strength of the human spirit...She led her people with dignity and grace, fostering a sense of community, cooperation, and shared values."
- **Cherokee Nation Principal Chief Chad Smith**: "We are a better people and a stronger tribal nation because of her example of Cherokee leadership, statesmanship, humility, grace, determination and decisiveness."
- **United States Interior Secretary Ken Salazar**: "Wilma Mankiller was a shining example of courage and leadership for all Americans."
- **Assistant United States Secretary of the Interior and Bureau of Indian Affairs Head Larry Echo Hawk**: "She willingly reached out beyond her tribal community and Indian Country in search of solutions to the social and economic challenges facing the Cherokee people, while sharing her knowledge and insights with anyone who needed them."

These excerpts from longer commentaries evince the esteem in which all manner of Americans held Chief Mankiller. By virtually all accounts, she was a beloved leader who left a profound legacy. See "Comments on death of ex-Cherokee Chief Mankiller," Associated Press, April 6, 2010, available at http://www.newson6.com/global/story.asp?s=12267182. Last visited April 6, 2010.

51. Mankiller and Wallis, *Mankiller: A Chief and Her People*, 94.

52. Naylor, *African Cherokees in Indian Territory*, 1.

53. Patrick Minges, *Beneath the Underdog: Race, Religion, and the "Trail of Tears,"* (Union Theological Seminary in the City of New York, 1994, 1998), 9-10.

54. Ibid.

55. Theda Purdue and Michael D. Green, *The Cherokee Removal: A Brief History with Documents* (Boston, Massachusetts and New York, New York: Bedford/St. Martin's, 2nd ed., 2005), 168. "[M]ost scholars think that the death toll was at least four thousand, and some suggest that the population loss may have been as high as eight thousand."

56. *Worcester v. Georgia*, 31 U.S. 515 (1832).

57. Letter from Lucy Ames Butler to Drusilla Burnap, January 2, 1839, The Fadjo Cravens II Collection, National Park Service, U.S. Department of the Interior, Fort Smith [Arkansas] National Historic Site.

58. "Cherokee Female Seminary, 1851—Native American Board School First," *The Brown Quarterly*, Vol. 4, No. 3, Fall 2001. (Native American Issue).

59. Some suggest the killing of the Treaty Party was an "execution," while oth-

ers liken it to an assassination. See, e.g., Purdue and Green, *The Cherokee Removal*, 168. "The unknown assailants probably saw themselves as executioners of an ancient Cherokee law, cited by John Ridge in 1826 and committed to writing in 1829, that made land cession a capital crime."); Ronald N. Satz, *American Indian Policy in the Jacksonian Era* (Norman, Oklahoma: University of Oklahoma Press, 2002). Originally published Lincoln, Nebraska: University of Nebraska Press, 1974), 221-222. "Continuing feuds between the National party and the Treaty party led to the brutal assassination of the three leaders of the latter group. . . .").

60. Purdue and Green, *The Cherokee Removal*, 58-59.

61. Constitution of the Cherokee Nation, Formed by a Convention of Delegates from the Several Districts, at New Echota. July 1827), reproduced in Purdue and Green, *The Cherokee Removal*, 60-70.

62. See, e.g, Pylant, James, "In Search of the Black Dutch," *American Genealogy Magazine* (Vol. 12, No. 1. March 1997), 11-30; Jimmy H. Crane, "The Elusive Black Dutch of the South," *Native Peoples Magazine*, available at http://www.nativepeoples.com/article/articles/164/1/The-Elusive-Black-Dutch-of-the-South/.

63. See generally, Ronald N. Satz, *American Indian Policy in the Jacksonian Era* (Norman, Oklahoma: University of Oklahoma Press, 2002; originally published Lincoln, Nebraska: University of Nebraska Press, 1974); Akers, "Removing the Heart of the Choctaw People," 127-140; Anthony F. C. Wallace, *The Long, Bitter Trail: Andrew Jackson and the Indians*. Eric Foner, consulting editor (New York, New York: Hill and Wang, 1993); Robert Vincent Remini, *Andrew Jackson & His Indian Wars* (New York, New York: Viking Press, 2001); Purdue and Green, *The Cherokee Removal*.

64. Ibid.

65. See, e.g., David Buice, *Lincoln's Unissued Proclamation*, 153-169 Prologue 1978 10(3) arguing that the failure of the Union and President Lincoln to make commitments to the Five Civilized Tribes spawned Confederate/tribal alliances and resulted in great hardships for Native Americans.

66. See generally, Murray R. Wickett, *Contested Territory—Whites, Native Americans and African Americans in Oklahoma, 1865-1907* 13. (Baton Rouge, Louisiana: Louisiana State University Press, 2000), 5-6.

67. United States Census Bureau, *A Census of the Population Growth from the First Census of the United States to the Twelfth, 1790-1900* (Washington, D.C.: Government Printing Office 1909); see also, F. B. Bullard, M.A., "'Civilization' and Southern Identity: A Cultural and Political History of the Cherokees of the Old South, 1540-1866," http://www.sagespirit.net/nativeamericanhistory.html

68. Diane Miller, "Frontier Freedom: Seeking the Underground Railroad in Indian Territory," *The Chronicles of Oklahoma*, 87 (Spring 2009), 76-93, citing Celia-Naylor-Ojurongbe, "Born and Railed Among These People, I Don't Want to Know Any Other": Slaves' Acculturation in Nineteenth-Century Indian Territory, in James F. Brooks, ed., *Confounding the Color Line: The Indian-Black Experience in North America* (Lincoln, Nebraska: University of Nebraska Press, 2002), 173.

69. For more on Joseph Vann (1798-1844), see, e.g., Henry Thompson Malone, *Cherokees of the Old South: A People in Transition* (Athens, Georgia: University of Georgia Press, 1956); William G. McLoughlin, *Cherokee Renascence in the New Republic* (Princeton, New Jersey: Princeton University Press, 1986); Theda Perdue, "The Conflict Within: The Cherokee Power Structure and Removal," *Georgia Historical Quarterly* 73, Fall 1989): 467-91.

70. See Art T. Burton, "Slave Revolt of 1842," *Oklahoma Historical Society's Encyclopedia of History & Culture*, http://digital.library.okstate.edu/encyclopedia/entries/S/SL002.html, citing Art T. Burton, "Cherokee Slave Revolt in 1842," *True West Magazine* (June 1996); Rudi Halliburton, Jr., *Red Over Black: Black Slavery among the Cherokee Indians* (Westport, Connecticut: Greenwood Press, 1977); Kaye M. Teall, *Black History in Oklahoma: A Resource Book* (Oklahoma City, Oklahoma: Oklahoma City Public Schools, 1971); and Morris L. Wardell, *A Political History of the Cherokee Nation, 1838-1907* (Norman, Oklahoma: University of Oklahoma Press, 1977).

71. *Constitution and Laws of the Choctaw Nation*, printed at Doaksville, 20, 1852; Wyatt F. Jeltz, "The Relations of Negroes and Choctaw and Chickasaw Indians," *The Journal of Negro History* (vol. 33, no. 1, Jan. 1948): 24-37.

72. See, e.g., http://www.historynet.com/sand-creek-massacre.htm. Last visited February 7, 2012.

73. *Proclamation for Neutrality by Principal Chief John Ross* on May 17, 1861, available at http://cherokeehistory.com/confed.html.

74. The reply of Cherokee Chief John Ross to Lt. Col. J.R. Kannady, commanding officer at Ft. Smith, Arkansas, reaffirming the neutrality of the Cherokee Nation, available at http://cherokeehistory.com/confed.html.

75. Instructions from Confederate Secretary of War L. P. Walker to Superintendent of Indian Affairs David Hubbard to form alliances with the tribes of the Indian Territory and recruit their warriors into the Confederate Military, available at http://cherokeehistory.com/confed.html.

76. Declaration of ratification of the treaty with the Confederated States of America by the Cherokee National Committee with concurrence of the National Council and approval of Chief John Ross, available at http://cherokeehistory.com/confed.html.

77. Theda Purdue, *Slavery and the Evolution of Cherokee Society 1540-1866* (Knoxville, Tennessee: The University of Tennessee Press, 1979), 144.

78. See, e.g., Art T. Burton, *Black, Buckskin, and Blue: African American Scouts and Soldiers on the Western Frontier* (Austin, Texas: Eakin Press, 1999), 109-117; see also, Richard Sias and Bob L. Blackburn, "Lincoln's Legacy in Oklahoma," *The Chronicles of Oklahoma*, Vol. LXXXVI, No. 4, Winter 2008-09): 481; Hannibal B. Johnson, *Acres of Aspiration—The All-black Towns in Oklahoma* (Austin, Texas: Eakin Press, 2002), 136-139.

79. "Battle Summaries: Honey Springs, National Park Service." http://www.nps.gov/history/hps/abpp/battles/ok007.htm. Last visited on May 25, 2009), citing Steve Cottrell, *Civil War in the Indian Territory* (Gretna, Louisiana: Pelican Press, 1995); Dudley Taylor Corinth, *The Sable Arm: Black Troops in the Union Army, 1861-1865* (Lawrence, Kansas: University of Kansas Press 1987), 75-78; Wiley Britton, *The Union Indian Brigade in the Civil War* (Kansas City, Kansas, F. Hudson Publishing, 1922), 282-83.

80. Historian Davis D. Joyce wonders whether too much has been made of Watie's tardy surrender. Perhaps, Joyce suggests, Watie simply did not know that the Civil War was over. E-mail from Davis Joyce to Hannibal B. Johnson, January 10, 2011.

81. W. Craig Gaines, *The Confederate Cherokees: John Drew's Regiment of Mounted Rifles* (Baton Rouge: Louisiana State University Press, 1989), 124.

82. Ibid.

83. Commissioner of Indian Affairs, Report, 1865; pp. 298-302; 318-19. mes-

sage to The Peace Council at Fort Smith on September 9, 1865, in connection with the negotiation of the Treaty of 1866.

84. See, e.g., Laurence M. Hauptman, *Between Two Fires: American Indians in the Civil War* (New York, New York: Free Press, 1995); Emmet Starr, *History of the Cherokee Indians and Their Legends and Folk Lore* (Oklahoma City, Oklahoma: Warden 1921); Thomas F. Andrews, "Freedmen in Indian Territory: A Post Civil War Dilemma," *Journal of the West* 1965 4(3): 367-76.

85. Murray R. Wickett, *Contested Territory—Whites, Native Americans and African Americans in Oklahoma, 1865-1907* (Baton Rouge, Louisiana: Louisiana State University Press, 2000).

86. Ibid., 12-13.

87. Katz, *Black Indians*.

88. Purdue, *Slavery and the Evolution of Cherokee Society, 1540-1866*, 144-145.

89. Treaty with the Cherokee, July 19, 1866, 14 Stat. 799; *Indian Affairs: Laws and Treaties*, Vol. II, Treaties. Charles J. Kappler ed., Washington, D.C.: Government Printing Office 1904), 942-945.

90. Ibid., 943-944.

91. Ibid.

92. Ibid., Art. VI, 944.

93. Ibid. at 945.

94. Circe Sturm, "Blood Politics, Racial Classification, and Cherokee National Identity: The Trials and Tribulations of the Cherokee Freedmen," *American Indian Quarterly* (vol. 22, no. 1 & 2, Winter/Spring, 1998): 230-258.

95. Ibid.

96. Interview with David Cornsilk in Tulsa, Oklahoma, October 18, 2008.

97. James Moody, *Myths of the Cherokee* (New York, New York: Dover Publications, Inc., 1995), 146-47, originally published by the Government Printing Office, Washington, D.C., in 1900, as part of the *Nineteenth Annual Report of the Bureau of American Ethnology to the Secretary of the Smithsonian Institution, 1897-98*; in Two Parts—Part I).

98. Interview with David Cornsilk in Tulsa, Oklahoma, October 18, 2008.

99. Naylor, *African Cherokees in Indian Territory*, 218. See also, Patricia Nelson Limerick, *The Legacy of Conquest: The Unbroken Past of the American West* (New York, New York: W.W. Norton, 1987); Scott B. Vickers, *Native American Identities: From Stereotype to Archetype in Art and Literature* (Albuquerque, New Mexico Press, 1998).

100. Adam Geller, "Past and future collide in fight over Cherokee identity," *Associated Press*, February 2, 10, 2007, available at http://usatoday.com

101. Richard T. Schaefer, *Racial and Ethnic Groups*, 11th ed. (Upper Saddle River, N.J.: Prentice Hall, 2007), 12-13.

102. Teresa A. Rendon, "Indian Identity," *The Oklahoma Bar Journal* 81:5, February 13, 2010): 359.

103. Ibid., 360.

104. Ibid.

105. See *Shaare Tefila Congregation v. Cobb*, 481 U.S. 615. 1987); *Saint Francis College v. Al-Khazraji*, 481 U.S. 604. 1987.

106. *Cherokee Nation v. United States*, 12 I.C.C. 570, 583. 1963).

107. Ibid., 643a. (Final Order).

108. David D. Friedman, *Law's Order: An Economic Account*, 1999. (unpublished manuscript), ch. 12, 7-8 of 25, available at http://www.daviddfriedman.com

109. African-Native American Genealogy Forum, http://afrigeneas.com. John Cornsilk, March 26, 2007, posting.
110. Cf. *Williams v. Walker-Thomas Furniture Co.*, 350 F.2d 445. D.C. Cir. 1965).
111. *Seminole v. Norton*, 223 F. Supp.2d 123. D.D.C. 2002).
112. *Seminole v. Norton*, 206 F.R.D. 1. D.D.C.), 2001.
113. *Seminole v. Norton*, 223 F. Supp. 2nd 123, 134. D.D.C. 2002).
114. *United States v. Dion*, 476 U.S. 734. 1986).
115. Nancy Hope Self, "The Building of Rail Roads in the Cherokee Nation," *The Chronicles of Oklahoma* (vol. 49, Summer 1971): 180-181.
116. Andrew Denson, *Demanding the Cherokee Nation: Indian Autonomy and American Culture, 1830-1900* (Lincoln, Nebraska & London, England: University of Nebraska Press, 2004), 174.
117. Ibid., 177-178.
118. The phrase "as long as grass grows or water runs" was used by President Andrew Jackson in an October 15, 1829, letter to his emissary to the Indians, Major David Haley. The President tasked Major Haley with assuaging Indian doubts about removal. This designated ambassador sought to secure Indians' willing compliance with the Jackson plan for an east-for-west land swap that would, ideally, both facilitate removal and placate the reluctant among the population to be removed. "There, beyond the limits of any state, [transplanted Indians will be] in possession of land of their own, which they shall possess as long as grass grows or water runs, I can and will protect them and be their friend and father." Letter from President Andrew Jackson to Major David Haley, October 15, 1829, cited in J. F. Holden, "THE B.I.T.: The Story of an Adventure in Railroad Building," *Chronicles of Oklahoma* (vol. 11, no. 1. March 1933): 639-641.
119. John Hope Franklin and John Whittington Franklin, eds., *My Life and an Era—The Autobiography of Buck Colbert Franklin* (Baton Rouge, Louisiana: Louisiana State University Press, 1997), 65-66; see also J. F. Holden, "THE B.I.T.: The Story of an Adventure in Railroad Building," *Chronicles of Oklahoma* (vol. 11, no. 1. March 1933): 643-645:

> There had been no railroads in the Indian country up to 1870, but beginning in that year the steel rails began to push their way into to the Territory.... The coming of the railroads into the Indian country was the beginning of the disintegration of the Indian nations, and foreshadowed the ending of the isolation of the Indian Territory. As the long lines of rail pushed their way farther and farther into the country white people followed them. Stations and towns were located, coal mines opened up, and merchants and tradesmen began doing business—all spelling the doom of the old free and self-governing national life and existence of the Indians.

120. Omnibus Railroad Act, 30 Stat. 990. March 2, 1899); see also, Wilkins, *American Indian Sovereignty*, 82.
121. "Our Indian Wards," *The American Indian* (CD-ROM, version 3.1, Guild Press of Indiana, date unknown); The Indian Territory, *Fort Smith Weekly New Era* (December 22, 1871): 22.
122. See, e.g., Debo, *And Still the Waters Run*, 11:

The Cherokees, Choctaws, and Chickasaws also admitted intermarried whites to citizenship. There had been considerable admixture of white blood in all the tribes before Removal, but for a time after the settlement in the West[,] white influence almost disappeared. After the Civil War, with the construction of the first railroads across Indian Territory and the rapid settlement of the Western frontier, this immigration and intermarriage began again.

123. Luther B. Hill, *A History of the State of Oklahoma: 1908* (Chicago, Illinois & New York, New York: The Lewis Publishing Company, 1908).

124. "The Indian Territory: Convention of the Colored People of the Choctaw Nation—They see the Shadow of the Coming Events and Prepare for it." Resolution:—Address, Etc., *Fort Smith Weekly New Era* (March 15, 1872), 2; "Something for the U. S. Government to Look Into," *Fort Smith Weekly New Era* (April 5, 1872), 2.

Chapter II

1. Gabrielle Tayac, gen. ed., *Indivisible—African-Native American Lives in the Americas* (Washington, D.C., and New York, New York: National Museum of the American Indian, The Smithsonian Institution, 2009), 21.

2. David Weber, *The Spanish Frontier in North America* (New Haven, Connecticut: Yale University Press, 1994), 36-37.

3. Katz, *Black Indians*.

4. Purdue, *Slavery and the Evolution of Cherokee Society, 1540-1866*, 36.

5. Ibid., 36-37.

6. Chang, *Race, Nation, and the Politics*.

7. Oklahoma Slave Narratives, http://freepage.genealogy.rootsweb.ancestry.com/~ewyatt/_borders/Oklahoma%20Slave%20Narratives/Slave%20Narrative%20Index.html. Last visited June 11, 2009.

8. See Hannibal B. Johnson, *Black Wall Street—From Riot to Renaissance in Tulsa's Historic Greenwood District* (Austin, Texas: Eakin Press, 1998); see also *Final Report of the Oklahoma Commission to Study the Tulsa Race Riot of 1921* (Oklahoma Historical Society, 2001), www.okhistory.org/trrc/freport.htm.

9. Franklin and Franklin, eds., *My Life and an Era*, xii-xxii.

10. John Hope Franklin, *From Slavery to Freedom: A History of African Americans* (New York, New York: A.A. Knopf, 1st ed., 1947).

11. See generally, John Hope Franklin, *Mirror to America: The Autobiography of John Hope Franklin* (New York, New York: Farrar, Straus and Giroux, 2005).

12. Franklin and Franklin, eds., *My Life and an Era*, 1-2.

13. T. Lindsay Baker and Julie P. Baker, eds., *The WPA Slave Narratives* (Norman, Oklahoma: University of Oklahoma Press, 1976), 109.

14. Ibid., 110-11.

15. Baker and Baker, eds., *The WPA Slave Narratives*, 109.

16. "Memorial of delegates from the Indian Territory protesting against the passage of the bill to organize the Territory of Oklahoma," 45th Cong., 2nd Session, Senate, Mis. Doc. 82, p. 2, June 12, 1878.

17. See, e.g., Tiya Miles, *Ties That Bind: The Story of an Afro-Cherokee Family in*

Slavery and Freedom (Berkeley and Los Angeles, California: University of California Press, 2005), Introduction, 4. "[I]n the social context of the Cherokee communities, people of African descent were not always defined as 'black' and 'enslaved'; sometimes they were defined as relatives."); Chang, *Race, Nation, and the Politics*, 23. "Not all Creek people—not even most—embraced [the black chattel slavery system]. . . . Some people of African descent lived as free and full members of Creek towns. Their numbers are unknown, but their presence was noted at the time and has been emphasized by historians."

18. Diane Miller, "Frontier Freedom: Seeking the Underground Railroad in Indian Territory," *Chronicles of Oklahoma* (87, Spring 2009): 84, citing, Celia-Naylor-Ojurongbe, "Born and Raised Among These People, I Don't Want to Know Any Other": Slaves' Acculturation in Nineteenth-Century Indian Territory, in James F. Brooks, ed., *Confounding the Color Line: The Indian-Black Experience in North America* (Lincoln, Nebraska: University of Nebraska Press, 2002), 173.

19. "Memorial of delegates from the Indian Territory protesting against the passage of the bill to organize the Territory of Oklahoma," 45th Cong., 2nd Session, Senate, Mis. Doc. 82, June 12, 1878.

20. Chang, *Race, Nation, and the Politics*, Introduction, 1.

21. Donald A. Grinde, Jr., and Quintard Taylor, "Red vs Black: Conflict and Accommodation in the Post Civil War Indian Territory, 1865-1907," *American Indian Quarterly* (vol. 8., no. 3, Summer 1984): 222-224.

22. See, e.g., Walton L. Brown, "The Forgotten Heritage: African-Amerindian Relations in America," *Proteus* (1992 9. 1): 11-17.

23. Murray R. Wickett, *Contested Territory—Whites, Native Americans and African Americans in Oklahoma, 1865-1907* (Baton Rouge, Louisiana: Louisiana State University Press, 2000), 196.

24. Grinde and Taylor, "Red vs Black," 211.

25. See, e.g., Michael Kolhoff, "Fugitive Communities in Colonial America," available at http://www.earlyamerica.com/review/2001_summer_fall/fugative.html. Last visited February 8, 2012.

26. Ibid., 212.

27. The Keetoowah Society became both an abolitionist and a revitalization movement. See, e.g., James Duncan, "The Keetoowah Society," 4 *Chronicles of Oklahoma* (1926): 251-55; Howard Q. Tyner, *The Keetoowah Society in Cherokee History*, M.A. Thesis, University of Tulsa, 1949; James E. Hendrix, "Redbird Smith and the Nighthawk Keetoowahs," 8 *Journal of Cherokee Studies* (1989): 22-39, 73-86.

28. James Mooney, *Myths of the Cherokees* (Smithsonian Institution, Bureau of American Ethnology, Washington, D.C.: Government Printing Office, 1900), 225.

29. Debo, *And Still the Waters Run*, 162-164.

30. "Sequoyans Gain Little Ground: Latest Returns Show But 17,703 Votes Cast of Which Over 3,000 Are Against the Constitution," *Muskogee Phoenix* (November 10, 1905), 1.

31. Wickett, *Contested Territory*, 182.

32. See, e.g., Naylor, *African Cherokees in Indian Territory*, 192-199; see also Wickett, *Contested Territory*, 196.

33. Naylor, *African Cherokees in Indian Territory*, 192-193.

34. Ibid., 175.

35. See, e.g., Rayford Logan, *The Betrayal of the Negro from Rutherford B. Hayes to Woodrow Wilson* (New York, New York: Da Capo Press, 1997, expanded edition of

the author's seminal work, *The Negro in American Life and Thought, The Nadir, 1877-1901* (New York, New York: Dial Press, 1945); James Loewen, *Lies My Teacher Told Me* (New York, New York: Touchstone, 1995); James Loewen, *Lies Across America* (New York, New York: Touchstone, 1999).

36. Roger L. Nichols, ed., *The American Indian Past and Present* (Norman, Oklahoma: University of Oklahoma Press, 2008, article by Nancy Shoemaker entitled "How Indians Got Red").

37. Shoshana Wasserman, *Native American Experience, Oklahoma Almanac 2007-2008: We Know We Belong to the Land—A Centennial Celebration* (Oklahoma City, Oklahoma: Oklahoma Department of Libraries, 2007), 14.

38. Mankiller and Wallis, *Mankiller—A Chief and Her People*, 138-39.

39. Debo, *And Still the Waters Run*, 159.

40. Ibid.

41. *Oklahoma Historical Society's Encyclopedia of History & Culture*, Oscar Ameringer. 1870-1943), http://digital.library.okstate.edu/encyclopedia/entries/A/AM014.htm. Last visited June 29, 2009.

42. Oscar Ameringer, *If You Don't Weaken: The Autobiography of Oscar Ameringer* (Norman, Oklahoma; University of Oklahoma Press, 1983), 232.

43. See, e.g., S. E. Ruckman, "For Indians, a time to protest," *Tulsa World*, (November 11, 2007), A9.

44. Not surprisingly, some Oklahomans recoiled at the mere hint of a counter-narrative on the birth of the state. Presented with a different mirror, they bristled at a reflection that looked eerily foreign. Historian Davis D. Joyce reported that his book, *Alternative Oklahoma: Contrarian View of the Sooner State* (Norman, Oklahoma: University of Oklahoma Press, 2007) debuted the year of the Oklahoma Centennial celebration, 2007. That year, he traveled the state speaking about the Centennial and promoting the book. He encountered significant resistance to his emphasis on alternative, rather than "mainstream," Oklahoma history. Among his alternative discussions was one on the difficulty of celebrating an invasion. E-mail from Davis D. Joyce to Hannibal B. Johnson, September 12, 2011.

45. Grinde and Taylor, "Red vs Black," 222.

46. In the 1870s, the federal government moved even more Indians to Oklahoma. Federal policymakers consolidated the Plains Indians, who had been scattered across the western plains, onto two large reservations, one in Indian Territory, the other in the Dakotas. Federal officials apparently felt that since all Indians were alike, why not clump them all together?

47. Naylor, *African Cherokees in Indian Territory*, 49.

48. Art T. Burton, *Cherokee Slave Revolt of 1842: American Indians as Slave Owners*, http://www.freerepublic.com/focus/news/655380/posts (March 28, 2002).

49. See, e.g., William McLoughlin, *The Cherokee Ghost Dance: Essays on the Southeastern Indians* (Atlanta, GA: Mercer University Press, 1984), 266; Purdue, *Slavery and the Evolution of Cherokee Society 1540-1866*, 36; and Kenneth W. Porter, *Relations Between Negroes and Indians Within the Present United States* (Washington, D.C.: The Association for Negro Life and History, 1931), 16.

50. Charles Evans and Clinton Orrin Bunn, *Oklahoma Civil Government* (Ardmore, Oklahoma: Bunn Brothers, 1908), 88.

51. Debo, *And Still the Waters Run*, 292.

52. Curtis Act, 30 Stat. 495 (1898).

53. Ibid., 110-111. Debo noted the Choctaw Nation likewise operated under a

usufructuary regime, and pointed out gross disparities existed between the land holdings of a few wealthy families and the Choctaw masses, even in the face of this "communal" land ownership system.).

54. Chang, *Race, Nation, and the Politics*, 20-21.

55. Robert D. Miller, "'A Few Hundred People Can't Do Anything with 75 Million!': The Cherokee Advocate and the Inevitability of Allotment," *The Chronicles of Oklahoma*, vol. LXXXVIII, no. 1 (Spring 2010): 41.

56. During the last quarter of the twentieth century, a number of African-American men policed Indian Territory as deputy U.S. marshals. Most were Freedmen, and many were part Indian. These men had been a vital part of life in the Five Civilized Tribes since the late eighteenth century, and were often both culturally and linguistically fluent. See Burton, *Black Gun, Silver Star*, 2-7.

57. Burton, *Black Gun, Silver Star*, 4. The accomplishments of Bass Reeves are all the more impressive when one recalls that he had once been enslaved and, not unlike many others on the western frontier, he never achieved literacy.

58. George O. Carney, "Historic Resources of Oklahoma's All-black Towns: A Preservation Profile," *The Chronicles of Oklahoma* (Summer 1991, vol. LXIX, no. 2): 118.

59. Johnson, *Acres of Aspiration*.

60. Steven J. Niven, Alexander K. Davis, *African American National Biography*. Henry Louis Gates, Jr., and Evelyn Brooks Higginbotham, eds. (Cambridge, Massachusetts and London, England: W.E.B. Du Bois Institute for African and African American Research at Harvard University and Oxford University Press, 2008); available online at Oxford African American Studies Center, http://www.oxfordaasc.com/article/opr/t0001/e1378. Last visited February 5, 2012.

61. Arthur L. Tolson, *The Black Oklahomans: A History, 1541-1972* (New Orleans, Louisiana; Edwards Printing Company, 1974), 42-43.

62. Ibid.

63. See, e.g., Johnson, *Acres of Aspiration*.

64. See, e.g., Franklin and Franklin, eds., *My Life and an Era*, 143.

65. Wickett, *Contested Territory*, 110.

66. Mellinger, "Discrimination and Statehood," *Langston City Herald*, June 13, 1893.

67. See, e.g., "Going to the Nation: The Idea of Oklahoma in Early Blues Recordings," http://www.journals.cambridge.org.

68. Betty Gerber, Ed.D., Executive Director of the Broken Arrow Historical Society Museum, January 2007, in Childers/Childress Family Association, Inc. Newsletter (Summer 2007. Martha Childress Ferris, ed.), 3.

69. Danney Goble, *Progressive Oklahoma: The Making of a New Kind of State* (Norman, Oklahoma: University of Oklahoma Press, 1980), 376-77.

70. See, e.g., Johnson, *Acres of Aspiration*, 197.

71. Roy E. Stafford, "The Negroes' Place," *The Daily Oklahoman*, September 13, 1907.

72. *The Oklahoma Eagle*, July 10, 1997, 1.

73. See, e.g., Johnson, *Black Wall Street*; Franklin and Franklin, eds., *My Life and an Era*.

74. James W. Loewen, *Sundown Towns: A Hidden Dimension of American Racism* (New York, New York: The New Press, 2005), 1-18. Dr. Loewen also discussed Tulsa as a sundown town in a speech at the John Hope Franklin Center for Reconciliation

Symposium, "Reconciliation in America: Moving Beyond Racial Violence," June 3, 2010.

75. The referenced postcards are included in Oklahoma Commission to Study the Tulsa Race Riot of 1921, *Tulsa Race Riot: A report by the Oklahoma Commission to Study the Tulsa Race Riot of 1921*, February 28, 2001, as follows: "Runing [*sic*] the Negro out of Tulsa." (Courtesy Oklahoma Historical Society), 18; "Charred Negro" (Courtesy Department of Special Collections, McFarlin Library, The University of Tulsa), 18; "Little Africa on Fire: Tulsa Race Riot" (Courtesy Department of Special Collections, McFarlin Library, The University of Tulsa), 21.

76. Scott Ellsworth, "The Tulsa Race Riot," 11, http://www.tulsareparations.org/TulsaRiot.htm. Last visited June 8, 2010; see also, Scott Ellsworth, *Death in a Promised Land* (Baton Rouge, Louisiana: Louisiana State University Press, 1982).

77. See, e.g., Alana J. Erickson, "Red Summer," in *Encyclopedia of African American Culture and History* (New York, New York: Simon & Schuster Macmillan, 1996); "For Action On Race Riot Peril—Radical Propaganda Among Negroes Growing, and Increase of Mob Violence Set Out in Senate Brief for Federal Inquiry," *New York Times*, October 5, 1919.

78. James Weldon Johnson, "1921 Tulsa race riot: NAACP report on 1921 Tulsa race riot," *The New Crisis*, Nov./Dec. 1999, http://findarticles.com/p/articles/mi_qa 3812/is_199911/ai_n8854233/?tag=content;col1. Last visited January 14, 2011.

79. James Weldon Johnson, ed., *The Book of American Negro Poetry* (San Diego, California; New York, New York; London, United Kingdom: A Harvest Book, Harcourt Brace & Company, 1969, originally published in 1931 by Harcourt Brace & Company), 168-69.

80. See, e.g., http://www.pbs.org/wnet/jimcrow/stories_events_birth.html. "The Rise and Fall of Jim Crow, Jim Crow Stories, The Birth of a Nation" (1915) PBS; http://www.filmsite.org/birt.html. AMC Filmsite, written and edited by Tim Dirks. Last visited January 13, 2011.

81. Thomas F. Dixon, Jr., *The Clansman: An Historical Romance of the Ku Klux Klan* (New York, New York: Doubleday, Page & Co., 1905).

82. Andrew Leiter, "Thomas Dixon, Jr.: Conflicts in History and Literature," http://docsouth.unc.edu/southlit/dixon_intro.html. Documenting the American South website. Last visited January 13, 2011.

83. The rosters of the Tulsa Ku Klux Klan are available at McFarlin Library, Special Collections, The University of Tulsa.

84. E-mail from Peggy Brooks-Bertram, Dr.H., Ph.D., to Hannibal B. Johnson, January 20, 2011. Peggy Brooks-Bertram, Dr.P.H., Ph.D., of Buffalo, New York, Co-Founder, Uncrowned Queens Institute for Research and Education on Women, Inc., has compiled material on Drusilla Dunjee Houston. 1876-1941. She was an Oklahoma native and activist in her own right who engaged in a broad array of intellectual pursuits. Few are aware of her central role in early Oklahoma race politics. Drusilla Dunjee Houston crafted an unpublished screenplay, *Spirit of the South—The Maddened Mob*, as a response to D. W. Griffith's *Birth of a Nation* and the writings of Thomas Dixon, some of which Griffith drew from to create his cinematically acclaimed film, now roundly condemned for its patent racism. Houston's unique work is available both in its original, handwritten form, and in a later typed and revised version. Drusilla Dunjee Houston also wrote a multi-volume history of ancient African peoples and civilizations, perhaps the first such treatment of African history by an African-American woman.

85. See, e.g., James Allen, Hilton Als, Congressman John Lewis, and Leon F. Litwack, *Without Sanctuary: Lynching Photography in America* (Sante Fe, New Mexico: Twin Palms Publishers, 2008).

86. James Weldon Johnson, ed., *The Book of American Negro Poetry* (San Diego, California; New York, New York; London, United Kingdom: A Harvest Book, Harcourt Brace & Company, 1969, originally published in 1931 by Harcourt Brace & Company), 168.

87. Wickett, *Contested Territory*, 154-155.

88. Abel Meeropol, aka Lewis Allan, "Strange Fruit," originally published as a poem in *The New York Teacher*, a union magazine, in 1936, and then later set to music by Meeropol. As performed by Billie Holliday, credits include: Lewis Allan (i.e., Meeropol), songwriter; Maurice Pearl, songwriter; Dwayne P. Wiggins, songwriter; Dwayne Wiggins Pub Designee, publisher; and WB Music Corp., publisher. "Strange fruit" is a metaphor for the numerous, mostly black, bodies hanged from tree in Southern lynchings.

89. See, generally, Charles N. Clark, *Lynching in Oklahoma: Vigilantism and Racism in the Twin Territories and Oklahoma* (Oklahoma City, Oklahoma: N.P., 2008).

90. See, e.g., James Allen, Hilton Als, *Without Sanctuary*.

91. See, generally, Kaye M. Teall, *Black History in Oklahoma: A Resource Book* (Oklahoma City, Oklahoma: Oklahoma City Public Schools, 1971).

92. Eddie Faye Gates, *They Came Searching: How Blacks Sought the Promised Land in Tulsa* (Austin, Texas: Eakin Press, 1997), 32.

93. Franklin and Franklin, eds., *My Life and an Era*, 199-200.

94. Interview with Eli Grayson, President of the California Muscogee. Creek) Association, in Tulsa, Oklahoma, June 20, 2009.

95. Eddie Faye Gates, *They Came Searching*, 91-93.

96. Johnson, *Black Wall Street*.

97. See S. Res. 39. June 13, 2005. "Apologizing to the victims of lynching and the descendants of those victims for the failure of the Senate to enact anti-lynching legislation.")

98. See, generally, Johnson, *Black Wall Street*; Scott Ellsworth, *Death in a Promised Land* (Baton Rouge, Louisiana: Louisiana State University Press, 1982); Eddie Faye Gates, *They Came Searching: How Blacks Sought the Promised Land in Tulsa* (Austin, Texas: Eakin Press, 1997); Mary E. Jones Parrish, *Events of the Tulsa Disaster*. The 1923 self-published account of an African-American woman who survived the 1921 Tulsa Race Riot.

99. *Final Report of the Oklahoma Commission to Study the Tulsa Race Riot of 1921* (Oklahoma City, Oklahoma: Oklahoma Historical Society, 2001), www.okhistory.org/trrc/freport.htm. The core findings of the Commission included:

- Black Tulsans had every reason to believe Dick Rowland would be lynched after his arrest on charges later dismissed and highly suspect from the start.
- They had cause to believe his personal safety, like the defense of themselves and their community, depended on them alone.
- As hostile groups gathered and their confrontation worsened, municipal and county authorities failed to take action to calm or contain the situation.
- At the eruption of violence, civil officials selected many men, all

of them white, and some of them participants in that violence, and made those men their agents as deputies.
- In that capacity, deputies did not stem the violence, but added to it, often through overt acts that were themselves illegal.
- Public officials provided firearms and ammunition to individuals, again all of whom were white.
- Units of the Oklahoma National Guard participated in the mass arrests of all, or nearly all, of Greenwood's residents, removed them to other parts of the city, and detained them in holding centers.
- Entering the Greenwood district, people stole, damaged, or destroyed personal property left behind in homes and businesses.
- People, some of them agents of government, deliberately burned or otherwise destroyed homes credibly estimated to have numbered 1,256, along with virtually every other structure—including churches, schools, businesses, even a hospital and library—in the Greenwood district.
- Despite duties to preserve order and to protect property, no government at any level offered adequate resistance, if any at all, to what amounted to the destruction of the neighborhood referred to commonly as "Little Africa" and politely as the "Negro quarter."
- Although the exact total can never be determined, credible evidence makes it probable many people, likely numbering between one and 300, were killed during the riot.
- Not one of these criminal acts was then, or ever has been, prosecuted or punished by government at any level—municipal, county, state, or national.
- Even after the restoration of order, it was official policy to release a black detainee only upon the application of a white person, and then only if that white person agreed to accept responsibility for that detainee's subsequent behavior.
- As private citizens, many whites in Tulsa and neighboring communities did extend invaluable assistance to the riot's victims, and the relief efforts of the American Red Cross, in particular, provided a model of human behavior at its best.
- Although city and county government bore much of the cost for Red Cross relief, neither contributed substantially to Greenwood's rebuilding. In fact, municipal authorities acted, initially, to impede rebuilding.

In the end, the restoration of Greenwood after its systematic destruction was left to the victims of that destruction.

100. See, e.g., Johnson, *Black Wall Street*.

101. John Hope Franklin and Alfred A. Moss, Jr., *From Slavery to Freedom: A History of African Americans* (Columbus, Ohio: McGraw-Hill, Inc., 1947, 2000).

102. Funding request letter to the Trustees of the Cuesta Foundation from Lee Clark-Johns, Co-chair, Program Committee, John Hope Franklin Center for Reconciliation, Inc., March 31, 2009.

103. On November 7, 1978, Article XXIII, Section 11 of the Oklahoma Constitution, defining race, was repealed by the people of Oklahoma.
104. See, e.g., Naylor, *African Cherokees in Indian Territory*, 196.
105. See, e.g., Keith L. Bryant, Jr., *Alfalfa Bill Murray* (Norman, Oklahoma: University of Oklahoma Press, 1968); Danney Goble, *Progressive Oklahoma: The Making of a New Kind of State* (Norman, Oklahoma: University of Oklahoma Press, 1980).
106. "The Negro and Indian to Figure as Political Issues," *Daily Oklahoman*, July 28, 1906.
107. African Americans protested the passage of Senate Bill One, with some demonstrations turning violent in Taft and Redbird. E. P. McCabe led a legal challenge, but the U.S. Supreme Court upheld the law's constitutionality. In a series of cases beginning in the mid-1940s, the United States Supreme Court declared various types of segregation on interstate railways unconstitutional. In 1965, the Oklahoma Legislature repealed all segregation statutes for public transportation. For more information on segregation in Oklahoma, see, e.g., Phillip Mellinger, "Discrimination and Statehood in Oklahoma," *The Chronicles of Oklahoma* (Autumn 1971), 49; James Scales and Danney Goble, *Oklahoma Politics: A History* (Norman, Oklahoma: University of Oklahoma Press, 1982); Kay Teall, *Black History in Oklahoma: A Resource Book* (Oklahoma City, Oklahoma: Oklahoma City Public Schools, 1971); Arthur Tolson, *The Negro in Oklahoma Territory, 1889-1907: A Study in Racial Discrimination* (Ph.D. dissertation, University of Oklahoma, 1966); *General Statutes of Oklahoma, 1908* (Kansas City, Missouri: Pipes Reed Book Company, 1908); *Journal of the House of Representatives of the Regular Session of the First Legislature of Oklahoma* (Guthrie, Oklahoma: Leader Printing and Manufacturing House, 1908); and *Journal of the Proceedings of the Senate of the First Legislature of the State of Oklahoma* (Muskogee, Oklahoma: Muskogee Printing Company, 1909).
108. Generally, each of the Five Civilized Tribes held their land communally, to the extent the tribes held title to the land. There was, however, an element of capitalism inherent in the usufructuary land tenure systems most tribes recognized. See, e.g., Robert D. Miller, "'A Few Hundred People Can't Do Anything With 75 Million!': The Cherokee Advocate and the Inevitability of Allotment," *The Chronicles of Oklahoma*, vol. LXXXVIII, no. 1 (Spring 2010), 28:

> Although the [Cherokee] Nation retained the title to Cherokee lands, individual members had usufruct rights and controlled the disposition of any improvements they made to the land. Consequently, the Cherokee system of land tenure did not resemble a communal system in which everyone received an equal share of the produce regardless of work performed. Because Cherokees already had incentives to improve their lands, reformers had no reason to introduce severalty to them in order to promote a system of individual rewards.

109. Chang, *Race, Nation, and the Politics*, 79-81.
110. Ibid., 81-82.
111. Ibid., 93-95.
112. See *Kappler's Indian Affairs: Laws and Treaties* Vol. II, Treaties: Treaty with the Cherokee, 1866, 942–950; Treaty with the Choctaw and Chickasaw, 1866,

Endnotes 353

918-931; Treaty with the Muscogee (Creek), 1866, 931-937; and Treaty with the Seminole, 1866, 910-915.

113. Mary Ellison, "Black Perceptions and Red Images: Indian and Black Literary Links," 44 *Phylon*, vol. 44, no. 1 (March 1983): 44-45.

114. Jack D. Forbes, "Mulattoes and People of Color in Anglo-North America: Implications for Black-Indian Relations," *Journal of Ethnic Studies* 1984 12(2): 17-61.

115. National Congress of American Indians, 57th Annual Session, *Many Nations, One Family*, November 12-17, 2000, St. Paul, Minnesota. Wilma Mankiller, transcription of session entitled, "Exploring the Legacy and Future of Black/Indian Relations"; transcription published 2001 by The Kansas Institute of African-American and Native-American Family History, with support from The Freedom Forum, http://web.mit.edu/wjohnson/www/kiaanafh/KIAANAFH_PORTAL_PAGE.html.

116. See, e.g., *Morton v. Mancari*, 417 U.S. 535, 554 (1974), upholding a BIA Indian hiring preference against claims of racial discrimination on the premise it is not race based, but rather a hiring criterion in furtherance of Indian self-government.

117. There are 565 federally recognized Native American tribes in the United States. Thirty-eight of those tribes maintain Oklahoma headquarters. See, e.g., Lenzy Krehbiel-Burton, "Summit of Tribal Leaders Scheduled," *Tulsa World* (November 22, 2010), A11.

118. See, e.g., Wilkins and Lomawaima, *Uneven Ground*, 64-97.

119. Pub. L. 570, Act of June 7, 1956, 70 Stat. 254.

120. "Federal Recognition: The Lumbee Tribe's Hundred Year Quest," http://www.lumbeetribe.com/recognition/index.htm

121. National Congress of American Indians, 57th Annual Session, *Many Nations, One Family*, November 12-17, 2000, St. Paul, Minnesota. Professor David Wilkins, transcription of session entitled, "Exploring the Legacy and Future of Black/Indian Relations"; transcription published 2001 by The Kansas Institute of African-American and Native-American Family History, with support from The Freedom Forum, http://web.mit.edu/wjohnson/www/kiaanafh/KIAANAFH_POR-TAL_PAGE.html.

122. Margo S. Brownell, *Who Is an Indian? Searching for an Answer to the Question at the Core of Federal Indian Law*, 34 Mich. J.L Reform 275, 288 (2001).

123. National Congress of American Indians, 57th Annual Session, *Many Nations, One Family*, November 12-17, 2000, St. Paul, Minnesota. Wilma Mankiller, transcription of session entitled, "Exploring the Legacy and Future of Black/Indian Relations"; transcription published 2001 by The Kansas Institute of African-American and Native-American Family History, with support from The Freedom Forum, http://web.mit.edu/wjohnson/www/kiaanafh/KIAANAFH_PORTAL_PAGE.html.

124. Carey Ross-Perhenick, J.D., M.B.A., "Tribal Citizenship—Inherent Tribal Decision or Federal Mandate? Misconceptions Surrounding the Freedmen of Cherokee Nation," Federal Indian Law (newsletter), Spring 2008, 10-11, citing *Nero v. Cherokee Nation of Oklahoma*, 892 F.2d 1457 (10th Cir. 1989).

125. Adrienne P. Samuels, "What Does Indian Blood Look Like?—A Century-Old Battle Boils as Black Indians Fight for Membership in Their Native American Tribe," *Ebony* (April 2008, 94): 100.

126. Interview with David Cornsilk, Tulsa, Oklahoma, October 18, 2008.

127. Wheeler-Howard Act (Indian Reorganization Act of 1934), 48 Stat. 984, 25 U.S.C. §461 *et. seq.*, P.L. 383 (73rd Congress, June 18, 1934).

128. Solicitor's Opinion M-27781, United States Department of the Interior, Office of the Solicitor, Washington, October 25, 1934, approved October, 25, 1934, Oscar L. Chapman, Assistant Secretary (Part V. Important Court Decisions, on Tribal Rights and Property), http://thorpe.ou.edu/solicitor.html. Last visited June 26, 2009.

129. *Vann v. Kempthorne*, 467 F. Supp. 2d 56. D.D.C. 2006); *Vann v. Kempthorne*, 534 F.3d 741. D.C. Cir. 2008.

130. See *Martinez v. Santa Clara Pueblo*, 46 U.S. 49 (1978), upholding the right of tribes to define citizenship criteria as part of sovereignty and in service of the federal goal of promoting Indian self-government.

131. Carla D. Pratt, "Tribes and Tribulations: Beyond Sovereign Immunity and Toward Reparation and Reconciliation for Estelusti," 11 Wash. & Lee R.E.A.L. J. 61, 113-114 (2005); See also, Eric Reitman, "An Argument for the Abrogation of Federally Recognized Indian Tribes' Sovereign Power over Membership," 92 Va. L. Rev. 793, 863 (2006); Terrion L. Williamson, "The Plight of 'Nappy-Headed' Indians: The Role of Tribal Sovereignty in the Systematic Discrimination against Black Freedmen by the Federal Government and Native-American Tribes," 10 *Mich. J. Race & Law* 233, 262-268.

132. See Letter from Chief Carl J. Artman, Assistant Secretary, Indian Affairs, United States Department of the Interior, Office of the Secretary to Principal Chief of the Cherokee Nation, The Honorable Chadwick Smith. August 9, 2007.

133. Artman served as United States Assistant Secretary of the Interior for Indian Affairs, with jurisdiction over the Office of Indian Affairs, Bureau of Indian Affairs, and the Bureau of Indian Education from 2007 to 2008. He also acted as Associate Solicitor for Indian Affairs at the Department of the Interior from 2005 to 2007.

134. Sean Murray, "Cherokees Pull Memberships of Freed Slaves," *Associated Press*, March 4, 2007.

135. Interview with Marilyn Vann in Tulsa, Oklahoma, October 15, 2008.

136. Francis G. Hutchins, *The Iroquois, New York and Federal Tribal Policy*, 2004, 481-482 (unpublished manuscript), available at www.madisoncounty.org

137. Ibid.

138. S. A. Ray, "A Race or a Nation? Cherokee National Identity and the Status of Freedmen's Descendants," http://law.bepress.com/expresso/eps/1570 (2006).

139. *Cohen's Handbook of Federal Indian Law*, Sec. 401[2][b] (2005 ed.). "[T]he Department of the Interior has taken the position that it may decline to continue government-to-government relations with a tribe's elected officials if it finds that the tribal membership laws underlying voter eligibility for the election violate [ICRA] or the tribe's own constitution." ICRA, the Indian Civil Rights Act of 1968, prohibits "banishment," which term might arguably be applied with respect to the treatment of the Freedmen. See Indian Civil Rights Act of 1968, 25 U.S.C. Sec. 1301 (1968).

140. Congress could also block the Secretary of Interior from acquiring and holding in trust land for the Cherokees. The Indian Reorganization Act (1934) authorizes the Secretary of the Interior to acquire land and hold it in trust "for the purpose of providing land for Indians." 25 U.S.C. Sec. 465. Within the meaning of

that statute, "Indian" includes "all persons of Indian descent who are members of any recognized tribe now under Federal jurisdiction." 25 U.S.C. Sec. 479. According to the United States Supreme Court, the word "now" refers to those tribes that were under federal jurisdiction when the IRA was enacted in 1934. See *Carcieri v. Salazar*, No. 07-526. United States Supreme Court, February 25, 2009. The Cherokees fall outside that stricture and thus, barring Congressional action, could be prevented from placing land in federal trust.

    141. http://www.african-nativeamerican.com/Petition.htm.

    142. Jim Myers, "Coburn: Congress should force Cherokees' decision," *Tulsa World* (August 8, 2007): A1; Jim Myers, "Tribe can change constitution, not [F}reedmen treaty, BIA says," *Tulsa World* (August 11, 2007), A1.

    143. Letter to The Honorable Eric Holder, United States Attorney General, from United States Congress members Diane E. Watson, Barney Frank, John Lewis, John Conyers, Jr., Barbara Lee, and Sheila Jackson Lee, April 30, 2009.

Chapter III

    1. This reference to "allotment" uses the term in a casual sense. The Muscogee (Creek) Nation held land in common, but permitted persons within the tribe to make use of land without benefit of legal title. The Dawes Commission ushered in the concept of allotment—division of tribal land into individual parcels, with formal, legal ownership vesting in the person(s) to whom the land was allotted.

    2. Oklahoma Slave Narratives, http://freepage.genealogy.rootsweb.ancestry.com/~ewyatt/_borders/Oklahoma%20Slave%20Narratives/Slave%20Narrative%20Index.html. Last visited June 12, 2009.

    3. Cited in Matthew Atkinson, "Red Tape: How American Laws Ensnare Native American Lands, Resources, and People," 23 *OK City Law Rev*, 379, 392 (1998). See also Jeff Arnold, "Act Ended Federal 'Kill Indian' Philosophy," *Southwest Times Record* (November 24, 2007): A1, noting that the Pratt statement was intended to counter a common maxim of the day: "[T]he only good Indian is a dead Indian."

    4. Patrick Minges, *The Keetoowah Society*, Introduction; available online at http://www.us-data.org/us/minges/keetoodi.html.

    5. Pratt, "Loving Indian Style," 425.

    6. Ibid.

    7. Antonio J. Waring, ed., *Laws of the Creek Nation* (Athens, Georgia: University of Georgia Press, University of Georgia Libraries Miscellanea Publications no. 1, 1960), law 20.

    8. Scott L. Malcomson, *One Drop of Blood: The American Misadventure of Race* (New York, New York: Farrar, Straus & Giroux, 2000), 90.

    9. *Laws of the Cherokee Nation*, Sept. 19, 1839, Manuscript and Archives Division, Oklahoma State University.

    10. Ibid., Mar. 16, 1858.

    11. Bill No. 52, Choctaw Nation, Indian Territory, Special Files, Choctaw and Chickasaw and Cherokee Freedmen, RG 48, Box 48, RDI.

    12. Pratt, "Loving Indian Style," 430-431.

    13. Wyatt F. Jeltz, "The Relations of Negroes and Choctaw and Chickasaw Indians," *The Journal of Negro History* (vol. 33, no. 1. January 1948): 24-37.

    14. Wickett, *Contested Territory*.

15. L. J. Abbott, "The Race Question in the Forty-sixth State," *Independent* (July 25, 1907), 208.

16. Wickett, *Contested Territory*, 6.

17. Chang, *Race, Nation, and the Politics*, 30-31. Chang points out that even among the Muscogee (Creek) Nation, plantation owners and so-called "traditionalists" treated enslaved Africans differently. Plantation owners referred to their slaves as este-vpuekv, meaning "livestock person"—a chattel slave. Traditionalists, on the other hand, often related to their slaves as though they were tenant farmers.

18. Katz, *Black Indians*, 135-136.

19. Wickett, *Contested Territory*, 6.

20. "Memorial of delegates from the Indian Territory protesting against the passage of the bill to organize the Territory of Oklahoma," 45th Cong., 2nd Session, Senate, Mis. Doc. 82, 2, June 12, 1878.

21. President Theodore Roosevelt, First Annual Message, December 3, 1901, http://www.digital history.uh.edu/native_voices_display.cfm?id=92.

22. Pratt, "Loving Indian Style," 456.

23. Morris L. Wardell, *A Political History of the Cherokee Nation, 1838-1907* (Norman, Oklahoma: University of Oklahoma Press, 1938), 333.

24. S. A. Ray, "A Race or a Nation? Cherokee National Identity and the Status of Freedmen's Descendants," http://law.bepress.com/expresso/eps/1570 (2006).

25. *Rowe v. Sartain*, 107 Okla. 199, 230 P. 919. Okla. 1924.

26. *Sango v. Willig*, 119 Okla. 128, 1926 OK 622, 249 P. 901 (Okla. 1926).

27. Circe Sturm, *Blood Politics: Race, Culture, and Identity in the Cherokee Nation of Oklahoma* (Berkeley, California: University of California Press, 2002), 189.

28. "Descendants of the Freedmen of the Five Civilized Tribes," http://www.freedmen5tribes.com.

29. Debo, *And Still the Waters Run*, 260.

30. See Bureau of Indian Affairs, Certificate of Degree of Indian or Alaska Native Blood, OMB Control #1076-0153 (expires July 31, 2011), available at http://www.bia.gov/idc/groups/public/documents/text/idc-001805.pdf. Last visited November 7, 2010.

31. Interview with Evan White in Chouteau, Oklahoma, July 31, 2009.

32. Pratt, "Loving Indian Style," 461-462.

33. Ibid.

34. Ann McMullen, "Blood and Culture: Negotiating Race in Twentieth-Century Native New England," in *Confounding the Color Line: The Indian-Black Experience in North America*. James F. Brooks ed. (Lincoln, Nebraska: University of Nebraska Press, 2002), 268.

35. Barack Obama, "A More Perfect Union," Speech delivered on March 18, 2008, in Philadelphia, Pennsylvania.

36. Jim Myers, "Obama selects Cherokee as senior adviser," *Tulsa World* (June 16, 2009), A13.

37. See, generally, Andres T. Tapia, *The Inclusion Paradox: The Obama Era and the Transformation of Global Diversity* (Lincolnshire, Illinois: Hewitt Associates, 2009).

38. Steve Hammons, "Who is a Cherokee? Many Americans have Indian in the family tree," *American Chronicle* (March 6, 2007), http://www.americanchronicle.com.

39. Keegan King, "Obama right on Cherokee Freedmen controversy," *The New Mexico Independent* (June 23, 2008), http://newmexicoindependent.com/924/obama-right-on-cherokee-freedmen-controversy. Last visited June 16, 2009.

Chapter IV

1. See U.S. Bureau of the Census, *Compendium of the Ninth Census of the United States, 1870* (Washington, D.C.: Government Printing Office 1872), 20-21; Bureau of the Census, *Extra Census Bulletin: The Five Civilized Tribes* (Washington, D.C.: Government Printing Office 1894), 4; Bureau of the Census, *Thirteenth Census of the United States: 1910, Population* (Washington, D.C.: Government Printing Office 1913), 464, 466.

2. See, e.g., Nina Lane Dunn, *Tulsa's Magic Roots* (Tulsa, Oklahoma: N.L.D. Corp. 1979), 35-36.

3. Debo, *And Still the Waters Run*, 91.

4. Ibid.

5. Homestead Act of 1862, Library of Congress, *A Century of Lawmaking for a New Nation: U.S. Congressional Documents and Debates, 1774-1875*, 392 Statutes at Large, 37th Congress, 2nd Session.

6. Leslie Jones, "Chitto Harjo and the Snake Rebellion," *The Chronicles of Oklahoma*, vol. LXXXVIII, no. 2 (Summer 2010): 170-171.

7. U.S. Congress, Report of the Select Committee to Investigate Matters Connected with Affairs in the Indian Territory (Hearings) 59th Congress, 2nd Sess., Senate Report No. 5013, pt. 2. (2 Vols., Washington, D.C.: Government Printing Office, 1907), Vol. II, 1251-1252.

8. Ch. 119, Laws 1887, 24 Stat. 388, 25 U.S.C. § 331 et seq. (2000).

9. Pub. L. 106–462, title I, § 106(a)(1), Nov. 7, 2000, 114 Stat. 2007.

10. *Indian Territory—Information for Home-Seekers and Investors*. Compiled by N.R. Baker and I. N. Ury; Muskogee, Indian Territory; Indian Territory Publishing Co. (entered in the Office of Librarian of Congress, 1901).

11. Curtis Act, 30 Stat. 495 (1898).

12. Dawes Commission Rolls: Five Civilized Tribes, Enrollment Cards of the Five Civilized Tribes, 1898-1914 Series: M1186 Rolls: 1-93. microfilm publication reproducing the enrollment cards prepared by the staff of the Commission to the Five Civilized Tribes between 1898 and 1914. These records are part of the Records of the Office of Indian Affairs, Record Group 75, and are housed in the National Archives-Southwest Region in Fort Worth, Texas); see http://www.censusmicrofilm.com/dawshist.htm. Last visited May 27, 2009.

13. Debo, *And Still the Waters Run*, ix. Citing Superintendent, Office Files, Report of A. M. Landman, 1935, 56-60.

14. See, e.g., Angie Debo, *The Rise and Fall of the Choctaw Republic* (Norman, Oklahoma: University of Oklahoma Press, 1934), 289, discussing the April 26, 1906, law winding up of the affairs of the Choctaw Nation.

15. See Kent Carter, "Dawes Commission," *Oklahoma Historical Society's Encyclopedia of Oklahoma History & Culture*, http://digital.library.okstate.edu/encyclopedia/entries/D/DA018.html, citing Jeffrey Burton, *Indian Territory and the United States, 1866-1906: Courts, Government, and the Movement for Oklahoma Statehood* (Norman, Oklahoma: University of Oklahoma Press, 1995); Kent Carter, *The Dawes Commission and the Allotment of the Five Civilized Tribes, 1893-1914* (Orem, Utah: Ancestry.com, 1999); Debo, *And Still the Waters Run*; *American Indian Policy in the Twentieth Century*, Vine Deloria, Jr., ed. (Norman, Oklahoma: University of Oklahoma Press, 1985); William T. Hagan, *Theodore Roosevelt and Six Friends of the Indian* (Norman, Oklahoma: University of Oklahoma Press, 1997); Frederick E. Hoxie, *A Final Promise: The Campaign to Assimilate the Indians, 1880-1920* (Lincoln,

Nebraska: University of Nebraska Press, 1984); see also, J. F. Holden, "THE B.I.T.: The Story of an Adventure in Railroad Building," *Chronicles of Oklahoma*, vol. 11, no. 1 (March 1933): 655. "In their negotiations with the Indians, particularly those in the Choctaw and Chickasaw nations, the Commission segregated from allotment all coal and asphalt lands—approximately 450,000 acres—and 1,400,000 acres of timber lands."

Chapter 5
1. Wickett, *Contested Territory*, 190.
2. Danney Goble, *Progressive Oklahoma: The Making of a New Kind of State* (Norman, Oklahoma: University of Oklahoma Press, 1980), 201; Wickett, *Contested Territory*, 189-202.
3. Wickett, *Contested Territory*, 202.
4. Ibid., 196.
5. S. Con. Res. 26.
6. Declaration of Independence, July 4, 1776.
7. Anthony F. C. Wallace, *Jefferson and the Indians: The Tragic Fate of the First Americans* (Cambridge, MA: Harvard University Press, 1999), excerpt available at http://www.hup.harvard.edu/features/waljef/intro3.html.
8. Organic Act, 1890 (May 2, 1890); Oklahoma, upon admission to the Union in 1907, allowed non-discriminatory voting, at least in theory.
9. See, e.g., David Pilgrim, "What Was Jim Crow?" Museum of Racism Memorabilia, Ferris State University, 2000, at http://www.ferris.edu/news/jimcrow/what.htm; Joseph Boskin, *Urban Racial Violence* (Beverly Hills, California, 1976), 14-15.
10. Johnson, *Acres of Aspiration*.
11. "Oklahoma Negro Issue Put Up To Roosevelt," *New York Times* (February 2, 1907), 4.
12. "Population of Oklahoma and Indian Territory 1907," Bulletin 89. (Washington, D.C.: GPO, 1907), 8-9.
13. R. Darcy, "Constructing Segregation: Race Politics in the Territorial Legislature, 1890-1907," *The Chronicles of Oklahoma* (vol. LXXXVI, no. 3, 260), 281.
14. See http://www.thedrewshow.com/reparations/JIM_CROW_LAWS_BY_STATE2004.doc
15. Among the abundant Jim Crow measures in Oklahoma were:

- 1890: Education: Every three years an election for school electors was to be held to vote for or against separate schools for white and "colored" children.
- 1897: Education: A separate district was established for colored children wherever there were at least eight black children. It is unlawful for any white child to attend a school for black children. or vice versa.
- 1907: Education: The original Oklahoma Constitution mandated the Oklahoma Legislature provide separate schools for white and "colored" children "with like accommodations" and "impartially maintained."
- 1907: Voting rights: The Oklahoma Constitution, as originally adopted at statehood, extended the franchise to African Americans. Oklahoma enfranchised her citizens over the age of twenty-one, with exceptions for felons, paupers, and lunatics. Soon thereafter, the Oklahoma Legislature passed literacy requirements that curtailed black voting.

- 1908: Education: Public schools within Oklahoma were to be operated under a plan of separation between the white and colored races. The penalties for violations of the statute included: Teachers could be fined between $10 and $50 for violating the law, and their teaching certificate cancelled for one year. Corporations that operated schools that did not comply with the law were guilty of a misdemeanor and could be fined between $100 and $500. White students who attended a colored school could be fined between $5 and $20 daily.
- 1908: Railroads: All railroad and streetcar companies were to provide separate coaches for white and black passengers, "equal in all points of comfort and convenience." The penalties for violations of the law included: Railway companies that violate the law were to be fined $100 to $1,000. Passengers who failed to comply could be charged with a misdemeanor punishable by a fine from $5 to $25. Conductors could be fined $50 to $500 for failing to enforce the law.
- 1908: Miscegenation: A person of African descent could not legally marry any person not of African descent. A violation of the law constituted a felony punishable by a fine of up to $500, and imprisonment from one to five years in the penitentiary.
- 1915: Public accommodations: Telephone companies were required to maintain separate booths for white and colored patrons.
- 1921: Miscegenation: A law prohibited marriage between Indians and Negroes.
- 1921: Education: Teaching white and black children in the same school constituted a misdemeanor. The penalty for a violation of the statute was the cancellation of the violator's teaching certificate without renewal for one year.
- 1921: Public accommodations: The law required the maintenance of separate accommodations for colored persons in public libraries in cities with a Negro population of 1,000 or more.
- 1925: Entertainment: An Oklahoma City ordinance prohibited black bands from marching with white bands in Oklahoma City parades. White Golden Gloves boxers were prohibited from sparring against black boxers.
- 1937: Public carriers: Public carriers were to be segregated.
- 1949: Health Care: Legislation called for a consolidated Negro institution to care for blind and deaf persons, and orphans.
- 1954: Public accommodations: Legislation required separate "white" and "colored" restrooms in mines.
- 1955: Miscegenation: Legislation prohibited the marriage of a person of African descent to a white person. Violation of the law could result in a fine of up to $500 and imprisonment for up to five years.
- 1957: Adoption: Legislation required adoption petitions state the race of both the petitioner and the child.

See, e.g., http://www.dougloudenback.com/maps/jimcrowhistory.htm. last visited July 1, 2010); "Oklahoma State Senate Passes Concurrent Resolution Denouncing Jim Crow Laws," February 5, 2008 (press release), http://www.oksenate.gov/news/press_releases/press_releases_2008/pr20080205c.html; see also, Jimmie Lewis Franklin, *The Blacks in Oklahoma* (Norman, Oklahoma: University of Oklahoma

Press, 1980); Jimmie Lewis Franklin, *Journey Toward Hope: A History of Blacks in Oklahoma* (Norman, Oklahoma: University of Oklahoma Press, 1982); Kaye M. Teall, *Black History in Oklahoma: A Resource Book* (Oklahoma City, Oklahoma: Oklahoma City Public Schools, 1971); Arthur L. Tolson, *The Black Oklahomans: A History, 1541-1972* (New Orleans, Louisiana: Edwards Printing Company, 1972).

16. Okla. Const. art. I, sec. 5.

17. Ibid.; see also, Thelma Ackiss Perry, "The Availability of Education in the Negro Separate School," *The Journal of Negro Education* (vol. 16, no. 3, Summer, 1947): 397-404.

18. Sixteenth Biennial Report of the Superintendent of Public Instruction of the State of Oklahoma, 1936, p. 5; see also, Thelma Ackiss Perry, "The Availability of Education in the Negro Separate School," *The Journal of Negro Education* (vol. 16, no. 3, Summer, 1947): 397-404. "[I]t is apparent that neither the quality nor the quantity of educational facilities for Negroes in Oklahoma is commensurate with the population which the State is responsible for serving.")

19. Rosenwald, born to poor parents in Springfield, Illinois, came to empathize with the plight of poor, southern African Americans. Without a high school diploma, he worked through the ranks of the clothing industry, landing at Sears in 1895. There, he ascended the corporate ladder, pioneering innovative practices such as the "satisfaction guaranteed" pledge, quality control systems, and mail order merchandising. In 1908, he rose to the company presidency, succeeding Richard Sears. That same year, the riot that inspired the NAACP erupted in Rosenwald's hometown of Springfield, Illinois. See Jeffrey Sosland, *A School in Every County—The Partnership of Jewish Philanthropist Julius Rosenwald & American Black Communities* (Washington, D.C.: Economics & Science Planning, 1995).

20. The 1928 Pioneers of American Industry dinner honored eight men: George Eastman, photography; Henry Ford, automobiles; Orville Wright and Glen Curtis; aviation; Thomas Edison, inventions; Charles Schwab, iron and steel; Harvey S. Firestone, rubber; and Julius Rosenwald, merchandising. See Jeffrey Sosland, *A School in Every County*.

21. Jeffrey Sosland, *A School in Every County*, cover and 13. Rosenwald spoke in 1911 of the philosophy underlying his focus on improving the condition of America's southern African-American population:

> As an American and as a Jew, I appeal to all high-minded men and women to join in a relentless crusade against race prejudice, indulgence in which will result in the blotting out of the highest ideals of our proud nation.
>
> . . . .
>
> Race prejudice is merely destructive; it offers nothing but a hopeless warfare and a blank pessimism. A nation divided against itself cannot stand; two nations cannot live side by side at dagger's point with one another, and maintain a healthy state of progress in either. Perpetual feud destroys what is best and most helpful in both.
>
> To my mind, no man can in any way render greater service to mankind than by devoting his energy toward removal of this mighty obstacle. The destruction of race prejudice is the beginning of the higher civilization.

22. At the commencement of Rosenwald's efforts in 1911, African-American illiteracy in the South approached fifty percent in some areas, often four or five times the proportion for whites. Per-pupil expenditures for African-American children lagged at about half the amount spent on whites. The abbreviated school year for African Americans in some areas amounted to as few as three months. Segregated school buildings for African Americans sat decrepit and dilapidated. Too often, students languished under the tutelage of poorly educated, untrained classroom teachers.

23. See Jeffrey Sosland, *A School in Every County*. In addition to funding school construction, Rosenwald built twenty-four Young Men's Christian Association (YMCA) facilities for urban African Americans. He contributed to medical care and training for African-American doctors and nurses. He also funded bus transportation to allow African-American students to attend rural schools, made significant contributions to African-American colleges such as Tuskegee Institute and Howard, Fisk, and Dillard Universities, and financed libraries in schools, colleges, and county seats.

Rosenwald's bold vision of African-American uplift and the diminution of race prejudice led him to fund initiatives that assisted in the creation of a corps of African-American intellectuals and leaders. The Rosenwald Fund helped establish the United Negro College Fund (UNCF) in 1944. Rosenwald fellowships supported advanced study for some 1,500 individuals, including such notables as W.E.B. Du Bois, Ralph Bunche, Ralph Ellison, Walter White, and Marian Anderson.

Rosenwald became, in many ways, a model philanthropist. He did more than merely write checks. He visited potential school sites. He networked with local community leaders, both African American and white. He modeled collaboration. In short, he practiced what he preached: diversity and inclusion.

24. In 1985, the National Register of Historic Places listed Julius Rosenwald Hall, located in Lima, one of Oklahoma's all-black towns. Built in 1921, Julius Rosenwald Hall is but one example of scores of school buildings in Oklahoma built with grant money from the Rosenwald Fund. Indeed, most of the all-black towns at one time proudly boasted a "Rosenwald School."

25. For a discussion on the Jewish concept of "chesed," see http://www.bible-researcher.com/chesed.html. Last visited December 20, 2010.

26. "The Hebrew word 'tzedakah' is commonly translated as 'charity' or 'tithe.' But this is misleading. 'Charity' implies that your heart motivates you to go beyond the call of duty. 'Tzedakah,' however, literally means 'righteousness'—doing the right thing. A 'tzaddik,' likewise, is a righteous person, someone who fulfills all his obligations, whether in the mood or not." *Ask Rabbi Simmons*, "Charity versus Tzedakah," About.com, Judaism, http://judaism.about.com/library/3_askrabbi_o/bl_simmons_charitytzedakah.htm. Last visited December 20, 2010.

27. Jeffrey Sosland, *A School in Every County*, cover and 61. For additional information on Julius Rosenwald, see Herb Stein, "A Model of Philanthropy," *Wall Street Journal* (February 24, 1998); "Special fund aided state black schools," *The Oklahoma Eagle*. Special supplement entitled Heritage—Celebrating Black History in Oklahoma (February 3, 2000), 6; George O. Carney, "Historic Resources of Oklahoma's All-Black Towns: A Preservation Profile," LXIX: *The Chronicles of Oklahoma*, vol. LXIX (Summer 1991): 125.

28. Marian E. Barnes, ed., *Talk That Talk Some More—On The Cutting Room Floor* (Austin, Texas: Eakin Press, 1993), 16. Excerpt from "A Portrait of Segregation,

Discrimination, and Degradation," remarks of Dr. John Hope Franklin, James B. Duke Professor of History Emeritus, Duke University, testifying before the United States Senate Judiciary Committee on the occasion of the nomination of Judge Robert Bork by President Ronald Reagan to fill a vacancy on the United States Supreme Court.

29. Oklahoma Constitution, article III.
30. Ibid., 4a.
31. *Guinn v. United States*, 248 U.S. 347 (1915).
32. Okla. Stats. Sec 5654 (1931); 26 Okla. Stats. Ann. tit. 74.
33. *Lane v. Wilson*, 307 U.S. 268 (1939).
34. Kennedy, Stetson, *Jim Crow Guide: The Way It Was* (Boca Raton, Florida: Florida Atlantic University Press, 1959/1990), 216-217.
35. The League of Women Voters, *Minority Report—A Survey of Civil Rights in Oklahoma City*, 1964.
36. See, e.g., *Alberty v. United States*, 162 U.S. 499 501 (1896), concluding that the offspring of an African American and an Indian is an African American.
37. Letter from Booker T. Washington to M. Gatewood Milligan, Jr. (a Presbyterian minister living in Victor, Colorado), April 27, 1914, 11, 13: 1914-15 *The Booker T. Washington Papers* (open book edition, Louis R. Harlan & Raymond W. Smock, eds., Susan Valenza and Sadie M. Harlan, asst. eds., Champaign, IL: University of Illinois Press 1984), available at http://www.historycooperative.org/btw/Vol.13/html/11.html. Last visited May 18, 2009.
38. Gary B. Nash, *Red, White, and Black: The peoples of early America* (Upper Saddle River, New Jersey: Prentice-Hall, 1974), 289-290.
39. See, e.g., Franklin and Franklin, eds., *My Life and an Era*, 143. "Here, many thousands of Indians . . . had, under the constitution of the state, been classified as Caucasian, thus preventing social contact and intermarriage with the Negro and making impossible the enrichment and predominance that intermarriage would have brought to him."
40. Wickett, *Contested Territory*, 196.
41. *Sammie Ispocogee v. Sam Ispocogee*, Case No. D-10830, Tulsa County District Court. Application for Additional Funds to Defend and Temporary Allowance for Support, May 20, 1933.
42. Ibid.
43. Ibid.
44. *Loving v. Virginia*, 388 U.S. 1 (1967).
45. *Pace v. Alabama*, 106 U.S. 583 (1883).
46. Adam Geller, "In fight over Cherokee identity, tribe's past and future collide," *The San Diego Union-Tribune*, http://www. Singonsandiego.com/news/nation/20070210-0915-fightingtobecherokee.html; see also Tiya Miles, *Ties That Bind: The Story of an Afro-Cherokee Family in Slavery and Freedom* (Berkeley and Los Angeles, California: University of California Press, 2005).
47. Sturm, "Blood Politics, Racial Classification, and Cherokee National Identity," 231.

Chapter VI
1. Gavin Off, "Tribal citizenship granted," *Tulsa World* (January 15, 2011), A1.
2. *Hub City News*, 5:7 (February 12, 2010), 5 (Southern California newspaper).

3. "Native American Spirituality: Freedom Denied Or, Blood Quantum: Native America's Dirty Little Secret," http://www.manataka.org/page1965.html. Last visited March 1, 2010.

4. *Hub City News*, 5:7 (February 12, 2010), 5 (Southern California newspaper).

5. The Absentee Shawnee were organized in 1936 as the "Absentee Shawnee Tribe of Indians of Oklahoma" under the Oklahoma Indian Welfare Act, a law that extended the 1934 Indian Reorganization Act to the tribes in Oklahoma. Taken together, these post-Dawes Commission enactments sought to revive tribal land holdings, governments, and culture. See, e.g., Absentee Shawnee Tribe of Oklahoma web site, http://www.absenteeshawneetribe-nsn.gov/Government.aspx. Last visited February 16, 2012; Pamela A. Smith, "Shawnee, Absentee," *Oklahoma Historical Society's Encyclopedia of History and Culture*, http://digital.library.okstate.edu/encyclopedia/entries/S/SH016.html. Last visited February 16, 2012.

6. Lydia Edwards, "Spotlight On Jon Velie: A Man On A Thirteen Year Mission," *The Modern American* (Spring 2005): 23.

7. Ibid.

8. Sturm, "Blood Politics, Racial Classification, and Cherokee National Identity," 233-239.

9. Wayne Greene, "Leader of Cherokee Nation affects all," *Tulsa World* (July 3, 2011), A1.

10. Ibid.

11. *The Oklahoman*, http://www.newsok.com, November 15, 2009.

12. Tom Kenworthy, "For Native American tribes, business diversifying pays," *USA Today*, November 28, 2007.

13. "Cherokees start jobs initiative for tribal members," *Associated Press* (May 19, 2011), http://newsok.com/cherokees-start-jobs-initiative-for-tribalmembers/article/3569407. Last visited May 19, 2011. In the spring of 2011, The Cherokee Nation of Oklahoma commenced a unique jobs initiative called "Jobs Well Done," said to be the first of its kind among tribes. The Cherokees' employment-boosting initiative will: (1) provide a one-stop shop connecting tribal citizens with programs that lead ultimately to employment; (2) connect individuals with appropriate jobs inside the Cherokee Nation or Cherokee Nation Businesses; (3) establish a day training program to provide immediate on-the-job experience and a remuneration—a paycheck; (4) offer vocational and educational assistance and counseling for career path development; and (5) emphasize internships within the Cherokee Nation or Cherokee Nation Businesses. Gaming, among other tribal enterprises, generates revenue sufficient to fund creative programs like this jobs initiative.

14. Cherokee Nation of Oklahoma, "Where the Casino Money Goes: Planting the Seed Corn for our Children's Future," http://www.cherokee.org/docs/Where_the_Money_Goes_2008.pdf, 2.

15. Clifton Adcock, "Cherokee Nation Enterprises revenue up despite recession," *Tulsa World*, June 16, 2009, A11.

16. Ibid., 1.

17. House Rule 25 5(a)(3)(A-W); Senate Rule 35 1(c)(1-23), exceptions to House & Senate, respectively, gift rules.

18. E-mail from David Cornsilk to Hannibal B. Johnson. Dec. 1, 2008, 05:24:10 p.m. CST, on file with author.

19. E-mail from Ann Dapice, Ph.D., to Hannibal B. Johnson, Dec. 8. 2008, 02:59:34 p.m. CST, on file with author; Elizabeth Larson, "Seeking Redress:

Disenrolled Indians have few options," http://lakeconews.conm/content/view/6569/764/. Last visited December 8, 2008.

20. The Indian Gaming Regulatory Act, Pub. L. 100-497, 25 U.S.C. Sec. 2701 et seq. (1988).

21. Ibid.

22. S. E. Ruckman, "Gaming expansion sites," *Tulsa World* (December 27, 2007), A4.

23. Conversation with Ross Swimmer, former Principal Chief of the Cherokee Nation, Tulsa, Oklahoma, January 14, 2008.

24. S. E. Ruckman, "Gaming growth: Tribes up their stakes," *Tulsa World* (December 27, 2007), A7.

25. Wayne Greene, "Gambling revenue now No. 4 in U.S.," *Tulsa World* (March 9, 2011), A1.

26. Clifton Adcock, "Tribes give state $105 million," *Tulsa World* (July 8, 2009), A1.

27. See Randy Ellis, "Oklahoma Indian gaming revenues soar," *The Oklahoman* (August 15, 2010), http://newsok.com/oklahoma-indian-gaming-revenues-soar/article/3485404. Last visited March 9, 2011. The three largest contributors to Oklahoma coffers in terms of Indian gaming compact revenues for fiscal year 2010 were the Chickasaw Nation ($33.3 million), the Choctaw Nation ($22.7 million), and the Cherokee Nation ($12.2 million).

28. Editorial, "Going strong: tribal gaming big business," *Tulsa World* (June 5, 2010), A18.

29. S. E. Rickman, "Chickasaw exec lauds gaming," *Tulsa World* (November 29, 2007), A5.

30. National Indian Gaming Association, 3, The Economic Impact of Indian Gaming in 2006 (report), available at http://www.indiangaming.org/info/pr/press-releases-2007/NIGA_econ_impact_2006.pdf.

31. "Indian casinos pull in a record $25 billion in '06," *Tulsa World* (June 5, 2007), A11.

32. Charles P. Pierce, "High Stakes," *The Boston Globe* (July 30, 2006).

33. Ibid.

34. *National Urban League, The State of Black America: Message to the President* (New York, New York: National Urban League 2009, annual publication).

35. "State of the World's Indigenous Peoples" Secretariat of the United Nations Permanent Forum on Indigenous Issues (January 14, 2010), http://www.un.org/esa/socdev/unpfii/documents/SOWIP_Press_package.pdf. Last visited April 22, 2010.

36. Stephanie Schorow, "Going for broke," *MIT News* (May 20, 2009), http://web.mit.edu/newsoffice/2009/vegas-tt0520.html. Last visited January 10, 2011.

37. Fred Gottheil, "Gambling, a cruel regressive tax," *Illinois Review* (December 30, 2010), http://illinoisreview.typepad.com/illinoisreview/2010/12/gambling-a-cruel-regressive-tax.html. Last visited January 10, 2011.

38. Charles P. Pierce, "High Stakes," *The Boston Globe* (July 30, 2006).

39. Adam Geller, "In fight over Cherokee identity, tribe's past and future collide," *The San Diego Union-Tribune*, http://www. Singonsandiego.com/news/nation/20070210-0915-fightingtobecherokee.html

40. The 2011 election for Cherokee Nation Principal Chief merits mention. It seemed as though incumbent Smith's challenger, Bill John Baker, Cherokee Nation

tribal council member and Tahlequah, Oklahoma, businessman, had overtaken three-term Principal Chief in a costly and contentious election on June 25, 2011.

In a series of perplexing twists, the initial tally—7,600 to 7,589—listed Bill John Baker as the apparent winner by eleven votes, but official figures released by the commission on June 27th declared current chief Chad Smith the victor by a 7,609—7,602 margin, or seven votes. The Cherokee Nation Election Commission changed initial results posted on its web site early on June 26th after spending all night June 25th and part of the morning of June 26th tabulating votes.

Baker filed a request with the Commission on June 29th for a full recount of the election, by show of hands. "We demand to know what caused the change in vote tally. We want to know who demanded the change and why," Baker said in a news conference on June 29th. "All Cherokees should demand to know the truth."

After a hand recount, Baker was certified as the official winner of the election by more than 266 votes on June 30th. Smith sought injunctive relief on July 1st from the Cherokee Nation Supreme Court, asking that the Commission be ordered to conduct a machine recount or, in the alternative, a new election. Smith claimed "fatal flaws" in the hand recount. Campaign officials for challenger Baker, on the other hand, accused a person named Terry Rainey, president of Automated Election Services, of altering numbers while inside the ballot vault, in an effort to name Smith the winner.

In the original count of the June 25th election, in which Smith was deemed to be the winner by seven votes, machines recorded 6,144 absentee votes. In the June 30th recount, which was done by hand, 5,870 absentee ballots were recorded. After the recount, Baker was declared the winner by 266 votes. The Smith campaign maintained that hundreds of absentee ballots may have been miscounted in the recount that named Baker chief-elect of the Cherokee Nation. According to members of the Smith campaign team, the machine count is more accurate than the hand recount.

Documents released by the Smith's own campaign indicated that the Supreme Court's independent count found 25 more actual absentee ballots than absentee ballot envelopes. Baker asserted that the only way for the number of absentee ballots to exceed the number of absentee ballot envelopes is by someone's intervention. On July 12th, the Cherokee Nation Supreme Court ordered a hand count of all ballots from the tribe's June 25th election, in an effort to determine exactly which candidate received the most votes. By design, the count only pertained to the proceedings before the Court: incumbent Chief Chad Smith's appeal of the outcome of the first recount, which named Baker Chief-elect.

The Cherokee Nation maintains a fourteen-county jurisdiction in Oklahoma. Its membership approaches 300,000, with many citizens living elsewhere and casting absentee ballots.

Smith rose to power in 1999 after unseating Joe Byrd, who succeeded Wilma Mankiller upon her retirement. Smith ran on, and is largely credited with, expanding Cherokee Nation business opportunity and success.

See, e.g., Murray Evans, "Cherokee Nation elects new leader," *The Associated Press* (June 27, 2011); Lenzy Krehbiel-Burton, "Cherokees elect new chief," *Tulsa World* (June 27, 2011), A1; Lenzy Krehbiel-Burton, "Cherokees await recount," *Tulsa World* (June 30, 2011), A1; Lenzy Krehbiel-Burton, "Chief looks to justices for recount," *Tulsa World* (July 5, 2011), A1; and Jarrel Wade, "Ballot tampering alleged in Cherokee chief election," *Tulsa World* (July 12, 2011), www.tulsaworld.com; Jarrel

Wade and Lenzy Krehbiel-Burton, "Cherokee Supreme Court orders hand count of ballots," *Tulsa World* (July 12, 2011), www.tulsaworld.com.

41. Proper cite: http://www.snowwowl.com/hhcherokeeFreedmen.html (a noncommercial Native American educational web site); http://www.indianz.com/News/2006/013060.asp.

42. S. A. Ray, "A Race or a Nation? Cherokee National Identity and the Status of Freedmen's Descendants," http://law.bepress.com/expresso/eps/1570 25. 2006).

43. Clifton Adcock, "Cherokee councilors not aware of $50,000 donation," *Tulsa World* (December 30, 2008).

44. Clifton Adcock, "Cherokees fund opponent of freedmen foe," *Tulsa World* (November 19, 2009), A10.

45. A 1994 United States Supreme Court case provided an opening for states to prevent non-Indian state residents from purchasing non-taxed Indian smoke shop cigarettes. The case upheld state regulations in New York that limited cigarette wholesalers to providing such outlets with only enough untaxed cigarettes to supply the residents of the reservation on which it operated. Similar state regulations of cigarette sales could have a significant impact on tribal revenues derived from the cigarette market. See *Department of Taxation and Finance of New York v. Milhelm Attea & Brothers*, 521 U.S. 61 (1994).

46. *Oklahoma Tax Commission v. Citizen Band, Potawatomi Indian Tribe of Oklahoma*, 498 U.S. 505 (1991).

47. Susan M. Browning, Deputy Director, *Government-To-Government Annual Report by Oregon Department of Revenue* (December 2006).

48. Omer Gillham, "Tribal Smoke Shop's Sales on Fire" (December 7, 2005), http://www.redorbit.com/news/science/323711/tribal_smoke_shops_sales_on_fire/.

49. Felicia S. Hodge, Dr.PH, Betty A. Geishirt Cantrell, MSSW, MBA, Roxanne Struthers, Ph.D., and John Casken, Ph.D., "American Indian Internet Cigarette Sales: Another Avenue for Selling Tobacco Products," *American Journal of Public Health*, (2004 February; 94(2)): 260-61.

50. Ibid.

51. See http://www.freedmen5tribes.com

53. See "Native American Tribes Population Rankings," http://www.americawest.com/pages/indrank.htm.

53. Interview with Marilyn Vann, October 15, 2008, Tulsa, Oklahoma.

54. E-mail from David Cornsilk to Hannibal B. Johnson (Dec. 1, 2008, 05:24:10 p.m. CST, on file with author).

Chapter VII

1. James Mooney, "Myths of the Cherokee," 15 (New York, New York: Dover Publications, Inc., 1995, originally published by the Government Printing Office, Washington, D.C., 1900, as part of the Nineteenth Annual Report of the Bureau of American Ethnology to the Secretary of the Smithsonian Institution, 1897-98): in two parts—Part I.

2. Wright, *Guide to the Indian Tribes of Oklahoma*.

3. Some question the legitimacy of the Cherokee Nation of Oklahoma as presently constituted. The tribe did not avail itself of the Oklahoma Indian Welfare Act of 1936 (the OIWA), federal legislation designed to allow Oklahoma tribes to reorganize and remove any disabilities suffered at the hands of prior federal law.

The OIWA provided a mechanism that allowed the Oklahoma tribes to regain a modicum of the political and sovereign authority lost when the Curtis Act (1898) dismantled the tribal governments of the Five Civilized Tribes. The 1906 Five Civilized Tribes Act granted the President of the United States the power to appoint the Principal Chief (an office rooted in the 1839 Cherokee Constitution). The 1970 Five Civilized Tribes Act gave the power to *select* (as opposed to *elect*) the Principal Chief back to the Cherokee people, together with the power to promulgate rules to affect the selection. The Principal Chief, so the argument goes, has no power beyond this ruling-making authority in furtherance of the popular selection of the occupant of the office of Principal Chief. Since the citizenship rolls of the Cherokee Nation were frozen in 1906, the current Nation, beyond the few centenarians who are original members, is, in essence, a descendancy organization. The primary role of its members is the popular selection of the largely toothless Principal Chief. See David Cornsilk, "What Is the Cherokee Nation of Oklahoma?," http://www.opednews.com/articles/1/opedne_david_co_080409_what_is_the_cno_3 f.htm.

A recent decision by the head of the Bureau of Indian Affairs, Larry EchoHawk, supports the position articulated by David Cornsilk. In *United Keetoowah Bank of Cherokee Indians v. Director, Eastern Oklahoma Region, Bureau of Indian Affairs* (June 24, 2009), Mr. EchoHawk, Assistant Secretary, Indian Affairs, United States Department of the Interior, noted, at footnote 2:

> The CNO [Cherokee Nation of Oklahoma] has long maintained there is no distinction between it and the historic CN [Cherokee Nation]. By closing the rolls in 1907, Congress effectively imposed a sunset provision on its relationship with the historic CN. The Federal relationship would exist so long as its members survived. This is consistent with Congress's expectation that the government of the historical CN, like the governments of the other Five Civilized Tribes, would not be permanent.... The CNO is a new political organization, therefore, because the historical CN no longer exists and the CNO government is a new government.

EchoHawk's decision put the Tahlequah-based United Keetoowah Band of Cherokee Indians on equal jurisdictional footing with the Tahlequah-based Cherokee Nation of Oklahoma. Neither, per the decision, is the historical Cherokee tribe. Rather, both are "successors in interest" to the original tribe. That status makes it unclear whether the tribes stand in the place of their predecessor in interest, the original Cherokee Nation. At issue is the power of the respective tribes to put land in trust. Gaming operations and other sovereign functions are permissible only on trust lands. Per the United States Supreme Court, in *Carcieri v. Salazar*, (No. 07-526), 497 F.3d 15, reversed, only tribes recognized by the Indian Reorganization Act of 1934 may hold land in trust. It is unclear whether tribes that are "successors in interest" (e.g., the United Keetoowah Band of Cherokee Indians, recognized in 1950, and the Cherokee Nation of Oklahoma, recognized in 1975) may stand in the place of their predecessors recognized by that 1934 Act.

4. Sturm, "Blood Politics, Racial Classification and Cherokee National Identity," 231.

5. Telephone interview with Reuben Gant in Tulsa, Oklahoma, June 22, 2009.

6. See, e.g., Letter from Congressman Barney Frank to United States Attorney

General Eric H. Holder, Jr., April 15, 2009; Letter from Congressional Representatives Diane E. Watson, Barney Frank, John Lewis, John Conyers, Jr., Barbara Lee, and Sheila Jackson Lee to United States Attorney General Eric H. Holder, Jr., April 30, 2009.

7. Petition to the Honorable Members of the Congressional Black Caucus presented by Verdie Triplett, Founder and Contact Person for the Choctaw Chickasaw Freedmen and other signatories (2007).

8. Jim Myers, "Actor touts freedmen rights," *Tulsa World* (September 27, 2008), A11.

9. Theda Perdue, *Slavery and the Evolution of Cherokee Society, 1540-1866*, (Knoxville, Tennessee: The University of Tennessee Press, 1979), 36.

10. William G. McLoughlin, "Red Indians, Black Slavery and White Racism: America's Slaveholding Indians," *American Quarterly* 26:4 (October 1974), 368.

11. Alexander Hewatt, "An Historical Account of the Rise and Progress of the Colonies of South Carolina and Georgia," *BiblioBazaar* 2006 (first published, London, England 1779), 2, 8.

12. R. Halliburton, Jr., *Red over Black: Black Slavery among the Cherokee Indians* (Westport, Connecticut: Greenwood Press, 1977), 190.

13. Bernard Vincent, "Slaveholding Indians: the Case of the Cherokee Nation," 7, http://www.unive.it/media/allegato/dep/Ricerche/1_Vincent1.pdf. Last visited May 19, 2009.

14. Ibid., 14.

15. See, e.g., http://www.freemasons-freemasonry.com/. Last visited June 1, 2010:

> Freemasonry is one of the world's oldest secular fraternal societies. Freemasonry is a society of men concerned with moral and spiritual values. Freemasons are taught its precepts by a series of ritual dramas, which follow ancient forms, and use stonemasons' customs and tools as allegorical guides. The essential qualification to become Freemason is a belief in a Supreme Being. A Freemason's duty as a citizen must always prevail over any obligation to other Masons, and any attempt to shield Freemasons who acted dishonourably or unlawfully, or to confer an unfair advantage on other Free[m]asons is contrary to this prime duty. The Freemasons refer to those who are not Freemasons as "cowans" because in architecture a cowan is someone apprenticed to bricklaying but not licensed to the trade of masonry.
>
> Freemasonry is an esoteric society only in that certain aspects are private; Freemasons state that Masonry is not, in the 21st century, a secret society but a "society with secrets." Some Freemasons describe Freemasonry as a "confidential" society in contrast to a secret society. Most modern Freemasons regard the traditional concern over secrecy as a demonstration of their ability to keep a promise and a concern over the privacy of their own affairs. Lodge meetings, like meetings of many other social and professional associations, are private occasions open only to members. The private aspects of modern Freemasonry deal with the modes of recognition amongst members and elements within

the ritual. In reality, Freemasons are proud of their true heritage and happy to share it, offering spokesmen, briefings for the media, and providing talks to interested groups upon request.

See also Christopher Hodapp, *Freemasons for Dummies* (Indianapolis, Indiana: Wiley, 2005).

16. Bernard Vincent, "Slaveholding Indians," 9, 10.
17. Ibid., 10.
18. Halliburton, *Red over Black*, 177.
19. Ibid.
20. Bernard Vincent, "Slaveholding Indians," 13.
21. Claudio Saunt, "'The English has now a mind to make slaves of them all!' Creeks, Seminoles, and the Problem of Slavery," *American Indian Quarterly* 22:1-2 (Winter-Spring 1998): 160.
22. William G. McLoughlin, "Red Indians, Black Slavery and White Racism: America's Slaveholding Indians," *American Quarterly* 26:4 (October 1974): 367, 380.
23. Purdue, *Slavery and the Evolution of Cherokee Society 1540-1866*, 142-143.
24. Some of the Freedmen retain citizenship because, in addition to having an ancestor on the Freedmen Roll, they have an ancestor on the "By Blood" section of the Dawes Rolls. It should also be noted that inclusion on the "By Blood" section of the Dawes Rolls does not necessarily signify the presence of Indian blood in an individual. So-called "Adopted Whites," white persons adopted into the Cherokee Nation pursuant to the Treaty of 1866, are listed on the "By Blood" section of the Dawes Rolls.
25. E-mail from Ann Dapice, Ph.D., to Hannibal B. Johnson (Dec. 8, 2008, 02:59:34 p.m. CST on file with author).
26. Jim Myers, "Controversy hurts tribe, chief says," *Tulsa World* (September 24, 2007), A1.
27. "Segregation Now, Segregation Forever," Inaugural Address, Governor George Wallace of Alabama, 1963.
28. The grandfather of Cherokee Nation Principal Chief Chadwick "Corntassel" Smith, Redbird Smith, was a Cherokee patriot who fought against the allotment of Indian lands. His grandmother, Rachel Quinton, was a Cherokee activist. His wife, Bobbie Gail Smith, is a full-blood, bilingual Cherokee who works to preserve the Cherokee language and culture. See www.chadsmith.com.
29. Jim Myers, "Bill could halt U.S. funds to Cherokees," *Tulsa World* (June 22, 2007), A5.
30. Jim Myers, "Controversy hurts tribe, chief says," *Tulsa World* (September 24, 2007), A1.
31. Aaron Sadler, "Freedmen Allies See Racism in Tribal Ouster," *Southwest Times Record* (September 29, 2007), A1.
32. Ronn Smith, "Freedmen urged to get more active," *Muskogee Daily Phoenix and Times-Democrat* (June 27, 2004), 1A.
33. Richard Reeb, "Tribalism and Racism—The Allure of Despotism (September 26, 2007), http://www.claremont.org,
34. See, e.g., NAACP resolution. ("NAACP supports the severance of United States government relations with the Cherokee Nation of Oklahoma until such time as the Cherokee Nation of Oklahoma restores full tribal citizenship to the Cherokee Freedmen."), August 6, 2007.

35. See H.R. 2824, 110th Congress (2007-2008), introduced June 21, 2007.
36. Jim Myers, "Bill could halt U.S. funds to Cherokees," *Tulsa World* (June 22, 2007), A5.
37. "NAACP chides Cherokees over freedmen issue," *Tulsa World* (August 25, 2007), A16.
38. Barbara Hoberock, "Chief pushes Congress to let courts act," *Tulsa World* (August 22, 2007), A11.
39. Ibid.
40. Jim Myers, "Votes strips housing funds," *Tulsa World* (September 7, 2007), A11.
41. Jim Myers, "Controversy hurts tribe, chief says," *Tulsa World* (September 24, 2007), A1.
42. Kenneth J. Cooper, "A Nation Divided," *The Louisiana Weekly* (March 19, 2007), http://www.louisianaweekly.com.
43. David Cornsilk, December 7, 2006, Indianz.com (web posting).
44. Sturm, "Blood Politics, Racial Classification and Cherokee National Identity," 253.
45. "Cherokee, Council for Community Action partner to provide genealogical assistance," *The Oklahoma Eagle* (June 27, 2008), A1.
46. Mankiller and Wallis, *Mankiller: A Chief and Her People*, 28.
47. Ibid., 123.
48. *Lucy Allen v. Cherokee Nation Tribal Council, et al.*, JAT-04-09 14-20 (Judicial Appeals Tribunal of the Cherokee Nation, March 7, 2006).
49. "Cherokee Emancipation Proclamation," Archives Division, Oklahoma Historical Society, Cherokee Volume 248 (February 18-19, 1863); see also David R. Wrone, "The Cherokee Act of Emancipation," *Journal of Ethnic Studies* 1973 1(3): 87-90, noting that the Cherokee emancipation, unlike that of the Union, applied to all slaves within the Cherokee Nation, not just those under Confederate control, and that those manumitted gained a stake in the communal property of the tribe.
50. Whitmore, *Trustee for the Cherokee Freedmen v. Cherokee Nation*, 30 Ct. Cl. 138 (Ct. Cl. 1895).
51. *Redbird v. United States*, 203 U.S. 76 (1906).
52. Solicitor's Opinion, Bureau of Indian Affairs, October 1, 1941, 1 Op. Sol. "On Indian Affairs" 1076 (U.S.D.I. 1979).
53. Public Law 87-775 (October 9, 1962).
54. Approved for Referendum by the Commissioner, Morris Thompson, on September 5, 1975, Seconded by the Principal Chief of the Cherokee Nation, Ross O. Swimmer, on October 2, 1975, approved by Referendum on June 26, 1976.
55. Cherokee Nation of Oklahoma Const. (approved 1975; adopted 1976).
56. Sturm, "Blood Politics, Racial Classification, and Cherokee National Identity," 241.
57. Ibid., 230-258; see also, *Cherokee Observer* (February/March 2007), 2 (letter to the editor from David Cornsilk).
58. Sturm, "Blood Politics, Racial Classification, and Cherokee National Identity," 242.
59. "Cherokee Nation, Guidelines: Rules and Regulations of the Registration [sic] Committee," http://www.cornsilks.com/cshiprulesswim.html.
60. Brendan I. Koerner, "Blood Feud," (September 1, 2005), available at http://www.velielaw.com.

61. Whitmore, *Trustee for the Cherokee Freedmen v. Cherokee Nation*, 30 Ct. Cl. 138, 180 (Ct. Cl. 1895), holding that the Freedmen were entitled to share in tribal proceeds and that Cherokee sovereignty could not be exercised in a manner inconsistent with treaty obligations to the United States of America); see also, *Red Bird v. United States*, 203 U.S. 76. 84 (1906), confirming, under the Treaty of 1866, the citizenship status of the Cherokee Nation Freedmen and their entitlement to property rights on par with those of other Cherokee citizens; *Goat v. United States*, 224 U.S. 458, 468 (1912), affirming the citizenship rights accorded pursuant to the Treaty of 1866 with respect to Seminole Freedmen, noting: "Indeed, the [Seminole Nation] is essentially a nation of full bloods, save as to its colored citizens, who, under treaty provision [i.e., the Seminole Nation version of the Treaty of 1866], are on equal footing with the citizens by blood"; *Keetoowah Society v. Lane*, 41 App. D.C. 319, 322 (App. D.C. 1914), affirming, once again, Cherokee Freedmen rights, noting: "We do not think the right of these freedmen to participate in the lands and funds of the Cherokee Nation longer open to question."

62. E-mail from Ross Swimmer to Hannibal B. Johnson (May 18, 2009, 11:59:58 a.m. CST; on file with author).

63. Cherokee Nation of Oklahoma Resolution No. 21-88, Supporting the Guidelines: Rules and Regulations of the Cherokee Registration Committee (approved March 12, 1988), http://www.cornsilks.com/scip88.html.

64. Cherokee Nation of Oklahoma, Legislative Act 6-92, An Act Relating to the Process of Enrolling as a Member of the Cherokee Nation (adopted September 12, 1992), http://www.cornsilks.com/cshipLA6-92.html.

65. An Act Relating To The Process of Enrolling as a Member of the Cherokee Nation, http://www.cornsilks.com/chipsLA6-92.html?Chief.

66. National Congress of American Indians, 57th Annual Session, "Many Nations, One Family," November 12-17, 2000, St. Paul, Minnesota. Wilma Mankiller, transcription of session entitled "Exploring the Legacy and Future of Black/Indian Relations"; transcription published 2001 by The Kansas Institute of African-American and Native-American Family History with support from The Freedom Forum, http://web.mit.edu/wjohnson/www/kiaanafh/KIAANAFH_POR TAL_PAGE.html).

67. Affidavits of the longstanding BIA position are a part of the *Nero* case file. (*Nero* was apparently dismissed in 1989 on jurisdictional grounds.) See also, Bureau of Indian Affairs Solicitor's Opinion, October 1, 1941, 1 Op. Sol. "On Indian Affairs" 1076. U.S.D.I. (1979), where the BIA reaffirmed that the Cherokee Freedmen voting and membership rights were fixed by treaty and formal tribal actions.

68. Doug Struck, "Slave descendants say they deserve Indians' benefits," *The Baltimore Sun* (July 29, 1984).

69. The rule of hypodescent has allowed for distinctions among those whom it deems "black" based on, essentially, blood quantum. Thus persons were classified as "quadroons" (one-quarter African ancestry), "octoroons" (one-eighth African ancestry), and so on. Moreover, additional monikers attached to persons with some African heritage: mulatto, half-breed, metissee, bi-racial, interracial, multi-racial, Eurafrican, half-caste, zambo, and griffe, just to name a few. See, e.g., http://www.mixedfolks.com/names.htm. Last visited January 5, 2010.

70. A powerful variant on the rule of hypodescent finds expression in parts of the African-American community. This minority view holds that embracing one's

multi-racial/multicultural identity is a means by which to deny one's blackness—to distance oneself from the history and struggle of persons of African descent. Stated differently, this minority view suggests that however slight one's "African blood," the failure to define oneself by that blood and embrace what it has historically meant is, in essence, a manifestation of internalized oppression—of self-hatred—and is tantamount to an acceptance of white supremacy and black inferiority. Similarly, questions arise in some circles as to whether some of the Freedmen are mere "race jumpers": African Americans seeking acceptance within the Native American fold, at least subconsciously, as a means of avoiding their own blackness and all that it portends.

71. Pauline Turner Strong and Barrik Van Winkle, "'Indian Blood': Reflections on the Reckoning and Refiguring of Native North American Identity," *Cultural Anthropology* 11, no. 4. (November 1996): 551.

72. Naylor, *African Cherokees in Indian Territory*, 219.

73. *Nero v. Cherokee Nation*, 892 F.2d 1457 (10th Cir. 1989).

74. *Riggs v. Ummerteske*, JAT 97-03, August 15, 2001.

75. John Velie, "Bureau of Indian Affairs Recognizes Cherokee Election Although Black Citizens Forbidden Right to Vote," http://www.African-nativeamerican.com.bia.htm (press release).

76. *Seminole Nation of Okla. v. Norton* (cases of 2001 [206 F.R.D. 1] [D.D.C. 2001 and 2002] [223 F. Supp. 122] [D.D.C. 2002]).

77. *Vann v. Kempthorne*, 534 F. 3d 741 (D.C. Cir. 2008).

78. See Jim Myers, "Freedmen, tribe alike see victory in ruling," *Tulsa World* (July 30, 2008), quoting Marilynn Vann, lead plaintiff, saying the "freedmen's treaty rights trump the right of our elected officials to oppress us"; quoting Chad Smith, Principal Chief of the Cherokee Nation: "This decision is a strong affirmation for tribes across the country, who rely upon federal courts to uphold tribal sovereignty when it comes under attack."

79. *Vann v. Kempthorne*, 534 F. 3d 741, 746-747 (D.C. Cir. 2008).

80. Ibid., 752.

81. Ibid., 766.

82. Adam Geller, "Past and future collide in fight over Cherokee identity," *USA Today* (February 10, 2007).

83. Ibid.

84. 11 C.N.C.A. Sec. 12.

85. *Lucy Allen v. Cherokee National Tribal Council, et al.*, JAT-04-09 (March 7, 2006).

86. Ibid.

87. Ibid., sy. 2-3.

88. *Brown v. Board of Education of Topeka*, 347 U.S. 483 (1954).

89. "Law professor receives $50,000 award for work on race relations project," Kansas University News Release, July 2, 2008, available at http://www.news.ku.edu/2008/july/2/leeds.shtml.

90. Oklahoma Senator Judy Eason-McIntyre & Oklahoma State Representative Jabar Shumate, "An Open Letter to Chad Smith, Principal Chief of the Cherokee Nation of Oklahoma," Letters to the Editor, *The Oklahoma Eagle* (April 13, 2006).

91. "Indian mascot name issue is being revived," *Tulsa World* (January 29, 2009), A5.

92. Some, including Ed Crittenden, former advisor of Chief Byrd, believe that Chief Smith's motivation for excluding the Freedmen is political—as a means to build a political base. See, e.g., "Congressional Black Caucus Briefed on Cherokee

Freedmen at 37th Annual Legislative Conference," *The Cherokee Observer*, vol. 16, no. 1, (January 2008), 1, 7.

93. *Raymond Nash v. Cherokee Nation Registrar*, Consolidated Cases No. CV-07-40, et. al. (D.C., Cherokee Nation, January 14, 2011), 1, class action lawsuit on behalf of the Freedmen.

94. S. E Ruckman, "Cherokee kick out freedmen," *Tulsa World* (March 4, 2007), A1.

95. Ibid.

96. Sean Murphy & Evelyn Nieves, "Cherokee accused of racism by black tribesmen," *The Scotsman* (March 6, 2007), available at http://thescotsman.scotsman.com.

97. E-mail from Louis Gray to Hannibal B. Johnson (Nov. 23, 2008, 07:46:24 p.m. CST, on file with author).

98. http://www.leonardpeltier.net.

99. Tulsa Indian Coalition Against Racism (TICAR) web site, http://www.ticarok.org.

100. E-mail from Louis Gray to Hannibal B. Johnson (Nov. 23, 2008, 07:46:24 p.m. CST, on file with author).

101. S. E. Ruckman, "Survey finds indication of overt, subtle racism," *Tulsa World* (October 2, 2007); "S. E. Ruckman, FBI hate crime report shows Indians remain most often assaulted," *Native American Times*, http://nativetimes.bizweb5.tulsaconnect.com (Nov. 24, 2008, 07:09 a.m. CST).

102. "Congressional Black Caucus Briefed on Cherokee Freedmen at 37th Annual Legislative Conference," *The Cherokee Observer*, vol. 16, no. 1 (January 2008), 1, 7.

103. Ibid.

104. John Velie, Velie Law Firm, Address at the Descendants of Freedman of the Five Civilized Tribes "First Annual Treaty Celebration Banquet," April 23, 2010, Bartlesville, Oklahoma.

105. Ibid.

106. See, e.g., "The Nuremberg Laws," Jewish Virtual Library, http://www.jewishvirtuallibrary.org; Geoffrey Pridham & Jeremy Noakes, *Documents on Nazism: 1919-1945* (London, England: Jonathan Cape 1974).

107. John Velie, Velie Law Firm, Address at the Descendants of Freedman of the Five Civilized Tribes "First Annual Treaty Celebration Banquet," April 23, 2010, Bartlesville, Oklahoma.

108. "Cherokee vote is scrutinized," *Tulsa World* (March 14, 2007), A4.

109. "The Shame of the Cherokee Nation," *The New York Times* (June 8, 2007, editorial).

110. "Cherokee Nation blasted for ousting Freedmen," April 4, 2007, Indianz.com, www.indianz.com/News/2007/002217.asp.

111. S. A. Ray, "A Race or a Nation? Cherokee National Identity and the Status of Freedmen's Descendants," http://law.bepress.com/expresso/eps/1570, 69 (2006).

112. Treaty of 1866 (Cherokee), Article 9.

113. Cherokee Nation Const., art. III, Sec. 5. 1839, as amended 1866.

114. "Why Freedmen Descendants Without an Indian Ancestor Listed on the Base Rolls Are Not Eligible for Citizenship in the Cherokee Nation," Cherokee Nation publication, available online at http://freedmen.cherokee.org/Portals\/13/Docs/Briefing%20on%20History%20and%20Cases.pdf.

115. P.L. 129 (April 26, 1906), The "Five Tribes Act": An Act to provide for the final disposition of the affairs of the Five Civilized Tribes in the Indian Territory, and for other purposes.

116. "Why Freedmen Descendants Without an Indian Ancestor Listed on the Base Rolls Are Not Eligible for Citizenship in the Cherokee Nation," Cherokee Nation publication available online at http://freedmen.cherokee.org/PortalsV/13/Docs/Briefing%20on%20History%20and%20Cases.pdf, 3.

117. Ibid.

118. See, e.g., *Gritts v. Fisher*, 224 U.S. 640 (1912), holding that children born to enrolled members of the Cherokee Nation after September 1, 1902, and living on March 4, 1906, are entitled to enrollment as members of the tribe, and to participation in the allotment and distribution of its lands and funds under Congressional legislation. The Freedmen Roll of the Final Rolls in 1906 included children who, by virtue of being children, could not have been alive in 1867.

119. See Wilkins and Lomawaima, *Uneven Ground*, 98-116. This work offers a robust discussion of plenary power.

120. U.S. Const. art. II, sec. 2, cl. 2; U.S. Const. art. I, sec. 8, cl. 3.

121. *United States v. Dion*, 476 U.S. 734, 738-740 (1986).

122. Indeed, a "win" for the Cherokee Nation on the claim that the Treaty of 1966 has been abrogated may well be a pyrrhic victory. It may temporarily allow the Cherokee Nation to exclude its Freedmen, but there would undoubtedly be other ramifications. What treaties might Congress then wish to avoid, based on less than clear and unequivocal intent to abrogate? What consequences might such unpredictability and instability of treaty rights and obligations entail for the Cherokee Nation?

123. Sturm, "Blood Politics, Racial Classification, and Cherokee National Identity," 245.

124. *Raymond Nash v. Cherokee Nation Registrar*, Consolidated Cases No. CV-07-40, et. al., (D.C., Cherokee Nation, January 14, 2011), 3, class action lawsuit on behalf of the Freedmen.

125. Gavin Off, "Tribal citizenship granted," *Tulsa World* (January 15, 2011), A1.

126. Ibid., A7.

127. Gavin Off, "Tribe appeals citizen ruling," *Tulsa World* (January 26, 2011), A7.

128. Chris Casteel, "Freedmen Cherokee citizenship in limbo," *Tulsa World* (January 30, 2011), A9.

129. *Cherokee Nation Registrar v. Raymond Nash*, Case No. SC-2011-02 (Supreme Court of the Cherokee Nation, August 22, 2011).

130. Telephone conversation with Marilyn Vann, August 28, 2011.

131. According to Cherokee Nation Judicial History (http://www.cherokeecourts.org/History.aspx):

> The Cherokee Nation Judicial Appeals Tribunal. JAT) was created by Article VII of the 1975 Constitution. The District Court was re-established by Legislative Act in 1990 after the 10th Circuit Federal Court of Appeals case decided Ross v Neff which held that the State of Oklahoma did not have criminal jurisdiction over Indian country within the Cherokee Nation.
> In June of 2006, the Judicial Appeals Tribunal issued its opinion in case number JAT-05-04. The Court found that the 1999 Constitution of the Cherokee Nation had been effective since July 26, 2003. The changes of the 1999 Constitution to the Judicial Branch are the Judicial Appeals Tribunal became the Supreme Court and added two more justices to the bench, bring-

ing the count up to five. The District Court received original and general jurisdiction.

132. Marilyn Vann, President—Descendants of Freedmen, "CNO tribal court blocks freedmen from voting in chief election. Emergency meeting, demonstration, date set, August 23, 2011" (press release).

133. *Cherokee Nation Registrar v. Raymond Nash*, Case No. SC-2011-02 (Supreme Court of the Cherokee Nation, August 22, 2011), 6.

134. Ibid., 8.

135. Ibid., 8-9.

136. Ibid., 9.

137. Marilyn Vann, President—Descendants of Freedmen, "CNO tribal court blocks freedmen from voting in chief election. Emergency meeting, demonstration, date set, August 23, 2011" (press release).

138. Kenneth J. Cooper, "Cherokee Supreme Court Denies Citizenship Rights To Cherokee Freedmen, Cherokee Freedmen Descendants," www.facebook.com, August 26, 2011.

139. Lenzy Krehbiel-Burton, "Freedmen descendants decry tribal court ruling," *Tulsa World* (August 24, 2011), A9.

140. Tria Robinson, "Cherokee Freedmen Descendants," Facebook comment posted 8:57 a.m., August 23, 2011.

141. Robert Warrior, "Cherokees flee the moral high ground over Freedmen." (News from Indian Country Op-Ed on Cherokee Freedmen), Turtle Talk, http://turtletalk.wordpress.com/2011/08/23/news-from-indian-country-op-ed-on-cherokee-freedmen/. Last visited August 23, 2011.

142. Lenzy Krehbiel-Burton, "Freedmen descendants decry tribal court ruling," *Tulsa World* (August 24, 2011), A14.

143. Kenneth J. Cooper, "Cherokee Supreme Court Denies Citizenship Rights To Cherokee Freedmen, Cherokee Freedmen Descendants," www.facebook.com, August 26, 2011.

144. Wright, *Guide to the Indian Tribes of Oklahoma*.

145. Angie Debo, *The Road to Disappearance: A History of The Creek Indians* (Norman, Oklahoma: University of Oklahoma Press 1941), 115-116; see also, Kathryn E. Holland, "The Creek Indians, Blacks, and Slavery," *Journal of Southern History* 1991 57(4): 601-636.

146. Chang, *Race, Nation, and the Politics*, 23.

147. Ibid., 18-19, referencing additional works on Muscogee (Creek) nationality, including Steven C. Hahn, *The Invention of the Creek Nation, 1670-1763* (Lincoln, Nebraska: University of Nebraska Press 2004) and Claudio Saunt, *New Order of Things: Property, Power, and the Transformation of the Creek Indians, 1733-1816* (Cambridge, England: Cambridge University Press, 1999).

148. John R. Swanton, *Early History of the Creek Indians & Their Neighbors* (Gainesville, Florida: University Press of Florida, 1998), 215 (originally published in 1922 by the Smithsonian Institution, Bureau of American Ethnology, Bulletin 73).

149. H. B. Cushman, *History of the Choctaw, Chickasaw and Natchez Indians*, Angie Debo ed. (Norman, Oklahoma: University of Oklahoma Press, 1999), 13. (First edition published in 1899; abridged edition by Angie Debo published in 1962 by Redlands Press.)

150. Ibid., 18-19, 298-299; see also Waselkov and Braund, eds., *William Bartram on the Southeastern Indians*, 142.

151. See generally http://muscogeecreektribalcourt.org/.

152. United States Department of Interior Census Office, Extra Census Bulletin: The Five Civilized Tribes In Indian Territory—The Cherokee, Chickasaw, Choctaw, Creek, and Seminole Nations (Washington, D.C.: Department of the Interior, United States Census Printing Office 1893).

153. United States Department of Interior Census Office, 27, Extra Census Bulletin. Washington, D.C.: United States Census Printing Office 1894.

154. See generally, http://www.muscogeenation-nsn.gov/ (the official tribal web site of the Muscogee [Creek] Nation), last visited December 31, 2010; see also, Chang, *Race, Nation, and the Politics*.

155. See generally, http://muscogeecreektribalcourt.org/.

156. Muscogee (Creek) resistance to occupation and domination is thought to be the origin of the familiar phrase "God willing and the Creek don't rise." This figure of speech is used to mean, essentially, "I will accomplish this task barring unforeseen contingencies." Benjamin Hawkins, a politician and Indian diplomat, is said to have used the phrase in print in the late 18th century. On one occasion, the President of the United States reportedly summoned Hawkins from his post in the South, to which Hawkins replied, "God willing and the Creek don't rise." Hawkins capitalized the word "Creek," indicating reference to the Muscogee (Creek) Indians, not a body of water, as is commonly assumed by users of the phrase. See, e.g., Williams, Nicole, Origin of the Phrase "God willing and the Creek Don't Rise" [Internet] (Version 3. Knol. 2009 Jul 31. Available from: http://knol.google.com/k/nicole-williams/origin-of-the-phrase-god-willing-and/2syhui1zwwxai/5. Last visited June 5, 2011.

157. See, e.g., Walter R. Borneman, *1812: The War That Forged a Nation* (New York, New York: Harper Perennial, 2004); Robert Remini, *Andrew Jackson and the Course of American Empire, 1767-1821* (New York, New York: Harper & Row, 1977), chapter 13; Steve Rajtar, *Indian War Sites* (Jefferson, North Carolina: McFarland and Company, Inc., 1999); http://www.nps.gov/hobe/.

158. See, e.g., "Creek Indian Tribe," Access Genealogy, Indian Tribal Records, http://www.accessgenealogy.com/native/tribes/creek/creekhist.htm.

159. Gary Lee, "Trail of Tears," *Washington Post*, August 1, 1999, 4, available online at http://www.washingtonpost.com/wp-srv/travel/features/trailoftears080199.htm. Last visited June 21, 2009.

160. Ibid., 8-9.

161. Johnson, *Acres of Aspiration*, 215.

162. Angie Debo, "The Road to Disappearance: a History of the Creek Indians," *Civilization of the American Indian Series*, v. 22 (Norman, Oklahoma: University of Oklahoma Press, 1941).

163. For an overview of the life of Cow Tom, see, e.g., Jonathan Greenberg, *Staking A Claim—Jake Simmons, Jr. and the Making of an African American Oil Dynasty* (New York, New York: Atheneum, 1990), Prologue—An Ancestry of Freedom, 13-33.

164. Thomas Jessup was a general during the Second Seminole War. He is most famous for capturing Seminole leader Osceola under a flag of truce in 1837. After Osceola's capture, General Jessup continued the war effort, fighting the Battle of Loxahatchee in January of 1838. By May of that year, General Jessup asked for, and was granted, relief of command by President Zachary Taylor.

165. Military writer Ethan Allen Hitchcock kept a diary in 1842, in which he wrote about his experiences in Indian Territory. He spoke of Cow Tom often in the diary, taking particular note of Cow Tom as the voice of Chief Yargee.

166. See Muriel H. Wright, George H. Shirk, and Kenny A Franks, *Mark of Heritage* (Norman, Oklahoma: University of Oklahoma Press, 1976).

167. Letter from D. N. McIntosh to Commissioner Dennis Cooley, March 18, 1866, M234-231: M245.

168. Cow Tom is listed as "Cow Mikko" on the Treaty of 1866. "Mikko," a Muscogee (Creek) word, means "chief."

169. See Felix S. Cohen, 104 *Handbook of Federal Indian Law* (1982).

170. Title 27, § 1-103(A) of the M.C.N.C.A. provides: "In all cases, the Muscogee (Creek) Nation Court shall apply the Constitution and duly enacted laws of the Muscogee Nation, the common law of the Muscogee people as established by customs and usage, and the Treaties and Agreements between the Muscogee nation and the United States. Tile 27, § 1-101(A)(1) in pertinent part state ,"The authority of the Muscogee nation to adopt this title is based upon . . . the Treaty of 1866."

171. "Indian Affairs: Laws and Treaties," Vol. II, *Treaties*, 931-933, Charles J. Kappler, ed. (Washington, D.C.: Government Printing Office, 1904).

172. See Greenberg, *Staking A Claim*.

173. Ibid.

174. Angie Debo, *The Road to Disappearance* (Norman, OK: University of Oklahoma Press, 1941), 290.

175. Minutes of the September 27, 1870, meeting of the General Council of the Indian Territory, Gilcrease Museum, Tulsa, Oklahoma, library, box 39, volume 84, 1-2. The minutes reference the authority for the Council emanates from the Treaty of 1866, citing Article 12 of the Cherokee Treaty of 1866 by way of example, but noting that the treaties with the other members of the Five Civilized Tribes contain similar passages. Article 12 of the Cherokee Treaty of 1866 provides:

ARTICLE 12.

The Cherokees agree that a general council, consisting of delegates elected by each nation or tribe lawfully residing within the Indian Territory, may be annually convened in said Territory, which council shall be organized in such manner and possess such powers as hereinafter prescribed.

First. After the ratification of this treaty, and as soon as may be deemed practicable by the Secretary of the Interior, and prior to the first session of said council, a census or enumeration of each tribe lawfully resident in said Territory shall be taken under the direction of the Commissioner of Indian Affairs, who for that purpose is hereby authorized to designate and appoint competent persons, whose compensation shall be fixed by the Secretary of the Interior, and paid by the United States.

Second. The first general council shall consist of one member from each tribe, and an additional member for each one thousand Indians, or each fraction of a thousand greater than five hundred, being members of any tribe lawfully resident in said Territory, and shall be selected by said tribes respectively, who may assent to the establishment of said general council; and if none should be thus formally selected by any nation or tribe so assenting, the said nation or tribe shall be represented in said general council by the chief or chiefs and headmen of said tribes, to be taken in the order of their rank as recognized in tribal usage, in the same number and proportion as above indicated. After the said census shall have been taken and completed, the superintendent of Indian affairs shall publish and declare to each tribe assenting to the establishment of such council the number of members of such council to which they shall be entitled under the provisions of this article, and the persons entitled to represent said tribes shall meet at such time and place as he shall approve; but thereafter the time and place of the sessions of said council shall be determined by its action: *Provided*, That no session in any one year shall exceed the term of thirty days: *And provided*, That special sessions of said council may be called by the Secretary of the Interior whenever in his judgment the interest of said tribes shall require such special session.

Third. Said general council shall have power to legislate upon matters pertaining to the intercourse and relations of the Indian tribes and nations and colonies of freedmen resident in said Territory; the arrest and extradition of criminals and offenders escaping from one tribe to another, or into any community of freedmen; the administration of justice between members of different tribes of said Territory and persons other than Indians and members of said tribes or nations; and the common defence [sic] and safety of the nations of said Territory.

All laws enacted by such council shall take effect at such time as may therein be provided, unless suspended by direction of the President of the United States. No law shall be enacted inconsistent with the Constitution of the United States, or laws of Congress, or existing treaty stipulations with the United States. Nor shall said council legislate upon matters other than those above indicated: *Provided, however*, That the legislative power of such general council may be enlarged by the consent of the national council of each nation or tribe assenting to its establishment, with the approval of the President of the United States.

Fourth. Said council shall be presided over by such person as may be designated by the Secretary of the Interior.

Fifth. The council shall elect a secretary, whose duty it shall be to keep an accurate record of all the proceedings of said council, and who shall transmit a true copy of all such proceedings, duly certified by the presiding officer of such council, to the Secretary of the Interior, and to each tribe or nation represented in said council, immediately after the sessions of said council shall terminate. He shall be paid out of the Treasury of the United States an annual salary of five hundred dollars.

Sixth. The members of said council shall be paid by the United States the sum of four dollars per diem during the term actually in attendance on the sessions of said council, and at the rate of four dollars for every twenty miles necessarily traveled by them in going from and returning to their homes, respectively, from said council, to be certified by the secretary and president of the said council.

176. Interview of Mary Grayson, Works Progress Administration Slave Narratives, Tulsa, Oklahoma, 1937, http://www.african-nativeamerican.com/mary_grayson.htm. Last visited May 20, 2009.

177. "55 Burial Ground Form," Works Progress Administrations Indian-Pioneer History Project for Oklahoma, 275-77 (May 24, 1937).

178. See, e.g., Deon Hampton, "Monument is planned to mark Trail of Tears," *Tulsa World* (July 20, 2009), A14.

179. Nina Lane Dunn, *Tulsa's Magic Roots* (Tulsa, Oklahoma: N.L.D. Corp. 1979), 58.

180. "A Brief History of Brookside," http://brooksidetheplacetobe.com/index.php?/about-us.html?74a4a300. Last visited June 2, 2009.

181. John Bartlett Meserve, "The Perrymans," *Chronicles of Oklahoma*, 15:2 (June 1937), 178.

182. See Abstract of Creek Freedmen Census Cards. J. B. Campbell ed., Muskogee, OK: (December 1, 1915); see also Abstract of Creek Indian Census Cards. J. B. Campbell ed., Muskogee, OK: (April 3, 1915).

183. One prominent Muscogee (Creek) family that rivals the Perrymans in terms of power, position, and prestige is the Childers/Childress clan. The Childers migrated to Oklahoma from Alabama. Examples of the family's sphere of influence include two notable men from different eras: Ellis Buffentan Childers and Ernest Childers. In the post-Civil War period, Ellis Buffentan Childers, born on January 10, 1866, to Napoleon B. Childers and Sophia Melford, became a leading citizen. E.B. took on a prominent role in the Muscogee (Creek) House of Warriors, became a noteworthy farmer/rancher, and practiced law with the Childers & Mingo firm. Decades later, another man named Childers earned the Medal of Honor for his heroic actions in World War II. Ernest Childers, born in Broken Arrow, retired from the United States Army as a Lieutenant Colonel, and died in 2005. See, e.g., H. F. and E. S. O'Beirne, *The Indian Territory, Its Chiefs, Legislators and Leading Men* (St. Louis, Missouri: 1892).

184. Nina Lane Dunn, *Tulsa's Magic Roots* (Tulsa, Oklahoma: N.L.D. Corp. 1979), 54.

185. Telephone interview with Monetta Trepp in Tulsa, Oklahoma, June 27, 2009; http://www.travelok.com. Last visited June 27, 2009.

186. United States Department of Interior Census Office, 7 Extra Census Bulletin (Washington, D.C.: United States Census Printing Office 1894). Lequest Choteau Perryman was the great-great-great uncle of Damario Solomon-Simmons.

187. Curtis Act, Act of June 28, 1898, 30 Stat. L. 495.

188. General Allotment Act (Dawes Act), Act of February 8, 1887, Stat. L., vol. XXIV, pp. 388-391.

189. See, e.g., D. C. Gideon, *Indian Territory, Descriptive, Biographical and Genealogical* (New York, New York: Lewis Publishing Company, 1901); Michael D. Green, "Pleasant Porter," *Encyclopedia of North American Indians*, ed. Frederick E. Hoxie (Boston, MA: Houghton Mifflin, 1997); John B. Meserve, "Chief Pleasant Porter," *The Chronicles of Oklahoma* (September 1931), 9.

190. See Dunn Roll confirmation and acknowledgement at http://freepages.genealogy.rootsweb.ancestry.com/~ewyatt/DUNN%20ROLL/Given%20Name%20Alpha/J%20%20W%20Dunn.html. Last visited November 9, 2010.

191. Kent Carter, "Snakes & Scribes, The Dawes Commission and the Enrollment of the Creeks," Part 2, *The U.S. National Archives & Records Administration* (Spring 1997, 29:1) 2.
192. *Plessy v. Ferguson*, 163 U.S. 537 (1896).
193. Ibid.
194. Kent Carter, *The Dawes Commission and the Allotment of the Five Civilized Tribes 1893-1914* (Orem, Utah: Ancestry.com 1999), 49.
195. Const. of the Muscogee (Creek) Nation art III, Sec. 2.
196. See, e.g., Brendan I. Koerner, "Blood Feud," http://www.velielaw.com/show Article.asp?articleid=45.
197. For details on Ron Graham's efforts to attain Muscogee (Creek) citizenship, see *Ron Graham v. Muscogee (Creek) Nation of Oklahoma Citizenship Board*, Case No. CV 2003-53, in the District Court of the Muscogee (Creek) Nation, Okmulgee District. Trial Brief, including Findings of Face and Conclusions of Law) filed by Attorneys Damario Solomon and Selim Fiagome on August 26, 2005.
198. Relevant legal provisions include:

Article II, Section 1 of the Muscogee (Creek) Constitution:
Each Muscogee (Creek) Indian by blood shall have the opportunity for citizenship in The Muscogee (Creek) Nation.

Article III, Section 1 of the Muscogee (Creek) Constitution:
The Principal Chief shall appoint, subject to majority approval of the Muscogee (Creek) National Council, a Citizenship Board comprised of five. 5) citizens who shall be charged with the responsibility of the establishment and maintenance of a Citizenship Roll, showing degree of Muscogee (Creek) Indian blood based upon rolls prepared pursuant to the Act of April 26, 1906,. 34 Stat. 137). . . .

Article III, Section 2 of the Muscogee (Creek) Constitution:
Persons eligible for citizenship in the Muscogee (Creek) Nation shall consist of Muscogee (Creek) Indians by blood whose names appear on the final rolls as provided by the Act of April 26, 1906 (34 Stat. 137), and persons who are lineal descendants of those Muscogee (Creek) Indians by blood whose names appear on the final rolls as provided by the act of April 26, 1906. 34 Stat.137). . . .

Article III, Section 3 of the Muscogee (Creek) Constitution:
(a) All persons eligible for citizenship shall register as an applicant for citizenship; and
(b) The Citizenship Board shall certify citizenship, and the declaration of citizenship may be affirmed at any time with the name of the individual being entered on the citizenship roll, and the persons being recognized as a citizen of The Muscogee (Creek) Nation, provided that:
> the person is a Muscogee (Creek) Indian by blood whose name appears on the final rolls as provided by the Act of April 26, 1906,. 34 Stat. 137), or the person is a lineal descendant of a Muscogee (Creek) Indian by blood whose name appears on the final rolls as provided by the Act of April 26, 1906,. 34 Stat. 137). . . .

Endnotes 381

Act of April 26, 1906. 34 Stat. 137)
Section 3 of the Act of April 26, 1906 provides, in pertinent part:

That the approved roll of Muscogee (Creek) freedmen shall include only those persons whose names appear on the roll prepared by J.W. Dunn, under authority of the United States prior to March fourteenth, eighteen hundred and sixty-seven , and their descendants born since said roll was made, and those lawfully admitted to citizenship in the Muscogee (Creek) Nation subsequent to the date of the preparation of said roll, and their descendants born since such admission, except such, if any, as have heretofore been enrolled and their enrollment approved by the Secretary of the Interior.

Muscogee (Creek) Citizenship Code Prior to August 23, 2001, provided in pertinent part:
(1) Each Muscogee (Creek) Indian by blood shall have the opportunity for citizenship in the Muscogee (Creek) Nation, and in pursuance thereof, the Citizenship Board shall [emphasis added]:

A. Utilize records of the former Muscogee (Creek) Nation Election Board, the former Muscogee (Creek) Constitution Commission, the United States Bureau of Indian Affairs, and other suitable records, to identify persons who are Muscogee (Creek) Indian by blood.

B. Utilize records of and meeting with organizations of Muscogee (Creek) Indians by blood to identify persons who are Muscogee (Creek) Indian by blood.

C. Contact by mail every person identified to the Citizenship Board as a Muscogee (Creek) Indian by blood, in order to provide adequate information and necessary forms for their application for citizenship.

D. Upon the request of any application for citizenship, convene a hearing as an evidentiary proceeding to determine whether that person is a Muscogee (Creek) Indian by blood. In such proceedings, the burden of proof shall be upon the applicant[s], to demonstrate a preponderance of evidence that they are a Muscogee (Creek) Indian by blood. The applicant and any member of the Citizenship Board may subpoena witnesses.

(2) Evidence of Degree of Muscogee (Creek) Indian blood shall be based upon the Degree of Muscogee (Creek) Indian blood shown for all direct ancestors on the final rolls prepared pursuant to the Act of April 26, 1906. 34 Stat. 137); and based upon direct ancestors enrolled on previous tribal enrollment hereinafter-listed [one of which is "The Loyal Muscogee (Creek) Roll of 1870," which is [composed] of those Muscogee (Creek) citizens who sided with the United States of America—the Union—during the Civil War], notwithstanding the lack of a listed Degree of Muscogee (Creek) Indian blood on such other enrollment.

Muscogee (Creek) Citizenship Code After Adoption of NCA 01-135 and NCA 02-078 provided in pertinent part:
  A. Opportunity for Citizenship. As provided in the Muscogee Nation Constitution at Article II, Section 1, "Each Muscogee (Creek) Indian by blood shall have the opportunity for citizenship in the Muscogee (Creek) Nation."
  B. In order to implement this Code, the Citizenship Board shall utilize the 8x10 Certificates of Degree of Indian Blood of the United States Department of the Interior, and other suitable records.

Article II of the Muscogee (Creek) Treaty of 1866. 14 Stat. 785) provides in pertinent part:
  The Muscogee (Creek)s hereby covenant and agree that henceforth neither slavery nor involuntary servitude . . . shall ever exist in said Nation; and inasmuch as there are among the Muscogee (Creek)s many persons of African descent . . . it is stipulated that hereafter these persons, lawfully residing in said Muscogee (Creek) country, under their laws and usages, or who have been thus residing in said country, and may return within one year from the ratification of this treaty, and their descendants and such others of the same race as may be permitted by the laws of said Nation to settle within the limits of the jurisdiction of the Muscogee (Creek) Nation as citizens [thereof], shall have and enjoy all the rights and privileges of native citizens, including an equal interest in the soil and national funds; and the laws of said Nation shall be equally binding upon and give equal protection to all such persons . . . .

199. Interview with Ron Graham, Tulsa, Oklahoma, June 30, 2011.
200. Interview with Eli Grayson, President of the California Muscogee (Creek) Association, in Tulsa, Oklahoma, June 20, 2009.
201. Adrienne P. Samuels, "What Does Indian Blood Look Like? A Century-old Battle Boils as Black Indians Fight for Membership in Their Native American Tribes," *Ebony* (April 2008): 102.
202. Interview with Vanessa Adams-Harris, Tulsa, Oklahoma, November 11, 2010.
203. Interview with Robert Trepp in Tulsa, Oklahoma, June 7, 2009.
204. Interview with Eli Grayson, President of the California Muscogee (Creek) Association, in Tulsa, Oklahoma, June 20, 2009.
205. Interview with Eli Grayson, President of the California Muscogee (Creek) Association, in Tulsa, Oklahoma, June 20, 2009.
206. *Hub City News*, 5:7 (February 12, 2010), 5 (Southern California newspaper).
207. See Daniel F. Littlefield, Jr., *African and Creeks: From the Colonial Period to the Civil War* (Westport, Connecticut: Greenwood Press 1979), 145.
208. Wright, *Guide to the Indian Tribes of Oklahoma*.
209. Work Projects Administration, *Slave Narratives: A Folk History of Slavery in the United States* (August 18, 1936, interview of Frank Berry, Seminole Freedmen), http://www.fullbooks.com/Slave-Narratives-A-Folk-History-of-Slaveryx16701.html
210. Brent Staples, "The Seminole Tribe, Running From History," *The New York Times* (April 21, 2002).

211. John R. Swanton, *Early History of the Creek Indians & Their Neighbors* (Gainesville, Florida: University Press of Florida 1998), 400 (originally published in 1922 by the Smithsonian Institution, Bureau of American Ethnology, Bulletin 73).
212. Ibid., 170-181.
213. See, e.g., Seminole History, myflorida.com, http://dhr.dos.state.fl.us/facts/history/seminole/.
214. Swanton, *Early History of the Creek Indians*, 80-109.
215. John R. Swanton, *The Indians of the Southeastern United States* (Washington, D.C.: Library of Congress, 1979), 115 (reprint of Smithsonian Institution Bureau of American Ethnology Bulletin 137, 1946).
216. Waselkov and Braund, eds., *William Bartram on the Southeastern Indians*, 51.
217. Swanton, *Early History of the Creek Indians*, 97.
218. Daniel F. Littlefield, Jr., *Africans and Seminoles: From Removal to Emancipation* (Westport, Connecticut: Greenwood Press, 1977), 174-175.
219. Jean West, "Seminoles and Slaves: Florida's Freedom Seekers," http://www.slaveryinamerica.org/history/hs_es_siminole.htm; see also, J.K. Mahon, *History of the Second Seminole War, 1835-1842* (Gainsville, Florida: University of Florida Press, 1967); Joseph Opala, *A Brief History of the Seminole Freedmen* (Austin, Texas: University of Texas at Austin, African and Afro-American Studies and Research Center, 1980).
220. The Estelusti Foundation seeks to preserve and publish the history of the enslaved African and African-Native Americans who lived among the Five Civilized Tribes, particularly within what is now the State of Oklahoma. Among other offerings, The Estelusti Foundation maintains significant Internet resources, including links to Indian Pioneer Papers maintained by The University of Oklahoma, Western History Collections. The Indian-Pioneer Papers, an oral history collection spanning the years 1861 to 1936, include typescripts of interviews with thousands of Oklahomans that were conducted by federal government workers during the 1930s. The Papers' subject matter encompasses the settlement of Oklahoma and Indian Territories as well as general aspects of life and living in early Oklahoma. The Estelusti Foundation Web site also includes a feature called "Vignettes of Indian Territory," biographical sketches of some of the Freedmen trailblazers who endured enslavement, jostled with "Jim Crow," and petitioned for protection as citizens within the nations of their birth.
221. Charles J. Kappler ed., *Indian Affairs: Laws and Treaties*, Vol. II, Treaties (Washington, D.C.: Government Printing Office, 1904), 910-13.
222. *Davis v. United States*, No. 98-6161 (10th Cir., September 21, 1999).
223. *Seminole Nation of Fla. & Seminole Nation of Okla. v. United States*, 38 Ind. Cl. Comm. 91 (Dockets 73 & 151).
224. See Indian Claims: Distribution of Funds to Seminole Indians, Pub.L.No. 101-277, 104 Stat. 143 (1990)
225. See, e.g., William Glaberson, "Who Is a Seminole, and Who Gets to Decide?" *The New York Times* (January 29, 2001).
226. See Distribution Act, Act of April 30, 1990, Pub. L. No. 101-277 §2(a)(1), 104 Stat. 143.
227. Ibid.
228. See Plan for the Use of the Seminole Nation of Okla. Indian Judgment Funds in Docket Nos. 73 & 151 Before the Indian Claims Comm'n, 56 Fed. Reg. 32480, 32480 (1991).

229. See Pratt, "Loving Indian Style," 445, fns. 201, 202.
230. Brent Staples, "The Seminole Tribe, Running From History," *The New York Times* (April 21, 2002).
231. Distribution Act, § 4(a), 104 Stat. at 144.
232. See, e.g., *Davis v. United States*, No. CIV-96-1988-M, slip op. at 10 (W.D. Okla. Mar. 20, 1998); *Davis v. United States*, 192 F.3rd 951 (10th Cir. 1999); and *Davis v. United States*, 199 F. Supp 2nd 1164 (W.D. Okla. 2002); *Davis v. United States*, No. 02-6198 (10 Cir., September 10, 2003)
233. *Seminole Nation of Oklahoma v. Norton*, 206 F.R.D. 1(D.D.C. 2001).
234. Ibid., 223 F. Supp. 2d 122. D.D.C. 2002).
235. Const. of the Seminole Nation of Oklahoma art. II.
236. "Treaty With the Seminole," Mar. 21, 1866, U.S.-Seminole Nat., 14 Stat. 755, 1866 WL 4729, *2.
237. See Seminole Nation web site, http://www.seminolenation.com/services_judgmentfund.htm. Last visited May 23, 2009.
238. Letter to The Honorable Eric Holder, United States Attorney General, from United States Congress members Diane E. Watson, Barney Frank, John Lewis, John Conyers, Jr., Barbara Lee, and Sheila Jackson Lee, April 30, 2009.
239. Wright, *Guide to the Indian Tribes of Oklahoma*.
240. H. B. Cushman, *History of the Choctaw, Chickasaw and Natchez Indians*, Angie Debo, ed. (Norman, OK: University of Oklahoma Press, 1999), 18 (first edition published in 1899; abridged edition by Angie Debo published in 1962 by Redlands Press).
241. Iwasaki Yoshitaka, "Freedmen in the Indian Territory after the Civil War: The Dual Approaches of the Choctaw and Chickasaw Nations," *Nanzan Review of American Studies*, vol. 30 (2008): 91-108, http://www.ic.nanzan-u.ac.jp/AMERICA/kanko/documents/16IWASAKI_000.pdf (Proceedings of the NASSS 2008), 94-95. Last visited July 5, 2011.
242. Ibid., Proceedings of the NASSS 2008, at 91, 99-100.
243. "Estelusti—The Lives of The Freedmen of Indian Territory: The Slave Narratives of Indian Territory," http://www.african-nativeamerican.com/estelusti.htm (Frances Banks interview).
244. The act of adoption is set forth in the annual report of the Commissioner of Indian Affairs for 1884. See H. Ex. Doc. No. 1, pt. 5, 48th Cong., 2d Sess., at 36-37; see also, Yoshitaka, "Freedmen in the Indian Territory after the Civil War, " 91-108, Proceedings of the NASSS 2008, at 91, 101-103.
245. Charles J. Kappler ed., *Indian Affairs: Laws and Treaties*, Vol. I, Laws, Chapter 1362: Commission to the Five Civilized Tribes—Ratification of agreement with the Choctaw and Chickasaw Indians, Compiled to December 1, 1902 (Washington, D.C.: Government Printing Office, 1904).
246. Charles J. Kappler ed., *Indian Affairs: Laws and Treaties*, Vol. II, Treaties (Washington, D.C.: Government Printing Office, 1904), 918-920.
247. Daniel F. Littlefield, Jr. & Mary Ann Littlefield, "The Beams Family: Free Blacks in Indian Territory," *The Journal of Negro History*, vol. 61, no. 1. (January 976): 16-36.
248. "The Choctaw Freedmen of Oklahoma," http://www.african-nativeamerican.com/8-chocfreed.htm
249. Senate Bill 73, a measure elevating *Swing Low, Sweet Chariot* to special status in Oklahoma, passed the Senate on February 24, 2011. Oklahoma Governor Mary Fallin signed the legislation into law on April 25, 2011, at the 19th biennial

A. C. Hamlin Legislative Black Caucus awards banquet sponsored by the six-member Oklahoma Legislative Black Caucus. Governor Fallin, who was being honored as the state's first woman governor, announced her intention to sign the legislation, Senate Bill 73, onstage at the National Cowboy Museum, in front of hundreds of witnesses. The legislation, sponsored primarily by Representative Jabar Shumate and Senator Judy Eason-McIntyre, both of Tulsa, and promoted by every member of the caucus, designates the spiritual *Swing Low, Sweet Chariot* as Oklahoma's official state Gospel Song. According to the African-American Registry, Wallis Willis, a Choctaw Freedmen who lived in Indian Territory, wrote the spiritual on December 21, 1840. Willis found inspiration in Oklahoma's Red River, a trigger for his reflections on the Jordan River, site of the biblical tale of Prophet Elijah's heavenly ascension by chariot. Many believe the song secreted references to the Underground Railroad. The world-famous Fisk Jubilee Singers recorded the song in 1909. *Swing Low, Sweet Chariot* earned a place on the National Recording Registry and is listed among the Songs of the Century. See, generally, Barbara Hoberock, "Fallin signs bill making 'Swing Low' the state's gospel song," *Tulsa World* (April 27, 2011), tulsaworld.com. Last visited April 28, 2011; Barbara Hoberock, "Bill to establish state gospel song passes through Senate," *Tulsa World* (February 25, 2011), A11; Melanie Eversly, "Story behind spiritual 'Sweet Chariot' emerges," *USA Today* (August 15, 2006); http://www.negrospirituals.com/history.htm. Last visited February 25, 2011; African-American Registry, http://www.aaregistry.org/poetry/view/swing-low-sweet-chariot-wallace-willis. Last visited February 25, 2011.

250. Katy June-Friesen, "Using government documents, author Angela Walton-Raji traced her ancestors to the slaves owned by American Indians," Smithsonian.com (February 17, 2010), http://www.smithsonianmag.com/history-archaeology/An-Ancestry-of-African-Native-Americans.html. Last visited February 22, 2010.

251. Const. of the Choctaw Nation of Oklahoma, art. II, sec. 1.

252. Ibid.; see also Const. of the Choctaw Nation of Oklahoma, art. XXI.

253. Dawes enrollment card, Chickasaw Nation, Freedmen Roll, listing Ardena Darneal, roll no. 3748, field no. 929, enrollment approved by the Secretary Interior on April 10, 1898.

254. Interview with Verdie Triplett (telephonic), May 25, 2009.

255. Choctaw Chickasaw Freedmen Association, http://www.choctawchickasaw freedmen.com/confpage.htm

256. Richard Green, "Beyond the Divide: Chickasaw-Choctaw Warfare," http://www.chickasaw.net/history_culture/print/index_754.htm; "The Choctaw Trail of Tears," http://www.thebicyclingguitarist.net/studies/trailoftears.htm.

257. Wright, *Guide to the Indian Tribes of Oklahoma*.

258. "Estelusti—The Lives of The Freedmen of Indian Territory: The Slave Narratives of Indian Territory," http://www.african-nativeamerican.com/estelusti.htm.

259. Daniel F. Littlefield, Jr. *The Chickasaw Freedmen—A People Without a Country* (Westport, Connecticut: Greenwood Press, 1980), preface.

260. See, e.g., Yoshitaka, "Freedmen in the Indian Territory after the Civil War," 91-108.

261. Arrell M. Gibson, *The Chickasaws* (Norman, Oklahoma: University of Oklahoma Press 1971), 283.

262. Quoted in Opinion of Solicitor Nathan R. Margold (October 1, 1941), Opinions of the Solicitor of the Department of the Interior Relating to Indian

Affairs 1917-1974 (Washington, D.C.: United States Government Printing Office), http://thorpe.ou.edu/solicitor.html. Last visited July 5, 2011; see *United States v. The Choctaw Nation*, 38 Ct. Cl. 558. 1943); see also Yoshitaka, "Freedmen in the Indian Territory after the Civil War," 91-108.

263. Littlefield, *The Chickasaw Freedmen*, 218-19.
264. Ibid., preface.
265. Ibid.
266. "Biographical Directory of the United States Congress, 1774-Present," http://bioguide.congress.gov/scripts/biodisplay.pl?index=D0002142. Last visited May 29, 2009.
267. Letter from Columbus Delano, Secretary of the Interior, to William A. Buckingham, Chairman of the Senate Committee on Indian Affairs, about Senate Bill No. 680, a measure providing relief for certain person of African descent resident in the Choctaw and Chickasaw Nations, dated May 2, 1874, 43rd Congress, 1st Session, Senate Miscellaneous Document No. 118, available at http://www.estelusti.com/new_page_72.htm. Last visited May 28, 2009.
268. Littlefield, *The Chickasaw Freedmen*, preface.
269. Ibid.
270. Ibid.
271. Even the *New York Times* recounted the exploits of the inimitable King Blue:

> During the past ten days the peaceably inclined Indians living along the eastern border of the Chickasaw Nation have been terrorized by a band of Negro Indians led by Old King Blue....King Blue is nearly sixty years old, very strong physically, and a natural leader of surprising tact. He was chosen King of the negro colony that came into this reservation at the close of the civil war, and he exercises an absolute tyranny over his followers.

"The Chickasaw Nation: What Civilization, Industry, and Energy Have Done For Them," *New York Times* (July 12, 1896), 32.
272. "The Eloquent Protest of the Chickasaw Freedmen," http://www.african-nativeamerican.com/chickmem.htm
273. Curtis Act, 30 Stat. 495 (1898).
274. See, e.g., Angie Debo, *The Rise and Fall of the Choctaw Republic* (Norman, Oklahoma: University of Oklahoma Press 1961); Arrell M. Gibson, *The Chickasaws* (Norman, OK: University of Oklahoma Press, 1971); Gaston Litton, *History of Oklahoma at the Golden Anniversary of Statehood* (New York, New York: Lewis Historical Publishing Company, 1957), 1.
275. See, e.g., Littlefield, *The Chickasaw Freedmen*, 219.
276. Equity Case 7071, *Bettie Ligon v. Douglas H. Johnson, Breen McCurtain, and James Garfield, Secretary of the Interior* (United States Court for the Southern District of Indian Territory at Ardmore), available at http://freepages.genealogy.rootsweb.ancestry.com/~ewyatt/Equity%20case%207071/1.html. Last visited May 25, 2009.
277. Ibid.
278. Littlefield, *The Chickasaw Freedmen*, 93.
279. "Choctaw and Chickasaw Freedmen Seek Enrollment," *Indian Citizen* (April 18, 1907), 1.
280. Ibid.

281. Sen. Rpt. No. 5013, pt. 2. 1907.
282. Sen. Doc. 257, 59th Congress, 2nd session, Hearings Before the Committee on Indian Affairs on the Choctaw and Chickasaw Indians (January 23, 1907), available at http://www.archive.org/details/choctawchikasawi01united. Last visited May 29, 2009.
283. Telephone interview with Terry J. Ligon, Freedmen advocate, in San Francisco, California, May 28, 2009.
284. Act of March 3, 1901, 31 Stat. 1447, vol. 1, at 114.
285. United States Code, Title 8, Sec. 1401(a)(2).
286. Littlefield, *The Chickasaw Freedmen*, 227.
287. Const. of the Chickasaw Nation, art. II, sec. 1.

Conclusion

1. Frederick Douglass, West India Emancipation Speech of August 1857, cited in *Black on Black*, Arnold Adoff, ed. (New York, New York: Macmillan, 1968), 1.
2. Howard Zinn, *The Southern Mystique* (New York, New York; Alfred A. Knopf 1964), 262-63.
3. See generally, Tiya Miles, *Ties That Bind: The Story of an Afro-Cherokee Family in Slavery and Freedom* (Berkeley and Los Angeles, California: University of California Press, 2005).
4. Interview with Marilyn Vann in Tulsa, Oklahoma, October 15, 2008.
5. See, e.g., Michelle Alexander, "The New Jim Crow," *The Nation* (March 15, 2010), http://www.npr.org/templates/story.php?storyId=124687663&sc=emaf. Last visited March 30, 2010. Alexander argues that the war on drugs has created a racial "undercaste." In this modern Jim Crow system, disproportionate numbers of African Americans are incarcerated and disenfranchised. Moreover, much of the supposed "black progress" is a myth. Be it poverty, child poverty, or unemployment statistics, African Americans are no better off than they were in 1968, the year an assassin's bullet felled Dr. Martin Luther King, Jr. Many of us feel better about our circumstances, though: "Affirmative action . . . has put a happy face on this racial reality. Seeing black people graduate from Harvard and Yale and become CEOs or corporate lawyers—not to mention president of the United States—causes us all to marvel at what a long way we've come." See also Michelle Alexander, *The New Jim Crow: Mass Incarceration in the Age of Colorblindness* (New York, New York: The New Press, 2010).
6. Remarks by President Bill Clinton, June 14, 1997, cited in *One America in the 21st Century: Forging a New Future, The President's Initiative on Race*, The Advisory Board's Report to the President, 1.
7. Eddie N. Williams & Robert McC. Adams, *African Americans and the Living Constitution*, John Hope Franklin & Genna Rae McNeil, eds. (Washington, D.C.: Smithsonian Institution Press, 1995), xiv (Foreword).
8. See, e.g., Gerald M. Sider, *Lumbee Indian Histories: Race, Ethnicity, and Indian Identity in the Southern United States* (New York, New York: Cambridge University Press 1993). Sider, an anthropologist, argues racial classifications were designed by the dominant white society to further concentrate its power, wealth, privilege, and land holdings.
9. E-mail to author from Calvin C. Moore, J.D., Ph.D., dated August 19, 2010. Dr. Moore, addressing "post-racialism" primarily in the context of black-white relations, noted in part:

> From a subjective standpoint, it appears that white America is moving towards a post-racialism that says "as long as your norms, value system, educational and job performance, presentation of self and social behavior conform to that of middle-class white America, we will look beyond your race."
>
> Ah, but there's the rub: that post-racialism, however well-meaning, is not completely benign, as it can perpetuate forms of rationalized racism. Rationalized racism essentially says "Yes, we will overlook your race to the extent of your conformity, but we will nonetheless sanction you in direct proportion to your failure to conform." As such, you will suffer inequities in the job market[,] not because of racial discrimination, but because of deficiencies in educational preparedness. Housing segregation does not occur because of race, but because of undesirable cultural patterns associated with ghetto communities. Heightened suspicion towards black males is a real byproduct of black male violence being six times that of the white norm. It is only when these objective facts no longer hold that blacks will cease to suffer those sanctions that inhibit their full integration into society.
>
> Of course the objective reality of black-white inequities leads to finger-pointing as to whose fault this is: blacks and liberals point to persistent structural inequalities that are perpetuated by the white-dominated power structure, while conservatives focus on entrenched cultural and behavioral patterns among blacks that inhibit their progress in spite of barriers having been removed. That argument goes on without resolution.
>
> The reality, however, is that because of objective reality, we are not post-racial in any sense of the term. The ideal is planted, however, and that is a start.

See also, Terry Smith, "Election Shows Post-Racial America Is a Long Way Off," *AOL News* (November 9, 2010), http://www.aolnews.com/opinion/article/opinion-election-shows-post-racial-america-is-a-long-way-off/19707823. Last visited November 9. 2010; "Shirley Sherrod and a 'post-racial' America," *Los Angeles Times* (July 22, 2010), http://articles.latimes.com/2010/jul/22/opinion/la-ed-sherrod-20100723. Last visited November 10, 2010; Keith Richburg, "Jimmy Carter was right. 'Post-racial' America is still a forlorn hope," *The Observer* (September 20, 2009), http://www.guardian.co.uk/commentisfree/cifamerica/2009/sep/20/jimmy-carter-barack-obama-racism. Last visited November 10, 2010.

10. S. A. Ray, "A Race or a Nation? Cherokee National Identity and the Status of Freedmen's Descendents," http://law.bepress.com/expresso/eps/1570 52. 2006).

11. Ibid.

12. Ibid.

13. Ibid.

14. The resolution's "Whereas" clauses canvass the relationship between the United States and Native Americans:

> Whereas the ancestors of today's Native Peoples inhabited the land of the present-day United States since time immemorial and for thousands of years before the arrival of peoples of European descent;

Whereas the Native Peoples have for millennia honored, protected, and stewarded this land we cherish;

Whereas the Native Peoples are spiritual peoples with a deep and abiding belief in the Creator, and for millennia their peoples have maintained a powerful spiritual connection to this land, as is evidenced by their customs and legends;

Whereas the arrival of Europeans in North America opened a new chapter in the histories of the Native Peoples;

Whereas, while establishment of permanent European settlements in North America did stir conflict with nearby Indian Tribes, peaceful and mutually beneficial interactions also took place;

Whereas the foundational English settlements in Jamestown, Virginia, and Plymouth, Massachusetts, owed their survival in large measure to the compassion and aid of the Native Peoples in their vicinities;

Whereas in the infancy of the United States, the founders of the Republic expressed their desire for a just relationship with the Indian Tribes, as evidenced by the Northwest Ordinance enacted by Congress in 1787, which begins with the phrase, "The utmost good faith shall always be observed toward the Indians";

Whereas Indian Tribes provided great assistance to the fledgling Republic as it strengthened and grew, including invaluable help to Meriwether Lewis and William Clark on their epic journey from St. Louis, Missouri, to the Pacific Coast;

Whereas Native Peoples and non-Native settlers engaged in numerous armed conflicts;

Whereas the United States Government violated many of the treaties ratified by Congress and other diplomatic agreements with Indian Tribes;

Whereas this Nation should address the broken treaties and many of the more ill-conceived Federal policies that followed, such as extermination, termination, forced removal and relocation, the outlawing of traditional religions, and the destruction of sacred places;

Whereas the United States forced Indian Tribes and their citizens to move away from their traditional homelands and onto federally established and controlled reservations, in accordance with such Acts as the Indian Removal Act of 1830;

Whereas many Native Peoples suffered and perished—
- (1) during the execution of the official United States Government policy of forced removal, including the infamous Trail of Tears and Long Walk;
- (2) during bloody armed confrontations and massacres, such as the Sand Muscogee (Creek) Massacre in 1864 and the Wounded Knee Massacre in 1890; and
- (3) on numerous Indian reservations;

Whereas the United States Government condemned the traditions, beliefs, and customs of the Native Peoples and endeavored to assimilate them by such policies as the redistribution of land under the General Allotment Act of 1887 and the forcible removal of Native children from their families to faraway boarding schools where their Native practices and languages were degraded and forbidden;

Whereas officials of the United States Government and private United States citizens harmed Native Peoples by the unlawful acquisition of recognized Tribal land, the theft of resources from such territories, and the mismanagement of Tribal trust funds;

Whereas the policies of the United States Government toward Indian Tribes and the breaking of covenants with Indian Tribes have contributed to the severe social ills and economic troubles in many Native communities today;

Whereas, despite continuing maltreatment of Native Peoples by the United States, the Native Peoples have remained committed to the protection of this great land, as evidenced by the fact that, on a per capita basis, more Native people have served in the United States Armed Forces and placed themselves in harm's way in defense of the United States in every major military conflict than any other ethnic group;

Whereas Indian Tribes have actively influenced the public life of the United States by continued cooperation with Congress and the Department of the Interior, through the involvement of Native individuals in official United States Government positions, and by leadership of their own sovereign Indian Tribes;

Whereas Indian Tribes are resilient and determined to preserve, develop, and transmit to future generations their unique cultural identities;

Whereas the National Museum of the American Indian was established within the Smithsonian Institution as a living memorial to the Native Peoples and their traditions; and

Whereas Native Peoples are endowed by their Creator with certain unalienable rights, and that among those are life, liberty, and the pursuit of happiness.

15. At least one prominent Native American leader thinks the Brownback resolution is insufficient as an apology to Native Americans for the misdeeds of the federal government. A.D. Ellis, Principal Chief of the Muscogee (Creek) Nation, wants a presidential apology. Chief Ellis noted: "I won't accept it unless it is from the president himself. It's long overdue. Brownback's letter was nice, but it's meaningless. I've written the White House several times, requesting one, but each time, I've just received a standard form letter." Lenzy Krehbiel-Burton, "Summit of tribal leaders scheduled," *Tulsa World* (November 22, 2010), A11.

16. Joseph V. Monteville, "Reconciliation—Applied Healing," John Hope Franklin Center for Reconciliation Symposium—"Hope & Healing: Black, White, and Native American," June 1-3, 2011, Tulsa, Oklahoma, featured lecture by Joseph V. Monteville, Senior Associate, Center for the Study of Jewish-Christian-Muslim Relations, Merrimack College; Distinguished Diplomat in Residence, American University; Chair, Center for World Religions, Diplomacy, and Conflict Resolution, George Mason University.

17. http://www.jhfcenter.org/john-hope-franklin/. The author works closely with the John Hope Franklin Center for Reconciliation on a number of initiatives.

18. http://www.hopeinthecities.org/abt; see also, Rob Corcoran, *Trustbuilding: An Honest Conversation on Race, Reconciliation, and Responsibility* (Charlottesville and London: University of Virginia Press 2010). Rob Corcoran is the founder of Hope in the Cities. The author graduated from a Hope in the Cities community fellowship program held in Richmond, Virginia, called "Connecting Communities" in 2003-2004).

19. Rob Corcoran, *Trustbuilding*, 262.

20. Part of the responsibility for examining one's own background and that of others is to search out an inclusive history and insist upon a curriculum that captures the lived experience of a variety of peoples and cultures. See, e.g., Greg Guedel, "Washington State Schools Improve Tribal History Curriculum," *Native American Legal Update* (June 21, 2010), discussing Washington's efforts to expand the amount and availability of resources with which to teach Native-American history in school curricula. http://www.nativelegalupdate.com/2010/06/articles/washington-state-schools-improve-tribal-history-curriculum/. Last visited January 3, 2010.

21. Frederick Douglass, Speech at dedication of Manassas (Virginia) Industrial School, September 3, 1894.

22. "One America in the 21st Century: Forging a New Future, The President's Initiative on Race," *The Advisory Board's Report to the President* (1998), 15.

23. Inaugural Address, President Barack Obama, January 20, 2009.

24. Statement of Cherokee Nation Principal Chief Chad Smith, John Hope Franklin Center for Reconciliation, "Reconciliation in America" Symposium, *Hope & Healing: Black, White, and Native American*, Tulsa, Oklahoma, June 2, 2011. (Point/Counterpoint session, "The Status of the Freedmen Among the Five Civilized Tribes," featuring Chief Smith and Jon Velie, Esq., Attorney and Freedmen Counsel, and facilitated by Hannibal B. Johnson, Esq.); see also, Wayne Greene, "Symposium looks at issue of freedmen," *Tulsa World* (June 3, 2011), A1; Lenzy Krehbiel-Burton, "Courts have final say of freedmen, candidates agree," *Tulsa World* (June 7, 2011), A5. Cherokee Nation Principal Chief Chad Smith, speaking at a candidates forum at Rogers State University in Claremore, Oklahoma, noted: "The force of the courts is supreme. What is within our control, however, is what happens the day after the decision is made. Regardless of the outcome, the day after will give us a chance to reconcile and start building bridges." The remarks came in advance of the election for Principal Chief of the Cherokee Nation of Oklahoma on June 25, 2011.

Appendix A

1. Brendan I. Koerner, "Blood Feud," September 1, 2005, available at http://www.velie.law.com.

2. Meeting of the Descendants of the Five Civilized Tribes, December 6, 2008, Tulsa, Oklahoma.

3. K. M. Armstrong & Bob Curry, *Chickasaw Rolls: Annuity Rolls of 1857-1860 and the 1855 Chickasaw District Roll of 1856* (Westminster, Maryland: Heritage Books, Inc., 1995).

4. Dr. Jack Forbes, Powhatan-Renape/Delaware-Lenape, a leading scholar on

the relationships between and among African Americans and Native Americans, noted: "We must recognize that one of the fundamental human rights of individuals and of groups includes the right to self-identification and self-definition." *Indivisible—African-Native American Lives in the Americas*, Gabrielle Tayac, gen. ed. (Washington, D.C., and New York, New York: National Museum of the American Indian, The Smithsonian Institution, 2009), 183.

5. About 69 Choctaw Freedmen left the Choctaw Nation before the adoption of the Choctaw Freedmen in 1885. Some 6,000 Choctaw Freedmen remained in Indian Territory. See, e.g., "1885 Choctaw Freedmen Who Elected To Leave the Nation," available at http://www.african-nativeamerican.com/leave.htm

Appendix B

1. E-mail from David Cornsilk to Hannibal B. Johnson (Dec. 1, 2008, 05:24:10 p.m. CST; on file with author).

Index

Act for the Protection of the People of Indian Territory, 68
Act in Regard to Free Negroes, 33
Adair, W. P., 52, 59
Adams, T. J., 222
Adams-Harris, Vanessa, 230
African-American Genealogical Society of Northern California, 259
African Americans:
    all-black towns, 72, 74, 133, 138, 144, 315
    as bondservants, 4
    civil rights, 307-325
    citizenship, 11, 69, 103
    education, 136, 137
    federal benefits, 9
    segregation of, 61, 127, 128, 139
    on Trail of Tears, 27, 28
    population, 134
    violence against, 63, 77, 79, 80, 82, 84, 104, 133
African-Americans and Native Americans:
    bond between, 1, 4, 15
    relationship between, 1, 4, 5, 6, 16, 30, 67, 128, 140, 142
    racism toward, 6
    slavery, 128, 129, 130
Akers, Donna L., 21
Alexander, Isaac, 253
alienability, *see* land transfer
Allen, Lucy, 187, 188, 291
American Anti-Slavery Society, 309
American Indian Religious Freedom Act, 298
American Red Cross, 83

Ameringer, Oscar, 64, 65
Anoatubby, Bill, 155
anti-slavery, 312, 314
Area Council for Community Action (ACCA), 175
Armstrong, Charles, 52
Artman, Carl J., 95, 98
Atoka Agreement, 255
Austin, Ellis, 116
Ayllon, Lucas Vasquez de, 54

Baker, John, 201
Baldwin, William, Jr., 135
Ballinger, Webster, 257
Baltimore Sun, 183
Banks, Frances, 242
Barnett, Ida B. Wells, 78
Barnett, Ketch, 212
Barnett, Ross, 233, 322
Bartram, William, 14, 235
Battle of Honey Springs, 36
Battle of Horseshoe Bend, 208
Beams, William, 244
Beaver, Ollie V., 141
Beaver, Samuel C., 141
Bell, John, 26, 28
Benge, John, 28
Benton, Stanley, 116
Berrey, John, 154
Berry, Frank, 234
Bethune, Mary McLeod, 319
Betty Ligon v. Douglas H. Johnson, Breen McCurtain, and James Garfield, Secretary of the Interior, *see* Equity Case 7071

Birth of a Nation, The, 77, 78, 316
Bixby, Tams, 122
Black Beaver, 52
Black Dispatch, 77
blood quantum, 6, 42, 43, 86, 87, 88, 89, 90, 96, 97, 101, 107, 108, 109, 111, 112, 114, 115, 149, 170, 178, 179, 182, 189, 223, 225, 227, 232, 233, 240, 241, 277, 280
Blue, King, 253
Boren, Dan, 286
Boudinot, Elias, 25, 30, 52
Bowlegs, Billy, 239
Bowles, William Augustus, 239
Brotherhood of Sleeping Car Porters, 317
Brown, John, 312
Brown, John F., 59
Brown v. Board of Education, 190, 314, 320
Brownback, Sam, 267, 268
Buckingham, William A., 251
Bureau of Indian Affairs, 4, 41, 92, 95, 97, 109, 110, 111, 112, 177, 179, 180, 183, 185, 186, 195, 204, 226, 238, 240, 251, 282, 286, 293, 294, 297, 298, 303, 305
Burgess, Jane Perryman, 215
Burke Act, 121, 295
Burks, Mary Fair, 319
Burnap, Drusilla, 28
Burney, Ben, 55
Burney, Wesley C., 55
Bushyhead, Dennis Wolf, 151
Butler, Elizur, 24, 28, 30
Butler, Lucy Ames, 28, 29
Byrd, Joe, 27, 171

California Muscogee (Creek) Association (CMCA), 230
Cannon, Rufus, 245
Cardin, Sanford R. "Sandy," 270
Carlisle Industrial Indian School, 102
Carnegie, Andrew, 83
Carr, Samuel, 209
Carter, Hannibal C., 70
Carter, Ken, 223
casinos/gaming, 96, 149-150, 152-153, 154, 155, 156, 157, 158, 159, 160, 161, 162, 163, 164, 172, 193, 196, 291, 305

census card, *see* Dawes enrollment cards
Certificate of Degree of Indian Blood (CDIB), 41, 97, 110, 111, 112, 174, 180, 181, 182, 185, 233, 238, 239, 240, 241, 260-262, 291
Chahtah, 242
Chang, David A., 60, 204, 205
Chapman v. King, 319
Charles and Lynn Schusterman Family Foundation, 270
Checote, Sam, 212
Cherokee Advocate, 68, 69
Cherokee Female Seminary, 30
Cherokee Historical Society, 282
Cherokee Nation: 2, 6, 17, 38, 43, 46, 47, 54, 55, 58, 64, 90, 103, 108, 113, 114, 119, 123, 124, 161, 182, 188, 191, 193, 201, 206, 208, 214, 221, 223, 235, 266, 302, 305, 306
  and Civil War, 33, 34, 35, 36
  Constitution, 7, 22, 30, 41, 95, 170, 174, 176, 177, 178, 180, 181, 183, 185, 186, 188, 189, 190, 191, 192, 198, 200, 201, 202, 284, 285, 286
  economic activity, 152, 153, 155, 282
  education, 31
  and federal benefits, 173, 277, 286
  and Freedmen, 7, 8, 9, 11, 41, 42, 44, 45, 92, 93, 94, 96, 98, 104, 111, 142-143, 149, 150, 151, 154, 160, 165, 166, 167, 169, 171, 172, 174, 176, 179, 180, 181, 184, 192, 195, 199, 204, 217, 224, 247, 280, 281, 283, 284-286, 287-291
  loss of lands, 22, 23
  membership in tribe, 7, 178, 185, 190
  political contributions, 158-159
  as political entity, 197
  and racism, 109, 175, 194, 196
  removal to Oklahoma, 21, 22, 23, 25, 26, 27, 28, 29, 294, 301; *also see* Trail of Tears
  and slavery, 5, 19, 32, 36, 39, 40, 59, 61, 62, 66, 105, 106, 142, 168, 169, 203, 278
  sovereignty, 23, 24, 95, 170, 172, 173, 186, 187, 202, 288, 293
  tribal funding, 152
Cherokee Nation Businesses, 158

Index   395

Cherokee Nation Enterprises, 153
Cherokee Nation Supreme Court (Judicial Appeals Tribunal), 9, 184, 185, 189, 190, 201
Cherokee Nation v. Georgia, 23, 24, 25, 293, 301
Cherokee Nation v. Nash et al., 7, 200, 204
Cherokee Nation v. United States, 44
Cherokee Phoenix, 22, 25, 185
Cherokee Tribal Council, 68, 69, 93, 111, 158, 170, 176, 178, 181, 182, 188, 189, 193, 282, 286, 289
Cheyenne Tribe, 33, 302, 305
Chickasaw Freedmen Associatio, 253
Chickasaw Nation: 2, 5, 6, 13, 17, 21, 25, 34, 35, 36, 38, 39, 45, 47, 55, 56, 57, 59, 60, 67, 86, 97, 104, 105, 106, 109, 119, 124, 152, 153, 154, 155, 196, 205, 206, 242, 243, 244, 247, 248, 249, 250, 251, 252, 253, 254, 255, 256, 257, 258, 259, 260, 276, 277, 301, 305, 327
Chikasah, 242
Chivington, John, 33
Choctaw Freedmen Oak Hill Industrial Academy, 245
Choctaw Nation: 2, 5, 6, 13, 17, 21, 32, 33, 34, 35, 36, 38, 39, 47, 55, 57, 58, 59, 60, 63, 65, 97, 104, 106, 109, 119, 124, 152, 153, 154, 155, 167, 203, 205, 206, 208, 230, 241, 242, 243, 244, 245, 246, 247, 248, 249, 250, 251, 252, 254, 255, 256, 257, 258, 259, 277, 279, 301, 305, 327, 334
Choctaw-Chickasaw Freedmen Association of Oklahoma, 247
Choctaw-Chickasaw Freedmen Project, 259
civil rights, 4, 80, 94, 99, 112, 113, 134, 139, 142, 154, 165, 167, 171, 178, 184, 186, 187, 194, 225, 237, 251, 298, 302, 307, 311, 314, 315, 317, 318, 319, 321, 322, 323
Clansman, The, 77
Clay, Henry, 310
Clinton, Bill, 56, 85, 130, 185, 204, 264-265, 272, 340

Cloud, Thomas, 59
Coburn, Tom, 98
Colbert, Frank, 249
Colbert, Julie, 249
Congress for Racial Equality (CORE), 318, 320
Congressional Black Caucus, 167, 172, 195, 241, 247, 283
Connor, James, 52
Connor, John, 52
Conser, Peter, 116
Constant, Mrs. D. C. (Antoinette Snow), 117
Coolidge, Calvin, 296
Cooper, Kenneth J., 173, 202, 204
Corbray, Rachael, 229
Corcoran, Rob, 270
Cornsilk, David, 41, 42, 160, 171, 174, 175, 180, 232, 287-291
Coronado, Francisco Vasquez de, 300
Cotch-chochee, 233
Cow Mikko, 233
Cow Tom, 210, 211, 212, 213, 214, 225, 237
Crain, Ambrose, 145
Cripps, John, 200, 201
Crittendon, Henry, 245
Currin, Green I., 80
Curtis Act of 1898, 68, 73, 122, 220, 255, 295, 302
Cushman, H. B., 205, 206

Daily Oklahoman, 75, 86
Darneal, Ardena, 246
Darneal, Silas, 246
Davis, Lucinda, 57, 58
Davis, Sylvia, 194, 239, 240
Dawes, Henry Laurens, 121
Dawes academy, 56
Dawes Act, 106, 121, 295
Dawes Blood Rolls, 5, 6, 8, 41, 43, 96, 97, 107, 108, 109, 110, 111, 112, 120, 124, 170, 175, 177, 178, 180, 182, 183, 189, 190, 192, 199, 202, 216, 217, 224, 225, 226, 228, 232, 233, 241, 246, 277, 278, 281, 285
    Final Rolls, 124, 171, 174, 175, 180
Dawes enrollment cards, 123, 145
Dawes Commission, 5, 8, 41, 69, 88,

89, 90, 106, 115, 121, 122, 123, 124, 125, 166, 170, 174, 185, 188, 191, 197, 217, 220, 221, 222, 223, 237, 253, 256, 277, 302
de la Harpe, Jean-Baptiste Benard, 300
de Soto, Hernando, 14, 15, 54, 55, 167, 300
Deas, Edward, 26
Debo, Angie, 20, 64, 119, 204, 210, 214
Delano, Columbus, 251, 252
Delano, John, 251
Democrats, and Indian/black tensions, 86
Descendants of Freedmen of the Five Civilized Tribes, 95, 194, 280, 282
Dixon, Thomas, 77, 78
DNA mapping, 43
Douglas, Stephen, 310, 311, 312
Douglass, Frederick, 263, 272
Dred Scott v. Sandford, 311
Du Bois, W.E.B., 314, 315
Dunjee, Roscoe, 77
Dunn, J. W., 222
Dunn Roll, 222
Dyer, L. C., 317
Dyer Anti-Lynching Bill, 317, 324

Eastern Band of Cherokee Indians, 26
Eisenhower, Dwight D., 321
Elliot Academy, 245
Ellsworth, Scott, 76
Equity Case 7071, 256, 257, 258, 259
Estelusti Foundation, 236, 259
Ewing, Jim Pathfinder, 149
Executive Order 8802, 318
Executive Order 13007, 299, 303
Executive Order 13175, 299, 304

Farmer, James, 318, 319
FEMA Tribal Policy, 299
Field, Richard, 52
First Kansas Colored Volunteer Infantry Regiment, 36
Fite, Julian, 282
Five Civilized Tribes, 6, 9, 11, 18, 20, 25, 38, 39, 43, 44, 47, 53, 58, 59, 60, 67, 68, 73, 94, 97, 99, 100, 102, 104, 105, 106, 107, 109, 112, 119, 121, 122, 124, 125, 127, 132, 172, 177, 180, 199, 202, 206, 210, 212, 220, 228, 229, 230, 234, 237, 239, 241, 242, 245, 246, 247, 248, 249, 255, 258, 259, 263, 273, 275, 277, 278, 279, 288, 291, 295, 301, 302
 barriers to citizenship, 103
 and Civil War, 32, 33, 34, 35
 exclusion of Freedmen, 89
 and slavery, 32, 37, 66
Fletcher, Alphonse, Sr., 190
Fort Butler, 25
Fort Cass, 25
Fort Coffee, Oklahoma, 26, 246
Fort Gibson, 30, 36, 301
Fort Smith, Arkansas, 34, 37, 44, 48
Fountain Baptist Church (Ebenezer Baptist Church), 209
Franklin, Buck Colbert, 56, 58, 83
Franklin, Buck Colbert, Jr., 56
Franklin, Fannie, 101
Franklin, Fred, 101
Franklin, John Hope, 56, 83, 84, 85, 137, 248
Franklin, Richard, 101
Franklin, Thamore, 101
Freedmen, 95, 172, 177, 194, 248, 277, 279, 280, 282
 definition of, 5, 9, 89, 107, 109, 123
 and federal treatment, 99, 250, 251
 land allotments, 6, 87, 120, 231, 232, 243
 petition to Congress, 97
 population, 160, 250
 response to detractors, 275-279
 tribal membership/citizenship, 6, 45, 46, 73, 104, 106, 111, 112, 149, 151, 158, 173, 174, 176, 178-179, 180, 212, 224, 243, 245, 246, 249, 250, 252, 253, 256, 259, 260
Freedmen Roll, 5, 8, 93, 97, 108, 109, 110, 111, 123, 166, 170, 178, 180, 183, 191, 196, 216, 221, 223, 225, 227, 237, 238, 239, 241, 246, 247, 256, 257, 277, 280
Freedmen's Oklahoma Immigration Association, 70, 71
From Slavery to Freedom: A History of African Americans, 56, 85

Index

Fry, Robert, 142
Fugitive Slave Law, 310

Gant, Reuben, 166
Gant, Richard, 166
Garrison, William Lloyd, 309
General Allotment Act of 1887, 121
General Council of Indian Territory, 214
Georgia, 22, 24, 29, 168, 208, 293, 294, 301, 319; voiding laws of Cherokee Nation, 23, 25
Glover, Danny, 167
Gover, Kevin, 185
Graham, Creasy, 228, 229
Graham, Ron, 225, 226, 227, 228, 229, 230, 232
Graham, Sissy, 227
Graham, Theodore "Blue," 226, 229
Grant, Ulysses S., 251
Gray, Louis, 193
Gray, Thelma DeEtta Perryman, 81
Grayson, Eli, 149, 229, 230, 232, 233
Grayson, Fannie (Nero), 229
Grayson, George Washington, 214
Grayson, Mary, 215
Greenwood Chamber of Commerce, 84
Greenwood Cultural Center, 84
Greenwood District, 76, 81, 82, 83, 84, 85, 316
Griffith, D. W., 77, 78, 316
Guinn v. United States, 138, 316

Hall, Amos T., 320
Hall, J. M., 142
Hall, Squire, 245
Hamlin, A. C., 80
Hammons, Diane, 200
Harding, Warren G., 76, 317
Harjo, Chitto, 120, 121
Harjo, Talof, *see* Pleasant Porter
Harjo, Yarteker, 59
Harrison, Benjamin, 72
Haskell, Charles Nathaniel, 67
Henderson v. United States, 320
Hirsch, Emil G., 136
History of the Choctaw, Chickasaw and Natchez Indians, 206
Hodge, D. M., 59

Hoktee, 229
Holcomb, Curtis W., 71
Holder, Eric, 98, 325
Hollis, Jess, 139
Homestead Act of 1862, 120
Hope in the Cities, 270
Houston, Drusilla Dunjee, 77, 78
Howell, Ethel G., 166
Hubbard, David, 34
Human Genome Project, 43
Hutton, Joe, 227, 228
hypodescent, 139, 140, 183, 184, 222, 228, 257

"If We Must Die," 76
Indian Appropriation Act, 294
Indian Civil Rights Act, 298, 302
Indian Claims Commission Act, 297
Indian Citizenship Act (Snyder Act), 259, 296, 302
Indian Claims Commission, 237, 238
Indian Gaming Association, 155
Indian Gaming Regulatory Act, 154, 298, 303
Indian Citizen, 256
Indian Health Service, 111, 179, 282, 298
Indian Removal Act, 23, 236, 301
Indian Reorganization Act, 93, 96, 296
Indian Self-determination and Education Assistance Act, 298, 303
Indian Territory, 2, 20, 26, 29, 30, 32, 34, 37, 40, 44, 46, 47, 59, 61, 62, 64, 66, 67, 68, 70, 71, 87, 88, 103, 105, 107, 118, 119, 120, 122, 124, 132, 134, 150, 176, 203, 211, 214, 216, 217, 221, 222, 232, 237, 255, 256, 257, 258, 295, 301, 302
Initiative on Race, 56
Initiatives of Change USA, 270
internment camps, 25
Irene Morgan v. Commonwealth of Virginia, 319, 320
Island, Harry, 210, 211, 212, 237
Ispocogee, Sam, 140, 141
Ispocogee, Sammie, 140, 141, 142

Jackson, Andrew, 21, 23, 24, 236, 326
Jefferson, Rose, 214

Jessup, Thomas, 211
Jim Crow, 4, 16, 79, 81, 82, 86, 87, 110, 118, 128, 129, 130, 131, 134, 135, 137, 138, 139, 140, 142, 194, 263, 315
John Hope Franklin Center for Reconciliation, 84, 85, 268, 269, 273
John Hope Franklin Reconciliation Park, 84, 85, 269
Johnson, Fred, 225
Johnson, James Weldon, 76, 316
Johnson, Lyndon B., 298, 323, 324
Johnson, Robert, 237
Johnson v. McIntosh, 300
Joliet, Louis, 300
Jones, Evan, 62
Jones, John B., 62
Jones, Mozella Franklin, 56
Journeycake, Charles, 52
Journeycake, Isaac, 52
Judicial Appeals Tribunal, *see* Cherokee Nation Supreme Court

Katz, William Loren, 1, 54
Keating, Frank, 75
Keen, Ralph, Jr., 200, 203
Keen, Taylor, 193
Keetoowah Society, 61, 62
Kennedy, Henry H., Jr., 8, 9
Kennedy, John F., 322, 323
Kennedy, Robert F., 324
Kern, Terrance, 7
Ketcher, John, 158
Ketchum, James, 52
Keys, Riley, 214
Kidd, Meredith Helm, 122
King, Martin Luther, Jr., 317, 319, 321, 322, 324
King, Primus, 319
King, Rodney, 324
Kirkwood, Samuel J., 71
Kollar-Kotelly, Judge, 46
Ku Klux Klan (KKK), 76, 77, 316, 322

land allotment, 5, 88, 108, 109, 119, 120, 124, 145, 169, 212, 223, 241, 243, 246, 280, 295
land transfer, 109
Langston City Herald, 72, 74

Langston University, 72, 84
Lea Act, 296
Lee, Albert J., 257
Lee, Gary, 209
Lee, Lila, 209
Lee, Robert E., 37
Leeds, Stacy L., 190
Lewis, Jackson, 230
Lewis, John, 137
Liberator, The, 309
Ligon, Betty, 256, 259
Ligon, Terry J., 259
Lincoln, Abraham, 36, 136, 311
Littlefield, Daniel, 196, 233
Littlejohn, Robert, 9, 11
Loewen, James W., 75
Lone, I. W., 139
Louisiana Purchase, 21
Love, Bob, 256
Love, Kiziah, 249
Loving v. Virginia, 142
Lucas, Hettie Reynolds, 246
Lucy Allen v. Cherokee National Tribal Council, et. al., 189, 190, 285, 289
Lumbee Act, 91
Luper, Clara, 321
lynching, 77, 78, 79, 80, 82
"Lynching, The," 78
Lyons, Thomas D., 141, 142

Malcolm X, 323
Mankiller, Wilma, 22, 27, 63, 90, 92, 175, 181, 182, 183
Margold, Nathan R., 93
Marquette, Jacques, 300
Marshall, John, 24, 29, 293, 301
Marshall, Thurgood, 317, 320, 324
Martin, Joseph L., 188
Martin, William, 188
McCabe, Edward P., 71, 72, 73, 144
McCaleb, Neal, 185
McDaniel, James, 52
McGilbray, Rose, 229
McIntosh, William, 208
McIntyre, Judy Eason, 191, 192
McKay, Claude, 76, 78
McKennon, Archibald S., 122
McLaurin v. Oklahoma, 320
McNeal, Joe, 147

Memorial of the Chickasaw Freedmen, 253-255
Menawa (Great Warrior), 208
Meredith, James, 322
Miles, Tiya, 142
miscegenation, 102, 103, 104, 112, 113, 142
Moody, James, 41
Mooney, James, 302
Moore, Calvin C., 266
Moore, John R., 59, 214
Moore's Ford Memorial Committee, 269
Morgan, Lewis Henry, 16
Morton v. Mancari, 3
Morton, Samuel, 16
Murray, William H. "Alfalfa Bill," 86
Muscogee Creek Indian Freedmen Band, 229
Muscogee (Creek) Nation: 2, 6, 21, 23, 39, 57, 59, 61, 67, 71, 81, 104, 105, 106, 109, 119, 120, 123, 124, 149, 152, 153, 154, 155, 172, 204, 205, 206, 207, 208, 209, 210, 211, 212, 213, 214, 215, 217, 220, 221, 222, 223, 224, 225, 226, 227, 228, 229, 230, 231, 232, 233, 234, 235, 236, 237, 241, 301, 305

National Association for the Advancement of Colored People (NAACP), 76, 172, 315, 317, 318, 320, 321
National Congress of American Indians, 90
National Council (Cherokee), 30
National Gambling Impact Study, 157
National Negro Business League, 83
National Party, 25
National Urban League, 135, 315
Native-American Graves Protection and Repatriation Act, 303
Native-American Languages Act, 298, 303
Native Americans:
    African American relationship, 53, 102, 128, 140, 141, 142;
    Civil War, 31, 33, 34, 35, 37
    economic development, 152, 154, 156, 159

Freedmen, 6, 41, 128, 149, 151, 154, 167, 196
    gambling, 149-150, 152-153, 154, 157
    political support, 2, 3, 4;
    racism, 4, 6, 17, 20, 151, 194
    religion, 103, 298
    relocation of, 21, 25, 102, 294, 297, 301
    slaveholders, 5, 87, 105, 106;
    social problems, 157
    tobacco, 159
    tribal membership, 43, 122, 124
    U.S. treatment of, 24, 91, 102, 152, 155, 267-268, 296, 297, 302, 305-306
    whites, 68, 107
Naylor, Celia E., 11
Negrophobia, 20
Nelly, 244
Nelson, L. W., 80
Nelson, Laura, 80
Nero, Roger H., 184, 291
Nero v. Cherokee Nation of Oklahoma, 189, 284
New Echota, 25
New York Times, 133, 195
Newell, Felton, 159
Nuremberg Laws, 194, 195

Obama, Barack, 2, 113, 115, 158, 204, 272, 324
Oklahoma:
    all-black towns, 72, 74, 133, 138, 144;
    Constitution: "Definition of Races," 86
    creation of all-black state, 72;
    economy, 80, 155
    opposition to white settlers, 60;
    segregation, 69, 110, 132, 134, 135, 137, 141
    settlement of by Indians, 59;
    voter literacy laws, 138
Oklahoma Daily Leader, 64
Oklahoma Indian Welfare Act, 297
Oklahoma Renters Union, 64
Oklahoma Slave Narratives, 56, 101
Oklahoma State University-Tulsa, 84

Oklahoma Supreme Court, 108
Oklahoma, and Senate Bill One, 87
Oktars-sars-har-jo (Chief Sands), 212, 233
Omnibus Railroad Act of 1899, 47
"one drop" rule, 184
ONEOK Field, 84
Opothleyoholo, 233
Organic Act of 1890, 132
Osceola, 234, 236
Overton, B. F., 59

Pace v. Alabama, 142
Page, Sarah, 82
Pardo, Juan, 54, 167
Parker, Joe, 183
Parks, Fanny, 246
Parks, Rosa, 321
Patterson, Frederick D., 319
Payne, Elmer, 227
Payton, Kenneth, 149
Peabody Institute, 56
Peace Council, 37
Peltier, Leonard, 193
Perdue, Theda, 35, 54
Perryman, George, 217
Perryman, Joseph M., 214
Perryman, Legus C., 214, 215, 217
Perryman, Lequest Choteau, 206, 220
Perryman, Lewis, 217
Perryman, Lydia, 221
Perryman, Molly, 215
Perryman, Moses (Mose), 214, 215, 217
Perryman, Sandford, 214
Perryman family, 214, 216, 217, 218, 219, 231
Pitchlynn, P. P., 59
Plessy v. Ferguson, 314
Porter, Pleasant, 59, 214, 220, 221
Pratt, John G., 52
Pratt, Richard Henry, 102
President's Initiative on Race, 85
Presidential Medal of Freedom, 85
Prigg v. Pennsylvania, 309

Qualla Reservation, North Carolina, 26

racial Darwinism, 16
Racial Integrity Act, 142

railroad rights-of-way, 46, 47
Railroad Enabling Act, 294
Randolph, Asa Philip, 317, 318
Ray, James Earl, 324
Ray, S. A., 266, 267
Raymond Nash v. Cherokee Nation Registrar, 9
Redbird v. United States, 177
Reeves, Bass, 69, 126
Rendon, Teresa, 43
Rentiesville, Oklahoma, 36
Resolution 21-88, 181, 182
Reynolds, Levi, 246
Ridge, John Rollin, 52
Ridge, John, 25, 30
Ridge, Major, 25, 30
Riggs, Bernice, 184, 288, 291
Riggs v. Ummerteskee, 291
Riley, Howard, 200
Road to Disappearance: A History of the Muskogee (Creek) Indians, The, 210
Robinson, Tria, 203
Roger Williams University, 56
Roosevelt, Franklin D., 318
Roosevelt, Theodore, 106, 133
Rosenwald, Julius, 135, 136, 137
Rosenwald Fund, 136
Ross, Allen, 214
Ross, Daniel H., 59
Ross, John, 25, 26, 29, 30, 33, 34, 45, 168
Ross, Lewis, 26
Ross, William Potter, 45, 214
Ross's Landing, 26
Rowe v. Sartain, 109
Rowland, Dick, 82
runaway slaves, 32, 33

Samuels, Jim, 215
San Miguel de Guadalupe, 54
Sango v. Willig, 109
Santa Clara v. Martinez, 189
Sarcoxie, Sr., John, 52
Sarwanoge, Mary, 230
Scott, Winfield, 25, 27
Seminole Nation: 2, 6, 21, 25, 33, 34, 35, 38, 39, 46, 47, 59, 61, 67, 71, 79, 97, 104, 105, 106, 112, 119, 124, 172, 186, 193, 194, 204, 205, 224,

Index 401

234, 235, 236, 237, 238, 239, 240, 241, 277, 301, 306
   Estelusti Tribe, 238, 239, 240, 241
   Judgment Fund Program, 238, 239, 240, 241
Seminole Nation of Oklahoma v. Norton, 46, 186, 240
Senate Congressional Resolution 26, 128-129
Senate Indian Affairs Committee, 98
Sequoyah, 50, 59, 62
Shade, Hastings, 186
Shawnee Nation, 112
"shocks the conscience" contracts, 45, 46
Shumate, Jabar, 191, 192
Simmons, Jake, 214
Sipuel v. Board of Regents of the University of Oklahoma, 320
Sirhan, Bishara Sirhan, 324
Slave Narratives: A Folk History of Slavery in the United States, 234
Slave Revolt of 1842, 33
Slavery by Europeans, 55
Smith, Bessie, 74
Smith, Chad, 158, 171, 172, 173, 174, 185, 186, 190, 191, 192, 193, 197, 201, 273, 282, 289
Snake Rebellion, 121
Solomon-Simmons, Damario, 225
Southwest Times Record, 282
Spanish explorers, 14
Spears, Franklin & Chappelle, 83
Spirit of the South—The Maddened Mob, 78
Springwater, Dennis, 183
Stafford, Roy E., 75
State of the World's Indigenous People, 156
Stevens, Ernest L., Jr., 155
Stidham, George Washington, 214
Stowe, Harriet Beecher, 310
Sturm, Circe, 40
Sumner, Charles, 311
sundown town, 75
Sweatt v. Painter, 320
Swimmer, Ross, 152, 179, 180, 182
Swing Low, Sweet Chariot, 245

Taney, Roger, 311

Tappan, Arthur, 309
Tappan, Lewis, 309
Tecumseh, 208
Teehee, Kimberly, 113
Thompson, Pleas, 175
Tiblow, Henry, 52
Till, Emmett, 320-321
Tisne, Charles du, 300
Trail of Tears, 13, 22, 27, 28, 72, 102, 168, 209, 264, 278, 280, 294, 301
treaties, 22, 37
   Treaty of 1866, 7, 8, 9, 38, 39, 40, 41, 43, 44, 45, 47, 46, 71, 73, 93, 94, 98, 96, 101, 106, 171, 175, 177, 179, 182, 183, 186, 187, 193, 197, 198, 199, 200, 201, 202, 204, 212, 213, 214, 217, 220, 221, 222, 224, 225, 232, 233, 237, 239, 240, 241, 243, 245, 249, 250, 251, 252, 254, 280, 281, 283, 289, 290, 294
   Treaty of Fort Jackson (Treaty with the Creeks, 1814), 208
   Treaty of Indian Springs, 208
   Treaty of New Echota, 25, 26, 30
Treaty Party, 25
Trepp, Monetta, 217, 231
Trepp, Robert, 231, 232
Triplett, Verdie, 167, 246, 247
Trotter, Monroe, 315
Trustbuilding: An Honest Conversation on Race, Reconciliation, and Responsibility, 270
Tulsa Drillers, 84
Tulsa Indian Coalition Against Racism (TICAR), 192, 193
Tulsa Race Riot, 56, 75, 76, 77, 82, 83, 84, 85, 269, 316
Tulsa Tribune, 82
Tulsa World, 155
Turner, Nat, 309
Tuskegee Institute, 136

Uncle Tom's Cabin, 310
Underground Railroad, 32
United Keetoowah Band, 96
United Negro College Fund (UNCF), 319
United States and tribal funding, 155
United States Constitution, 3, 4, 8, 24,

40, 48, 129, 130, 138, 172, 202, 224, 265, 289, 293, 296, 301, 308, 309, 311, 313, 318
United States Supreme Court:
  and racial discrimination, 43;
  and Fifteenth Amendment, 138;
  and miscegenation law, 142
  and treaty abrogation, 199
United States v. Kagama, 3
United States v. Nice, 3
usufructuary land use, 68, 120

Van Buren, Martin, 21, 25, 26
Vann, Joseph, 32, 33
Vann, Marilyn, 95, 160, 186, 196, 200, 201, 202, 264, 280-283, 291
Vann et al. v. Salazar, 8, 9
Vann v. Kempthorne, 186, 187, 201, 284, 285, 286
Velie, Jonathan, 8, 150, 151, 193, 194, 195, 202
Vickers, Scott B., 42

Walker, L. P., 34
Walker, Mary, 109
Wallace, George, 233, 289
Walton, Sallie, 245
Walton-Raji, Angela, 245
Warrior, Robert, 203
Washington, Booker T., 83, 135, 136, 137, 140, 314, 315

Washington Post, 209
Watie, Saladin, 52
Watie, Stand, 25, 30, 36
Watson, Diane, 159, 172, 195, 196
Watt, Mel, 173
Watts Riots, 323
Weatherford, William (Red Eagle), 208
Webbers Falls, Oklahoma, 32
Wheeler, Perry, 180, 181
Wheeler-Howard Act, 93
Where the Casino Money Goes, 153
white supremacy, 16, 17, 86, 103, 121, 125, 128, 131, 142, 232, 312, 317
White, Evan, 112
White, Walter, 78
Whitmore v. Cherokee Nation, 177, 180
Wilkins, David, 90, 91, 92
Williams, Heather, 92, 93
Willis, Wallis, 245
Wilson, Louisa Perryman, 216
Wilson, Margaret Ann, 256
Wilson, Woodrow, 77
Women's Political Council (WPC), 319
Woodson, Carter G., 1
Worcester v. Georgia, 24, 29, 293, 301
Worcester, Samuel Austin, 24, 28

Yamasee Tribe, 235, 236
Yargee, James, 101, 210, 211
Young, John, 52
Zinn, Howard, 17, 263, 264

About the Author

Hannibal B. Johnson, Esq., is a graduate of Harvard Law School. He did his undergraduate work at the University of Arkansas, where he completed a double major in economics and sociology. Johnson is an attorney, author, and independent consultant specializing in diversity and inclusion issues and nonprofit leadership and management. Johnson has served as an adjunct professor at the University of Tulsa College of Law, and now teaches business law in the MBA program at Oklahoma State University–Tulsa and a number of undergraduate liberal studies courses at the University of Oklahoma–Tulsa.

Johnson is past president of Leadership Tulsa, the Metropolitan Tulsa Urban League, and the Northeast Oklahoma Black Lawyers Association. He served as Chairman of the board of directors of The Community Leadership Association, an international leadership organization, during 2001-2002, and he is a founding director of the Oklahoma Appleseed Center for Law and Justice. He serves on the Oklahoma Advisory Committee for the United States Commission on Civil Rights, and as Chairman of the board of directors of the Oklahoma Department of Libraries. Johnson directed Anytown, Oklahoma, a statewide human relations camp for teens, for more than a decade. He serves on the board of the Foundation for Tulsa Schools, and on the Advisory Board of the Mayborn Literary Nonfiction Writers Conference of the Southwest. Johnson, a member of the Rotary Club of Tulsa, also serves on the Institutional Review Board for Oklahoma State University Center for Health

Sciences and the Tulsa Public Schools Fine Arts Advisory Board. He is a member of the Programs Committee for the John Hope Franklin Center for Reconciliation and serves as chair of the JHF Symposium National Advisory Committee. In 2004, Mr. Johnson graduated with the inaugural class of the national "Connecting Community Fellowship Program" based in Richmond, Virginia.

Johnson's books include: *Black Wall Street—From Riot to Renaissance in Tulsa's Historic Greenwood District*; *Up From the Ashes—A Story About Community*; *Acres of Aspiration—The All-Black Towns in Oklahoma*; *Mama Used To Say—Wit & Wisdom From The Heart & Soul*; *No Place Like Home—A Story About an All-Black, All-American Town*; and *IncogNegro—Poetic Reflections on Race & Diversity in America*. Johnson's play, *Big Mama Speaks—A Tulsa Race Riot Survivor's Story*, has been performed at the Tulsa Performing Arts Center and Philbrook Museum of Art, and it was selected for the 2011 National Black Theatre Festival in Winston-Salem, North Carolina. Johnson is a contributing writer to the *Encyclopedia of African-American History* (New York, New York: Facts on File, Inc. 2010), penning two articles: "Langston, Oklahoma, and the "Birth of the All-Black Town Movement"; and "Edward Preston McCabe—The Father of the All-Black Town Movement."

Johnson's honors include: the Don Newby/Ben Hill award from Tulsa Metropolitan Ministry; the Keeping The Dream Alive award from the Dr. Martin Luther King, Jr., Commemoration Society; the Outstanding Service to the Public Award from the Oklahoma Bar Association; the Ten Outstanding Young Tulsans award from the Tulsa Jaycees; the Distinguished Leadership Award from the National Association for Community Leadership; the 2005 Ralph Ellison Literary Award from the Black Liberated Arts Center; the 2006 Oklahoma Human Rights Award from the Oklahoma Human Rights Commission; induction into the 100 Black Men of Tulsa, Inc. Hall of Honor in 2007; and the Goodwill Appreciation Award from the Islamic Society of Tulsa in 2008.

Johnson lives and works in Tulsa, Oklahoma.